The Political Economy of the Indigenous Peoples of the World, Volume I

Sangaralingam Ramesh

The Political Economy of the Indigenous Peoples of the World, Volume I

Land, Sovereignty, and the Foundations of Indigenous Economies

palgrave
macmillan

Sangaralingam Ramesh
University College London
London, UK

University of Oxford
Oxford, UK

ISBN 978-3-032-24040-8 ISBN 978-3-032-24041-5 (eBook)
https://doi.org/10.1007/978-3-032-24041-5

This Palgrave Macmillan imprint is published by the registered company Springer Nature Switzerland AG
The registered company address is: Gewerbestrasse 11, 6330 Cham, Switzerland

For my father and my mother,
Nallathamby Sangaralingam and Pathmarani Sangaralingam
Inuvil and Karinagar, Ceylon.

Preface

This volume, *The Political Economy of the Indigenous Peoples of the World: Volume 1*— Foundations, Colonisation, and Worldviews, emerges from the need to examine how Indigenous peoples have engaged with, been affected by, and actively resisted dominant global economic systems. Initially conceived as a single comprehensive manuscript, the scope and richness of the material led to the decision to divide the work into two volumes. This first volume lays the historical, philosophical, and theoretical foundations for understanding the economic life of Indigenous peoples across the globe. It focuses on Indigenous economic systems prior to and during the early phases of colonization, the impact of European expansion, and the deep cultural, ecological, and political frameworks that shaped Indigenous governance and livelihood. Volume 1 traces the development of Indigenous socio-economic systems across different world regions and contrasts them with European economic ideologies, including mercantilism, capitalism, and communism. It explores Indigenous governance models, land stewardship practices, and spiritual worldviews, which often stand in contrast to extractive, commodified forms of economic life. These systems—whether based on kinship, reciprocity, ecological balance, or ceremonial exchange—are neither static nor monolithic. Rather, they represent adaptive, sustainable, and deeply rooted responses to specific social and environmental contexts. A particular strength of this volume is its comparative approach. It situates Indigenous economic practices alongside ancient economic philosophies from India, China, and

Greece, as well as against the backdrop of neoclassical economics and Marxist thought. In doing so, the volume not only critiques the historical processes of colonial dispossession and the imposition of Western economic models but also opens space for a serious intellectual reckoning with alternative economic rationalities. Volume 1 also introduces the foundational critiques that underpin the emergent framework of Symbiotic Gaian Economics (SGE), an original contribution to political economy that is developed fully in the concluding chapter of Volume 2. This new economic ideology draws on Indigenous relational ontologies and ecological ethics to propose an alternative vision of human and planetary flourishing.

While this volume is grounded in rigorous interdisciplinary research—drawing from political economy, anthropology, Indigenous studies, environmental history, and legal theory—it remains committed to amplifying Indigenous voices, worldviews, and intellectual traditions. It seeks not to speak for Indigenous peoples but to honour their perspectives, struggles, and aspirations by situating them at the centre of economic analysis. Volume 2, Resistance, Resurgence, and the Struggle for Economic Justice, continues the conversation by focusing on contemporary challenges facing Indigenous communities—neoliberalism, climate change, global governance, and the politics of recognition—as well as the resurgence of Indigenous-led movements, legal reforms, and economic alternatives. Together, the two volumes aim to provide a comprehensive, decolonial, and pluralistic account of Indigenous political economy that is both analytically rigorous and politically engaged. Volume 1 is a foundation; Volume 2 is a continuation. Both volumes share a single purpose: to reimagine economic futures that are just, relational, and grounded in the wisdom and resilience of Indigenous peoples. This work is offered in humility and solidarity with those whose lives, land, and knowledge continue to challenge the narrow paradigms of the global economic order.

Oxford, UK Sangaralingam Ramesh

Acknowledgements

I would like to thank Wyndham Hacket Pain, Senior Editor (Economics) at Palgrave Macmillan for his assistance in turning an idea into reality. I would also thank Raju Heggidi (Production Editor) for his help in facilitating and managing the production of the book.

Contents

List of Tables

CHAPTER 1

Introduction

1 Overview of Indigenous Histories, Socio-Economic Structures, and the Impact of Colonization

Introduction

The political economy of Indigenous peoples is shaped by centuries of resistance, survival, and negotiation within global systems of domination and extraction. This book emerges from a pressing need to rethink mainstream economic narratives that have marginalized Indigenous experiences, epistemologies, and institutions. Across continents and generations, Indigenous communities have faced the violent expansion of settler colonial states, the imposition of capitalist property regimes, and the commodification of land, labour, and life itself. Yet their responses have been neither uniform nor passive. Instead, Indigenous peoples have asserted distinct economic logics and political practices grounded in reciprocal relations with land, community responsibility, and cultural continuity. This first chapter lays the conceptual groundwork for the volume by asking: What does it mean to examine Indigenous economies through a political economy lens? How can we understand land, sovereignty, and resource governance not as abstract economic variables, but as lived and contested realities shaped by colonialism, global capital, and Indigenous agency? The chapter begins by introducing the theoretical and

S. Ramesh, *The Political Economy of the Indigenous Peoples of the World, Volume I*, https://doi.org/10.1007/978-3-032-24041-5_1

methodological frameworks that inform this analysis, particularly decolonial thought, world-systems theory, and Marxian political economy. Each of these perspectives contributes to a richer understanding of how Indigenous dispossession has been structured, legitimized, and resisted through time. The chapter also establishes the importance of historical continuity. While global capitalism and state expansion have intensified in the modern era, they are not new phenomena in Indigenous experience. The transformation of Indigenous economies must be situated within long-term processes of empire-building, racial capitalism, and settler colonialism. As such, we highlight the need to view Indigenous political economies as neither pre-modern nor obsolete, but as evolving systems capable of offering sustainable, relational, and alternative models of economic life. Throughout this chapter, we also examine the limitations of existing development paradigms and human rights frameworks, including the uneven impact of international instruments like the United Nations Declaration on the Rights of Indigenous Peoples (UNDRIP). While these frameworks have advanced recognition in some contexts, they often fall short in confronting the material realities of extractive development and land appropriation. In contrast, Indigenous-led economic models—rooted in land-based knowledge systems, governance traditions, and collective stewardship—offer pathways towards not only decolonization but also economic transformation.

In laying this foundation, the chapter sets the stage for the rest of the volume. Subsequent chapters evaluate further into the mechanisms of settler colonialism, imperial expansion, and capitalist accumulation. We examine the historical and contemporary structures that sustain Indigenous dispossession while also tracing the resurgence of Indigenous economies that challenge and reimagine global economic orders. Together, these inquiries aim to foreground Indigenous voices, epistemologies, and visions as central—not peripheral—to the study of political economy.

1.1 Indigenous Peoples Across the Globe: Diversity and Commonalities

Indigenous peoples across the globe exhibit immense diversity in terms of culture, language, and lifestyle, reflecting the vast array of environments and histories they inhabit. There are approximately 476 million Indigenous people worldwide, living in over 90 countries and constituting about 6% of the global population.[1] This diversity is marked by distinct languages, traditions, and ways of interacting with the natural world. For instance, the Sami people of northern Europe maintain a reindeer-herding culture adapted to Arctic conditions, while the Indigenous groups of the Amazon Basin, such as the Yanomami, practice sustainable agriculture and hunting within dense tropical rainforests.[2] Despite these differences, many Indigenous societies share core values that distinguish their worldviews from non-Indigenous populations. A central concept across numerous Indigenous groups is kinship, which extends beyond family relationships to include a sense of relationality with the land, animals, and spiritual entities. For example, the concept of "all my relations" in many North American Indigenous cultures emphasizes interconnectedness and the obligation to maintain balance within the ecosystem.[3] This kinship principle underpins a sense of stewardship, where land is not owned but is instead a shared resource and a responsibility to be managed for the benefit of current and future generations.[4] Such values are present across continents; for instance, in Australia, the Aboriginal "Dreaming" connects people to ancestral lands and emphasizes the duty of care towards these lands as an enduring legacy.[5] Economically, Indigenous societies vary widely in their forms of subsistence, ranging from hunter-gatherer to agrarian, pastoral, and maritime systems. Hunter-gatherer societies, such as the San people of southern Africa, rely on intricate knowledge of local flora, fauna, and seasonal patterns to sustain their communities without farming or animal husbandry. Their subsistence strategies involve deep ecological knowledge and careful resource management, contributing to biodiversity and ecosystem health.[6] In contrast, agrarian societies like

[1] United Nations. (2021). Indigenous Peoples at the United Nations. Available at: https://www.un.org/development/desa/indigenouspeoples/.

[2] Krupnik, I., Mason, R., & Horton, M. (2004). Northern Ethnographic Landscapes: Perspectives from Circumpolar Nations. Smithsonian Institution Press.

[3] Deloria, V. (2001). Power and Place: Indian Education in America. Fulcrum Publishing.

[4] Atalay, S. (2006). Indigenous Archaeology as Decolonizing Practice. American Indian Quarterly, 30(3), 280–310.

[5] Rose, D. B. (1996). Nourishing Terrains: Australian Aboriginal Views of Landscape and Wilderness. Australian Heritage Commission.

[6] Lee, R. B., & Daly, R. (2004). The Cambridge Encyclopedia of Hunters and Gatherers. Cambridge University Press.

the Maya of Mesoamerica developed sophisticated farming techniques, including terracing and crop rotation, to support densely populated settlements.[7] These systems were based on sustainable practices that often allowed these communities to flourish for centuries.

Pastoral Indigenous groups, like the Maasai of East Africa, rely on livestock for their livelihood, which requires extensive mobility and adaptation to diverse ecological zones. This pastoralism is well suited to semi-arid environments and involves seasonal migrations that prevent overgrazing and maintain the ecological balance.[8] Finally, maritime societies, such as the Polynesians, showcase advanced navigational skills and an intimate understanding of the marine environment. These communities have developed fishing techniques, sea-route navigation, and knowledge of marine biodiversity that are vital for their sustenance and cultural practices.[9] Indigenous societies represent a rich tapestry of cultural and economic adaptations to their surroundings, each grounded in shared principles of kinship, communal responsibility, and environmental stewardship. This diversity, however, is unified by a worldview that emphasizes interconnectedness with the land and non-human entities, highlighting a relational approach to existence that contrasts with more individualistic or extractive paradigms found in many colonial societies. Such values are not merely cultural artifacts but form the basis of Indigenous resistance to environmental degradation and the imposition of foreign economic models that threaten their ways of life.[10]

1.2 Traditional Socio-Economic Structures of Indigenous Communities

The socio-economic systems of Indigenous communities prior to colonization were remarkably diverse, locally adapted, and rooted in holistic

[7] Fedick, S. L. (1996). The Managed Mosaic: Ancient Maya Agriculture and Resource Use. University of Utah Press.

[8] Galaty, J. G. (1992). "Pastoralists Past and Present: Reinterpreting Family and Flock in East Africa". In B. Glazier (Ed.), Pastoralism in the Horn of Africa. New York University Press.

[9] Kirch, P. V. (2000). On the Road of the Winds: An Archaeological History of the Pacific Islands before European Contact. University of California Press.

[10] Alfred, T. (2009). Peace, Power, Righteousness: An Indigenous Manifesto. Oxford University Press.

relationships with land, kinship, and cosmology. Rather than being driven by the pursuit of individual accumulation or market efficiency, these economies emphasized collective well-being, reciprocity, and sustainable coexistence with the environment. Indigenous communities across the world developed complex systems of environmental management based on intimate ecological knowledge passed down through generations, often encoded in oral traditions, ceremonies, and spiritual practices.[11,12] For instance, the Yolngu people of northern Australia practiced intricate forms of seasonal mobility and resource sharing, governed by clan relationships and spiritual laws known as *Rom*.[13] Their land tenure and economic practices are inextricably linked to kin-based obligations and custodianship, challenging Western notions of private property and individual profit.[14] Similarly, among the Andean Quechua communities, the use of vertical ecological zonation, allocating crops to different altitudinal zones, demonstrated deep agroecological knowledge and ensured resilience in the face of environmental variability.[15] In North America, the Haudenosaunee (Iroquois Confederacy) organized agricultural production and distribution communally, using polyculture systems such as the "Three Sisters" planting of corn, beans, and squash to enhance soil fertility and mutual plant support.[16] Land was not owned in a Western legal sense but held collectively and used according to principles of stewardship and intergenerational responsibility. In Africa, many Indigenous systems incorporated philosophies like *Ubuntu*, which placed human relations and communal obligations at the centre of economic life.[17] These

[11] Berkes, F. (2012). *Sacred ecology* (3rd ed.). Routledge.

[12] Descola, P. (1994). *In the society of nature: A native ecology in Amazonia*. Cambridge University Press.

[13] Morphy, H. (1991). *Ancestral connections: Art and an Aboriginal system of knowledge*. University of Chicago Press.

[14] Altman, J. C. (2001). Sustainable development options on Aboriginal land: The hybrid economy in the twenty-first century. Centre for Aboriginal Economic Policy Research, ANU.

[15] Brush, S. B. (1976). Man's use of an Andean ecosystem. *Human Ecology*, 4(2), 147–166.

[16] Mount Pleasant, J. (2016). The science behind the Three Sisters mound system: An agronomic assessment of an Indigenous agricultural system in the Northeast. *Agronomy Journal*, 108(4), 1624–1632.

[17] Mbiti, J. S. (1990). *African religions and philosophy* (2nd ed.). Heinemann.

socio-economic structures also featured sophisticated governance institutions. Among the Dene in sub-Arctic Canada, decisions about resource use, hunting rights, and territory were made through consensus and social negotiation, underpinned by kinship and seasonal knowledge.[18] Rather than being "primitive" or static, as often characterized in colonial narratives, these systems were adaptive and resilient, shaped by centuries of interaction with diverse and often harsh environments. However, western colonial frameworks, rooted in capitalist assumptions about land as property and economy as market exchange, frequently failed to recognize these systems as legitimate or rational. This led to widespread dispossession, marginalization, and the disruption of Indigenous livelihoods.[19,20] However, as scholars increasingly acknowledge, these Indigenous models offer vital insights into sustainable economic organization and the governance of common resources, especially in the context of contemporary ecological crises and growing inequality.[21,22]

Sustainable Economic Practices and Resource Management

Indigenous communities across the world have historically developed complex and sustainable relationships with their environments, grounded in deep ecological knowledge, intergenerational stewardship, and cultural norms. These practices continue to influence contemporary sustainability discourse, particularly in debates on climate adaptation, biodiversity conservation, and alternative development models. In pre-colonial northern Australia, Yolngu sea rights illustrate how Indigenous marine tenure was structured around ecological cycles and kin-based governance. Access to fishing grounds and harvesting of resources such as trepang (sea

[18] Helm, J. (2000). *The People of Denendeh: Ethnohistory of the Indians of Canada's Northwest Territories*. McGill-Queen's University Press.

[19] Ostrom, E. (1990). *Governing the commons: The evolution of institutions for collective action*. Cambridge University Press.

[20] Sahlins, M. (1972). *Stone Age economics*. Aldine-Atherton.

[21] De la Cadena, M., & Blaser, M. (Eds.). (2018). *A world of many worlds*. Duke University Press.

[22] Berkes, F. (2012). *Sacred ecology* (3rd ed.). Routledge.

cucumber) was not only seasonal but embedded in ceremonial responsibilities that reinforced sustainable practices.[23] This has modern parallels in Indigenous Protected Areas (IPAs) and sea country management plans where Yolngu and other Aboriginal groups collaborate with the state to co-manage biodiversity while asserting custodianship.[24] In the Andean highlands, Quechua and Aymara communities practiced vertical ecological zonation, a spatial strategy that diversified crop production across multiple altitudes, minimizing risks from frost and drought. The integration of native crops such as potatoes, quinoa, and maize was coupled with sophisticated irrigation systems and soil conservation terraces, enhancing food security and ecological resilience.[25] This tradition persists in present-day agroecological initiatives, where Indigenous farmers not only preserve but also adapt ancestral techniques, such as intercropping, polyculture, and water-harvesting systems, to address contemporary climatic instability, biodiversity loss, and economic marginalization. These practices are not static relics of the past but are actively transformed to meet new environmental and social conditions. For instance, Quechua communities in the Peruvian Andes continue to use vertical archipelagos and native crop varieties to buffer against unpredictable weather and global market volatility.[26,27] Similarly, in Central America, Mayan milpa systems have been revitalized through participatory agroecological projects that integrate traditional ecological knowledge (TEK) with scientific research to enhance soil fertility and food security.[28] These cases highlight the dynamic resilience of Indigenous agroecology and their relevance to

[23] Morphy, H. (1991). Ancestral Connections: Art and an Aboriginal System of Knowledge. University of Chicago Press.

[24] Altman, J., & Kerins, S. (2012). People on Country: Vital Landscapes, Indigenous Futures. Federation Press.

[25] Brush, S. B. (1976). *Man's Use of an Andean Ecosystem*. Human Ecology, 4(2), 147–166.

[26] Brush, S. B. (2004). Farmers' Bounty: Locating Crop Diversity in the Contemporary World. Yale University Press.

[27] Zimmerer, K. S. (2014). Conservation booms with agricultural expansion: Sustainability and shifting environmental governance in Latin America. Annual Review of Environment and Resources, 39, 237–265. https://doi.org/10.1146/annurev-environ-101813-013212.

[28] Altieri, M. A., & Toledo, V. M. (2011). The agroecological revolution in Latin America: rescuing nature, ensuring food sovereignty and empowering peasants. Journal of Peasant Studies, 38(3), 587–612. https://doi.org/10.1080/03066150.2011.582947.

broader discourses on sustainable development and climate adaptation. Furthermore, the Iroquois Confederacy (Haudenosaunee) employed intercropping systems centred on the "Three Sisters": maize, beans, and squash. This polyculture created a mutually reinforcing ecological niche, corn provided a stalk for the beans to climb, beans fixed nitrogen in the soil, and squash suppressed weeds and conserved moisture. Such practices were accompanied by communal storage systems and decision-making councils that regulated resource use and collective welfare through coordinated seasonal planning, consensus-based governance, and customary laws. For example, agricultural surpluses, such as maize, beans, and squash, were stored in shared granaries under the supervision of clan leaders or elders, who were responsible for distributing food during times of scarcity or for ceremonial use. Resource allocation decisions were made collectively in village councils, where members debated the timing of planting and harvesting, land rotation schedules, and the equitable division of labour. These decisions were guided by oral traditions, social norms, and long-standing ecological knowledge, ensuring that overuse was avoided and that community needs were met in a sustainable and equitable manner.[29,30,31] Recent scholarship has argued for the relevance of these methods in sustainable agriculture, especially in marginal environments facing the stress of monoculture and land degradation. Studies have shown that Indigenous polycultures such as the Three Sisters system not only enhance biodiversity but also improve soil health, reduce pest pressures, and ensure greater food security compared to input-intensive monoculture systems.[32] These traditional techniques rely on ecological interactions and resource complementarities that support

[29] Mount Pleasant, J., 2016. *The science behind the Three Sisters mound system: An agronomic assessment of an Indigenous agricultural system in the Northeast*. Agronomy Journal, 108(2), pp. 1086–1100. https://doi.org/10.2134/agronj2015.06.0326.

[30] Mason, R.E., Savoie, K., DeMent, M. and Garibay, J., 2022. *Reclaiming Indigenous agricultural practices: Agroecological contributions of the Three Sisters polyculture*. Agriculture and Human Values, 39, pp. 115–130. https://doi.org/10.1007/s10460-021-10244-y.

[31] Morphy, H., 1991. *Ancestral connections: Art and an Aboriginal system of knowledge*. Chicago: University of Chicago Press.

[32] Mason, R.E., Savoie, K., DeMent, M. and Garibay, J., 2022. *Reclaiming Indigenous agricultural practices: Agroecological contributions of the Three Sisters polyculture*. Agriculture and Human Values, 39, pp. 115–130. https://doi.org/10.1007/s10460-021-10244-y.

long-term productivity without dependence on chemical inputs, making them particularly well-suited for communities in ecologically vulnerable or degraded regions.[33,34] For example, the Three Sisters intercropping system, cultivating maize, beans, and squash together, exemplifies how different species contribute to a shared ecological niche: maize provides a stalk for bean vines to climb, beans fix nitrogen into the soil to enhance fertility, and squash offers ground cover that retains moisture and suppresses weeds.[35,36] In Andean regions, vertical ecological zonation allows farmers to exploit distinct microclimates by growing complementary crops, like potatoes at higher altitudes and maize or quinoa lower down, thus diversifying risk and optimizing land use efficiency.[37,38] These examples illustrate how Indigenous agroecological systems are structured around synergies between species and environmental conditions, yielding resilient and sustainable agricultural outcomes. Agroecological frameworks influenced by Indigenous practices are increasingly recognized as critical pathways for climate-resilient farming systems, especially in regions where industrial agriculture has produced significant social and environmental harms. In northeastern Brazil, the expansion of industrial soybean cultivation has led to deforestation, biodiversity loss, and the displacement of Indigenous communities, spurring movements towards

[33] Altieri, M.A. and Toledo, V.M., 2011. The agroecological revolution in Latin America: Rescuing nature, ensuring food sovereignty and empowering peasants. *Journal of Peasant Studies*, 38(3), pp. 587–612. https://doi.org/10.1080/03066150.2011.582947.

[34] Mount Pleasant, J., 2016. The science behind the Three Sisters mound system: An agronomic assessment of an Indigenous agricultural system in the Northeast. *Agronomy Journal*, 108(2), pp. 1086–1100. https://doi.org/10.2134/agronj2015.06.0326.

[35] Mount Pleasant, J., 2016. The science behind the Three Sisters mound system: An agronomic assessment of an Indigenous agricultural system in the Northeast. *Agronomy Journal*, 108(2), pp. 1086–1100. https://doi.org/10.2134/agronj2015.06.0326.

[36] Mason, R.E., Savoie, K., DeMent, M. and Garibay, J., 2022. Reclaiming Indigenous agricultural practices: Agroecological contributions of the Three Sisters polyculture. *Agriculture and Human Values*, 39, pp. 115–130. https://doi.org/10.1007/s10460-021-10244-y.

[37] Brush, S.B., 2004. *Farmers' Bounty: Locating Crop Diversity in the Contemporary World*. New Haven: Yale University Press.

[38] Zimmerer, K.S., 2014. Conservation booms with agricultural expansion: Sustainability and shifting environmental governance in Latin America. *Annual Review of Environment and Resources*, 39, pp. 237–265. https://doi.org/10.1146/annurev-environ-101813-013212.

agroforestry rooted in traditional knowledge.[39] In India's Punjab region, decades of Green Revolution farming have resulted in severe groundwater depletion, soil degradation, and heightened farmer distress, conditions prompting renewed interest in traditional crop diversification and low-input sustainable practices.[40,41] Similarly, in the U.S. Midwest, large-scale monoculture has been linked to nutrient runoff, reduced soil fertility, and rural economic decline, leading to growing adoption of polyculture and regenerative techniques inspired by Indigenous systems such as the Three Sisters intercropping model.[42,43] These cases highlight the failures of conventional agriculture and the rising importance of agroecological alternatives grounded in cultural and ecological resilience. Moreover, other examples of sustainable indigenous agricultural practices can also be found. For example, among the Māori of Aotearoa (New Zealand), the concept of kaitiakitanga, a relational ethic of guardianship over land and water, guided customary practices of fishing, foraging, and land rotation. Seasonal restrictions (rahui) were imposed to allow regeneration of depleted resources, enforced through social consensus and spiritual sanctions.[44] This ethic now informs the legal recognition of natural entities such as the Whanganui River and Te Urewera as legal persons, co-governed by Indigenous and government authorities.[45] In West Africa, the Sahelian pastoralist systems of the Fulani offer another

[39] Altieri, M.A. and Toledo, V.M., 2011. The agroecological revolution in Latin America: Rescuing nature, ensuring food sovereignty and empowering peasants. *Journal of Peasant Studies*, 38(3), pp. 587–612. https://doi.org/10.1080/03066150.2011.582947.

[40] Shiva, V., 1991. *The Violence of the Green Revolution: Third World Agriculture, Ecology, and Politics*. London: Zed Books.

[41] Mazoyer, M. and Roudart, L., 2006. *A History of World Agriculture: From the Neolithic Age to the Current Crisis*. London: Earthscan.

[42] Mount Pleasant, J., 2016. The science behind the Three Sisters mound system: An agronomic assessment of an Indigenous agricultural system in the Northeast. *Agronomy Journal*, 108(2), pp. 1086–1100. https://doi.org/10.2134/agronj2015.06.0326.

[43] Mason, R.E., Savoie, K., DeMent, M. and Garibay, J., 2022. Reclaiming Indigenous agricultural practices: Agroecological contributions of the Three Sisters polyculture. *Agriculture and Human Values*, 39, pp. 115–130. https://doi.org/10.1007/s10460-021-10244-y.

[44] Roberts, M., Norman, W., Minhinnick, N., Wihongi, D., & Kirkwood, C. (1995). Kaitiakitanga: Maori perspectives on conservation. *Pacific Conservation Biology*, 2(1), 7–20.

[45] Charpleix, L. (2018). The Whanganui River as Te Awa Tupua: Place-based law in a legally pluralistic society. *The Geographical Journal*, 184(1), 19–30.

example of adaptive Indigenous management. Livelihoods based on transhumance (seasonal mobility) respond to rainfall variability and pasture availability. The communal negotiation of grazing corridors and wells ensures equitable access, while avoiding ecological exhaustion.[46] Contemporary pressures from land enclosure, climate change, and state policies have disrupted these patterns, yet recent policy shifts have begun to revalue Indigenous seasonal mobility as a rational strategy for resilience.[47] Across these cases, Indigenous resource management is characterized by relationality, the understanding that humans, non-human life, and land are interconnected through reciprocal obligations. This stands in contrast to extractivist logic which separates society from nature and prioritize short-term gains. As climate change intensifies and biodiversity loss accelerates, the relevance of Indigenous sustainability frameworks is increasingly acknowledged not only by anthropologists and ecologists, but also by multilateral institutions such as the Intergovernmental Science-Policy Platform on Biodiversity and Ecosystem Services (IPBES), the Food and Agriculture Organization (FAO) of the United Nations, and the Convention on Biological Diversity (CBD). These bodies have highlighted the importance of Indigenous and local knowledge in conserving ecosystems, enhancing climate resilience, and supporting food security. For instance, it has become evident[48] that Indigenous-managed lands often exhibit higher biodiversity and lower degradation rates compared to adjacent lands, while FAO[49] has incorporated traditional agroecological systems into its global framework for sustainable food systems. Similarly, the CBD's post-2020 Global Biodiversity Framework explicitly calls for the

[46] Turner, M. D. (2004). Political ecology and the moral dimensions of "resource conflicts": The case of farmer–herder conflicts in the Sahel. *Political Geography*, 23(7), 863–889.

[47] Catley, A., Lind, J., & Scoones, I. (Eds.). (2013). *Pastoralism and Development in Africa: Dynamic Change at the Margins*. Routledge.

[48] Intergovernmental Science-Policy Platform on Biodiversity and Ecosystem Services (IPBES), 2019. *Summary for Policymakers of the Global Assessment Report on Biodiversity and Ecosystem Services*. Bonn: IPBES Secretariat. https://doi.org/10.5281/zenodo.3553579.

[49] Food and Agriculture Organization (FAO), 2021. *Indigenous Peoples' Food Systems: Insights on Sustainability and Resilience from the Frontline of Climate Change*. Rome: FAO.

inclusion of Indigenous peoples in conservation planning and the recognition of their land rights and knowledge systems as crucial to halting biodiversity loss.[50]

Role of Social Structures in Economic Governance

Indigenous economic systems were embedded in social relations. Kinship ties, clan obligations, and tribal councils shaped production, distribution, and conflict resolution. In many societies, such as the Dene of Canada, land and resource use was organized through extended kin networks that governed access based on customary law and reciprocal obligations.[51] In Aotearoa (New Zealand), Māori *hapū* (sub-tribes) held collective authority over land (*whenua*), fisheries, and forests, making economic decisions through consensus and guided by ancestral principles like *kaitiakitanga* (guardianship).[52] Similarly, among the Tuareg in the Sahel, trade and mobility across the desert were historically coordinated by traditional leaders known as *amenokal*, who exercised political and spiritual authority over confederations of nomadic clans. These leaders regulated access to key trans-Saharan caravan routes, such as those linking Timbuktu, Agadez, and Ghat, which were essential for the movement of salt, dates, textiles, and slaves. The *amenokal* not only managed territorial passage rights but also mediated disputes between clans, secured tribute or tolls from passing caravans, and maintained diplomatic relationships with neighbouring ethnic groups and colonial authorities. Their ability to negotiate inter-group alliances and adjudicate conflict was crucial for sustaining both trade and Tuareg autonomy in a harsh and politically fragmented environment. For example, *amenokals* often forged strategic alliances with Arab traders, Hausa merchants, and even colonial administrators to secure safe passage and favourable trade conditions across the central Sahara. They also brokered truces between rival Tuareg confederations such as the Kel Ahaggar and the Kel Adagh to prevent disruptions along critical trade corridors. These leaders acted as mediators in disputes

[50] Convention on Biological Diversity (CBD), 2022. *Global Biodiversity Outlook 5*. Montreal: Secretariat of the CBD.

[51] Helm, J., 1981. *The People of Denendeh: Ethnohistory of the Dene*. Iowa City: University of Iowa Press.

[52] Durie, M., 1998. *Te Mana, Te Kāwanatanga: The Politics of Māori Self-Determination*. Auckland: Oxford University Press.

over grazing rights, water access, and caravan tolls, resolving conflicts through customary law and clan-based councils. Such diplomatic and legal authority enabled Tuareg societies to maintain control over vast desert territories despite the encroachment of colonial borders and the erosion of nomadic lifeways under post-colonial state regimes.[53] Indigenous governance systems, such as kinship networks, clan obligations, tribal councils, and traditional leadership roles, decentralized power and promoted economic resilience by embedding accountability and reciprocity within social relationships, in stark contrast to the centralized, hierarchical, and extractive nature of colonial economic systems.[54]

Spiritual Foundations of Economic Activity

In Indigenous worldviews, the economy was inseparable from spiritual and moral systems. Land, animals, and natural features were considered sentient and sacred, and economic activity was regulated through ritual and cosmological relationships. Among the Inuit, hunting practices involve ceremonies that honour the spirits of animals, reinforcing respectful and sustainable interaction with ecosystems.[55] In Amazonian societies, such as the Achuar of Ecuador and Peru, subsistence practices like hunting and swidden agriculture are inseparably bound to a cosmology in which non-human beings, animals, plants, rivers are seen as sentient and morally engaged persons. Hunting is not merely an economic activity, but a deeply ritualized practice governed by spiritual taboos and shamanic mediation; hunters must respect the "owners" of animal species (aents), and improper conduct, such as overhunting or disrespect for animal spirits, can lead to illness or failure in the hunt.[56,57] Agricultural cycles are similarly ritualized, with planting and harvesting coordinated through seasonal ceremonies and dream-guided instructions from plant

[53] Keenan, J., 2005. *The Lesser Gods of the Sahara: Social Change and Political Transformation among the Tuareg of Algeria*. London: Frank Cass.

[54] Ostrom, E., 1990. *Governing the Commons: The Evolution of Institutions for Collective Action*. Cambridge: Cambridge University Press.

[55] Berkes, F., 2012. *Sacred Ecology*. 3rd ed. New York: Routledge.

[56] Descola, P., 1994. *In the Society of Nature: A Native Ecology in Amazonia*. Cambridge: Cambridge University Press.

[57] Rival, L., 1998. *The Social Life of Trees: Anthropological Perspectives on Tree Symbolism*. Oxford: Berg.

spirits. These practices reflect a relational ontology in which humans are not separate from nature but part of a network of reciprocal obligations that sustain ecological balance.[58,59] Such ontologies, sometimes termed "relational ontologies" differ fundamentally from Western economic logic, which views nature as inert and commodifiable.[60] Moreover, similar to other indigenous beliefs, the African philosophy of *Ubuntu*, common in Nguni-speaking societies, reflects a similar ethic: "I am because we are". This collectivist orientation governs wealth redistribution, communal labour, and intergenerational care, anchoring economic decisions in social cohesion and shared survival.[61] Traditional Indigenous socio-economic structures were holistic, collective, and ecologically attuned. They prioritized relational balance over extractive growth and operated through decentralized governance deeply rooted in social and spiritual life. While these systems were disrupted or suppressed under colonial regimes, they continue to offer living alternatives to dominant economic models, particularly relevant in an age of climate breakdown and social inequality. Engaging seriously with these frameworks is not only a matter of historical redress but offers pathways towards more sustainable and just futures.

1.3 Indigenous Knowledge Systems and Technological Practices

Indigenous knowledge systems encompass a wide array of medicinal, agricultural, and ecological understandings developed through generations of lived experience, observation, and cultural transmission. These systems are highly localized and adapted to specific ecological contexts, forming the backbone of Indigenous technological innovation. In the Andean highlands, for example, Quechua and Aymara communities developed complex vertical ecological zonation farming systems that maximized ecological niches by cultivating different crops, such as potatoes, maize, and quinoa, across multiple altitudinal belts to reduce risk from

[58] Viveiros de Castro, E., 2004. *Exchanging Perspectives: The Transformation of Objects into Subjects in Amerindian Ontologies. Common Knowledge*, 10(3), pp. 463–484.

[59] Kohn, E., 2013. *How Forests Think: Toward an Anthropology Beyond the Human*. Berkeley: University of California Press.

[60] De la Cadena, M. and Blaser, M. eds., 2018. *A World of Many Worlds*. Durham: Duke University Press.

[61] Mbiti, J.S., 1990. *African Religions and Philosophy*. 2nd ed. Oxford: Heinemann.

climate variability.[62] Complementing this zonation system were elaborate terracing and irrigation networks, such as those at Moray in Peru, which modulated microclimates and moisture levels to sustain intensive cultivation.[63] Indigenous water management techniques are another key example of technological ingenuity. In sub-Saharan Africa, the Zai pits used by Sahelian farmers, particularly in Burkina Faso and Mali, illustrate how traditional ecological knowledge can rehabilitate degraded land. These small, hand-dug basins concentrate water and organic matter around crops, increasing yields under arid conditions.[64] Similarly, among the Indigenous peoples of the Amazon Basin, raised-field agriculture has been rediscovered as a sustainable technique. These elevated plots, constructed to avoid flooding and enhance nutrient retention, demonstrate effective long-term landscape modification.[65] Fishing and aquaculture practices also reflect deep ecological insight. The Yolngu people of northern Australia traditionally implemented sea tenure systems based on kinship and seasonal knowledge, allowing for sustainable harvesting of fish and shellfish without overexploitation.[66] In the Pacific, Hawaiian fishponds (loko iʻa) are among the most sophisticated Indigenous aquaculture systems, relying on tidal flows and rock enclosures to trap and cultivate fish while allowing smaller fry to escape, thus ensuring reproduction.[67] Despite this wealth of empirical knowledge, colonial powers routinely dismissed Indigenous systems as unscientific, even as they extracted and appropriated components for their own ends. Medicinal plants used by Indigenous peoples were catalogued by European botanists and often commercialized without compensation or recognition. The use

[62] Brush, S.B., 2004. *Farmers' Bounty: Locating Crop Diversity in the Contemporary World*. New Haven: Yale University Press.

[63] Erickson, C.L. (2000). *The Lake Titicaca Basin: A Pre-Columbian Built Landscape*. In: B.L. Turner II, W.B. Meyer (Eds.), *Global Land Use and Land Cover Change*. University of Arizona Press.

[64] Reij, C., Tappan, G. and Smale, M., 2009. *Agroenvironmental Transformation in the Sahel: Another Kind of "Green Revolution"*. Washington, DC: IFPRI.

[65] Denevan, W.M., 2001. *Cultivated Landscapes of Native Amazonia and the Andes*. Oxford: Oxford University Press.

[66] Morphy, H., 1991. *Ancestral Connections: Art and an Aboriginal System of Knowledge*. Chicago: University of Chicago Press.

[67] Kittinger, J.N., Bambico, T.M., Minton, D., Miller, A., Mejia, M., Kalei, N. and Wilcox, B.A., 2015. Restoring coupled social–ecological systems in a Hawaiian community: A social–ecological approach to fishpond restoration. *Ecology and Society*, 20(1), p. 36.

of cinchona bark by Quechua peoples for treating malaria was co-opted and synthesized into quinine by colonial pharmaceutical industries.[68] Similarly, Indigenous Australian fire management practices, long used to reduce bushfire risk and enhance biodiversity, were historically criminalized but are now being reintegrated into national land management policies due to their proven ecological benefits.[69] These patterns reflect a broader political economy in which Indigenous technological practices were simultaneously devalued and exploited. While colonial narratives framed Indigenous peoples as backward or primitive, they often depended on the very systems they sought to erase. In contemporary times, there is a growing recognition of the critical role Indigenous knowledge can play in addressing global challenges such as climate change, food insecurity, and biodiversity loss.[70] However, ensuring that such recognition leads to equitable collaboration rather than renewed forms of appropriation remains an ongoing struggle, as Indigenous knowledge is frequently integrated into environmental, agricultural, and pharmaceutical policies without adequate compensation, consent, or representation of Indigenous voices. For example, traditional ecological practices are often cited in climate resilience frameworks or sustainable development programs, yet Indigenous communities are rarely included as equal partners in research agendas or policy design.[71,72] This dynamic risks reproducing extractive relationships under the guise of inclusion, where knowledge is valued but the knowledge-holders remain marginalized, echoing patterns of colonial exploitation within modern institutional frameworks.

[68] Greene, S., 2004. *Indigenous People Incorporated? Culture as Politics, Culture as Property in Pharmaceutical Bioprospecting. Current Anthropology*, 45(2), pp. 211–237.

[69] Gammage, B., 2011. *The Biggest Estate on Earth: How Aborigines Made Australia.* Sydney: Allen & Unwin.

[70] IPBES (Intergovernmental Science-Policy Platform on Biodiversity and Ecosystem Services), 2019. *Summary for Policymakers of the Global Assessment Report on Biodiversity and Ecosystem Services.* Bonn: IPBES Secretariat.

[71] Greene, S., 2004. Indigenous People Incorporated? Culture as Politics, Culture as Property in Pharmaceutical Bioprospecting. *Current Anthropology*, 45(2), pp. 211–237.

[72] Smith, L.T., 2012. *Decolonizing Methodologies: Research and Indigenous Peoples.* 2nd ed. London: Zed Books.

1.4 The Onset of Colonization and Its Transformative Impact

The initial encounters between Indigenous societies and European colonizers were shaped by profound asymmetries in technology, worldviews, and intentions. In the Americas, the arrival of Spanish and Portuguese expeditions in the late 15th and early sixteenth centuries led to immediate disruption. The Aztec and Inca empires, with complex governance structures and advanced agricultural systems, were rapidly overthrown through a combination of military force, strategic alliances, and the catastrophic introduction of Old-World diseases such as smallpox.[73] Similar patterns were repeated in North America, Australia, and parts of Africa and Asia, where Indigenous populations were dramatically reduced, often by over 90%, within decades of first contact due to the combined effects of introduced diseases, violent conflict, land dispossession, and forced assimilation.[74,75] In North America, for instance, the introduction of smallpox, measles, and influenza decimated Indigenous communities such as the Mandan and Cherokee, with mortality rates exceeding 80% in some areas by the early nineteenth century. In Australia, British colonization led to catastrophic population losses among Aboriginal peoples due to diseases like smallpox, likely introduced in 1789, as well as widespread violence and displacement.[76] Similar devastation occurred in Southern Africa, where settler colonialism, land expropriation, and epidemics severely reduced Khoisan and Nguni populations. In the Andaman Islands and parts of Southeast Asia, the arrival of European powers brought lethal pathogens and social disruption to previously isolated groups. These demographic collapses had enduring socioeconomic consequences, dismantling traditional governance systems, reducing generational knowledge transmission, and creating conditions for colonial dominance and economic marginalization. The loss of a significant portion of the population meant that Indigenous economies,

[73] Crosby, A.W., 1972. *The Columbian Exchange: Biological and Cultural Consequences of 1492*. Westport: Greenwood Press.

[74] Diamond, J., 1997. *Guns, Germs, and Steel: The Fates of Human Societies*. New York: W.W. Norton.

[75] Crosby, A.W., 1972. *The Columbian Exchange: Biological and Cultural Consequences of 1492*. Westport: Greenwood Press.

[76] Reynolds, H., 1996. *Aboriginal Sovereignty: Reflections on Race, State and Nation*. Sydney: Allen & Unwin.

which relied on communal labour and shared stewardship of land, could no longer sustain pre-existing systems of production and trade. For example, in parts of the Americas, the drastic population decline following European contact led to the abandonment of agricultural lands and trade networks, forcing Indigenous communities into dependency on colonial economies and labour systems.

Land dispossession was central to the colonial project. In North America, the Doctrine of Discovery and later legal instruments such as the Indian Removal Act (1830) justified the systematic appropriation of Indigenous territories.[77] In Australia, the legal doctrine of terra nullius denied Aboriginal peoples any proprietary rights, facilitating vast land seizures.[78] These processes disrupted subsistence economies and severed spiritual ties to land, a cornerstone of Indigenous cosmologies. Resource exploitation followed closely behind. Colonial powers extracted minerals, timber, and agricultural produce for imperial markets, often using coerced or unpaid Indigenous labour. In the Congo Free State, rubber extraction under Belgian rule resulted in widespread atrocities and population decline.[79] In the Andes, Indigenous communities were conscripted into mit'a labour systems in silver mines such as Potosí, leading to demographic collapse and economic dislocation.[80]

The socio-economic consequences of colonization extended far beyond immediate violence. Traditional governance systems, such as tribal councils, chieftaincies, and consensus-based decision-making, were frequently dismantled or subordinated to colonial administrative structures. Christian missionaries often replaced Indigenous religious institutions, and colonial education systems promoted European languages and values, marginalizing local knowledge.[81] Cultural suppression was not incidental but deliberate. In Canada and Australia, policies of forced

[77] Banner, S., 2005. *How the Indians Lost Their Land: Law and Power on the Frontier*. Cambridge, MA: Harvard University Press.

[78] Reynolds, H., 1996. *Aboriginal Sovereignty: Reflections on Race, State and Nation*. Sydney: Allen & Unwin.

[79] Hochschild, A., 1998. *King Leopold's Ghost: A Story of Greed, Terror, and Heroism in Colonial Africa*. Boston: Houghton Mifflin.

[80] Bakewell, P., 1984. *Miners of the Red Mountain: Indian Labour in Potosí, 1545–1650*. Albuquerque: University of New Mexico Press.

[81] Smith, L.T., 2012. *Decolonizing Methodologies: Research and Indigenous Peoples*. 2nd ed. London: Zed Books.

assimilation included the removal of Indigenous children into boarding schools, where they were forbidden to speak their languages or practice their traditions, a legacy now recognized as cultural genocide.[82] These disruptions laid the foundation for long-term economic marginalization. Indigenous communities today often face higher rates of poverty, unemployment, and health disparities, a direct legacy of historical dispossession and systemic exclusion.[83] While colonialism sought to erase Indigenous autonomy, resilience and resistance have remained constants. From armed uprisings such as the Mapuche resistance in Chile to modern legal battles over land rights, Indigenous peoples have continuously asserted sovereignty and cultural identity in the face of persistent challenges.

1.5 Colonialism and the Legacy of Economic Dependence

Colonial regimes across the globe systematically restructured Indigenous economies to serve imperial interests, resulting in deep-rooted economic dependencies that persist today. One of the central mechanisms of this transformation was the erosion of Indigenous self-sufficiency through land dispossession, forced labour regimes, and trade monopolies. These processes not only extracted wealth from Indigenous communities but also integrated them into global capitalist systems on highly unequal terms. In Latin America, Spanish and Portuguese colonial authorities implemented the encomienda and mita systems, which coerced Indigenous populations into mining and agricultural labour. In Potosí, Bolivia, the silver mines relied heavily on the forced labour of Indigenous Andeans under the mita, generating vast profits for the Spanish Crown while dismantling local subsistence economies.[84] Similarly, in Africa, colonial powers such as Belgium in the Congo instituted violent labour regimes

[82] Truth and Reconciliation Commission of Canada, 2015. *Honouring the Truth, Reconciling for the Future: Summary of the Final Report of the Truth and Reconciliation Commission of Canada.* Ottawa: TRC.

[83] Anderson, I., Baum, F., & Bentley, M. (2007). *Beyond Bandaids: Exploring the Social Determinants of Aboriginal Health.* Darwin: Cooperative Research Centre for Aboriginal Health.

[84] Bakewell, P., 1984. *Miners of the Red Mountain: Indian Labour in Potosí, 1545–1650.* Albuquerque: University of New Mexico Press.

that forced Indigenous people to harvest rubber, vividly recounted in Hochschild's study of the Congo Free State.[85]

In Australia, the introduction of settler colonial economic models disrupted Indigenous trade networks and customary land management practices. Colonial authorities appropriated vast tracts of Aboriginal land, criminalized traditional economies, and instituted welfare-based dependencies that undermined economic autonomy.[86] In North America, Indigenous communities were displaced onto reservations, where federal policies restricted subsistence practices and introduced dependency on government rations and subsidies, leading to long-term underdevelopment.[87] Trade restrictions and monopolistic control were also common features. In British-controlled India, for instance, the East India Company manipulated markets to favour British textile imports while undermining Indigenous weaving industries, creating widespread deindustrialization and economic dependency.[88] Similarly, in the Americas, colonial authorities tightly controlled Indigenous access to markets, often limiting them to specific goods and imposing taxes payable only in colonial currency or commodities. The long-term consequences of these imposed economic structures are stark. Many Indigenous communities today face persistent poverty, limited access to capital and markets, and ongoing reliance on state transfers or extractive industries. These outcomes are not coincidental but the cumulative legacy of colonial economic restructuring that prioritized imperial profits over Indigenous well-being and autonomy.[89]

[85] Hochschild, A. (1998) King Leopold's Ghost: A Story of Greed, Terror and Heroism in Colonial Africa. Boston: Houghton Mifflin.

[86] Reynolds, H., 1996. *Aboriginal Sovereignty: Reflections on Race, State and Nation*. Sydney: Allen & Unwin.

[87] Truth and Reconciliation Commission of Canada, 2015. *Honouring the Truth, Reconciling for the Future: Summary of the Final Report of the Truth and Reconciliation Commission of Canada*. Ottawa: TRC.

[88] Diamond, J., 1997. *Guns, Germs, and Steel: The Fates of Human Societies*. New York: W.W. Norton.

[89] Smith, L.T., 2012. *Decolonizing Methodologies: Research and Indigenous Peoples*. 2nd ed. London: Zed Books.

2 The Role of Political Economy in Examining Indigenous Contexts

2.1 Defining Political Economy in the Indigenous Context

Political economy, as a field of study, examines the relationships between economic systems, political institutions, and power structures. At its core, it interrogates how resources are produced, distributed, and controlled, and by whom. Traditionally applied to the analysis of capitalist economies and state institutions, the political economy framework becomes particularly illuminating when applied to Indigenous contexts, where economic life is deeply entwined with sociopolitical organization, land tenure systems, and cultural autonomy. For Indigenous peoples, political economy is not merely a matter of material exchange; it involves complex negotiations over sovereignty, territorial rights, and recognition within broader national and global systems. Indigenous economies have historically been embedded in kinship networks, communal governance, and reciprocal exchange systems, yet colonialism has forcibly integrated them into state-centric capitalist structures often designed without their consent or benefit.[90,91] A political economy lens helps reveal the asymmetrical power relations that continue to marginalize Indigenous communities. For instance, in Australia, the Community Development Programme (CDP) has been critiqued for reproducing colonial labour hierarchies by obligating remote Aboriginal communities to participate in unpaid or low-paid labour schemes under threat of welfare sanctions.[92] Similarly, in Canada, resource extraction projects on Indigenous lands, such as oil pipelines, are frequently negotiated between state and corporate actors with limited consultation or benefit to Indigenous nations, despite constitutional and treaty rights guaranteeing participation and

[90] Altman, J.C. (2005). Economic futures on Aboriginal land in remote and very remote Australia: Hybrid economies and joint ventures. In D. Austin-Broos & G. Macdonald (Eds.), Culture, Economy and Governance in Aboriginal Australia. Sydney University Press.

[91] Smith, L.T., 2012. Decolonizing Methodologies: Research and Indigenous Peoples. 2nd ed. London: Zed Books.

[92] Fowkes, L., & Sanders, W. (2016). Financial penalties in the remote Community Development Programme: Social security penalties or participation incentives? CAEPR Working Paper No. 111. ANU Centre for Aboriginal Economic Policy Research.

compensation.[93] Applying political economy also highlights the structural causes of Indigenous poverty, land alienation, and underdevelopment. In Latin America, neoliberal reforms in the 1980s and 1990s encouraged the privatization of communal Indigenous lands, disrupting traditional governance and introducing new dependencies on volatile market economies.[94] These transitions disproportionately impacted Indigenous farmers, who lacked access to credit, legal representation, and infrastructure necessary to compete in commodified agricultural markets.[95] Moreover, political economy offers a framework for understanding resistance and resurgence. Across the globe, Indigenous movements for self-determination, from the Zapatistas in Chiapas to the Idle No More movement in Canada, can be seen as struggles to reclaim not only land but control over economic decision-making, cultural reproduction, and political voice.[96,97] In this sense, political economy is not just a lens for critique, but also a tool for articulating alternatives grounded in Indigenous knowledge systems and values. Understanding the political economy of Indigenous peoples thus requires a rethinking of standard economic categories. Concepts like "wealth", "labour", and "ownership" must be recontextualized within Indigenous worldviews, which often prioritize collective well-being, spiritual stewardship, and intergenerational equity over individual accumulation. By foregrounding power relations and historical processes, the political economy approach enables a deeper grasp of both the constraints and the possibilities Indigenous communities face in their ongoing pursuit of economic and political justice.

[93] Coulthard, G.S., 2014. Red Skin, White Masks: Rejecting the Colonial Politics of Recognition. Minneapolis: University of Minnesota Press.

[94] Bryan, J. (2012). Rethinking territory: social justice and neoliberalism in Latin America's extractive frontiers. Geography Compass, 6(2), 63–78.

[95] Kay, C., 2001. Neoliberalism, Peasant Agriculture and Rural Livelihoods: Threat or Opportunity? Latin AmericanPerspectives, 28(3), pp. 16–38.

[96] Escobar, A., 2008. Territories of Difference: Place, Movements, Life, Redes. Durham: Duke University Press.

[97] Simpson, L.B., 2017. As We Have Always Done: Indigenous Freedom through Radical Resistance. Minneapolis: University of Minnesota Press.

2.2 *Key Political Economy Themes in Indigenous Studies*

Land and resource rights have been at the core of Indigenous political economy, as control over land forms the material basis of cultural survival, economic activity, and political autonomy. Legal battles such as *Delgamuukw v. British Columbia* (1997) in Canada and the *Mabo v. Queensland* (No. 2) decision (1992) in Australia redefined the scope of Indigenous land rights by challenging colonial-era doctrines like terra nullius. Terra nullius, meaning "land belonging to no one", was a colonial legal fiction used to justify the occupation of Indigenous territories by falsely claiming they were uninhabited or lacked recognizable systems of law and land ownership. In Latin America, Bolivia's 2009 constitution formally recognized Indigenous territories (Tierras Comunitarias de Origen), yet practical enforcement remains uneven.[98] Economic sovereignty and self-determination involve Indigenous peoples reclaiming control over economic development to ensure culturally grounded and ecologically sustainable livelihoods. For instance, the Yolngu people in Australia have developed community-owned enterprises tied to land and sea management, while resisting assimilation into extractive capitalist systems.[99] Similarly, the Zapatista movement in Chiapas, Mexico, exemplifies a form of Indigenous economic autonomy that challenges state-led neoliberal models.[100] Global markets and policies increasingly shape Indigenous economies through mechanisms such as carbon offset markets, intellectual property regimes, and foreign investment. While the REDD+ (Reducing Emissions from Deforestation and Forest Degradation) initiative is praised for integrating forest conservation into climate finance, critics argue it can reinforce land alienation and bypass community governance.[101] This happens because carbon credits are

[98] Bebbington, A., 2009. The new extraction: Rewriting the political ecology of the Andes?. NACLA Report on the Americas, 42(5), pp. 12–20.

[99] Altman, J.C., 2005. Economic futures on Aboriginal land in remote and very remote Australia: Hybrid economies and joint ventures. In: D. Austin-Broos and G. Macdonald, eds. Culture, Economy and Governance in Aboriginal Australia. Sydney: Sydney University Press, pp. 211–234.

[100] Esteva, G., 1992. Development. In: W. Sachs, ed. The Development Dictionary: A Guide to Knowledge as Power. London: Zed Books, pp. 6–25.

[101] Larson, A.M., 2010. Making the 'rules of the game': Constituting territory and authority in Nicaragua's indigenous communities. Land Use Policy, 27(4), pp. 1143–1152.

typically issued to those holding formal title and meeting costly monitoring, reporting, and verification requirements, which channel power and payments to states, concessionaires, or external project developers, restrict customary access and livelihood practices, and sideline locally rooted decision-making institutions. Moreover, trade agreements like NAFTA and development interventions by institutions such as the World Bank have often advanced policies that prioritize foreign investment and resource extraction, such as mining, logging, and large-scale agriculture, while undermining Indigenous systems of land stewardship, disrupting local economies, and disregarding collective land rights. These externally driven projects frequently result in environmental degradation, displacement, and the erosion of Indigenous territorial sovereignty, despite being framed as engines of economic development.[102,103] These themes reveal the importance of integrating power, history, and resistance into the analysis of Indigenous economies. A political economy framework not only uncovers the structural barriers to Indigenous self-determination, such as land dispossession, marginalization from state policy, and dependency on welfare systems, but also highlights the alternative modes of life Indigenous peoples are actively constructing through practices rooted in relational economies, cultural resurgence, and autonomous governance. For example, many communities are building hybrid economies that combine traditional subsistence practices with selective engagement in market activities, establishing Indigenous-controlled schools and legal systems, and reclaiming land to reassert environmental stewardship and territorial sovereignty. These efforts challenge capitalist development models and assert Indigenous visions of well-being that prioritize kinship, reciprocity, and connection to land.

2.3 Analysing Power Dynamics: State vs. Indigenous Autonomy

Throughout history, state power has systematically constrained Indigenous autonomy by centralizing control over economic resources and governance structures. This dynamic manifests in policies that enforce

[102] Kay, C., 2006. Rural poverty and development strategies in Latin America. Journal of Agrarian Change, 6(4), pp. 455–491.

[103] Escobar, A., 1995. Encountering Development: The Making and Unmaking of the Third World. Princeton: Princeton University Press.

forced integration, suppress customary law, and limit access to traditional lands and subsistence activities. Across settler colonial contexts like Canada, Australia, and Latin America, Indigenous economies have been subordinated to state interests through legal frameworks and market-driven development. In Australia, the Northern Territory Emergency Response (2007), often referred to as "the Intervention", exemplified coercive state measures. While framed as a response to social issues, the policy imposed compulsory land leases and undermined local governance without proper consultation, effectively marginalizing Indigenous economic decision-making.[104] In the United States, the Dawes Act of 1887 partitioned collective tribal lands into individual allotments, eroding communal landholding systems and enabling non-Native land acquisition.[105] Such mechanisms often parallel broader patterns of extractivism. In Ecuador and Bolivia, oil and mining concessions have frequently been granted on Indigenous territories without free, prior, and informed consent, sparking mobilizations like the 2000–2002 Indigenous uprisings in Ecuador and the TIPNIS protest in Bolivia.[106,107] These conflicts underscore the power imbalance between state-sanctioned corporate interests and Indigenous claims to territorial sovereignty. Despite these challenges, Indigenous communities have continuously resisted marginalization and asserted economic and political rights. The Zapatista movement in Chiapas, Mexico, launched in 1994, established autonomous zones with alternative governance and economies based on Indigenous principles and collective ownership.[108] Similarly, in Canada, the Wet'suwet'en Nation's resistance to pipeline construction has brought global attention to Indigenous land rights and governance, highlighting the resilience of customary law systems against state encroachment.

[104] Altman, J.C., 2007. The Howard Government's Northern Territory Intervention: Are Neo-Paternalism and Indigenous Development Compatible? Topical Issue 16/2007, Centre for Aboriginal Economic Policy Research, ANU.

[105] Banner, S., 2005. How the Indians Lost Their Land: Law and Power on the Frontier. Cambridge, MA: Harvard University Press.

[106] Bryan, J., 2012. Rethinking Territory: Social and Environmental Conflicts over Resource Governance in Latin America. Journal of Latin American Geography, 11(1), pp. 7–31.

[107] Escobar, A., 2008. Territories of Difference: Place, Movements, Life, Redes. Durham: Duke University Press.

[108] Esteva, G., 2010. The Oaxaca Rebellion. Journal of Peasant Studies, 37(1), pp. 187–212.

These cases demonstrate that Indigenous autonomy is not merely about preserving culture but about reclaiming power over economic futures. Applying a political economy lens reveals the structural inequalities embedded in state-Indigenous relations and affirms the significance of Indigenous-led resistance as a form of political and economic reassertion.

2.4 *Relevance of Political Economy in Modern Indigenous Advocacy*

Indigenous communities around the world are increasingly employing political economy frameworks to articulate and advocate for their economic rights and policy reforms. These frameworks help explain how historical and contemporary power structures shape access to land, resources, and decision-making processes, providing a strategic basis for Indigenous movements that challenge neoliberal and colonial development paradigms.[109,110] One notable example is the Idle No More movement in Canada, which mobilized Indigenous peoples across the country against proposed federal legislation that threatened treaty rights and environmental protections. The movement foregrounded a critique of extractive economic models and demanded Indigenous sovereignty over lands and resources.[111] Similarly, in Latin America, the Zapatista movement in Chiapas, Mexico, has constructed an autonomous economic model rooted in Indigenous traditions, collective ownership, and resistance to neoliberal capitalism. Following their 1994 uprising, the Zapatistas established self-governing territories known as caracoles, where decision-making occurs through participatory assemblies and councils of elders. Within these territories, they operate agricultural cooperatives, artisan workshops, and community-run health and education systems that function outside of state control and corporate influence. For example, Zapatista coffee cooperatives export fair-trade coffee directly to solidarity networks abroad, bypassing exploitative intermediaries and maintaining community control over production and profits. Their education system, known as escuelas autónomas, prioritizes Indigenous languages, histories,

[109] Coulthard, G.S., 2014. Red Skin, White Masks: Rejecting the Colonial Politics of Recognition. Minneapolis: University of Minnesota Press.

[110] Smith, L.T., 2012. Decolonizing Methodologies: Research and Indigenous Peoples. 2nd ed. London: Zed Books.

[111] Simpson, L.B., 2017. As We Have Always Done: Indigenous Freedom through Radical Resistance. Minneapolis: University of Minnesota Press.

and epistemologies, challenging the colonial curriculum of state institutions. These practices form an alternative political economy that not only sustains material livelihoods but also reinforces cultural autonomy and political self-determination, resisting both state assimilation policies and dependency on global market forces.[112,113]

Beyond grassroots movements, Indigenous communities have launched numerous self-determined economic initiatives. In Australia, community-led ranger programs combine environmental stewardship with employment, enabling economic participation while maintaining cultural obligations to Country.[114] These initiatives often reject the narrow metrics of mainstream development by emphasizing relational well-being, environmental responsibility, and cultural continuity. At the international level, institutions like the United Nations Permanent Forum on Indigenous Issues (UNPFII), the International Labour Organization (ILO), and the United Nations Declaration on the Rights of Indigenous Peoples (UNDRIP) have played pivotal roles in legitimizing Indigenous economic claims. UNDRIP, adopted in 2007, affirms the rights of Indigenous peoples to freely pursue their economic, social, and cultural development and to maintain and strengthen their economic institutions.[115] Similarly, ILO Convention 169 emphasizes Indigenous control over development processes and resource management, setting global benchmarks for economic autonomy and consultation. Through these multi-level engagements, from grassroots to international forums, Indigenous peoples are reshaping the discourse on economic development, asserting rights that are collective, relational, and rooted in ancestral knowledge.

[112] Esteva, G. (2010) 'The Zapatistas and People's Power', Socialism and Democracy, 24(2), pp. 65–78.

[113] Holloway, J. (2002) Change the World Without Taking Power: The Meaning of Revolution Today. London: Pluto Press.

[114] Altman, J.C., 2007. Neo-paternalism and the destruction of CDEP. Arena Magazine, (89), pp. 32–35.

[115] United Nations, 2007. United Nations Declaration on the Rights of Indigenous Peoples (UNDRIP). [online] Available at: https://www.un.org/development/desa/indigenouspeoples/declaration-on-the-rights-of-indigenous-peoples.html.

3 Outline of the Book's Aims, Including the Question of European Dominance and Innovation

3.1 Aims and Objectives of the Book

This volume begins from the empirical reality, demonstrated across multiple regions and case studies, that Indigenous economies are institutionally embedded: land operates as a living nexus of spiritual, legal, ecological and economic relations; authority is distributed through kinship, clan and inter-polity compacts; and production and exchange are governed by customary law, ritual obligations and stewardship rather than by price alone.[116,117,118] To make this concrete, the volume details how tenure rules (e.g., seasonal access, clan guardianship, usufruct rights) allocate use and responsibility; how ritual calendars and ecological indicators structure planting, harvesting and hunting; and how dispute-resolution institutions, councils, elders, and consensus procedures, lower coordination costs and sustain cooperation across generations. Treating land and sovereignty as foundational institutions, rather than mere "factors" of production, allows us to trace mechanisms of change under colonization, globalization and state-led market integration: enclosure to cadastral title; collective governance to administrative units; commons to concessions; and Indigenous law to statutory or corporate codes. The analysis also foregrounds Indigenous innovation and adaptation: redesigns of tenure (e.g., layered customary-and-statutory arrangements), inter-group diplomacy (treaties, compacts and co-governance boards), and hybrid institutions (ranger programs, Indigenous trusts, guardianship roles) that protect country, sustain livelihoods and negotiate with states and firms on Indigenous terms.[119,120] Throughout, the volume centres institutional

[116] Polanyi, K. (1944) The Great Transformation: The Political and Economic Origins of Our Time. New York: Farrar & Rinehart. (Later eds. Beacon Press, 1957/2001).

[117] Ostrom, E. (1990) Governing the Commons: The Evolution of Institutions for Collective Action. Cambridge: Cambridge University Press.

[118] Scott, J.C. (1998) Seeing Like a State: How Certain Schemes to Improve the Human Condition Have Failed. New Haven, CT: Yale University Press.

[119] Sahlins, M. (1972) Stone Age Economics. Chicago: Aldine-Atherton.

[120] Graeber, D. (2011) Debt: The First 5,000 Years. Brooklyn, NY & London: Melville House.

and ecological realism, how people actually coordinate in specific places, over the stylised universals of abstract models. The volume also interrogates the structural roots of European ascendancy. Rather than treating "dominance" as endogenous genius, it documents how industrial capitalism, legal dispossession and imperial extraction co-produced European growth through the appropriation of land, labour, crops and knowledge (for example, potatoes, maize, cassava; cinchona/quinine), consistent with evidence on the demographic and urban impacts of New World crops and the wider comparative history of uneven development.[121,122] The narrative provides a process account: (i) territorial claims backed by violence and law; (ii) conversion of commons into tradeable assets; (iii) mobilization of coerced/cheap labour; (iv) long-distance commodity chains and insurance/finance innovations to extract surpluses; and (v) epistemic appropriation of indigenous knowledge (navigation, medicine, agronomy). In counterpoint, comparative syntheses show biodiversity and ecosystem outcomes are frequently better on Indigenous-managed lands, underscoring the effectiveness of Indigenous institutions in sustaining species richness, carbon stocks and landscape heterogeneity,[123,124] The implication is that Indigenous political economies are neither "premodern" nor inefficient; they are complex, adaptive and often ecologically superior systems that mainstream models have struggled to represent on their own terms.

Why is Indigenous Political Economy More Realistic Than Neoclassical or Marxist Perspectives?

Neoclassical economics typically models atomized agents with stable preferences, complete contracting and prices as sufficient statistics, while orthodox Marxist analysis often collapses institutional diversity into a

[121] Nunn, N. & Qian, N. (2011) 'The potato's contribution to population and urbanization: Evidence from a historical experiment', Quarterly Journal of Economics, 126(2), pp. 593–650.

[122] Pomeranz, K. (2000) The Great Divergence: China, Europe, and the Making of the Modern World Economy. Princeton, NJ: Princeton University Press.

[123] Garnett, S.T. et al. (2018) 'A spatial overview of the global importance of Indigenous lands for conservation', Nature Sustainability, 1(7), pp. 369–374.

[124] IPBES (2019) Global Assessment Report on Biodiversity and Ecosystem Services. Bonn: Intergovernmental Science-Policy Platform on Biodiversity and Ecosystem Services.

base–superstructure logic organized primarily around class and accumulation. Both lenses illuminate mechanisms, but both under-specify the meso-level where Indigenous economies live: legal pluralism (coexisting Indigenous, statutory and international law), collective choice (councils, clan mandates), ritual authority (legitimacy through ceremony and custodianship), polycentric governance (overlapping jurisdictions) and ecological feedbacks (rules tuned to water, fire and species cycles).[125,126] Building on the evidence assembled in Volume 1, these will be the first-order variables shaping production, allocation and distribution. We also evaluate outcomes in terms of capabilities, stewardship and intergenerational responsibility, not only utility or surplus, so that success is measured by maintained livelihoods, intact ecosystems, cultural continuity and political self-determination.[127] This produces a behavioural account that is institutionally embedded, ecologically situated, socially mediated, historically contingent and plural.

From Foundations to a New Model: Symbiotic Gaian Economics (SGE)

Volume 1 therefore contributes in two ways to the development of an alternative economic model, SGE. Firstly, it maps the institutional grammar of Indigenous economies (tenure mosaics, authority structures, relational ecologies) and lays the groundwork for an alternative framework developed across both volumes, facilitating the formulation of Symbiotic Gaian Economics (SGE). SGE synthesises Indigenous relational ontologies with institutional political economy to propose a model in which:

(a) **Symbiosis**—the mutual flourishing among human and more-than-human communities, is the central coordination principle, making reciprocity and consent primary design criteria for institutions.
(b) **The Gaian constraint**—biophysical limits and Earth-system interdependence—binds economic choice, so budget constraints

[125] Ostrom, E. (1990) Governing the Commons: The Evolution of Institutions for Collective Action. Cambridge: Cambridge University Press.

[126] Scott, J.C. (1998) Seeing Like a State: How Certain Schemes to Improve the Human Condition Have Failed. New Haven, CT: Yale University Press.

[127] Sen, A. (1999) Development as Freedom. Oxford: Oxford University Press. (US ed.: New York: Alfred A. Knopf, 1999).

include water, soil, biodiversity and climate stability alongside money; and

(c) **Governance**—is polycentric and consent-based, privileging Indigenous jurisdiction, commons stewardship and knowledge sovereignty.

In SGE, "efficiency" is recast as resilience with reciprocity (systems that absorb shocks without exporting harm), and prosperity as a capability set sustained within ecological thresholds. The volume clarifies operational implications such as multi-criteria accounting (ecological–social–financial), consent and veto as governance primitives, and rule sets that reward restoration and caretaking.[128,129,130,131] Volume 2 will focus on building on the foundations laid in Volume 1, Volume 2 turns to present-day arenas where institutions are actively being defended, leveraged and redesigned: enterprise development; labour and value chains; climate and biodiversity finance (REDD+[132], offsets, biocredits[133]); data and digital economies[134]; public law and international norms.[135,136]; and multi-level regulatory regimes. We ask when price-based solutions work (e.g., when rights are secure and monitoring is locally governed),

128 Polanyi, K. (1944) The Great Transformation: The Political and Economic Origins of Our Time. New York: Farrar & Rinehart. Later eds. Beacon Press, 1957/2001).

129 Ostrom, E. (1990) Governing the Commons: The Evolution of Institutions for Collective Action. Cambridge: Cambridge University Press.

130 Sen, A. (1999) Development as Freedom. Oxford: Oxford University Press. (US ed.: New York: Alfred A. Knopf, 1999).

131 Escobar, A. (2018) Designs for the Pluriverse: Radical Interdependence, Autonomy, and the Making of Worlds. Durham, NC: Duke University Press.

132 UN-REDD Programme (2009) UN-REDD Programme Strategy 2011–2015. Geneva: UN-REDD Programme.

133 Convention on Biological Diversity (CBD) (2022) Global Biodiversity Framework: COP15 Decision. Montreal: CBD Secretariat.

134 Kukutai, T. and Taylor, J. (eds.) (2016) Indigenous Data Sovereignty: Toward an Agenda. Canberra: ANU Press.

135 United Nations General Assembly (UNGA) (2007) United Nations Declaration on the Rights of Indigenous Peoples, A/RES/61/295 (13 September 2007). New York: United Nations.

136 International Labour Organisation (1989) C169—Indigenous and Tribal Peoples Convention, 1989 (No. 169). Geneva: ILO.

how they misfire (e.g., when MRV—Monitoring, Reporting, Verification—and title regimes recentralize control), and why polycentric, community-governed approaches often outperform standard toolkits, extending insights from polycentric climate governance.[137] The volume stress-tests carbon and biodiversity markets, showing how MRV rules and title requirements can recentralize control unless designed around free, prior and informed consent (FPIC), Indigenous jurisdiction and community benefit-sharing.[138,139,140] Also detailed will be the implementation architectures: Indigenous-led funds and trusts; revenue-sharing formulas tied to community-defined indicators; guardianship/rights-of-nature roles with enforcement powers; and benefit agreements aligned to cultural and ecological priorities. Finally, we advance Indigenous data sovereignty as a precondition for equitable participation in digital and knowledge economies, specifying protocols for governance of data, genetic resources and traditional knowledge.[141]

Symbiotic Gaian Economics (SGE): From Diagnosis to Design

Volume 2 develops SGE into an applied framework with three layers.

Firstly, normative axioms: reciprocity, sovereignty, consent, intergenerational justice and Earth-system integrity define legitimate economic action. These axioms operationalize "do no harm" beyond the human community, embedding obligations to place and kin, including non-human relations. Secondly, institutional design: polycentric governance, rights-of-nature/guardianship, layered tenure, FPIC and data sovereignty are treated as productive infrastructure, not "constraints", they lower transaction costs by clarifying decision rights, improve monitoring

[137] Ostrom, E. (2010) 'Polycentric systems for coping with collective action and global environmental change', Global Environmental Change, 20(4), pp. 550–557.

[138] United Nations General Assembly (UNGA) (2007) United Nations Declaration on the Rights of Indigenous Peoples, A/RES/61/295 (13 September 2007). New York: United Nations.

[139] Corbera, E. & Schroeder, H. (2011) 'Governing and implementing REDD+', Environmental Science & Policy, 14(2), pp. 89–99.

[140] Fletcher, R., Dressler, W., Büscher, B. & Anderson, Z.R. (2016) 'Questioning REDD+ and the future of market-based conservation', Conservation Biology, 30(3), pp. 673–675.

[141] Kukutai, T. & Taylor, J. (eds) (2016) Indigenous Data Sovereignty: Toward an Agenda. Canberra: ANU Press.

through local knowledge, and align incentives with long-run stewardship.[142,143,144] Thirdly, policy and finance tools: community-controlled enterprises and trusts; equitable benefit-sharing; Indigenous-led funds; territorial monitoring and ranger programs; jurisdiction-compatible carbon/biodiversity finance; and community protocols for data and genetic resources. It will be shown how these tools are braided: finance flows are conditioned on FPIC and guardianship; monitoring embeds community indicators; contracts reference customary law alongside statute.[145,146,147] The two volumes move from grounding principles (Volume 1) to applied transformations and futures (Volume 2). Volume 1 provides the evidential and conceptual base, why land and sovereignty are constitutive, how embedded institutions organize economic life and how extraction shaped European ascent. Volume 2 shows those grammars in action: in courts and legislatures (UNDRIP implementation; FPIC jurisprudence), in contracts (benefit agreements, supply-chain standards), in finance (trusts, revenue-sharing, Indigenous-led funds), in conservation (territorial monitoring, hybrid ranger programs) and in the digital sphere (data governance, community protocols). The result is an alternative framework for evaluating and analysing human economic activity, which is realistic, Symbiotic Gaian Economics, that is at once analytically rigorous and operational—an approach capable of guiding policy and practice beyond the limits of neoclassical abstraction and Marxist mono-institutionalism.

[142] Ostrom, E. (2010) 'Polycentric systems for coping with collective action and global environmental change', Global Environmental Change, 20(4), pp. 550–557.

[143] United Nations General Assembly (UNGA) (2007) United Nations Declaration on the Rights of Indigenous Peoples, A/RES/61/295 (13 September 2007). New York: United Nations.

[144] Kukutai, T. & Taylor, J. (eds) (2016) Indigenous Data Sovereignty: Toward an Agenda. Canberra: ANU Press.

[145] Corbera, E. & Schroeder, H. (2011) 'Governing and implementing REDD+', Environmental Science & Policy, 14(2), pp. 89–99.

[146] Fletcher, R., Dressler, W., Büscher, B. & Anderson, Z.R. (2016) 'Questioning REDD+ and the future of market-based conservation', Conservation Biology, 30(3), pp. 673–675.

[147] IPBES (2019) Global Assessment Report on Biodiversity and Ecosystem Services. Bonn: Intergovernmental Science-Policy Platform on Biodiversity and Ecosystem Services. (Summary for Policymakers available at: ipbes.net).

3.2 *Framing the Question of European Dominance and Technological Innovation*

Explaining Europe's global dominance is not a matter of a single cause but of multiple, interacting processes, ecological endowments, institutional configurations, technological trajectories, and imperial extraction, unfolding unevenly over centuries.[148,149,150] A widely known account, popularized as "guns, germs, and steel", argues that Eurasia's east–west axis, suites of domesticable plants and animals, and pathogen pools generated durable surpluses, urbanization, and military-technological advantages.[151,152] Yet as many historians and political economists note, ecological determinism under-explains key dynamics: it can obscure colonial violence, the role of legal-financial architectures, and the sophistication of non-European institutions.[153,154,155] By attributing historical development primarily to geography or environment, this perspective risks overlooking how power, coercion, and institutional design actively shaped global inequalities and trajectories of growth. Alternative perspectives emphasize institutional and cultural mechanisms within Europe. Competition among polities, merchant law, and scientific cultures sustained cumulative discovery and diffusion, while secure, if contested, property and contract enforcement reduced transaction costs and encouraged

[148] Pomeranz, K. (2000) The Great Divergence: China, Europe, and the Making of the Modern World Economy. Princeton, NJ: Princeton University Press.

[149] North, D.C. (1990) Institutions, Institutional Change and Economic Performance. Cambridge: Cambridge University Press.

[150] Mokyr, J. (2002) The Gifts of Athena: Historical Origins of the Knowledge Economy. Princeton, NJ: Princeton University Press.

[151] Diamond, J. (1997) Guns, Germs and Steel: The Fates of Human Societies. New York: W.W. Norton.

[152] McNeill, W.H. (1976) Plagues and Peoples. Garden City, NY: Anchor Press/ Doubleday.

[153] Pomeranz, K. (2000) The Great Divergence: China, Europe, and the Making of the Modern World Economy. Princeton, NJ: Princeton University Press.

[154] Acemoglu, D. and Robinson, J.A. (2012) Why Nations Fail: The Origins of Power, Prosperity, and Poverty. New York: Crown (Random House).

[155] Scott, J.C. (1998) Seeing Like a State: How Certain Schemes to Improve the Human Condition Have Failed. New Haven, CT: Yale University Press.

investment.[156,157] At the same time, scholars of empire stress that European industrialization was co-produced through coercive integration into global commodity chains and the large-scale extraction of land, labour, and knowledge: plantation slavery in the Atlantic world, dispossession in settler colonies, and imperial trade monopolies channelled value and raw materials into European cores.[158,159,160,161] The Columbian Exchange reconfigured bio-geographies and food systems; New World crops such as the potato measurably increased Old World population and urbanization, altering labour supplies and market development.[162,163] In short, "dominance" emerges as a joint product of internal innovation and external expropriation, not a linear tale of endogenous European superiority.[164,165] Volume 1 recentres Indigenous systems to correct this imbalance. Complex administration, record-keeping, and environmental management were not exclusive to Eurasia. The Andean world combined highland–lowland complementarity with state infrastructure, roads, storage, and labour organization, documented in work

156 North, D.C. (1990) Institutions, Institutional Change and Economic Performance. Cambridge: Cambridge University Press.

157 Mokyr, J. (2002) The Gifts of Athena: Historical Origins of the Knowledge Economy. Princeton, NJ: Princeton University Press.

158 Williams, E. (1944) Capitalism and Slavery. Chapel Hill: University of North Carolina Press.

159 Inikori, J.E. (2002) Africans and the Industrial Revolution in England: A Study in International Trade and Economic Development. Cambridge: Cambridge University Press.

160 Beckert, S. (2014) Empire of Cotton: A Global History. New York: Alfred A. Knopf.

161 Crosby, A.W. (1972) The Columbian Exchange: Biological and Cultural Consequences of 1492. Westport, CT: Greenwood Publishing.

162 Nunn, N. and Qian, N. (2011) 'The potato's contribution to population and urbanization: Evidence from a historical experiment', Quarterly Journal of Economics, 126(2), pp. 593–650.

163 Crosby, A.W. (1972) The Columbian Exchange: Biological and Cultural Consequences of 1492. Westport, CT: Greenwood Publishing.

164 Pomeranz, K. (2000) The Great Divergence: China, Europe, and the Making of the Modern World Economy. Princeton, NJ: Princeton University Press.

165 Acemoglu, D. and Robinson, J.A. (2012) Why Nations Fail: The Origins of Power, Prosperity, and Poverty. New York: Crown (Random House).

on the Inca and the "vertical archipelago".[166,167] In North America, the Haudenosaunee developed federated, consensus-oriented governance with codified diplomatic practices and robust mechanisms for accountability.[168] In Australia, long-standing fire-stick farming (cultural burning) engineered mosaics that promoted biodiversity and reduced catastrophic fires, evidence of sophisticated ecological management.[169] These examples, alongside comparative analyses of commons governance, show that Indigenous polities devised polycentric institutions and local knowledge systems that solved coordination and stewardship problems at scale.[170,171] Contemporary syntheses further observe that biodiversity outcomes are often better on Indigenous-managed lands, reinforcing the effectiveness of these institutions.[172,173] Reframing European ascent in this way also clarifies the knowledge economy of empire. Europeans appropriated Indigenous botanical, navigational, and medical knowledge, from cinchona (quinine) to canoe and kayak designs adapted for exploration and trade; such transfers underwrote imperial expansion into disease-endemic and difficult geographies.[174,175] The upshot is an

[166] D'Altroy, T.N. (2014) The Incas. 2nd edn. Malden, MA: Wiley-Blackwell.

[167] Murra, J.V. (1972) 'El "control vertical" de un máximo de pisos ecológicos en la economía de las sociedades andinas', in Murra, J.V. (ed.) Visita de la Provincia de León de Huánuco. Huánuco: Universidad Nacional Hermilio Valdizán, pp. 427–476.

[168] Johansen, B.E. (1982) Forgotten Founders: How the American Indian Helped Shape Democracy. Boston, MA: The Harvard Common Press.

[169] Gammage, B. (2011) The Biggest Estate on Earth: How Aborigines Made Australia. Sydney: Allen & Unwin.

[170] Ostrom, E. (1990) Governing the Commons: The Evolution of Institutions for Collective Action. Cambridge: Cambridge University Press.

[171] Scott, J.C. (1998) Seeing Like a State: How Certain Schemes to Improve the Human Condition Have Failed. New Haven, CT: Yale University Press.

[172] Garnett, S.T., Burgess, N.D., Fa, J.E., Fernández-Llamazares, Á., Molnár, Z., Robinson, C.J., Watson, J.E.M., Zander, K.K., Austin, B., Brondizio, E.S., et al. (2018) 'A spatial overview of the global importance of Indigenous lands for conservation', Nature Sustainability, 1(7), pp. 369–374.

[173] IPBES (2019) Global Assessment Report on Biodiversity and Ecosystem Services. Bonn: Intergovernmental Science-Policy Platform on Biodiversity and Ecosystem Services. (Official PDF available via UN DESA/IBPES sites.)

[174] Crosby, A.W. (1972) The Columbian Exchange: Biological and Cultural Consequences of 1492. Westport, CT: Greenwood Press.

[175] D'Altroy, T.N. (2014) The Incas. 2nd edn. Malden, MA: Wiley-Blackwell.

account in which technological change and state capacity coevolve with imperial infrastructures and dispossession, while Indigenous institutions appear not as static "traditions" but as innovative, adaptive systems that persist, hybridise, or are suppressed under colonial rule.[176,177] Volume 2 then asks what this reframing implies today. Legacies of dispossession shape access to capital, jurisdiction over resources, and participation in value chains; contemporary regimes, from mining and forestry to climate finance, are structured by legal instruments[178,179] and operational doctrines such as Free, Prior and Informed Consent (FPIC).[180] Evidence from carbon markets underscores that market instruments can centralize control unless designed around community authority, credible benefit-sharing, and locally governed monitoring, reporting, and verification (MRV).[181,182] Meanwhile, Indigenous data sovereignty debates highlight the informational foundations of economic power in the digital era, setting protocols for the governance of data, genetic resources, and traditional knowledge.[183] Across enterprise development, renewable energy, land restoration, and digital knowledge commons, Indigenous-led initiatives are reconfiguring institutions once used to

[176] Scott, J.C. (1998) Seeing Like a State: How Certain Schemes to Improve the Human Condition Have Failed. New Haven, CT: Yale University Press.

[177] Graeber, D. (2011) Debt: The First 5,000 Years. Brooklyn, NY and London: Melville House.

[178] UNDRIP (United Nations Declaration on the Rights of Indigenous Peoples): United Nations (2007) United Nations Declaration on the Rights of Indigenous Peoples (UNDRIP). New York: United Nations.

[179] International Labour Organization (1989) C169—Indigenous and Tribal Peoples Convention, 1989 (No. 169). Geneva: ILO.

[180] United Nations General Assembly (UNGA) (2007) United Nations Declaration on the Rights of Indigenous Peoples, A/RES/61/295 (13 September). New York: United Nations. (Resolution text and PDF available from UN websites.)

[181] Corbera, E. and Schroeder, H. (2011) 'Governing and implementing REDD+', Environmental Science & Policy, 14(2), pp. 89–99.

[182] Fletcher, R., Dressler, W., Büscher, B. and Anderson, Z.R. (2016) 'Questioning REDD+ and the future of market-based conservation', Conservation Biology, 30(3), pp. 673–675.

[183] Kukutai, T. and Taylor, J. (eds) (2016) Indigenous Data Sovereignty: Toward an Agenda. Canberra: ANU Press.

enclose them, demonstrating that durable innovation rests on institutional pluralism, jurisdictional clarity, and the alignment of incentives with stewardship.[184,185]

3.3 A Comparative View: Indigenous Resilience and Adaptation

Across regions, Indigenous societies have resisted, negotiated and innovated under colonial pressure, preserving core principles while reshaping socio-economic practice. In the Andes, long-term investments in terracing, canal irrigation and high-altitude storage (qollqa) stabilized yields and buffered climatic shocks across ecological tiers, while road networks and labour organization integrated dispersed communities in a "vertical archipelago" that linked highland and lowland production systems.[186,187] These infrastructures were not merely technical fixes but institutional arrangements, allocating rights and obligations, synchronizing planting with ritual calendars, and distributing risk intergenerationally. In North America, the Haudenosaunee (Iroquois) developed a federated, consensus-oriented polity under the Great Law of Peace, with codified diplomatic protocols, clan responsibilities and checks on power. Their "Three Sisters" polyculture (maize, beans, squash) exemplified agroecological design: beans fixed nitrogen, maize provided structure, and squash reduced evapotranspiration, raising productivity and dietary diversity while lowering labour risk.[188,189] Labour risk was lowered because the complementary growth cycles and mutual support of the crops reduced the need for intensive weeding, fertilizing, and replanting, enabling more efficient use of time and energy across the growing season.

[184] Ostrom, E. (2010) 'Polycentric systems for coping with collective action and global environmental change', Global Environmental Change, 20(4), pp. 550–557.

[185] Escobar, A. (2018) Designs for the Pluriverse: Radical Interdependence, Autonomy, and the Making of Worlds. Durham, NC: Duke University Press.

[186] Murra, J.V. (1972) 'El "control vertical" de un máximo de pisos ecológicos en la economía de las sociedades andinas', in Murra, J.V. (ed.) Visita de la Provincia de León de Huánuco. Huánuco: Universidad Nacional Hermilio Valdizán, pp. 427– 476.

[187] D'Altroy, T.N. (2014) The Incas. 2nd edn. Malden, MA: Wiley-Blackwell.

[188] Johansen, B.E. (1982) Forgotten Founders: How the American Indian Helped Shape Democracy. Boston, MA: The Harvard Common Press.

[189] Kimmerer, R.W. (2013) Braiding Sweetgrass: Indigenous Wisdom, Scientific Knowledge and the Teachings of Plants. Minneapolis, MN: Milkweed Editions.

The constitutional architecture and polyculture together show how governance and ecology were co-designed to sustain abundance and peace. In Australia, long-standing cultural burning ("fire-stick farming") produced patchy, fine-grained mosaics that promoted biodiversity, enhanced habitat heterogeneity and reduced the intensity of late-season fires. Ethnographic, historical and biogeographic evidence indicates that these fire regimes were deliberate, seasonal and knowledge-intensive, coordinated through kinship obligations and country-specific custodianship.[190,191] These practices clash with colonial imaginaries of "wilderness" and highlight sophisticated environmental governance embedded in law and ceremony. Such cases counter stereotypes of Indigenous economies as static or "subsistence-level" by evidencing complex institutional design (polycentric authority, rule-bounded access, conflict resolution) and deep ecological expertise (place-based monitoring, species-fire relationships, soil and water management). They also expose a recurring political economy of knowledge extraction: botanical, agronomic and medicinal knowledges were commercialized and legally decontextualized via colonial science, trade and intellectual property regimes, from cinchona (quinine) to crop germplasm and ethnobotanical pharmacopeias.[192,193,194] In Volume 1, these comparisons are used to map the institutional grammar of Indigenous economies, tenure mosaics, authority structures, inter-community compacts and customary law, and to show how these institutions underpin economic life and ecological stewardship. This is consistent with extensive evidence that communities can and do craft robust rules for governing commons, especially where local legitimacy and monitoring capacities

[190] Gammage, B. (2011) The Biggest Estate on Earth: How Aborigines Made Australia. Sydney: Allen & Unwin.

[191] Bowman, D.M.J.S., Balch, J., Artaxo, P., Bond, W.J., Carlson, J.M., Cochrane, M.A., D'Antonio, C.M., DeFries, R.S., Doyle, J.C., Harrison, S.P. and Johnston, F.H. (2011) 'The human dimension of fire regimes on Earth', Journal of Biogeography, 38(12), pp. 2223–2236.

[192] Crosby, A.W. (1972) The Columbian Exchange: Biological and Cultural Consequences of 1492. Westport, CT: Greenwood Press.

[193] Dutfield, G. (2000) Intellectual Property Rights, Trade and Biodiversity. London: Earthscan.

[194] Hayden, C. (2003) When Nature Goes Public: The Making and Unmaking of Bioprospecting in Mexico. Princeton, NJ: Princeton University Press.

are strong.[195,196] Contemporary syntheses likewise find that biodiversity outcomes are frequently stronger on Indigenous-managed lands, underscoring institutional effectiveness in conservation and carbon stewardship.[197,198] In Volume 2, the same comparative lens evaluates strategy and reform under current policy and market conditions. We examine Indigenous-controlled enterprises and trusts; revenue-sharing and impact-benefit agreements in resource sectors; territorial monitoring and ranger programs; climate and biodiversity finance; community banking and cooperatives; and digital data sovereignty. Evidence shows that when jurisdiction is clear and governance remains polycentric and consent-based, e.g., through Free, Prior and Informed Consent (FPIC), institutions align incentives with stewardship, lower transaction costs and improve compliance and monitoring.[199,200,201] Conversely, climate-market instruments such as REDD+ can recentralize control unless monitoring, reporting and verification (MRV), title rules and benefit-sharing are designed around community authority.[202,203] This is because, without robust safeguards, external actors, such as states, NGOs, or private investors, may

[195] Ostrom, E. (1990) Governing the Commons: The Evolution of Institutions for Collective Action. Cambridge: Cambridge University Press.

[196] Scott, J.C. (1998) Seeing Like a State: How Certain Schemes to Improve the Human Condition Have Failed. New Haven, CT: Yale University Press.

[197] Garnett, S.T., Burgess, N.D., Fa, J.E., Fernández-Llamazares, Á., Molnár, Z., Robinson, C.J., Watson, J.E.M., Zander, K.K., Austin, B., Brondizio, E.S., et al. (2018) 'A spatial overview of the global importance of Indigenous lands for conservation', Nature Sustainability, 1(7), pp. 369–374.

[198] IPBES (2019) Global Assessment Report on Biodiversity and Ecosystem Services. Bonn: Intergovernmental Science-Policy Platform on Biodiversity and Ecosystem Services.

[199] O'Faircheallaigh, C. (2013) 'Community development agreements in the mining industry: An emerging global phenomenon', Community Development, 44(2), pp. 222–238.

[200] Ostrom, E. (2010) 'Polycentric systems for coping with collective action and global environmental change', Global Environmental Change, 20(4), pp. 550–557.

[201] Kukutai, T. and Taylor, J. (eds) (2016) Indigenous Data Sovereignty: Toward an Agenda. Canberra: ANU Press.

[202] Corbera, E. and Schroeder, H. (2011) 'Governing and implementing REDD+', Environmental Science & Policy, 14(2), pp. 89–99.

[203] Fletcher, R., Dressler, W., Büscher, B. and Anderson, Z.R. (2016) 'Questioning REDD+ and the future of market-based conservation', Conservation Biology, 30(3), pp. 673–675.

retain decision-making power over land use and financial flows, sidelining Indigenous and local communities. For example, REDD+ projects that prioritize carbon sequestration metrics without involving traditional land stewards in governance have been criticized for reinforcing top-down conservation models and displacing customary land rights. Embedding community authority ensures that environmental benefits do not come at the cost of social justice or local sovereignty. Empirical work on Indigenous economic development similarly finds that durable gains track to self-determination and institution-building, rather than externally imposed programs, because decision rights, cultural legitimacy and knowledge systems co-determine performance.[204,205] This means that when Indigenous communities have the authority to govern their own affairs—developing laws, managing resources, and designing economic strategies that reflect their values and traditions—they are more likely to achieve sustained development outcomes. In contrast, top-down interventions often fail because they overlook local priorities, disrupt established governance systems, and lack community buy-in. For example, in the U.S. and Canada, tribes that reclaimed jurisdiction over economic and legal institutions, such as the Navajo Nation's local government reforms, have shown stronger performance in areas like employment, education, and infrastructure. The through-line across both volumes is that resilience is institutional, not merely cultural, rooted in governance arrangements that can be scaled, hybridized and defended in law, policy and markets.

3.4 Roadmap of the Book

Volume 1 opens with Chapter 1: Introduction, which establishes core concepts, land, sovereignty and foundational institutions, within colonial and environmental contexts, treating land as a socially embedded, legally plural and ecologically co-produced nexus rather than a mere

[204] Cornell, S. (2006) Indigenous Peoples, Poverty and Self-Determination in Australia, New Zealand, Canada and the United States. Joint Occasional Papers on Native Affairs (JOPNA) 2006–02. Tucson, AZ & Cambridge, MA: Native Nations Institute and Udall Center/Harvard Project. (Working paper.)

[205] Cornell, S. and Kalt, J.P. (2000) 'Where's the glue? Institutional and cultural foundations of American Indian economic development', Journal of Socio-Economics, 29(5), pp. 443–470.

"factor" of production.[206,207,208] Chapter 2: The Economics of Indigenous Peoples and Ancient Economic Thought develops the analytical lens by setting Indigenous institutions and exchange logics alongside classical and ancient traditions (South and East Asian, Mediterranean) and modern political economy, foregrounding reciprocity, stewardship and intergenerational obligation as durable economic principles.[209,210,211] Chapter 3: Historical Context and the Rise of European Expansion and Chapter 4: Technological and Strategic Superiority: An Analysis revisit European dominance by juxtaposing environmental and institutional theses[212,213] with evidence of Indigenous technological and organizational sophistication (Andean roads and storage; Haudenosaunee governance; Aboriginal fire regimes), and by detailing extractive mechanisms,

206 Polanyi, K. (1944) The Great Transformation: The Political and Economic Origins of Our Time. New York: Rinehart.

207 Ostrom, E. (1990) Governing the Commons: The Evolution of Institutions for Collective Action. Cambridge: Cambridge University Press.

208 Scott, J.C. (1998) Seeing Like a State: How Certain Schemes to Improve the Human Condition Have Failed. New Haven, CT: Yale University Press.

209 Sen, A. (1999) Development as Freedom. Oxford: Oxford University Press.

210 North, D.C. (1990) Institutions, Institutional Change and Economic Performance. Cambridge: Cambridge University Press.

211 Escobar, A. (2018) Designs for the Pluriverse: Radical Interdependence, Autonomy, and the Making of Worlds. Durham, NC: Duke University Press.

212 Diamond, J. (1997) Guns, Germs and Steel: The Fates of Human Societies. New York: W.W. Norton.

213 Mokyr, J. (2002) The Gifts of Athena: Historical Origins of the Knowledge Economy. Princeton, NJ: Princeton University Press.

slavery, dispossession, chartered monopolies and knowledge appropriation, that translated Indigenous land, labour and insight into European growth.[214,215,216,217,218,219,220,221]. Chapter 5: Land Rights and Resource Management in Indigenous Societies consolidates the institutional analysis around access, enforcement, monitoring and ecological stewardship, including layered customary–statutory arrangements and conflict resolution. Chapter 6: Governance, Self-Determination, and European Imperial Systems examines how decision rights were reallocated under empire and the pathways by which Indigenous polities defend or regain authority, compacts, co-management and legal pluralism, setting criteria for legitimate governance.[222,223] Chapter 7: Conclusion—Reclaiming the Past, Reimagining the Future bridges to Volume 2 by deriving implications for restitution, commons stewardship, knowledge sovereignty and decolonized institutional design. Volume 2 begins with Chapter 1: Introduction (contemporary political economy, globalization, environmental finance and the legal architecture), then turns to structural conditions in Chapter 2: Economic Marginalization and

[214] Williams, E. (1944) Capitalism and Slavery. Chapel Hill: University of North Carolina Press.

[215] Inikori, J.E. (2002) Africans and the Industrial Revolution in England: A Study in International Trade and Economic Development. Cambridge: Cambridge University Press.

[216] Beckert, S. (2014) Empire of Cotton: A Global History. New York: Alfred A. Knopf.

[217] Crosby, A.W. (1972) The Columbian Exchange: Biological and Cultural Consequences of 1492. Westport, CT: Greenwood Press.

[218] Nunn, N. and Qian, N. (2011) 'The potato's contribution to population and urbanization: Evidence from a historical experiment', Quarterly Journal of Economics, 126(2), pp. 593–650.

[219] D'Altroy, T.N. (2014) The Incas. 2nd edn. Malden, MA: Wiley-Blackwell.

[220] Murra, J.V. (1972) 'El "control vertical" de un máximo de pisos ecológicos en la economía de las sociedades andinas', in Murra, J.V. (ed.) Visita de la Provincia de León de Huánuco. Huánuco: Universidad Nacional Hermilio Valdizán, pp. 427–476.

[221] Gammage, B. (2011) The Biggest Estate on Earth: How Aborigines Made Australia. Sydney: Allen & Unwin.

[222] Ostrom, E. (1990) Governing the Commons: The Evolution of Institutions for Collective Action. Cambridge: Cambridge University Press.

[223] North, D.C. (1990) Institutions, Institutional Change and Economic Performance. Cambridge: Cambridge University Press.

Structural Inequalities (historical dispossession, labour regimes, access barriers) and to knowledge/market interfaces in Chapter 3: Impact of Globalization and the Commodification of Indigenous Knowledge (IP, biocultural rights, value-chain positioning). Chapter 4: Cultural Preservation Amid Technological Change focuses on adaptation and continuity, including protocols for digital and genetic data governance.[224] Chapter 5: Environmental Justice and Indigenous Movements assesses climate and biodiversity instruments (REDD+, biocredits), and conditions under which polycentric governance improves outcomes.[225,226,227] Chapter 6: Theories on European Dominance and Indigenous Displacement consolidates historical/theoretical debates to illuminate present inequalities. Chapter 7: Future Perspectives and Policy Recommendations operationalises design principles—FPIC implementation, benefit-sharing, Indigenous-led finance and metrics beyond GDP[228,229]—and Chapter 8: Conclusion synthesises both volumes into forward-looking models for just, sustainable development, noting evidence that biodiversity outcomes are often strongest on Indigenous-managed lands.[230,231] This chapter (V1): Introduction: Frames land as a living nexus of spiritual–legal–ecological relations and sovereignty as place-based jurisdiction

224 Kukutai, T. and Taylor, J. (eds) (2016) Indigenous Data Sovereignty: Toward an Agenda. Canberra: ANU Press.

225 Corbera, E. and Schroeder, H. (2011) 'Governing and implementing REDD+', Environmental Science & Policy, 14(2), pp. 89–99.

226 Fletcher, R., Dressler, W., Büscher, B. and Anderson, Z.R. (2016) 'Questioning REDD+ and the future of market-based conservation', Conservation Biology, 30(3), pp. 673–675.

227 Ostrom, E. (1990) Governing the Commons: The Evolution of Institutions for Collective Action. Cambridge: Cambridge University Press.

228 Stiglitz, J.E., Sen, A., and Fitoussi, J.-P. (2009) Report by the Commission on the Measurement of Economic Performance and Social Progress. Paris: Commission on the Measurement of Economic Performance and Social Progress.

229 Raworth, K. (2017) Doughnut Economics: Seven Ways to Think Like a 21st-Century Economist. London: Random House Business.

230 Garnett, S.T., Burgess, N.D., Fa, J.E., Fernández-Llamazares, Á., Molnár, Z., Robinson, C.J., Watson, J.E.M., Zander, K.K., Austin, B., Brondizio, E.S., et al. (2018) 'A spatial overview of the global importance of Indigenous lands for conservation', Nature Sustainability, 1(7), pp. 369–374.

231 IPBES (2019) Global Assessment Report on Biodiversity and Ecosystem Services. Bonn: Intergovernmental Science-Policy Platform on Biodiversity and Ecosystem Services.

embedded in kinship and custodianship. It surveys how enclosure, cadastral titling and conservation regimes reconfigured tenure while documenting persistent community governance capacities, monitoring, and sanctioning consistent with commons theory.[232,233,234,235,236] Chapter 2 (V1): The Economics of Indigenous Peoples and Ancient Economic Thought, positions Indigenous economic institutions alongside ancient and classical traditions and modern political economy. Themes include reciprocity and obligation, authority and legitimacy, ecological stewardship as productive infrastructure, and the capabilities approach to welfare, contrasting with narrow utility or output metrics.[237,238,239] Chapter 3 (V1), historical Context and the Rise of European Expansion reconstructs geopolitical, epidemiological and commercial conjunctures enabling European oceanic expansion, tying metropolitan legal–financial architectures (chartered companies, insurance, bills of exchange) to long-distance commodity chains and the channelling of colonial surplus into

[232] Polanyi, K. (1944) The Great Transformation: The Political and Economic Origins of Our Time. New York: Rinehart.

[233] Ostrom, E. (1990) Governing the Commons: The Evolution of Institutions for Collective Action. Cambridge: Cambridge University Press.

[234] Scott, J.C. (1998) Seeing Like a State: How Certain Schemes to Improve the Human Condition Have Failed. New Haven, CT: Yale University Press.

[235] Garnett, S.T., Burgess, N.D., Fa, J.E., Fernández-Llamazares, Á., Molnár, Z., Robinson, C.J., Watson, J.E.M., Zander, K.K., Austin, B., Brondizio, E.S., et al. (2018) 'A spatial overview of the global importance of Indigenous lands for conservation', Nature Sustainability, 1(7), pp. 369–374.

[236] IPBES (2019) Global Assessment Report on Biodiversity and Ecosystem Services. Bonn: Intergovernmental Science-Policy Platform on Biodiversity and Ecosystem Services.

[237] North, D.C. (1990) Institutions, Institutional Change and Economic Performance. Cambridge: Cambridge University Press.

[238] Sen, A. (1999) Development as Freedom. Oxford: Oxford University Press.

[239] Escobar, A. (2018) Designs for the Pluriverse: Radical Interdependence, Autonomy, and the Making of Worlds. Durham, NC: Duke University Press.

European state and urban growth.[240,241,242,243,244] Chapter 4 (V1): Technological and Strategic Superiority—An Analysis, tests claims of European "superiority" against Indigenous infrastructural and ecological systems (Inca road network and qollqa; Haudenosaunee federalism; Aboriginal fire mosaics), then analyses how Europeans aggregated maritime, military and informational advantages, converting Indigenous knowledge and crops into strategic capacity and demographic change.[245,246,247,248,249] Chapter 5 (V1): Land Rights and Resource Management in Indigenous Societies. Maps tenure mosaics (seasonal access, usufruct, clan guardianship), dispute resolution, local monitoring and sanctioning, and the performance of layered customary–statutory arrangements in contemporary claims over land, water, forests and biodiversity.[250,251] Chapter 6 (V1): Governance, Self-Determination,

[240] Diamond, J. (1997) Guns, Germs and Steel: The Fates of Human Societies. New York: W.W. Norton.

[241] Williams, E. (1944) Capitalism and Slavery. Chapel Hill: University of North Carolina Press.

[242] Inikori, J.E. (2002) Africans and the Industrial Revolution in England: A Study in International Trade and Economic Development. Cambridge: Cambridge University Press.

[243] Beckert, S. (2014) Empire of Cotton: A Global History. New York: Alfred A. Knopf.

[244] Crosby, A.W. (1972) The Columbian Exchange: Biological and Cultural Consequences of 1492. Westport, CT: Greenwood Press.

[245] Mokyr, J. (2002) The Gifts of Athena: Historical Origins of the Knowledge Economy. Princeton, NJ: Princeton University Press.

[246] D'Altroy, T.N. (2014) The Incas. 2nd edn. Malden, MA: Wiley-Blackwell.

[247] Murra, J.V. (1972) 'El "control vertical" de un máximo de pisos ecológicos en la economía de las sociedades andinas', in Murra, J.V. (ed.) Visita de la Provincia de León de Huánuco. Huánuco: Universidad Nacional Hermilio Valdizán, pp. 427–476.

[248] Gammage, B. (2011) The Biggest Estate on Earth: How Aborigines Made Australia. Sydney: Allen & Unwin.

[249] Nunn, N. and Qian, N. (2011) 'The potato's contribution to population and urbanization: Evidence from a historical experiment', Quarterly Journal of Economics, 126(2), pp. 593–650.

[250] Ostrom, E. (1990) Governing the Commons: The Evolution of Institutions for Collective Action. Cambridge: Cambridge University Press.

[251] Scott, J.C. (1998) Seeing Like a State: How Certain Schemes to Improve the Human Condition Have Failed. New Haven, CT: Yale University Press.

and European Imperial Systems. Traces reallocations of decision rights under imperial rule and the institutional pathways through which self-determination is defended or restored—inter-polity compacts, co-management, legal pluralism and recognition—specifying criteria for legitimate governance and durable compliance.[252,253] Chapter 7 (V1): Conclusion—Reclaiming the Past, Reimagining the Future. Synthesises institutional diagnostics and sets the bridge to V2: restitution (land-back, benefit-sharing), commons stewardship, knowledge sovereignty and policy architectures that embed consent and reciprocity, previewing polycentric, measurement-aware design.[254,255] Chapter 1 (V2): Introduction. Orients the reader to contemporary political economy—globalization, neoliberal governance, environmental finance—and the legal architecture[256,257] structuring participation, consent and enforcement. Chapter 2 (V2): Economic Marginalization and Structural Inequalities. Analyses pathways from historical dispossession and coerced labour to current market access barriers and jurisdictional ambiguity, identifying leverage points for institutional repair. Chapter 3 (V2): Impact of Globalization and the Commodification of Indigenous Knowledge. Examines value-chain positioning, IP/biocultural rights and the politics of recognition—when market integration empowers communities versus recentralizes control.[258,259] Chapter 4 (V2): Cultural Preservation

[252] North, D.C. (1990) Institutions, Institutional Change and Economic Performance. Cambridge: Cambridge University Press.

[253] Ostrom, E. (1990) Governing the Commons: The Evolution of Institutions for Collective Action. Cambridge: Cambridge University Press.

[254] Ostrom, E. (2010) 'Polycentric systems for coping with collective action and global environmental change', Global Environmental Change, 20(4), pp. 550–557.

[255] Stiglitz, J.E., Sen, A., and Fitoussi, J.-P. (2009) Report by the Commission on the Measurement of Economic Performance and Social Progress. Paris: Commission on the Measurement of Economic Performance and Social Progress.

[256] UNGA (United Nations General Assembly) (2007) United Nations Declaration on the Rights of Indigenous Peoples, A/RES/61/295 (13 September). New York: United Nations.

[257] International Labour Organisation (1989) C169—Indigenous and Tribal Peoples Convention, 1989 (No. 169). Geneva: ILO.

[258] Dutfield, G. (2000) Intellectual Property Rights, Trade and Biodiversity. London: Earthscan.

[259] Hayden, C. (2003) When Nature Goes Public: The Making and Unmaking of Bioprospecting in Mexico. Princeton, NJ: Princeton University Press.

Amid Technological Change. Details media, language and digital infrastructures; proposes governance for data, genetic resources and knowledge commons that protect sovereignty while enabling innovation.[260] Chapter 5 (V2): Environmental Justice and Indigenous Movements. Evaluates climate/biodiversity instruments (REDD+, biocredits), MRV protocols and movement-driven reforms; identifies conditions under which polycentric governance outperforms centralized models.[261,262,263] Chapter 6 (V2): Theories on European Dominance and Indigenous Displacement. Revisits historical and institutional theses to explain present-day uneven development and illuminate durable policy levers linking history to reform. Chapter 7 (V2): Future Perspectives and Policy Recommendations. Operationalizes FPIC; designs benefit-sharing and Indigenous-led finance (trusts, funds, co-ops); advances metrics beyond GDP (capabilities, ecological integrity, intergenerational well-being).[264,265] Chapter 8 (V2): Conclusion. Integrates both volumes into a forward-looking blueprint, hybrid governance, commons-based management and jurisdiction-compatible finance, linking courts, markets, climate negotiations and community enterprises, with empirical support that Indigenous-managed lands sustain biodiversity and carbon.[266,267]

[260] Kukutai, T. and Taylor, J. (eds) (2016) Indigenous Data Sovereignty: Toward an Agenda. Canberra: ANU Press.

[261] Corbera, E. and Schroeder, H. (2011) 'Governing and implementing REDD+', Environmental Science & Policy, 14(2), pp. 89–99.

[262] Fletcher, R., Dressler, W., Büscher, B. and Anderson, Z.R. (2016) 'Questioning REDD+ and the future of market-based conservation', Conservation Biology, 30(3), pp. 673–675.

[263] Ostrom, E. (2010) 'Polycentric systems for coping with collective action and global environmental change', Global Environmental Change, 20(4), pp. 550–557.

[264] Stiglitz, J.E., Sen, A., and Fitoussi, J.-P. (2009) Report by the Commission on the Measurement of Economic Performance and Social Progress. Paris: Commission on the Measurement of Economic Performance and Social Progress.

[265] Raworth, K. (2017) Doughnut Economics: Seven Ways to Think Like a 21st-Century Economist. London: Random House Business.

[266] Garnett, S.T., Burgess, N.D., Fa, J.E., Fernández-Llamazares, Á., Molnár, Z., Robinson, C.J., Watson, J.E.M., Zander, K.K., Austin, B., Brondizio, E.S., et al. (2018) 'A spatial overview of the global importance of Indigenous lands for conservation', Nature Sustainability, 1(7), pp. 369–374.

[267] IPBES (2019) Global Assessment Report on Biodiversity and Ecosystem Services. Bonn: Intergovernmental Science-Policy Platform on Biodiversity and Ecosystem Services.

4 Conclusion

This chapter has outlined the intellectual, historical, and methodological foundations necessary for understanding the political economy of Indigenous peoples in a global context. Beginning with a synthesis of the central themes of Volume 1 and the reasons for expanding the analysis into this second volume, we established the need to situate Indigenous experiences within broader systems of power, colonialism, capitalism, and global governance. By foregrounding a political economy approach, the chapter emphasized how land, sovereignty, labour, and resource control remain at the heart of Indigenous struggles worldwide. The examination of key theoretical frameworks, decolonial theory, world-systems analysis, and Marxist critiques demonstrated that Indigenous dispossession cannot be reduced to isolated historical injustices. Rather, it must be understood as structurally embedded within global processes of accumulation, extraction, and state formation. These frameworks also highlight the endurance of colonial logics in contemporary economic systems, from forms of racialized labour control to the governance of natural resources by multinational corporations and states. Equally important is recognizing that Indigenous peoples are not simply passive subjects of these systems. The chapter traced long histories of Indigenous resistance, cultural resurgence, and political mobilization, illustrating how communities reinterpret and challenge imposed economic structures. Movements for self-determination, assertions of land and water rights, and the revitalization of Indigenous legal orders show that Indigenous political economies are dynamic, adaptive, and deeply rooted in collective responsibilities to land and kin relations. These movements also intersect with global struggles for environmental justice and sustainable development, revealing the central role Indigenous peoples play in confronting planetary crises. Finally, the chapter examined the contemporary landscape of Indigenous political economy, marked by contradictions between neoliberal development pressures and Indigenous-led economic alternatives grounded in relationality, stewardship, and interdependence. The rise of international human rights frameworks—such as UNDRIP—has altered the terrain of advocacy and governance, yet these mechanisms remain uneven in their influence and implementation. Understanding these tensions is essential for analysing how global structures enable or obstruct Indigenous economic futures. Taken together, the themes explored in this chapter provide the conceptual scaffolding for the rest of this volume. They also raise critical questions that guide the transition to Chapter 2, where the focus shifts to a deeper examination of settler colonialism, imperial expansion, and the global capitalist system as interlocking structures. Chapter 2 investigates how these systems were constructed, how they function, and how they continue to shape Indigenous economic realities today. By analysing these historical trajectories and structural forces, we gain clearer insight into why Indigenous dispossession persists—and why Indigenous resurgence remains a vital and transformative force within the global political economy.

References

Acemoglu, D. and Robinson, J.A., 2012. Why Nations Fail: The Origins of Power, Prosperity, and Poverty. New York: Crown Publishing Group.

Alfred, T. (2009). Peace, Power, Righteousness: An Indigenous Manifesto. Oxford University Press.

Altieri, M.A. and Nicholls, C.I., 2020. *Agroecology and the emergence of a post COVID-19 agriculture*. Agriculture and Human Values, 37, pp. 525–526.

Altieri, M.A. and Toledo, V.M., 2011. *The agroecological revolution in Latin America: Rescuing nature, ensuring food sovereignty and empowering peasants*. Journal of Peasant Studies, 38(3), pp. 587–612.

Altman, J. C. (2001). *Sustainable development options on Aboriginal land: The hybrid economy in the twenty-first century*. Centre for Aboriginal Economic Policy Research, ANU.

Altman, J.C., 2001. Exploring Sustainable Development Options on Aboriginal Land: The Hybrid Economy in the Twenty-First Century. CAEPR Discussion Paper No. 226, ANU.

Altman, J.C. (2005). Economic futures on Aboriginal land in remote and very remote Australia: Hybrid economies and joint ventures. In D. Austin-Broos & G. Macdonald (Eds.), Culture, Economy and Governance in Aboriginal Australia. Sydney University Press.

Altman, J.C., 2007. The Howard Government's Northern Territory Intervention: Are Neo-Paternalism and Indigenous Development Compatible? Topical Issue 16/2007, Centre for Aboriginal Economic Policy Research, ANU.

Altman, J.C., 2007. Neo-paternalism and the destruction of CDEP. Arena Magazine, (89), pp. 32–35. (Replaces: Altman, 2007 CAEPR Topical Issue 16/2007).

Anderson, I., Baum, F. and Bentley, M., 2007. *Beyond Bandaids: Exploring the Social Determinants of Aboriginal Health*. Darwin: Cooperative Research Centre for Aboriginal Health.

Atalay, S. (2006). Indigenous Archaeology as Decolonizing Practice. American Indian Quarterly, 30(3), 280–310.
Bakewell, P., 1984. *Miners of the Red Mountain: Indian Labour in Potosí, 1545–1650*. Albuquerque: University of New Mexico Press.
Banner, S., 2005. *How the Indians Lost Their Land: Law and Power on the Frontier*. Cambridge, MA: Harvard University Press.
Bebbington, A., 2009. The new extraction: Rewriting the political ecology of the Andes?. NACLA Report on the Americas, 42(5), pp. 12–20.
Beckert, S. (2014) Empire of Cotton: A Global History. New York: Alfred A. Knopf.
Berkes, F. (2012). *Sacred ecology* (3rd ed.). Routledge.
Blaut, J.M., 1993. The Colonizer's Model of the World: Geographical Diffusionism and Eurocentric History. New York: Guilford Press.
Bowman, D.M.J.S., Balch, J., Artaxo, P., Bond, W.J., Carlson, J.M., Cochrane, M.A., D'Antonio, C.M., DeFries, R.S., Doyle, J.C., Harrison, S.P. and Johnston, F.H. (2011) 'The human dimension of fire regimes on Earth', Journal of Biogeography, 38(12), pp. 2223–2236.
Brush, S. B. (1976). Man's use of an Andean ecosystem. *Human Ecology*, 4(2), 147–166
Brush, S.B., 2004. *Farmers' Bounty: Locating Crop Diversity in the Contemporary World*. New Haven: Yale University Press.
Bryan, J. (2012). Rethinking territory: social justice and neoliberalism in Latin America's extractive frontiers. Geography Compass, 6(2), 63–78.
Bryan, J., 2012. Rethinking territory: social and environmental conflicts in Bolivia's indigenous lands. Journal of Latin American Geography, 11(1), pp. 7–31.
Convention on Biological Diversity (CBD), 2022. *Global Biodiversity Outlook 5*. Montreal: Secretariat of the CBD.
Corbera, E. & Schroeder, H. (2011) 'Governing and implementing REDD+', Environmental Science & Policy, 14(2), pp. 89–99.
Cornell, S. (2006) Indigenous Peoples, Poverty and Self-Determination in Australia, New Zealand, Canada and the United States. Joint Occasional Papers on Native Affairs (JOPNA) 2006–02. Tucson, AZ & Cambridge, MA: Native Nations Institute and Udall Center/Harvard Project. (Working paper.)
Cornell, S. and Kalt, J.P. (2000) 'Where's the glue? Institutional and cultural foundations of American Indian economic development', Journal of Socio-Economics, 29(5), pp. 443–470.
Coulthard, G.S. (2014). Red Skin, White Masks: Rejecting the Colonial Politics of Recognition. Minneapolis: University of Minnesota Press.
Crosby, A.W., 1972. *The Columbian Exchange: Biological and Cultural Consequences of 1492*. Westport: Greenwood Press.
D'Altroy, T.N. (2014) The Incas. 2nd edn. Malden, MA: Wiley-Blackwell.

De la Cadena, M., & Blaser, M. (Eds.). (2018). *A world of many worlds*. Duke University Press.
Deloria, V. (2001). Power and Place: Indian Education in America. Fulcrum Publishing.
Denevan, W.M., 2001. *Cultivated Landscapes of Native Amazonia and the Andes*. Oxford: Oxford University Press.
Descola, P. (1994). *In the society of nature: A native ecology in Amazonia*. Cambridge University Press.
Diamond, J., 1997. *Guns, Germs, and Steel: The Fates of Human Societies*. New York: W.W. Norton.
Durie, M., 1998. *Te Mana, Te Kāwanatanga: The Politics of Māori Self-Determination*. Auckland: Oxford University Press.
Dutfield, G. (2000) Intellectual Property Rights, Trade and Biodiversity. London: Earthscan.
Erickson, C.L. (2000). *The Lake Titicaca Basin: A Pre-Columbian Built Landscape*. In: B.L. Turner II, W.B. Meyer (Eds.), *Global Land Use and Land Cover Change*. University of Arizona Press.
Escobar, A., 1995. Encountering Development: The Making and Unmaking of the Third World. Princeton: Princeton University Press.
Escobar, A. (2008). Territories of Difference: Place, Movements, Life, Redes. Durham: Duke University Press.
Escobar, A. (2018) Designs for the Pluriverse: Radical Interdependence, Autonomy, and the Making of Worlds. Durham, NC: Duke University Press.
Esteva, G., 1992. Development. In: W. Sachs, ed. The Development Dictionary: A Guide to Knowledge as Power. London: Zed Books, pp. 6–25.
Esteva, G., and Prakash, M.S., 1998. Grassroots Post-Modernism: Remaking the Soil of Cultures. London: Zed Books. (Replaces: Esteva, 2010 Journal of Peasant Studies).
Fedick, S. L. (1996). The Managed Mosaic: Ancient Maya Agriculture and Resource Use. University of Utah Press.
Fletcher, R., Dressler, W., Büscher, B. & Anderson, Z.R. (2016) 'Questioning REDD+ and the future of market-based conservation', Conservation Biology, 30(3), pp. 673–675.
Food and Agriculture Organization (FAO), 2021. *Indigenous Peoples' Food Systems: Insights on Sustainability and Resilience from the Frontline of Climate Change*. Rome: FAO.
Fowkes, L., & Sanders, W. (2016). Financial penalties in the remote Community Development Programme: Social security penalties or participation incentives? CAEPR Working Paper No. 111. ANU Centre for Aboriginal Economic Policy Research.

Galaty, J. G. (1992). "Pastoralists Past and Present: Reinterpreting Family and Flock in East Africa". In B. Glazier (Ed.), Pastoralism in the Horn of Africa. New York University Press.

Gammage, B., 2011. *The Biggest Estate on Earth: How Aborigines Made Australia*. Sydney: Allen & Unwin.

Garnett, S.T., Burgess, N.D., Fa, J.E., Fernández-Llamazares, Á., Molnár, Z., Robinson, C.J., Watson, J.E.M., Zander, K.K., Austin, B., Brondizio, E.S., et al. (2018) 'A spatial overview of the global importance of Indigenous lands for conservation', Nature Sustainability, 1(7), pp. 369–374.

Graeber, D. (2011) Debt: The First 5,000 Years. Brooklyn, NY & London: Melville House.

Greene, S., 2004. Indigenous People Incorporated? Culture as Politics, Culture as Property in Pharmaceutical Bioprospecting. *Current Anthropology*, 45(2), pp. 211–237.

Hayden, C., 2003. When Nature Goes Public: The Making and Unmaking of Bioprospecting in Mexico. Princeton University Press.

Helm, J., 1981. *The People of Denendeh: Ethnohistory of the Dene*. Iowa City: University of Iowa Press.

Helm, J. (2000). *The People of Denendeh: Ethnohistory of the Indians of Canada's Northwest Territories*. McGill-Queen's University Press.

Hochschild, A., 1998. *King Leopold's Ghost: A Story of Greed, Terror, and Heroism in Colonial Africa*. Boston: Houghton Mifflin.

Intergovernmental Science-Policy Platform on Biodiversity and Ecosystem Services (IPBES), 2019. *Summary for Policymakers of the Global Assessment Report on Biodiversity and Ecosystem Services*. Bonn: IPBES Secretariat.

ILO (International Labour Organization) (1989) Indigenous and Tribal Peoples Convention (No. 169). Geneva: ILO.

Inikori, J.E. (2002) Africans and the Industrial Revolution in England: A Study in International Trade and Economic Development. Cambridge: Cambridge University Press.

IPBES (2019) Global Assessment Report on Biodiversity and Ecosystem Services. Bonn: Intergovernmental Science-Policy Platform on Biodiversity and Ecosystem Services. (Summary for Policymakers available at: ipbes.net).

Johansen, B.E. (1982) Forgotten Founders: How the American Indian Helped Shape Democracy. Boston, MA: The Harvard Common Press.

Kay, C. (2001). Neoliberalism, Peasant Agriculture and Rural Livelihoods: Threat or Opportunity? Latin American Perspectives, 28(3), 16–38.

Kay, C., 2006. Rural poverty and development strategies in Latin America. Journal of Agrarian Change, 6(4), pp. 455–491.

Keenan, J., 2005. *The Lesser Gods of the Sahara: Social Change and Political Transformation among the Tuareg of Algeria*. London: Frank Cass.

Kimmerer, R.W. (2013) Braiding Sweetgrass: Indigenous Wisdom, Scientific Knowledge and the Teachings of Plants. Minneapolis, MN: Milkweed Editions.

Kirch, P. V. (2000). On the Road of the Winds: An Archaeological History of the Pacific Islands before European Contact. University of California Press.

Kittinger, J.N., Bambico, T.M., Minton, D., Miller, A., Mejia, M., Kalei, N. and Wilcox, B.A., 2015. Restoring coupled social–ecological systems in a Hawaiian community: A social–ecological approach to fishpond restoration. *Ecology and Society*, 20(1), p. 36.

Kohn, E., 2013. *How Forests Think: Toward an Anthropology Beyond the Human*. Berkeley: University of California Press.

Krupnik, I., Mason, R., & Horton, M. (2004). Northern Ethnographic Landscapes: Perspectives from Circumpolar Nations. Smithsonian Institution Press.

Kukutai, T. & Taylor, J. (eds) (2016) Indigenous Data Sovereignty: Toward an Agenda. Canberra: ANU Press.

Larson, A.M., 2010. Making the 'rules of the game': Constituting territory and authority in Nicaragua's indigenous communities. Land Use Policy, 27(4), pp. 1143–1152.

Lee, R. B., & Daly, R. (2004). The Cambridge Encyclopedia of Hunters and Gatherers. Cambridge University Press.

Mann, C.C., 2005. 1491: New Revelations of the Americas Before Columbus. New York: Knopf.

Marks, R.B., 2007. The Origins of the Modern World: A Global and Environmental Narrative from the Fifteenth to the Twenty-First Century. 2nd ed. Lanham: Rowman & Littlefield.

Mason, R.E., Savoie, K., DeMent, M. and Garibay, J., 2022. *Reclaiming Indigenous agricultural practices: Agroecological contributions of the Three Sisters polyculture*. Agriculture and Human Values, 39, pp. 115–130.

Mazoyer, M. and Roudart, L., 2006. *A History of World Agriculture: From the Neolithic Age to the Current Crisis*. London: Earthscan.

Mbiti, J. S. (1990). *African religions and philosophy* (2nd ed.). Heinemann.

McNeill, W.H. (1976) Plagues and Peoples. Garden City, NY: Anchor Press/Doubleday.

Mokyr, J. (2002) The Gifts of Athena: Historical Origins of the Knowledge Economy. Princeton, NJ: Princeton University Press.

Mokyr, J. (2009) The Enlightened Economy: An Economic History of Britain 1700–1850. New Haven, CT: Yale University Press.

Mokyr, J., 2010. The Enlightened Economy: An Economic History of Britain 1700–1850. New Haven: Yale University Press.

Morphy, H. (1991). *Ancestral connections: Art and an Aboriginal system of knowledge*. University of Chicago Press.

Mount Pleasant, J. (2016). The science behind the Three Sisters mound system: An agronomic assessment of an Indigenous agricultural system in the Northeast. *Agronomy Journal*, 108(4), 1624–1632.

Murra, J.V. (1972) 'El "control vertical" de un máximo de pisos ecológicos en la economía de las sociedades andinas', in Murra, J.V. (ed.) Visita de la Provincia de León de Huánuco. Huánuco: Universidad Nacional Hermilio Valdizán, pp. 427–476.

North, D.C. (1990) Institutions, Institutional Change and Economic Performance. Cambridge: Cambridge University Press.

Nunn, N. & Qian, N. (2011) 'The potato's contribution to population and urbanization: Evidence from a historical experiment', Quarterly Journal of Economics, 126(2), pp. 593–650.

O'Faircheallaigh, C. (2013) 'Community development agreements in the mining industry: An emerging global phenomenon', Community Development, 44(2), pp. 222–238.

Ostrom, E. (1990). *Governing the commons: The evolution of institutions for collective action*. Cambridge University Press.

Ostrom, E. (2010) 'Polycentric systems for coping with collective action and global environmental change', Global Environmental Change, 20(4), pp. 550–557.

Polanyi, K. (1944) The Great Transformation: The Political and Economic Origins of Our Time. New York: Farrar & Rinehart. (Later eds. Beacon Press, 1957/2001).

Pomeranz, K. (2000) The Great Divergence: China, Europe, and the Making of the Modern World Economy. Princeton, NJ: Princeton University Press.

Raworth, K. (2017) Doughnut Economics: Seven Ways to Think Like a 21st-Century Economist. London: Random House Business.

Reij, C., Tappan, G. and Smale, M., 2009. *Agroenvironmental Transformation in the Sahel: Another Kind of "Green Revolution"*. Washington, DC: IFPRI.

Reynolds, H., 1996. *Aboriginal Sovereignty: Reflections on Race, State and Nation*. Sydney: Allen & Unwin.

Rival, L., 1998. *The Social Life of Trees: Anthropological Perspectives on Tree Symbolism*. Oxford: Berg.

Rose, D. B. (1996). Nourishing Terrains: Australian Aboriginal Views of Landscape and Wilderness. Australian Heritage Commission.

Sahlins, M. (1972). *Stone Age economics*. Aldine-Atherton.

Scott, J.C. (1998) Seeing Like a State: How Certain Schemes to Improve the Human Condition Have Failed. New Haven, CT: Yale University Press.

Secretariat of the Convention on Biological Diversity (CBD), 2022. *Global Biodiversity Outlook* 5. Montreal: CBD.

Sen, A. (1999) Development as Freedom. Oxford: Oxford University Press. (US ed.: New York: Alfred A. Knopf, 1999).

Shiva, V., 1991. *The Violence of the Green Revolution: Third World Agriculture, Ecology, and Politics*. London: Zed Books.

Simpson, L.B. (2017). As We Have Always Done: Indigenous Freedom through Radical Resistance. Minneapolis: University of Minnesota Press.

Smith, L.T., 2012. *Decolonizing Methodologies: Research and Indigenous Peoples*. 2nd ed. London: Zed Books.

Stiglitz, J.E., Sen, A. and Fitoussi, J.-P. (2009) Report by the Commission on the Measurement of Economic Performance and Social Progress. Paris: Commission on the Measurement of Economic Performance and Social Progress.

Truth and Reconciliation Commission of Canada, 2015. *Honouring the Truth, Reconciling for the Future: Summary of the Final Report of the Truth and Reconciliation Commission of Canada*. Ottawa: TRC.

United Nations General Assembly (UNGA) (2007) United Nations Declaration on the Rights of Indigenous Peoples, A/RES/61/295 (13 September 2007). New York: United Nations.

United Nations, 2007. United Nations Declaration on the Rights of Indigenous Peoples (UNDRIP).

Urton, G., 2003. Signs of the Inka Khipu: Binary Coding in the Andean Knotted-String Records. Austin: University of Texas Press.

Viveiros de Castro, E., 2004. *Exchanging Perspectives: The Transformation of Objects into Subjects in Amerindian Ontologies. Common Knowledge*, 10(3), pp. 463–484.

Zimmerer, K.S., 2014. *Conservation booms with agricultural expansion: Sustainability and shifting environmental governance in Latin America*. Annual Review of Environment and Resources, 39, pp. 237–265.

CHAPTER 2

The Economics of Indigenous Peoples and Ancient Economic Thought

1 Introduction

Modern economic theory often presents itself as the universal framework for understanding value, exchange, and development. Yet this universality is both historically narrow and philosophically limiting. Dominant paradigms, whether neoclassical economics with its rational, utility-maximizing agent (homo economicus) or Marxian frameworks centred on production and class, are abstracted from specific ecological, spiritual, and political contexts. This chapter challenges that abstraction by recovering economic traditions rooted in Indigenous societies and ancient civilizations, which offer alternative foundations for organizing collective life, managing resources, and understanding prosperity.

Indigenous economies across the globe, from the Andean ayllu to the Dene caribou governance systems, are not pre-modern remnants but coherent systems of ecological stewardship, relational accountability, and consensual governance.[1,2] These systems embed the economy in land, law, kinship, and cosmology. Land is not a commodity, but a living entity;

[1] Berkes, F. (2012) Sacred Ecology: Traditional Ecological Knowledge and Resource Management. 3rd edn. London: Routledge.

[2] Nadasdy, P. (2003) Hunters and Bureaucrats: Power, Knowledge, and Aboriginal-State Relations in the Southwest Yukon. Vancouver: UBC Press.

S. Ramesh, *The Political Economy of the Indigenous Peoples of the World, Volume I*, https://doi.org/10.1007/978-3-032-24041-5_2

wealth is not surplus, but relational harmony. Decision-making is polycentric and legitimacy is grounded in ritual, consent, and community-based monitoring, features that resonate with Ostrom's design principles for sustainable commons governance.[3,4] Parallel to these traditions, ancient economic thought in India, China, and Greece articulated moral-political frameworks where economy served the ethical order. In India, Kautilya's Arthashastra presented a statecraft of taxation, irrigation, and famine relief rooted in dharma, or righteous duty.[5] In Confucian and Mencian thought, economic welfare, especially food security and land access, was fundamental to legitimate rule, entwining virtue with policy.[6,7] Even Greek thinkers such as Aristotle and Xenophon distinguished between natural household management (oikonomia) and unnatural money accumulation (chrematistike), reflecting early critiques of limitless accumulation.[8] These traditions stand in stark contrast to the abstraction of land, labour, and capital in modern economic theory. Neoclassical models depoliticise value and obscure histories of dispossession. Marxism, while incisive in its critique of class and enclosure, under-theorises non-material values, cosmological authority, and multi-species governance.[9,10] Both traditions often treat Indigenous and ancient systems as primitive or incomplete, rather than seeing them as full political economies with their own ontologies of value.

This chapter also introduces Symbiotic Gaian Economics (SGE), a future-oriented framework that synthesises Indigenous relationality, ancient moral economies, and Earth-system science. SGE treats

[3] Ostrom, E. (1990) Governing the Commons: The Evolution of Institutions for Collective Action. Cambridge: Cambridge University Press.

[4] Ostrom, E. (2010) 'Beyond markets and states: Polycentric governance of complex economic systems', American Economic Review, 100(3), pp. 641–672.

[5] Rangarajan, L. N. (trans.) (1992) Kautilya: The Arthashastra. New Delhi: Penguin Books.

[6] Elman, B. A. (2005) Classicism, Politics, and Kinship: The Ch'ing Imperial Examinations. Cambridge: Cambridge University Press.

[7] Bloom, I. (trans.) (2009) Mencius. New York: Columbia University Press.

[8] Finley, M. I. (1973) The Ancient Economy. Berkeley: University of California Press.

[9] Federici, S. (2004) Caliban and the Witch: Women, the Body and Primitive Accumulation. New York: Autonomedia.

[10] Kimmerer, R. W. (2013) Braiding Sweetgrass: Indigenous Wisdom, Scientific Knowledge and the Teachings of Plants. Minneapolis: Milkweed Editions.

economies as embedded within planetary boundaries,[11] governed through polycentric institutions, and guided by reciprocal obligations rather than extractive rights. It reframes development as resilience and regeneration, prioritises FPIC (Free, Prior and Informed Consent), and values capabilities and intergenerational well-being over growth.[12,13] Ultimately, this chapter aims to pluralise economic thought by foregrounding alternative epistemologies and governance systems. Rather than searching for a universal model, it calls for an economics grounded in relational justice, ecological integrity, and the legitimacy of multiple ontologies. In doing so, it reclaims Indigenous and ancient knowledge as vital for navigating the twenty-first century's ecological and political crises and beyond.

1.1 Indigenous Economic Practices: Governance, Sustainability, and Reciprocity

Relational Ontologies and Economic Life

Kinship and Economy: The Indivisibility of Social, Spiritual, and Material Relations

Across many Indigenous societies, economic life is not an autonomous sphere but braided with kinship, law, and spirituality. Exchange and production reproduce social relations as much as they provision material needs. Sahlins' account of "the domestic mode of production" foregrounded kin-ordered labour and reciprocity rather than wage contracts or profit maximization.[14] Subsequent work shows how kin networks allocate rights and duties in ways that lower transaction costs and smooth risk: labour is mobilized through obligations, not markets; credit is embedded in social reputation; and property is defined by responsibilities to relations, human and more-than-human, rather than absolute

[11] Rockström, J. et al. (2009) 'A safe operating space for humanity', Nature, 461(7263), pp. 472–475.

[12] Sen, A. (1999) Development as Freedom. Oxford: Oxford University Press.

[13] Raworth, K. (2017) Doughnut Economics: Seven Ways to Think Like a 21st-Century Economist. White River Junction: Chelsea Green Publishing.

[14] Sahlins, M. (1972) Stone Age Economics. Chicago, IL: Aldine-Atherton.

individual title.[15,16] Among many First Nations, for example, clan affiliation governs access to fisheries and forests while embedding sanctioning through shame, reputational loss, and ritual.[17] Such arrangements constitute a form of "commons governance" long misread by colonial legal orders as absence of ownership.[18,19] The spiritual economy is related to cosmology and reciprocity with land, water, and non-human life. Relational ontologies treat land and waters as kin and law-bearing entities. In Māori thought, whenua (land/placenta) signals the life-giving relation between people and place; mana and kaitiakitanga (authority/guardianship) entail duties of care that structure extraction, redistribution, and restoration.[20] In many North American nations, ceremonial calendars (first-salmon rites; disbursing feasts) align harvesting with obligations to non-human persons, linking abundance to right relationship.[21] These are not metaphorical add-ons; they are institutional constraints that regulate timing, intensity, and social distribution of use, akin to ecological "harvest control rules" anchored in cosmology. This embeddedness challenges the neoclassical abstraction of land as a fungible factor and echoes Polanyi's claim that economies are ordinarily "embedded" in social meanings.[22] In other words, land is not just an interchangeable input in production but a relational good bound up with kinship, law, and cosmology, so decisions about its use are governed by social obligations and cultural meanings that

[15] Polanyi, K. (1944) The Great Transformation: The Political and Economic Origins of Our Time. New York: Rinehart.

[16] Graeber, D. (2011) Debt: The First 5,000 Years. Brooklyn, NY and London: Melville House.

[17] Berkes, F. (2012) Sacred Ecology. 3rd edn. New York: Routledge.

[18] Ostrom, E. (1990) Governing the Commons: The Evolution of Institutions for Collective Action. Cambridge: Cambridge University Press.

[19] Scott, J. C. (1998) Seeing Like a State: How Certain Schemes to Improve the Human Condition Have Failed. New Haven, CT: Yale University Press.

[20] Durie, M. (1998) Te Mana, Te Kāwanatanga: The Politics of Māori Self-Determination. Auckland: Oxford University Press.

[21] Kimmerer, R.W. (2013) Braiding Sweetgrass: Indigenous Wisdom, Scientific Knowledge and the Teachings of Plants.
Minneapolis, MN: Milkweed Editions.

[22] Polanyi, K. (1944) The Great Transformation: The Political and Economic Origins of Our Time. New York: Rinehart.

markets and prices alone cannot capture.[23] Empirical syntheses show that such rule complexes often sustain biodiversity and carbon stocks at least as well as state-protected areas, suggesting that spiritual and legal reciprocity can be ecologically effective design.[24,25] Together, these dimensions show that Indigenous economies are constituted by relations and responsibilities. Value is measured not only in goods but in maintained relations; efficiency is judged by resilience and the continuity of life-giving ties rather than short-run output.[26,27]

Resource Governance and Collective Decision-Making

Indigenous systems of economic governance challenge the assumptions embedded in both neoclassical economics and centrally planned communist models. Where neoclassical economics presumes rational individual utility maximization within competitive markets, and communism emphasizes centralized planning to eliminate class-based exploitation, Indigenous resource governance is structured around collective stewardship, localized knowledge, and recursive moral economies. Among groups such as the Tłı̨chǫ Dene, Tuareg pastoralists, and Māori hapū/iwi, governance is embedded in social relations, spiritual obligations, and environmental feedback systems. The Tłı̨chǫ people of northern Canada historically governed caribou hunting through decentralized institutions rooted in kinship, seasonal mobility, and elder-guided decision-making. Rather than fixed quotas or state-imposed regulations, norms of restraint, enforced through shared knowledge and elder legitimacy, regulated harvest levels.[28] Post-treaty governance arrangements, such as

23 Polanyi, K. (1944) The Great Transformation: The Political and Economic Origins of Our Time. New York: Rinehart.

24 Garnett, S.T., Burgess, N.D., Fa, J.E., Fernández-Llamazares, Á., Molnár, Z., Robinson, C.J., Watson, J.E.M., Zander, K.K., Austin, B., Brondizio, E.S. et al. (2018) 'A spatial overview of the global importance of Indigenous lands for conservation', Nature Sustainability, 1(7), pp. 369–374.

25 IPBES (Intergovernmental Science-Policy Platform on Biodiversity and Ecosystem Services) (2019) Global Assessment Report on Biodiversity and Ecosystem Services. Bonn: IPBES Secretariat.

26 Sen, A. (1999) Development as Freedom. Oxford: Oxford University Press.

27 Berkes, F. (2012) Sacred Ecology. 3rd edn. New York: Routledge.

28 Berkes, F. (2012). Sacred Ecology: Traditional Ecological Knowledge and Resource Management (3rd ed.). Routledge.

the Wek'èezhìi Renewable Resources Board, integrate Indigenous law and Western statutory structures in co-management frameworks that continue to rely on consensus and knowledge-sharing.[29] This contrasts with neoclassical economic models, where resource use is governed by price signals and individual property rights, often failing to account for ecological interdependence and community values. Unlike in centrally planned systems where directives are imposed from above, the Tłı̨chǫ system is recursive and adaptive, shaped by seasonal feedback and elder counsel. Tuareg pastoralists of the Sahara and Sahel exemplify another form of adaptive governance. Their access to resources such as wells and pastures is negotiated through nested rights within confederation and lineage structures. Rights to use land shift with rainfall patterns and herd movements, illustrating a dynamic and flexible model of property relations that cannot be reduced to either private ownership or state allocation.[30,31] Reciprocity is not merely a moral norm but a functional requirement for survival in arid and uncertain environments. This fluidity challenges both capitalist market assumptions of static entitlements and communist models that rely on fixed production targets. Instead, Tuareg governance leverages decentralized decision-making, overlapping authorities, and social obligations to mitigate risk. In Aotearoa New Zealand, Māori economic governance revolves around mana whenua (authority over land) and rangatiratanga (chiefly leadership), reinforced through hapū/iwi structures, traditional social and political organization of Māori society. Co-governance arrangements resulting from Treaty of Waitangi settlements, such as the Waikato River Authority, embed Māori concepts like kaitiakitanga (guardianship) into environmental policy, affecting decisions on resource harvest, restoration, and eco-tourism.[32] These institutions operate in polycentric governance systems, where Māori and Crown entities share responsibility, reflecting the principles of clearly defined

[29] Nadasdy, P. (2003). Hunters and Bureaucrats: Power, Knowledge, and Aboriginal-State Relations in the Southwest Yukon. UBC Press.

[30] Scoones, I. (1995). Living with Uncertainty: New Directions in Pastoral Development in Africa. Intermediate Technology Publications.

[31] Niamir-Fuller, M. (1999). Managing Mobility in African Rangelands: The Legitimisation of Transhumance. Intermediate Technology Publications.

[32] Durie, M. (1998). Te Mana, Te Kāwanatanga: The Politics of Māori Self-Determination. Oxford University Press.

boundaries, local monitoring, graduated sanctions, and conflict resolution.[33,34] Graduated sanctions refer to a system where rule-breaking is met with proportionate and escalating penalties, allowing for education and correction before severe punishment is applied. Unlike communist central planning that often disregarded local knowledge, or market systems that privatized commons, Māori governance emphasizes enduring relationships with the land and intergenerational responsibility. Legitimacy in Indigenous governance is not secured through electoral mandates or bureaucratic authority but through embedded moral and spiritual authority, typically vested in elders, clan leaders, or councils. These figures enforce decisions not by coercion but through ritual, custom, and communal sanction. Seasonal ceremonies, naming protocols, and collective resource use rituals are mechanisms of compliance, serving both symbolic and practical functions.[35,36] Violations result in social consequences, loss of standing, exclusion from marriages, or diminished access to resources, sanctions more deeply felt than monetary penalties in many Indigenous contexts. These systems contrast sharply with neoclassical models that rely on market discipline and monetary incentives, often neglecting the cost of externalities and the role of cultural legitimacy in governance. Similarly, communist economic systems, while grounded in collective ownership, often failed to generate legitimacy at the local level, resulting in poor compliance and environmental degradation. For instance, the Soviet Union's collectivized agriculture destroyed traditional peasant knowledge systems and incentivized overuse of land, with catastrophic ecological consequences.[37] Polycentric and consent-based Indigenous governance systems offer redundancy and resilience.

[33] Ostrom, E. (1990). Governing the Commons: The Evolution of Institutions for Collective Action. Cambridge University Press.

[34] Ostrom, E. (2010). Beyond Markets and States: Polycentric Governance of Complex Economic Systems. American Economic Review, 100(3), 641–672.

[35] Berkes, F. (2012). Sacred Ecology: Traditional Ecological Knowledge and Resource Management (3rd ed.). Routledge.

[36] Scott, J. C. (1998). Seeing Like a State: How Certain Schemes to Improve the Human Condition Have Failed. Yale University Press.

[37] Scott, J. C. (1998). Seeing Like a State: How Certain Schemes to Improve the Human Condition Have Failed. Yale University Press.

The overlapping roles of clan structures, treaty boards, and village councils allow for adaptive learning and resistance to capture by elites.[38] These systems show that consensus is not the absence of power but a mode of binding leadership to collective obligations. Where states recognize Indigenous governance procedures, such as in the Tłı̨chǫ Agreement or Māori co-governance bodies, environmental and social outcomes tend to improve. Where such recognition is absent, extractive regimes intensify, leading to dispossession and ecological collapse. Empirical data supports these insights. Indigenous-managed fisheries in Canada have higher compliance and sustainability rates than state-managed equivalents.[39] Other evidence suggests that mobile pastoralist systems in Africa often outperform sedentary agricultural schemes in terms of resource use efficiency and ecological balance.[40] In Aotearoa, co-managed river ecosystems have shown improved water quality and biodiversity outcomes, attributed to the incorporation of Māori values.[41] These cases demonstrate that Indigenous economic governance is not merely cultural heritage—it is a living, functional alternative to dominant economic paradigms.

Sustainable Agriculture and Ecological Stewardship

Indigenous agricultural systems represent complex, ecologically embedded economies that resist reduction to the frameworks of either neoclassical economics or centrally planned communism. These systems are not primitive or static; rather, they are dynamic agroecological strategies rooted in Traditional Ecological Knowledge (TEK), which functions through feedback loops, long-term observation, and cultural transmission. Unlike neoclassical models that assume efficiency emerges from competitive specialization and market price signals, Indigenous systems prioritize diversity, resilience, and ecological balance. Unlike communism's tendency towards industrial-scale collectivism and monoculture,

[38] Ostrom, E. (2010). Beyond Markets and States: Polycentric Governance of Complex Economic Systems. American Economic Review, 100(3), 641–672.

[39] Berkes, F. (2012). Sacred Ecology: Traditional Ecological Knowledge and Resource Management (3rd ed.). Routledge.

[40] Niamir-Fuller, M. (1999). Managing Mobility in African Rangelands: The Legitimisation of Transhumance. Intermediate Technology Publications.

[41] Durie, M. (1998). Te Mana, Te Kāwanatanga: The Politics of Māori Self-Determination. Oxford University Press.

these systems centre polyculture, seasonal rhythms, and distributed governance. In the Andes, the "vertical archipelago" model captures how Andean societies organized ecological complementarity across altitudinal zones.[42] Highland communities cultivated potatoes, grains, and tubers, while accessing tropical fruits, coca, and fish from lowland allies. Storage systems such as qollqa stabilized food availability over multi-year cycles, absorbing shocks from frost or drought.[43] This decentralized yet coordinated system is incompatible with the logic of comparative advantage that drives neoclassical agriculture, which often erodes resilience through specialization. Instead of optimizing for marketable surplus, Andean economies optimized for nutritional security, climate risk distribution, and social cohesion. In North America, the Haudenosaunee "Three Sisters" agricultural system, maize, beans, and squash, embodies agroecological integration. Maize provides a structure for beans to climb; beans fix nitrogen into the soil; squash shades the ground, conserving moisture and deterring weeds. This intercropping system enhances yields per unit area, reduces labour, and diversifies diets.[44,45] It defies the neoclassical model of monoculture efficiency, which externalizes ecological costs such as soil degradation and pest vulnerability. Likewise, it contrasts with Soviet collectivized farms, where forced standardization and over-mechanization often destroyed soil fertility and reduced crop diversity.[46] In the Haudenosaunee model, labour is not exploited in service of surplus extraction but embedded in community rituals, ceremonies, and food-sharing systems that reinforce social norms and ecological knowledge. In the Sahel, transhumant pastoralism represents a mobile and adaptive strategy tuned to ecological variability. Pastoralists shift herds across ecological gradients in response to rainfall and pasture

[42] Murra, J. V. (1972). El "control vertical" de un máximo de pisos ecológicos en la economía de las sociedades andinas. In Ortiz de Zúñiga, J. (Ed.), Visita de la Provincia de León de Huánuco en 1562 (Vol. 2). Universidad Nacional Hermilio Valdizán.

[43] D'Altroy, T. N. (2014). The Incas (2nd ed.). Wiley-Blackwell.

[44] Johansen, B. E. (1982). Forgotten Founders: How the American Indian Helped Shape Democracy. The Harvard Common Press.

[45] Kimmerer, R. W. (2013). Braiding Sweetgrass: Indigenous Wisdom, Scientific Knowledge and the Teachings of Plants. Milkweed Editions.

[46] Scott, J. C. (1998). Seeing Like a State: How Certain Schemes to Improve the Human Condition Have Failed. Yale University Press.

growth, governed by customary rules and clan-based negotiations.[47,48] These systems generate ecological benefits, such as promoting grassland biodiversity and preventing overgrazing through rotational pressure. In contrast to neoclassical land tenure regimes that seek privatization and fixed boundaries, pastoralist governance is fluid, negotiated, and relational. When colonial and post-colonial regimes imposed sedentarism, land degradation and social fragmentation followed. Communist agrarian reforms similarly failed in such contexts, flattening complex tenure systems into bureaucratic grids, often leading to environmental collapse and food insecurity.[49] What links these diverse Indigenous systems is a foundation in TEK, Traditional Ecological Knowledge. TEK is neither folklore nor myth, but a cumulative body of knowledge passed through generations via story, ritual, taboo, and observation.[50] In agroecological terms, TEK systems achieve outcomes, biodiversity conservation, soil regeneration, pest control, that are now supported by empirical studies.[51] For instance, cultural burning practices among Aboriginal Australians created mosaic landscapes that reduced the risk of catastrophic fires while enhancing habitat heterogeneity.[52] These practices contradict industrial fire suppression policies based on centralized control and fuel accumulation. Whereas cultural burning applies frequent, low-intensity fires to manage vegetation and sustain ecological balance, industrial approaches often prevent all fires, allowing flammable materials to build up and increasing the likelihood of large, uncontrollable wildfires. Contemporary global data reinforces these insights. Indigenous-managed lands globally overlap with areas of highest biodiversity and often outperform

[47] Niamir-Fuller, M. (1999). Managing Mobility in African Rangelands: The Legitimization of Transhumance. Intermediate Technology Publications.

[48] Scoones, I. (1995). Living with Uncertainty: New Directions in Pastoral Development in Africa. Intermediate Technology Publications.

[49] Scott, J. C. (1998). Seeing Like a State: How Certain Schemes to Improve the Human Condition Have Failed. Yale University Press.

[50] Berkes, F. (2012). Sacred Ecology: Traditional Ecological Knowledge and Resource Management (3rd ed.). Routledge.

[51] Altieri, M. A., & Nicholls, C. I. (2017). Agroecology: A Transdisciplinary, Participatory and Action-Oriented Approach. CRC Press.

[52] Gammage, B. (2011). The Biggest Estate on Earth: How Aborigines Made Australia. Allen & Unwin.

state-protected areas in ecological indicators.[53] The Intergovernmental Science-Policy Platform on Biodiversity and Ecosystem Services confirms that biodiversity loss is lowest where Indigenous rights are secure and land is governed by customary institutions.[54] This empirical evidence refutes neoclassical assumptions that open-access resources inevitably lead to overexploitation (the so-called "tragedy of the commons"). Instead, where land tenure and monitoring are communally defined, ecological thresholds are maintained. Agroecological systems inspired by Indigenous practice offer tangible alternatives to capitalist agribusiness and state socialism. They are not backward but scalable, particularly when supported by legal recognition and participatory institutions. TEK-based systems produce not only food but also ecosystem services, climate resilience, and institutional memory. Where communism often erased cultural and ecological diversity in pursuit of industrial quotas, and capitalism commodifies land and labour, Indigenous economies prioritize balance, reciprocity, and multi-generational stewardship. As climate instability intensifies, these systems offer grounded design principles for food sovereignty and ecological governance in a warming world.

1.2 Ancient Indian and Chinese Economic Thought

Ancient India: Dharma, Artha, and Kautilyan Economics

Ancient Indian economic thought, particularly in the Sanskritic tradition, reflects a sophisticated integration of ethics, political authority, and material life. Unlike the modern separation of economics from morality and politics, as seen in neoclassical economics, which reduces human behaviour to preference maximization under constraints, ancient Indian frameworks viewed prosperity (artha) as legitimate only when aligned with dharma (ethical duty). This fusion created an embedded political economy where governance was simultaneously a material and moral obligation. The Dharmashastra corpus, especially texts like Manusmriti and Yājñavalkya Smṛti, outlines the obligations of rulers to maintain justice,

[53] Garnett, S. T., Burgess, N. D., Fa, J. E., Fernández-Llamazares, Á., Molnár, Z., Robinson, C. J., … & Leiper, I. (2018). A Spatial overview of the global importance of Indigenous lands for conservation. Nature Sustainability, 1(7), 369–374.

[54] IPBES. (2019). Summary for Policymakers of the Global Assessment Report on Biodiversity and Ecosystem Services. Intergovernmental Science-Policy Platform on Biodiversity and Ecosystem Services.

protect livelihoods, and ensure famine relief. The state was expected to uphold rajadharma, a code of righteous kingship, which included just taxation, prevention of exploitation, and investment in infrastructure like irrigation tanks, roads, and granaries.[55,56] The ideal king was not an extractive sovereign but a steward of social order, constrained by the moral logic of redistribution and public responsibility. This directly contrasts with the neoclassical notion of a minimal state or laissez-faire policies, where moral concerns are considered externalities. In communism, while redistribution is central, economic governance is driven by class conflict and centralized planning, often ignoring spiritual or ethical dimensions. Kautilya's Arthashastra, compiled circa fourth century BCE, represents the most systematic treatment of ancient Indian economic administration. Its realism and analytical precision mark a break from the purely prescriptive style of the Dharmashastra, resembling instead a treatise in political economy. Kautilya advocates a diversified tax base, land revenue, customs duties, resource monopolies (especially on salt, metals, and forest products), and emphasizes anti-corruption mechanisms, including undercover inspectors (spies) and public audits.[57] The text recommends price controls during famines, grain reserves for disaster relief, and public works to stimulate economic productivity, anticipating proto-Keynesian ideas about counter-cyclical investment and the role of the state in stabilizing output and consumption. Public welfare in the Arthashastra is not altruistic but instrumental: stability and prosperity are essential to state survival. Over-taxation is explicitly discouraged because it alienates the productive classes and undermines state revenue in the long run. Kautilya notes that "just as trees are tapped for sap, not cut at the root, so should the king collect revenue without hurting the taxpayers".[58] This insight reflects an incentive-compatible framework that recognizes economic behaviour is sensitive to institutional design, a core concern in contemporary political economy. Yet, despite its pragmatism, Kautilyan economics is not amoral. It remains embedded in the broader normative frame of dharma. The goal is not merely state expansion but the

[55] Sen, A. (1999). Development as Freedom. Oxford University Press.

[56] Olivelle, P. (2004). The Law Code of Manu. Oxford University Press.

[57] Rangarajan, L. N. (Trans.) (1992). Kautilya: The Arthashastra. Penguin Books.

[58] Rangarajan, L. N. (Trans.) (1992). Kautilya: The Arthashastra. Penguin Books.

preservation of social order and interdependence among castes, professions, and regions. The concept of varna (social order) and ashrama (life stages) undergirds economic roles and responsibilities, producing a system in which individuals contribute to societal welfare in ways aligned with both cosmic and civic order.[59] While modern economists would critique this as hierarchical and exclusionary, its normative function was to ensure that economic behaviour supported social cohesion, not unlike communism's aspiration to align economic activity with collective welfare, albeit through different institutional mechanisms. For comparison, neoclassical economics abstracts from political structure and ethical concerns, reducing taxation and redistribution to utility trade-offs. It lacks the embeddedness seen in Arthashastra or Dharmashastra thinking, where political authority is inextricably linked to moral legitimacy. On the other hand, communist models, particularly in Stalinist or Maoist forms, elevate the state as an economic planner but often disconnect it from localized ethical traditions, resulting in coercive top-down policies divorced from cultural legitimacy. The Indian model, by contrast, relies on a layered authority, king, minister, village council, tempered by custom, ritual, and scriptural constraints. In practice, ancient Indian economies demonstrated a remarkable degree of institutional complexity. Irrigation projects such as those in the Cauvery delta, temple-based redistribution in Tamil Nadu, and localized grain banking systems functioned as decentralized yet integrated welfare mechanisms.[60] During famines, inscriptions show that tax relief and grain disbursements were common, reinforcing the idea that economic management was a public responsibility embedded in ethical governance. Thus, the economic thought of ancient India offers a model of embedded governance where material administration is inseparable from ethical obligations. It provides historical precedent for a political economy that balances institutional pragmatism with normative purpose. As climate instability and inequality deepen, this integrated model, rooted in moral responsibility, public investment, and adaptive governance, offers valuable design principles for future economic systems seeking to reconcile prosperity with justice.

[59] Trautmann, T. R. (2012). Arthashastra: The Science of Wealth. Aleph Book Company.

[60] Ludden, D. (1999). An Agrarian History of South Asia. Cambridge University Press.

Ancient China: Confucian Harmony and Legalist Control

Ancient Chinese economic thought reflects two enduring paradigms of governance: the Confucian model of virtue-based legitimacy and the Legalist model of rule-based control. These frameworks shaped the political economy of Imperial China for over two millennia, creating an oscillating synthesis of ethical leadership and administrative centralization. Unlike neoclassical economics, which assumes individual rationality and market efficiency independent of governance, or communism, which relies on central planning and class struggle, Chinese thought positions political authority and ethical cultivation at the heart of economic order. Prosperity is not a spontaneous outcome of market interaction or production quotas but the result of calibrated governance that ensures moral order and institutional predictability.

Confucianism, grounded in the teachings of Kongzi (Confucius) and expanded by thinkers such as Mencius, views economic life as subordinate to social harmony and moral leadership. The ruler's virtue (ren, benevolence; yi, righteousness) is seen as the basis for just governance, which reduces uncertainty, discourages rebellion, and fosters productive agriculture. Texts like The Analects and Mencius advocate light taxation, grain storage systems, and strict adherence to rites (li) to foster stability and cultivate trust.[61] The state's role is not to engineer outcomes through coercion, but to lead by moral example, guiding subjects into proper roles and reciprocal obligations. Agriculture is central in this view, not merely for food security, but as the ethical backbone of the polity. Merchants are tolerated but morally suspect; wealth derived from commerce is acceptable only if it does not undermine agrarian stability.

In contrast, Legalist thought, articulated most forcefully by Han Feizi during the Warring States period, places little trust in moral cultivation. Legalism assumes that individuals pursue self-interest and respond best to explicit rewards and punishments. Thus, the state must impose order through codified law (fa), administrative standardization, and surveillance.[62] The Legalist model prioritises agriculture and warfare, the bases of state strength, and disciplines commercial activity through regulation and state monopolies. Merchant guilds, religious institutions, and local

[61] Elman, B. A. (2005). Classicism, Politics, and Kinship: The Ch'ing Imperial Examinations. Cambridge University Press.

[62] Liao, W. K. (Trans.). (1939/2003). The Complete Works of Han Fei Tzu: A Classic of Chinese Political Science. Arthur Probsthain.

elites are viewed as potential threats to state control and are suppressed or absorbed into the bureaucratic structure. The Qin Dynasty's brief but foundational rule exemplified this approach: weights and measures, currency, roads, and legal codes were unified across regions, facilitating administrative scale and extractive efficiency. These two models are not mutually exclusive. Historically, Chinese governance evolved as a dynamic fusion: Confucianism provided the moral language of state legitimacy, while Legalist techniques underpinned bureaucratic functionality. During the Han Dynasty, for example, Confucianism was officially adopted as state ideology, yet Legalist methods were retained to manage tax collection, labour mobilization, and standardization. This duality resonates with modern debates in political economy: is legitimacy built through values and participation, or through enforcement and efficiency? Compared to neoclassical economics, which abstracts the state as a background guarantor of contracts and treats economic activity as decentralized and self-regulating, both Confucian and Legalist traditions view the economy as an extension of political authority. In neoclassical models, taxation is often cast as distortionary, and government intervention is justified only to correct market failures. Confucian economics, by contrast, frames taxation as a moral obligation, with over-taxation leading to loss of legitimacy. Legalist economics sees taxation as a tool of statecraft, designed to optimise extraction while maintaining order. Relative to communism, Confucianism diverges sharply in its rejection of egalitarianism and its emphasis on hierarchical obligations. Communism aims to eliminate class distinctions through collectivization, while Confucianism preserves social hierarchy through moral duty. Legalism, however, shares communism's centralizing impulse, using state power to suppress intermediary institutions and enforce uniformity. Yet where communism is driven by ideological commitment to class struggle, Legalism is agnostic about justice and focused on control and performance.

Empirical data from China's historical economy underscores these philosophical foundations. The Qing Dynasty's long-run stability depended on both extensive granary systems, often tied to Confucian famine ethics, and an immense bureaucracy operating under Legalist principles of hierarchical command. Contemporary scholarship has shown that state granary systems during the Ming and Qing reduced famine mortality by up to 50% in well-governed regions.[63] Moreover, early Chinese land taxes were structured to reflect regional productivity and household conditions, anticipating principles of progressive taxation and social buffering absent from modern flat-tax proposals. The Confucian-led emphasis on food price stabilization also prefigures today's debates on food sovereignty and the role of the state in securing basic needs. In sum, ancient Chinese economic thought reveals a nuanced political economy grounded in governance quality, whether through moral leadership or institutional enforcement. Confucianism emphasizes ethics as the anchor of economic life; Legalism privileges rule-based mechanisms to overcome opportunism and fragmentation. Neither fits neatly within modern capitalist or communist paradigms, yet both offer enduring insights. In an era of global institutional erosion, ecological instability, and declining trust, these models remind us that economic systems are not merely technical artefacts but moral and political constructions that reflect how societies choose to order life, labour, and legitimacy.

Agrarianism, Stability, and Ethical Governance

Ancient Indian and Chinese economic traditions place agrarian stability at the core of political legitimacy. Unlike neoclassical economics, which abstracts individuals as utility-maximizing agents in competitive markets, or communism, which centralises redistribution via the state, classical Asian thought grounds political economy in ethical governance and ecological prudence. Material well-being is not a by-product of market forces or production quotas but a ruler's explicit moral duty. Agrarianism is not only economic policy but the foundation of social order and cosmic legitimacy. In the Confucian tradition, Mencius (372–289 BCE) articulates a clear position: governance without economic security is illegitimate. In Mencius 1A7, he argues that if people lack stable access to land and time for seasonal rest, they cannot be expected to cultivate virtue. His vision of the "well-field system" (jingtian), a model of communal farming with state-supported redistribution, aimed to guarantee a subsistence floor while curbing elite land concentration. These policies were accompanied by restrictions on hunting and fishing during

[63] Will, P. E., & Wong, R. B. (1991). Nourish the People: The State Civilian Granary System in China, 1650–1850. University of Michigan Center for Chinese Studies.

breeding seasons, ensuring ecological regeneration.[64] Grain storage, disaster relief, and fair taxation were not technocratic tools, but ethical obligations rooted in the concept of ren (benevolence). The moral logic is explicit, famine, unrest, or flight signal that a ruler has lost the tianming (Mandate of Heaven), legitimizing revolt. This contrasts sharply with neoclassical models, where food security is a function of income and market access. In the Confucian model, food provisioning is an institutional responsibility tied to moral accountability. It also differs from communist regimes like Maoist China, where collectivization was justified in the name of the masses but frequently disregarded agronomic knowledge and led to catastrophic outcomes, such as the Great Leap Forward, during which an estimated 30 million people died of famine.[65] Where Mencius links rule to welfare, Maoist policy often linked authority to ideological conformity, severing feedback between governance and outcomes. Confucian agrarianism is also ecologically embedded. Seasonal regulations on resource extraction, investment in riparian infrastructure, and promotion of frugality and restraint were integrated into the moral education of elites and commoners alike.[66] The agrarian state was not purely extractive but protective, maintaining dikes, storing grain, and preventing overexploitation. Similar patterns appear in Indian thought. The Dharmashastra texts and Arthashastra both articulate a state responsible for irrigation, famine relief, and land grants for the poor, tying sovereignty to stewardship.[67] The ethics of provisioning were inseparable from political power. These traditions prefigure modern ideas in development theory, especially Amartya Sen's capability approach. Sen argues that development should be assessed not by GDP but by the freedoms people must live well, including access to food, education, and public goods.[68] Classical Indian and Chinese thinkers reached a similar conclusion through moral philosophy, rulers are to be judged not by conquest or tribute, but by the flourishing of their people. Governance is successful when the commoners

[64] Bloom, I. (Trans.). (2009). Mencius. Columbia University Press.

[65] Dikötter, F. (2010). Mao's Great Famine: The History of China's Most Devastating Catastrophe, 1958–1962. Walker & Company.

[66] Elman, B. A. (2005). Classicism, Politics, and Kinship: The Ch'ing Imperial Examinations. Cambridge University Press.

[67] Trautmann, T. R. (2012). Arthashastra: The Science of Wealth. Aleph Book Company.

[68] Sen, A. (1999). Development as Freedom. Oxford University Press.

eat well, cultivate virtue, and remain loyal, not from fear, but because the state secures their subsistence. Contemporary scholarship supports these insights. Data from Qing China's granary system shows that regions with better-managed reserves experienced lower mortality during crop failures.[69] In early Indian polities, archaeological evidence from tank irrigation systems in Tamil Nadu points to sustained public investment in food security across centuries.[70] These systems required coordinated labour, redistribution, and knowledge transmission, features absent in market-led models and often undermined in command economies. Thus, agrarianism in ancient Asia was neither feudal nor static. It represented a political economy of ethical governance, where rulers were accountable for ecological stability, subsistence provisioning, and just land use. The moral language of classical texts should not obscure their practical relevance: they describe institutional strategies for preventing famine, resisting elite capture, and sustaining the commons. These traditions challenge modern paradigms by insisting that economic life is embedded in social and ecological obligations—and that power, to be legitimate, must feed.

1.3 Ancient Greek Economic Thought

Oikos and Polis: Household Management and the Public Sphere

Ancient Greek economic thought, particularly in the classical works of Aristotle and Xenophon, offers a normative vision of economic life grounded in ethics, moderation, and civic responsibility. Contrary to both neoclassical economics, which abstracts economic behaviour into utility-maximizing choices, and communism, which subordinates individual economic agency to collective ownership and state planning, the Greek tradition views the economy as a moral activity deeply embedded in social relationships. It is not a self-contained system governed by impersonal laws of supply and demand, but a realm of human action shaped by virtue, order, and the pursuit of the good life (eudaimonia). Aristotle draws a fundamental distinction between oikonomia and chrematistics in Politics I.8–10. Oikonomia, or household management, aims at sufficiency and stability; it is natural and necessary for the flourishing

[69] Will, P. E., & Wong, R. B. (1991). Nourish the People: The State Civilian Granary System in China, 1650–1850. University of Michigan Center for Chinese Studies.

[70] Ludden, D. (1999). An Agrarian History of South Asia. Cambridge University Press.

of family and city. Chrematistics, by contrast, is the art of acquiring wealth for its own sake, particularly through money lending, speculation, and commerce detached from need. Aristotle condemns this as "unnatural" because it turns means into ends, treating accumulation, rather than well-being, as the purpose of economic life. This concern anticipates modern critiques of financialized capitalism, where capital circulates without grounding in production or human needs. His rejection of usury, earning money from money, foreshadows contemporary debates on debt traps, rentierism, and financial instability.[71]

For Aristotle, economic activity is not morally neutral but must be subordinated to the goals of the polis, the political community. Justice, reciprocity, and moderation are essential. Trade is acceptable when it supports household self-sufficiency and civic peace, but dangerous when it undermines virtue or concentrates power in private hands. The emphasis on limits stands in stark contrast to neoclassical growth models, which celebrate expansion without inherent moral direction. At the same time, Aristotle's vision diverges from communism's insistence on collective ownership and material equality. He accepts inequality and private property but insists that both be regulated by civic norms and the common good.

Xenophon's Oeconomicus complements Aristotle by developing a practical ethics of household and land management. His dialogue portrays economic leadership as a moral craft that requires discipline, foresight, and cooperation. The household, in this view, is a training ground for civic responsibility, where economic order reflects and cultivates personal virtue.[72] Xenophon emphasizes the efficient use of land and labour, the value of education, and the importance of aligning economic roles with natural abilities. These views resonate with later Republican ideals that see property and productivity as tied to public service, not isolated wealth accumulation. Yet both thinkers operate within hierarchies of gender and slavery. The household is patriarchal, and much of its productive labour is performed by enslaved persons. Still, the economic thought embedded in their works insists that prosperity must be governed by ethics and directed towards collective stability. These limitations do not invalidate

71 Aristotle. (1962). Politics (T. A. Sinclair, Trans.). Penguin Books. (Original work c. 4th century BCE).

72 Xenophon. (1997). Oeconomicus (S. Waterfield, Trans.). Oxford University Press. (Original work c. 4th century BCE).

the core insight: that economic systems are judged not solely by output but by their contribution to human development and civic integrity. The moral economy of the Greeks sharply contrasts with both neoclassical and communist paradigms. Neoclassical theory, especially in its late-twentieth century formulation, reduces all value to preference satisfaction and prices. It lacks a normative theory of the good life or ethical limits to accumulation. Communism, on the other hand, often collapses the moral into the collective, coercing conformity and suppressing individual ethics in favour of bureaucratic plans. Ancient Greek thought avoids both extremes. It affirms economic freedom within ethical boundaries, property within civic duty, and inequality within mutual obligation. The Greeks lacked a true "economy" in the modern sense. But this absence reflects a fundamentally different orientation: for the Greeks, economic life was not an autonomous domain but a subset of ethics and politics. The economy served the polis, not the other way around. In this, Greek thought anticipates modern critiques of market fundamentalism, from Karl Polanyi's concept of embeddedness to Amartya Sen's focus on capabilities. Like them, Greek thinkers insisted that economies must be judged by their ability to support human flourishing, civic virtue, and social stability, not simply by growth or profit.

The Role of Slavery, Gender, and Exclusion in Classical Thought

Classical Greek economic thought, while rich in ethical reflection, was deeply embedded in hierarchies of status, gender, and legal identity. The normative frameworks of thinkers like Aristotle and Xenophon, discussed previously as advocates for moderation, civic virtue, and economic responsibility, were constructed within a society that categorically excluded large segments of the population from full economic and political participation. This exclusion was not incidental but foundational: the ideal of oikonomia, household self-sufficiency, and the functioning of the polis rested on the labour of enslaved persons, the confinement of women to the domestic sphere, and the marginalization of resident foreigners (metics).[73,74] In Athenian democracy, political rights were restricted to

[73] Finley, M. I. (1973). The Ancient Economy. University of California Press.

[74] Patterson, O. (1982). Slavery and Social Death: A Comparative Study. Harvard University Press.

adult male citizens, a group that comprised perhaps 10–15% of the population. Women were denied legal autonomy and political agency, assigned instead to roles of reproduction and domestic labour. Enslaved persons, both Greek and non-Greek, were treated as property and formed a critical economic underclass that sustained the material infrastructure of urban life, agriculture, mining, and household service.[75] Oikonomia, as described in Xenophon's Oeconomicus, assumes command over others, especially women and slaves, as the foundation of household order. The moral and managerial discourses of the time did not extend ethical concern to the enslaved or the structurally excluded; instead, virtue was defined by the capacity to govern dependents effectively. This structural exclusion presents a paradox. The same philosophical tradition that condemned excessive accumulation (chrematistics) and praised civic justice did not question the institution of slavery or the economic subordination of women. In fact, Greek conceptions of freedom and democracy were made possible by the simultaneous presence of unfreedom.[76] The citizen's leisure, essential for participation in politics, philosophy, and public life, was made possible by the uncompensated labour of those beneath them. Ethical economies, then, could be deeply unjust in their foundations. This disjunction challenges any romanticization of ancient models and raises the critical question: who is counted as an economic agent, and who is not? Neoclassical economics, while formally inclusive in its model of rational individuals, often erases power and structural inequality by assuming abstract agents with equal access to markets. It treats slavery, patriarchy, and dispossession as historical anomalies rather than systemic conditions with enduring consequences. Communism, in its Marxist formulations, critiques class exploitation but has often reproduced gendered hierarchies and, in many cases, ignored ethnic and cultural exclusion. For example, Stalinist collectivization campaigns uprooted Indigenous and nomadic communities in Central Asia and Siberia, treating them as backward elements in need of forced modernization. Classical Greek thought, with all its limitations, forces us to confront a central dilemma in political economy: ethics and hierarchy often coexist.

[75] Patterson, O. (1982). Slavery and Social Death: A Comparative Study. Harvard University Press.

[76] Finley, M. I. (1973). The Ancient Economy. University of California Press.

Embedded economies may foster virtue within a bounded moral community while perpetuating exploitation outside it. This is especially relevant for contemporary Indigenous economic debates. Many Indigenous governance systems emphasize reciprocity, community consent, and moral obligation, but these principles must be critically examined for how they include or exclude gendered, generational, or outsider roles. The lesson is double: ethical values are essential to just economies, but they must be universal in scope to avoid reproducing structural domination under the guise of tradition or virtue. Amartya Sen's capability approach offers a framework to navigate this tension. It shifts focus from aggregate output or resource control to the substantive freedoms individuals must lead lives they value. It is important that development and justice be measured by actual opportunities across gender, class, and community lines, not by abstract averages or formal equality.[77] In this light, the Greek model serves as both inspiration and warning: ethical economic design must be paired with inclusive moral boundaries.

1.4 Comparing Indigenous, Ancient, and Modern Economic Systems

Neoclassical Economics: Homo Economicus and Market Rationality

Neoclassical economics emerged in the late nineteenth century as a mathematical framework to model individual choice and resource allocation under scarcity. Central to this paradigm is homo economicus, a rational, self-interested actor seeking to maximize utility within a system of competitive markets. These markets, in turn, are assumed to generate efficient outcomes through price signals, which coordinate supply and demand by treating land, labour, and capital as interchangeable factors of production. While this abstraction enables formal modelling and prediction, it also strips economic life of its institutional, historical, and ecological contexts. Unlike Indigenous and ancient systems, which embed economic activity in kinship, ritual, and collective norms, neoclassical economics decontextualizes human behaviour. Preferences are treated as exogenous and stable, while land is reduced to a commodity, devoid of cultural meaning or ecological specificity. Labour becomes a variable input, not a form of lived identity or social relation. This framing marginalizes key determinants of actual behaviour, such as reciprocity,

[77] Sen, A. (1999). Development as Freedom. Oxford University Press.

inequality aversion, or customary obligation that are central in Indigenous and historical traditions. Empirical findings from behavioural economics increasingly challenge the universality of homo economicus. Studies consistently reveal that individuals prefer fairness over pure self-interest, punish norm violations even at personal cost, and cooperate conditionally based on trust and group identity.[78]

This reductionism can be critiqued by showing that historically, markets were embedded in social institutions.[79] Only with the rise of industrial capitalism did markets for land, labour, and money become "disembedded" from moral and political life. This transformation was not natural but enforced, often violently, by states seeking to commodify what had previously been governed by custom or law. In contrast, Indigenous economic systems treat land as a living entity, subject to spiritual obligations and governed by relational tenure regimes. Labour is embedded in reciprocal duties, often guided by elders, councils, or rituals. Ancient agrarian economies, from Kautilya's India to Confucian China, also bound economic roles to moral hierarchies, public welfare, and ecological stewardship, not just production or exchange. Neoclassical economics' analytical strength lies in its parsimony. By reducing complex systems to optimizing behaviour under constraints, it generates testable models and policy prescriptions. But when this becomes market determinism, treating prices as sufficient statistics for coordination, other dimensions of governance vanish. Institutions, legitimacy, knowledge systems, and cosmological commitments fall outside the model's scope. Yet these dimensions often explain outcomes better than marginal incentives. For example, studies of common-pool resource management show that locally crafted rules, social sanctions, and participatory monitoring outperform both centralized control and market privatization in maintaining ecological sustainability.[80] Similarly, other studies document how state-led schemes that ignore local knowledge, whether in Soviet collectivization, Tanzanian ujamaa villages, or modern development planning,

[78] Bowles, S., & Gintis, H. (2011). A Cooperative Species: Human Reciprocity and Its Evolution. Princeton University Press.

[79] Polanyi, K. (1944). The Great Transformation: The Political and Economic Origins of Our Time. Beacon Press.

[80] Ostrom, E. (1990). Governing the Commons: The Evolution of Institutions for Collective Action. Cambridge University Press.

frequently fail.[81] These failures are not simply informational but epistemological; formal market or administrative systems cannot substitute for the embedded, tacit knowledge held by communities. Indigenous economies, with their emphasis on ritual, oral transmission, and ecological feedback, offer forms of intelligence that challenge the technocratic assumptions of both neoliberalism and state socialism. This is not an argument against markets. Markets are powerful tools for coordination and innovation. But they must be re-embedded in institutional and ecological realities. Indigenous systems, ancient agrarian traditions, and even some modern alternatives, such as participatory budgeting or commons governance, illustrate how economic life can be shaped by norms, duties, and collective intelligence. The challenge is not to discard efficiency, but to redefine it, not as maximized output per input, but as resilience, equity, and ethical coherence. In this light, neoclassical economics is a partial lens, illuminating in some domains, but dangerously blind in others. A comparative political economy must recover what the model leaves out: history, hierarchy, reciprocity, and the living world.

Marxism and Indigenous Worldviews

Karl Marx's critique of capitalism, rooted in the dynamics of class struggle, offers a powerful lens for understanding the transformation of communal resources into private capital. Marx shows how enclosure, the legal and physical conversion of commons into private property, becomes the foundation of capitalist accumulation, separating people from means of subsistence and producing a proletariat dependent on wage labour.[82] This process is not merely economic but profoundly political, as it creates a class hierarchy between owners of capital and those who must sell their labour power to survive. The logic of commodification transforms land, labour, and time into abstract, alienable units, laying the groundwork for extraction, crisis, and inequality. Marx's analysis of primitive accumulation helps clarify the mechanisms of colonialism and the global structure of unequal exchange. In the Americas, Africa, and Asia, colonial regimes enclosed Indigenous lands, devalued non-capitalist modes of production, and inserted territories into circuits of

[81] Scott, J. C. (1998). Seeing Like a State: How Certain Schemes to Improve the Human Condition Have Failed. Yale University Press.

[82] Marx, K. (1976). Capital: A Critique of Political Economy, Volume I (B. Fowkes, Trans.). Penguin Books. (Original work) published 1867).

global capital. Historical research confirms that the Atlantic slave trade and plantation economies were not peripheral but central to the rise of industrial capitalism. It has been shown that enslaved labour in the Americas generated surpluses that financed British industrialization.[83] Similarly, others have argued that the global cotton empire, driven by slavery and colonial violence, was a foundational engine of capitalist development, not a deviation from it.[84] In this way, Marxist political economy enables a structural understanding of dispossession, commodification, and dependency. Where Marxism converges with Indigenous thought is in its critique of private property and its defence of collective control over land and resources. Marx rejected bourgeois rights frameworks that obscure class power and celebrated communal property forms as more equitable and rational. Similarly, many Indigenous economies organize land tenure collectively, guided by kinship obligations, ceremonial law, and ecological relationships. Both traditions resist the fragmentation of land into commodified units and emphasize the social consequences of property regimes. However, the philosophical foundations differ. Marx's materialism emphasizes labour and production as the basis of social life; Indigenous systems often emphasize relationality, interconnectedness between people, ancestors, animals, and place as the basis of law and economy.[85,86] Marxist theory, while effective at diagnosing exploitation and alienation, tends to under-specify cultural sovereignty, cosmology, and multi-species governance. Historical materialism privileges human productive forces and sees nature primarily as raw material shaped by labour. In contrast, Indigenous ontologies often reject the division between nature and society altogether. Land is not a commodity or input but a living entity to whom obligations are owed. Value is not derived from labour alone but from reciprocity, stewardship, and participation in ongoing cycles of renewal. Indigenous economies are based not on extraction but on the "honourable harvest", taking

[83] Inikori, J. E. (2002). Africans and the Industrial Revolution in England: A Study in International Trade and Economic Development. Cambridge University Press.

[84] Beckert, S. (2014). Empire of Cotton: A Global History. Knopf.

[85] Berkes, F. (2012). Sacred Ecology: Traditional Ecological Knowledge and Resource Management (3rd ed.). Routledge.

[86] Kimmerer, R. W. (2013). Braiding Sweetgrass: Indigenous Wisdom, Scientific Knowledge and the Teachings of Plants. Milkweed Editions.

only what is given, using all that is taken, and giving back in return.[87] Moreover, consent and legitimacy play a central role in Indigenous governance that is less prominent in Marxist frameworks. While Marx critiques the coercive foundations of capitalist property, he pays limited attention to non-state forms of law, customary governance, or plural systems of authority. Indigenous economies often rely on community deliberation, elder guidance, and spiritual protocols to guide decision-making, especially in relation to land. These dimensions are not captured by a purely materialist analysis but are central to the durability and resilience of Indigenous institutions. That said, Marxist tools remain invaluable in understanding how capitalism erodes these systems. From deforestation driven by commodity markets to the legal suppression of communal tenure, the logics of accumulation and commodification directly threaten Indigenous ways of life. Marxist insights have been extended by showing how the enclosure of the commons was gendered, violently targeting women's autonomy and collective reproductive labour.[88] This intersectional lens is vital for connecting land struggles, gender justice, and resistance to extractivism. Thus, Marxism and Indigenous economic thought both offer critiques of capitalist domination and propose alternatives to private property and accumulation. But they differ in fundamental ways; Marxism centres labour and class; Indigenous thought centres land, law, and relationship. Marx seeks to replace capitalist property with collective ownership under democratic planning. Indigenous economies seek to uphold sovereignty, relational accountability, and intergenerational caretaking. A truly decolonial political economy must therefore draw from both: the structural rigour of Marx and the cosmological depth of Indigenous traditions.

Indigenous Economics as Pluriversal Rationalities

Indigenous economic systems do not conform neatly to the dominant paradigms of capitalism or communism, both of which universalize singular rationalities, market price in the former, production and surplus in the latter. Each abstracts human relations into categories

[87] Kimmerer, R. W. (2013). Braiding Sweetgrass: Indigenous Wisdom, Scientific Knowledge and the Teachings of Plants. Milkweed Editions.

[88] Federici, S. (2004). Caliban and the Witch: Women, the Body and Primitive Accumulation. Autonomedia.

governed by exchange or control, flattening the diversity of socio-ecological arrangements that Indigenous societies maintain. In contrast, Indigenous economic thought articulates a pluriversal worldview, one in which multiple value systems, authorities, and ontologies coexist without reduction to a single metric or institutional form.[89,90]

Capitalism is structured around commodification and competition. It assumes individuals as rational actors, resources as inputs, and prices as signals. It rewards efficiency, scale, and innovation but often disregards ecological boundaries, kin obligations, or place-based knowledge. Communism, though critical of private property and class exploitation, centralizes planning under a singular authority, often suppressing local governance, ritual economies, and spiritual landscapes. Both systems presume a universal logic applicable across space and culture, a feature that Indigenous systems explicitly reject.

Indigenous economies operate through relationality, connections among humans, non-humans, ancestors, and land. Value emerges not from abstract exchange or centralized allocation but from reciprocal responsibility, maintained through ritual, story, and ecological stewardship. These systems often feature polycentric governance: overlapping institutions, clans, councils, elders, and cosmological entities; shared authority; adjusting decisions to local needs and moral constraints.[91] There is no fixed centre; legitimacy is distributed and contingent on context. This approach challenges the Eurocentric binary of capitalism versus communism by proposing an alternative frame: pluriversal rationalities. The question is not which system is universally correct, but which institutional designs honour the specific moral, ecological, and political realities of a given community.[92] Indigenous worlds are not "alternative" in the sense of deviation, they are ontologically distinct ways of ordering the economic and political. That is, they do not merely offer different strategies within the same framework of modern capitalism or

[89] Escobar, A. (2018). Designs for the Pluriverse: Radical Interdependence, Autonomy, and the Making of Worlds. Duke University Press.

[90] De la Cadena, M., & Blaser, M. (Eds.). (2018). A World of Many Worlds. Duke University Press.

[91] Ostrom, E. (2010). Beyond Markets and States: Polycentric Governance of Complex Economic Systems. American Economic Review, 100(3), 641–672.

[92] Escobar, A. (2018). Designs for the Pluriverse: Radical Interdependence, Autonomy, and the Making of Worlds. Duke University Press.

statecraft but instead express fundamentally different assumptions about what constitutes value, authority, land, and community. For example, many Indigenous communities treat land not as a commodity to be owned or traded, but as a living relative with whom humans have reciprocal responsibilities, a worldview that challenges the foundational logic of property rights in Western economics. These ontologies do not merely add culture to economics; they redefine what counts as economy in the first place. For example, in the Andean ayllu system, land is held collectively, and production is organized through rotating labour (minka, ayni) that binds participants to one another and to the mountain spirits (apus). Value lies in maintaining balance between people, seasons, and spirits, not in maximizing surplus. Similarly, in the Yolngu economies of Arnhem Land, Australia, governance over sea and land resources is coordinated through songlines and kin-based protocols that reflect deep ontologies of territory and ancestry. These forms of economic life cannot be reduced to utility or production; they are ethical, spiritual, and ecological systems of accountability. Such systems resonate with Sen's capabilities approach, which shifts the focus of economic evaluation from output to freedom: the real opportunities people have to live the lives they value.[93] Sen rejects both market fundamentalism and authoritarian planning, arguing for context-sensitive policies that enhance agency, equity, and well-being.[94] Pluriversal economics echoes this position but deepens it ontologically, insisting that freedom itself must be understood through the values and categories of each society, not imposed externally. Indigenous economics thus exposes the limitations of universal models and demands a methodological shift: from theory-driven generalization to situated design. Rather than asking whether markets or plans are more efficient, the question becomes: What enables reciprocity, justice, and ecological integrity here? What institutional arrangements are legitimate, intelligible, and accountable within this specific ontological context? In a time of climate crisis, ecological collapse, and cultural fragmentation, Indigenous economies offer models of resilience grounded in long-term relationships rather than extractive logic. They show that another economy is not only possible but already exists, plural, situated, and committed to life beyond capital and command.

[93] Sen, A. (1999). Development as Freedom. Oxford University Press.

[94] Sen, A. (1999). Development as Freedom. Oxford University Press.

1.5 Towards a New Framework: Introducing Symbiotic Gaian Economics

Principles of Symbiotic Gaian Economics

Symbiotic Gaian Economics (SGE) emerges as a transformative synthesis of Indigenous economic ontologies, ecological systems science, and pluralistic governance theory. It responds to the structural failures of both neoclassical capitalism and communism, neither of which adequately account for ecological limits, ontological diversity, or non-exploitative human–nature relations. Where neoclassical models prioritize individual utility maximization in a frictionless market and communism centralizes production under state control, SGE begins from a radically different premise: the economy is not separate from ecology, but a mode of participation within a living planet. SGE asserts four foundational principles: interdependence, reciprocity, ecological stewardship, and ontological plurality. This means that rather than viewing nature as an external resource to be extracted or managed, SGE sees human economies as embedded within and accountable to ecological systems. Economic decisions are evaluated not just by their efficiency or output, but by their capacity to sustain mutual relationships among humans and the more-than-human world. For example, agricultural practices would be judged not solely on yield, but on whether they preserve soil health, respect local biodiversity, and uphold community obligations across generations. These principles reflect both long-standing Indigenous economic practices and contemporary Earth-system science. In Indigenous worldviews, land is not inert property but a sentient, law-bearing entity. Relationships between people, animals, waters, and places are structured by reciprocal duties rather than extractive rights. These perspectives converge with ecological findings on planetary boundaries, which identify critical thresholds, climate, biodiversity, water, nutrient flows, that define the safe operating space for humanity.[95] Violating these boundaries undermines not just ecosystems but the institutional conditions of economic and political stability. Within SGE, land is not a commodity. It is a relative, a source of life, and a holder of law. This ontological stance radically alters economic metrics. Efficiency is not measured by marginal productivity or GDP growth but by resilience-with-reciprocity, the capacity of

[95] Rockström, J., et al. (2009). A safe operating space for humanity. Nature, 461(7263), 472–475.

socio-ecological systems to maintain function while regenerating life and honouring obligations to human and more-than-human beings. Wealth, similarly, is redefined as the distribution of capabilities across generations, consistent with ecological thresholds and cultural integrity.[96,97] Economic design thus moves from extraction to care, from growth to regeneration. SGE relies on polycentric governance, multiple, overlapping institutions that share responsibility across scales, from clan councils and watershed assemblies to treaty boards and intergovernmental panels.[98] This means that no single authority dominates decision-making; instead, governance is distributed across locally rooted and globally connected bodies. Clan councils, such as those in many First Nations communities in Canada, make decisions about land stewardship and customary law based on kinship responsibilities. Watershed assemblies, like the Ganga River Panchayats in India or the Yuba River Watershed Council in California, coordinate ecological management across entire catchment areas. Treaty boards, such as the Yukon River Inter-Tribal Watershed Council, facilitate cooperation between Indigenous nations and settler states to uphold environmental agreements. Intergovernmental panels, like the Intergovernmental Panel on Climate Change (IPCC), synthesize scientific knowledge and guide global action. These layers ensure that governance is adaptive, participatory, and grounded in place-based knowledge while responsive to broader planetary concerns. Authority is not monopolized but distributed, with accountability rooted in cultural legitimacy, ecological feedback, and the principle of Free, Prior and Informed Consent.[99] In such systems, guardianship institutions, tribal land trusts, Indigenous protected areas, biocultural councils are not symbolic; they are constitutional. They hold rights and duties that are simultaneously legal, ecological, and moral. For example, Māori iwi (tribes) in Aotearoa New Zealand have legal personhood recognition for the Whanganui River, which grants the river rights and establishes co-governance duties for both Indigenous and state authorities. In the Amazon, Indigenous federations like COICA

[96] Sen, A. (1999). Development as Freedom. Oxford University Press.

[97] Raworth, K. (2017). Doughnut Economics: Seven Ways to Think Like a 21st-Century Economist. Chelsea Green Publishing.

[98] Ostrom, E. (2010). Beyond Markets and States: Polycentric Governance of Complex Economic Systems. American Economic Review, 100(3), 641–672.

[99] United Nations General Assembly (UNGA). (2007). United Nations Declaration on the Rights of Indigenous Peoples. A/RES/61/295.

advocate for the protection of sacred territories, blending ecological stewardship with moral obligations to future generations. Similarly, the Sámi parliaments in Scandinavia hold a mandate to protect reindeer herding grounds, not only as a legal right but as a cultural and ecological responsibility rooted in ancestral land relationships. The SGE framework contrasts sharply with neoclassical economics, where land and labour are treated as disembedded inputs priced through market exchange. It also diverges from communist command economies, which subordinated ecology to industrial goals and frequently suppressed Indigenous governance structures. For example, the Soviet Union's collectivization campaigns in Central Asia devastated pastoral mobility and destroyed ecological feedback systems. In contrast, Indigenous grazing systems, when governed by local customary authorities, often outperform state and market systems in maintaining biodiversity and land health.[100] SGE also addresses the crisis of legitimacy that afflicts modern economic systems. Neoliberal governance often claims technocratic neutrality while advancing corporate interests; authoritarian socialism enforces ideological conformity at the expense of local autonomy. In SGE, legitimacy derives from consent, not merely procedural but relational. Institutions must be accountable to place-based communities, intergenerational stewardship norms, and the more-than-human world. This includes ritual, story, and law as mechanisms of governance, not just cultural "add-ons". Real-world analogues are already emerging. The Rights of Nature movements in Ecuador and Bolivia, the Māori guardianship (kaitiakitanga) over the Whanganui River, and Indigenous-led conservation in Canada and Australia exemplify principles of SGE in practice. These cases show that plural legal systems, when properly resourced and respected, can sustain both ecological integrity and cultural sovereignty. Symbiotic Gaian Economics is not a utopia. It is a grounded alternative rooted in ancient practices and contemporary necessity. It calls for institutional pluralism, ecological realism, and an ethical economy of interdependence. Rather than proposing a new orthodoxy, it opens space for rethinking what economies are for, and how they can be designed to serve life rather than undermine it.

[100] Berkes, F. (2012). Sacred Ecology: Traditional Ecological Knowledge and Resource Management (3rd ed.). Routledge.

Bridging Ancient and Indigenous Thought with Future Economics
Symbiotic Gaian Economics (SGE) is not a speculative abstraction, but a rigorous synthesis of Indigenous, ancient, and Earth-system-based economic philosophies, each grounded in historical practice and ethical governance. Where modern economic systems emphasize scale, abstraction, and instrumental rationality, SGE draws from traditions that explicitly tie material prosperity to moral responsibility, social consent, and ecological limits. From Kautilya's infrastructure-driven welfare state in ancient India to Mencius' insistence that rulers secure food and seasonal rest, these systems embedded economy in ethics and statecraft in ecological realism.[101,102,103] Indigenous economies extend this embedding by recognizing land as law-bearing, kin as governance, and reciprocity as obligation, not choice.[104] Gaia theory and Earth-system science now formalize these intuitions as planetary boundaries, defining the biophysical thresholds within which economies must operate to ensure continuity.[105,106] SGE integrates these plural strands into a coherent institutional and ethical framework tailored for the Anthropocene. It rejects the false binary between nature and economy, instead positioning provisioning systems within nested socio-ecological systems. Where neoclassical economics abstracts land into factor markets and communism subordinates' ecological knowledge to state productivity targets, SGE recentres Earth as subject, not object, of economic law. Like dharma in the Arthashastra, SGE treats economic activity as bounded by duty. Like Confucian governance, it links legitimacy to the flourishing of the many. But unlike both, it formalizes Earth feedbacks, carbon sinks, biodiversity loss, water cycles into governance parameters that constrain and shape economic design. SGE operationalizes this synthesis through institutional innovation. Guardianship councils, rights-of-nature frameworks, and Indigenous land trusts reorient authority towards intergenerational

[101] Rangarajan, L. N. (Trans.). (1992). Kautilya: The Arthashastra. Penguin Books.

[102] Bloom, I. (Trans.). (2009). Mencius. Columbia University Press.

[103] Elman, B. A. (2005). Classicism, Politics, and Kinship: The Ch'ing Imperial Examinations. Cambridge University Press.

[104] Berkes, F. (2012). Sacred Ecology: Traditional Ecological Knowledge and Resource Management (3rd ed.). Routledge.

[105] Lovelock, J. (1979). Gaia: A New Look at Life on Earth. Oxford University Press.

[106] Rockström, J., Steffen, W., Noone, K., Persson, Å., Chapin III, F. S., Lambin, E., et al. (2009). A safe operating space for Humanity. Nature, 461(7263), 472–475.

stewardship. These institutions are not nostalgic revivals but adaptive governance forms that outperform extractive regimes in resilience and biodiversity outcomes. Empirical studies confirm that Indigenous-managed lands harbour disproportionately high levels of biodiversity and carbon sequestration.[107] These outcomes are not accidental; they result from rule systems that encode reciprocity, seasonal restraint, and relational accountability. SGE also challenges the dominant metrics of economic success. GDP growth, the hallmark of both capitalist and socialist economic regimes, is inadequate for tracking social and ecological well-being. SGE turns to multidimensional frameworks: Sen's capability approach,[108] biodiversity integrity indices, and intergenerational well-being measures. For instance, Amartya Sen's capability approach shifts focus from income or GDP to what individuals are able to do and be, such as attaining education, participating in community life, or maintaining good health, emphasizing freedom and real opportunities.[109] Biodiversity integrity indices, such as the Biodiversity Intactness Index (BII), measure how much of an area's original biodiversity remains intact despite human activity, helping evaluate the ecological sustainability of economic systems. Intergenerational well-being measures, like New Zealand's Living Standards Framework or Bhutan's Gross National Happiness index, assess long-term societal health across generations, including indicators such as mental health, environmental quality, cultural vitality, and economic security, thereby aligning development with ecological and ethical responsibilities. Economic value is redefined in terms of sustenance, care, and regeneration, not surplus. Finance is redirected: not towards speculation or debt leverage, but towards soil restoration, cooperative enterprises, and biocultural infrastructure. Contracts embed Free, Prior and Informed Consent (FPIC), and benefit-sharing clauses ensure that value circulates within communities, not extracted from them. In the digital realm, SGE extends its logic into data governance. Indigenous data sovereignty is central to decolonial development.[110] SGE supports governance over

[107] Garnett, S. T., Burgess, N. D., Fa, J. E., Fernández-Llamazares, Á., Molnár, Z., Robinson, C. J., et al. (2018). A spatial Overview of the global importance of Indigenous lands for conservation. Nature Sustainability, 1(7), 369–374.

[108] Sen, A. (1999). Development as Freedom. Oxford University Press.

[109] Sen, A. (1999). Development as Freedom. Oxford University Press.

[110] Kukutai, T., & Taylor, J. (2016). Indigenous Data Sovereignty: Toward an Agenda. ANU Press.

information as a public and cultural good, resisting extractive data practices by states and corporations. Consent, purpose-limitation, and community benefit become embedded principles in the digital commons, just as they are in land and water governance. This integrated approach marks a decisive shift from domination to reciprocity, from command to coordination, and from extraction to care. It offers not a single blueprint, but a design philosophy rooted in diversity, resilience, and situated ethics. In contrast to one-size models of neoclassical equilibrium or central planning, SGE fosters plural systems adapted to local ecologies, cultures, and values, consistent with a world of many worlds.[111] As ecological collapse and social inequality deepen, the call for an economic paradigm that binds prosperity to planetary justice is no longer theoretical; it is urgent. Symbiotic Gaian Economics offers a path forward by learning from the past, honouring Indigenous and ancient wisdom, and grounding future economies in the living systems that sustain all life.

Implications for Development, Policy, and Global Governance

Symbiotic Gaian Economics (SGE) reorients development and governance around relational justice, ecological limits, and institutional plurality. Rather than treating economic expansion as a universal goal, SGE proposes a post-growth framework grounded in the long-standing practices of Indigenous stewardship, ancient moral economies, and Earth-system realism. It offers neither a central plan nor a market fundamentalism, but a pluralist design ethic: economies must be embedded in place, responsive to planetary boundaries, and accountable to living communities—human and more-than-human. In the SGE framework, policy is rooted in the principle of relational sovereignty. Secure land tenure, co-governance with Indigenous authorities, and Indigenous-led ecological monitoring are foundational elements, not afterthoughts, for environmental and economic policy.[112,113] Climate finance, biodiversity credits, and restoration funding are conditioned not only on emissions

[111] De la Cadena, M. and Blaser, M. (eds) (2018) A World of Many Worlds. Durham, NC: Duke University Press.

[112] Corbera, E., & Schroeder, H. (2011). Governing and implementing REDD+. Environmental Science & Policy, 14(2), 89–99.

[113] Fletcher, R., Dressler, W., Büscher, B., & Anderson, Z. R. (2016). Questioning REDD+ and the future of market-based conservation. Conservation Biology, 30(3), 673–675.

or acreage metrics, but on Free, Prior and Informed Consent (FPIC), equitable benefit-sharing, and culturally relevant indicators. These conditions ensure that global funds serve communities, not displace them, and that ecological repair supports, not undermines, sovereignty and self-determination. Macroeconomic priorities also shift. In place of growth measured by GDP, SGE advocates for resilience metrics: livelihood stability, ecological regeneration, cultural continuity, and lower material throughput.[114,115] This reframing is essential in a world where the ecological cost of growth now outweighs its social gains. Extraction-intensive development, whether capitalist or state socialist, has routinely degraded Indigenous lands, violated customary law, and undermined subsistence economies. By contrast, economies grounded in reciprocity and sufficiency demonstrate higher long-term resilience, particularly in maintaining biodiversity, carbon sinks, and cultural cohesion. Crucially, SGE also entails the decolonization of economic thought itself. It challenges the epistemological monopoly of Western frameworks by recognizing multiple ontologies of economy. In legal and policy terms, this means embedding legal pluralism within global governance, adapting trade rules, intellectual property regimes, and environmental treaties to protect biocultural rights, customary law, and Indigenous institutions. This is not simply inclusion but transformation: acknowledging that Indigenous economic systems are not pre-modern relics, but viable, coherent, and often more sustainable than dominant models. The global rise of polycentric governance, multiple, overlapping authorities at different scales, supports this transition. Such systems encourage experimentation, local adaptation, and mutual learning, especially in managing commons.[116] Indigenous co-management boards, transboundary water assemblies, and customary marine tenure regimes illustrate how plural institutions can govern shared resources more effectively than either markets or centralized states. These arrangements not only build resilience but also deepen legitimacy, by aligning decision-making with cultural values, ecological feedback, and democratic consent. Examples abound:

[114] Kallis, G. (2018). Degrowth. Agenda Publishing.

[115] Raworth, K. (2017). Doughnut Economics: Seven Ways to Think Like a 21st-Century Economist. Chelsea Green Publishing.

[116] Ostrom, E. (2010). Beyond Markets and States: Polycentric Governance of Complex Economic Systems. American Economic Review, 100(3), 641–672.

the Yurok Tribe's river restoration programs in California tie watershed health to cultural revival. Māori co-governance of the Whanganui River redefines legal personhood in relational terms. The Kayapó's use of community trusts and territorial monitoring in Brazil deters illegal logging more effectively than state enforcement. These are not anomalies; they are previews of pluriversal futures where development is measured by justice and regeneration, not output alone. SGE does not offer a universal blueprint. It offers instead a principled framework for designing diversity, a plural economics rooted in ethical constraint, ecological realism, and cultural sovereignty. In contrast to the homogenizing logics of both neoclassical and Marxist orthodoxies, it affirms that many worlds are possible, but only within one biosphere. Development, in this view, becomes not expansion but alignment: of governance with place, of finance with repair, and of economy with Earth.

2 Conclusion

This chapter has shown that Indigenous economies are not anomalies to be explained away by universal theories, but coherent systems organized around relational ontologies, consent-based authority, and ecological stewardship. Across the case materials surveyed here, kin-ordered production, commons governance, ritualized accountability, agroecological design, the economy appears as a domain of law and relationship rather than a free-standing sphere reducible to prices or plan targets. This is the chapter's central analytical dividend: once land is recognized as a living, law-bearing relation and not a fungible "factor", the coordinate system of analysis must shift accordingly. That shift renders familiar ideologies, neoclassical market rationalism and orthodox Marxist materialism, ill-suited as full accounts of Indigenous economic life. They illuminate mechanisms (marginal trade-offs; accumulation and enclosure) yet under-specify the institutional, cosmological, and ecological grammars that organise production, exchange, and stewardship in place. On the neoclassical side, the representative agent with stable preferences and complete contracting abstracts land from country, labour from kinship, and risk from ritual coordination; "prices as sufficient statistics" presumes away legitimacy, consent, and knowledge sovereignty.[117,118,119] Behavioural and institutional evidence instead shows that reciprocity, reputation, and shared rules lower transaction costs and stabilise expectations, precisely the features documented in Indigenous councils, clan jurisdictions, and harvest calendars.[120,121,122] Likewise, classical Marxism powerfully theorises primitive accumulation, displacement, and unequal exchange,[123,124,125] which helps explain how imperial value chains converted Indigenous land, labour, and knowledge into European growth. Yet a base–superstructure lens that privileges productive forces cannot by itself account for worlds in which law extends to more-than-human kin, obligations are cosmological as well as distributive, and value is judged by the continuity of relations and the integrity of ecosystems.[126,127] Both traditions, in different ways, universalise a single metric, price or surplus, and a single axis of coordination, competition or command, where the evidence assembled here shows polycentric authority, plural values, and multi-species accountability. Ancient economic traditions deepen this contrast. Kautilya's statecraft joins revenue, relief, and public works to an ethical horizon (artha

117 Polanyi, K. (1944) The Great Transformation: The Political and Economic Origins of Our Time. New York: Rinehart.

118 North, D.C. (1990) Institutions, Institutional Change and Economic Performance. Cambridge: Cambridge University Press.

119 Bowles, S. and Gintis, H. (2011) A Cooperative Species: Human Reciprocity and Its Evolution. Princeton, NJ: Princeton University Press.

120 Ostrom, E. (1990) Governing the Commons: The Evolution of Institutions for Collective Action. Cambridge: Cambridge University Press.

121 Scott, J. C. (1998) Seeing Like a State: How Certain Schemes to Improve the Human Condition Have Failed. New Haven, CT: Yale University Press.

122 Berkes, F. (2012) Sacred Ecology. 3rd edn. New York: Routledge.

123 Marx, K. (1976) Capital: Volume 1. London: Penguin.

124 Federici, S. (2004) Caliban and the Witch: Women, the Body and Primitive Accumulation. New York: Autonomedia.

125 Inikori, J.E. (2002) Africans and the Industrial Revolution in England: A Study in International Trade and Economic Development. Cambridge: Cambridge University Press.

126 Kimmerer, R.W. (2013) Braiding Sweetgrass: Indigenous Wisdom, Scientific Knowledge and the Teachings of Plants. Minneapolis, MN: Milkweed Editions.

127 Escobar, A. (2018) Designs for the Pluriverse: Radical Interdependence, Autonomy, and the Making of Worlds. Durham, NC: Duke University Press.

within dharma), portraying prosperity as inseparable from just rule, infrastructure, and famine insurance.[128,129] Confucian and Mencian writings insist that grain security, light taxation, and moral governance underwrite stability; Legalists, by contrast, design rule-bound standardization to overcome information and enforcement problems.[130,131,132] Greek authors distinguish oikonomia (the ethical management of a household aimed at sufficiency and well-being) from chrematistics (art of money making, pursuing wealth as an end to itself), warning against boundless accumulation.[133,134] Oikonomia (οἰκονομία), household management, denotes the art of provisioning the oikos (household) so its members can live well and participate in the civic life of the polis; its aim is use-value and sufficiency, not endless wealth, and it is embedded in ethics and politics, balancing needs over time, caring for dependents, and stewarding land, tools, and stores to sustain a stable, largely self-sufficient household. Chrematistics (χρηματιστική), by contrast, names the pursuit of wealth as an end, accumulating exchange-value without intrinsic limits; Aristotle treats certain forms (retail aimed purely at profit, lending at interest) as "unnatural", because money as a medium is made to "breed" money, severed from real use and human need. Hence the classical warnings: morally, unlimited acquisition disorders character and cultivates greed rather than virtue; civically, it subordinates public life and justice to private gain, with extreme inequalities corroding civic friendship and stability; teleologically, it mistakes means (money) for ends, whereas the proper end of oikonomia is living well. The tradition thus expresses a preference for self-sufficiency and moderation over speculative gain, a suspicion of usury and certain

128 Sen, A. (1999) Development as Freedom. Oxford: Oxford University Press.

129 Kautilya's statecraft joins revenue, relief, and public works to an ethical horizon (artha within dharma), portraying prosperity as inseparable from just rule, infrastructure, and famine insurance (Rangarajan, 1992; Sen, 1999).

130 Bloom, I. (2009) Mencius. New York: Columbia University Press.

131 Elman, B.A. (2005) On Their Own Terms: Science in China, 1550–1900. Cambridge, MA: Harvard University Press.

132 Liao, W.K. (trans.) (1939) The Complete Works of Han Fei Tzŭ: A Classic of Chinese Political Science. London: Arthur Probsthain.

133 Finley, M.I. (1973) The Ancient Economy. Berkeley, CA: University of California Press.

134 Waterfield, R. (ed./trans.) (1997) Conversations of Socrates (includes Oeconomicus). London: Penguin Classics.

trades as socially corrosive, and a "moral economy" ideal that prioritises provisioning for enough over maximization. A crucial caveat, however, is that the classical household economy rested on exclusions, slavery and the subordination of women and many non-citizens, so its ethical critique of limitless accumulation coexisted with profoundly unequal social foundations.[135,136] In modern terms, oikonomia approximates provisioning for well-being within ethical and ecological limits, while chrematistics resembles financialized accumulation detached from real needs, the worry being that when the latter dominates, societies erode virtue, justice, and civic stability, a concern that still echoes in debates over financialization and inequality. These canons echo Indigenous emphasis on stewardship and legitimacy, but they also reveal exclusions (slavery, gender hierarchy) that Indigenous cases help correct.[137] Taken together, the comparative lens used in this chapter demonstrates that economies have always been embedded in ethics, law, and ecology, a view that converges with the capabilities approach to evaluating well-being in substantive freedoms rather than output alone.[138] The ecological record strengthens the argument. Traditional Ecological Knowledge and diversified agroecosystems, Andean vertical archipelagos, Haudenosaunee "Three Sisters", Sahelian mobility, internalise climate and landscape variability through redundancy, complementarity, and adaptive governance.[139,140,141,142,143] Traditional

[135] Finley, M.I. (1973) The Ancient Economy. Berkeley, CA: University of California Press.

[136] Waterfield, R. (ed./trans.) (1997) Conversations of Socrates (includes Oeconomicus). London: Penguin Classics.

[137] Patterson, O. (1982) Slavery and Social Death. Cambridge, MA: Harvard University Press.

[138] Sen, A. (1999) Development as Freedom. Oxford: Oxford University Press.

[139] Murra, J.V. (1972) 'El "control vertical" de un máximo de pisos ecológicos en la economía de las sociedades andinas', in Murra, J.V. (ed.) Visita de la Provincia de León de Huánuco. Huánuco: Universidad Nacional Hermilio Valdizán, pp. 427–476.

[140] D'Altroy, T.N. (2014) The Incas. 2nd edn. Malden, MA: Wiley-Blackwell.

[141] Kimmerer, R.W. (2013) Braiding Sweetgrass: Indigenous Wisdom, Scientific Knowledge and the Teachings of Plants. Minneapolis, MN: Milkweed Editions.

[142] Niamir-Fuller, M. (1999) Managing Mobility in African Rangelands: The Legitimisation of Transhumance. London: Intermediate Technology Publications.

[143] Scoones, I. (1995) Living with Uncertainty: New Directions in Pastoral Development in Africa. London: Intermediate Technology Publications.

Ecological Knowledge (TEK) encodes long-run observation, experiment, and stewardship norms, such as seasonal indicators, sacred no-take zones, and rotating harvest rules, so communities can match use to ecosystem cycles; by coupling rules with ritual and kin obligations, TEK builds redundancy (backup food species, multiple water sources) and rapid feedbacks for adaptive decision-making.[144,145] In the Andean vertical archipelago, households and allied kin groups distribute fields and herds across stacked altitude "floors" (potatoes, quinoa, camelids high; maize and fruit lower), linking them by storage (qollqa) and road networks; this spreads climate risk and lets communities substitute across zones when frost, drought, or pests hit one band.[146,147] Climate risk is spread because different altitudinal zones are affected by climate events at different times and intensities, diversifying production across ecological tiers ensures that a single weather shock rarely devastates the entire food and resource base of a community. The Haudenosaunee "Three Sisters" polyculture interplants maize, beans, and squash so that beans fix nitrogen, maize provides a living trellis, and squash shades soil and suppresses weeds; the trio raises yields, stabilises soils and moisture, and diversifies diets, classic complementarity at the plot scale.[148] In the Sahel, mobile and transhumant systems (seasonal movement of herders and their livestock between fixed grazing areas) coordinate herd movement with patchy rains and forage through clan governance, customary corridors, and negotiated access at wells; mobility itself is the risk hedge, while communal rules and reciprocity with farming neighbours enable

[144] Berkes, F. (2012) Sacred Ecology. 3rd edn. New York: Routledge.

[145] Ostrom, E. (1990) Governing the Commons: The Evolution of Institutions for Collective Action. Cambridge: Cambridge University Press.

[146] Murra, J.V. (1972) 'El "control vertical" de un máximo de pisos ecológicos en la economía de las sociedades andinas', in Murra, J.V. (ed.) Visita de la Provincia de León de Huánuco. Huánuco: Universidad Nacional Hermilio Valdizán, pp. 427–476.

[147] D'Altroy, T.N. (2014) The Incas. 2nd edn. Malden, MA: Wiley-Blackwell.

[148] Kimmerer, R.W. (2013) Braiding Sweetgrass: Indigenous Wisdom, Scientific Knowledge and the Teachings of Plants. Minneapolis, MN: Milkweed Editions.

adaptive governance as rainfall shifts.[149,150] Together these designs institutionalise redundancy (multiple crops/zones/species), complementarity (mutually beneficial crop and land-use mixes), and adaptation (rules that update with ecological signals), turning environmental variability from a threat into a managed asset.[151,152,153,154,155] Contemporary syntheses show that biodiversity and carbon outcomes are often strongest on Indigenous-managed lands, indicating that reciprocity-and-duty rule sets are not only culturally meaningful but ecologically effective.[156,157] At planetary scale, Earth-system science tightens the constraint set: development consistent with a "safe operating space" must respect biophysical thresholds.[158] In that light, frameworks that treat the biosphere as an externality are analytically incomplete. These results motivate the need for a new economic model commensurate with the evidence. We can term this model Symbiotic Gaian Economics (SGE). Its premise is simple: economies are nested within living Earth systems and constituted by relations, human and more-than-human, governed by law, consent, and care.

[149] Niamir-Fuller, M. (1999) Managing Mobility in African Rangelands: The Legitimization of Transhumance. London: Intermediate Technology Publications.

[150] Scoones, I. (1995) Living with Uncertainty: New Directions in Pastoral Development in Africa. London: Intermediate Technology Publications.

[151] Murra, J.V. (1972) 'El "control vertical" de un máximo de pisos ecológicos en la economía de las sociedades andinas', in Murra, J. V. (ed.) Visita de la Provincia de León de Huánuco. Huánuco: Universidad Nacional Hermilio Valdizán, pp. 427–476.

[152] D'Altroy, T.N. (2014) The Incas. 2nd edn. Malden, MA: Wiley-Blackwell.

[153] Kimmerer, R.W. (2013) Braiding Sweetgrass: Indigenous Wisdom, Scientific Knowledge and the Teachings of Plants. Minneapolis, MN: Milkweed Editions.

[154] Niamir-Fuller, M. (1999) Managing Mobility in African Rangelands: The Legitimisation of Transhumance. London: Intermediate Technology Publications.

[155] Scoones, I. (1995) Living with Uncertainty: New Directions in Pastoral Development in Africa. London: Intermediate Technology Publications.

[156] Garnett, S.T. et al. (2018) 'A spatial overview of the global importance of Indigenous lands for conservation', Nature Sustainability, 1(7), pp. 369–374.

[157] IPBES (2019) Global Assessment Report on Biodiversity and Ecosystem Services. Bonn: Intergovernmental Science-Policy Platform on Biodiversity and Ecosystem Services.

[158] Rockström, J. et al. (2009) 'A safe operating space for humanity', Nature, 461(7263), pp. 472–475.

Three axioms follow. First, symbiosis: mutual flourishing is a design criterion, so institutions must reward reciprocity, repair, and restraint.[159,160] Second, the Gaian constraint: economic choice is bounded by planetary limits; valuation therefore tracks capabilities and ecological integrity, not GDP alone.[161,162,163,164] In practice, this means judging policies by whether they secure human well-being within Earth's "safe operating space", meeting needs while staying inside boundaries for climate, biodiversity, freshwater and soils, rather than by expanding output irrespective of biophysical thresholds. Third, polycentric consent: decision rights are distributed across scales and grounded in Free, Prior and Informed Consent (FPIC), legal pluralism, and guardianship institutions that personate rivers, forests, and species as subjects of law.[165,166,167] Where neoclassical analysis asks whether prices clear and Marxist analysis asks who controls surplus, SGE asks whether institutions keep the web of relations intact, within biophysical thresholds, and with the consent of those, human and non-human, who bear the consequences. This is not a romantic archaism. It is a design language synthesizing: (i) Indigenous jurisprudence of country and consent; (ii) ancient insights that prosperity is inseparable from ethical governance and provisioning infrastructures; and (iii) Earth-system constraints that render extractive growth strategies self-defeating. In practice, SGE re-specifies "efficiency" as resilience

[159] Kimmerer, R.W. (2013) Braiding Sweetgrass: Indigenous Wisdom, Scientific Knowledge and the Teachings of Plants. Minneapolis, MN: Milkweed Editions.

[160] Berkes, F. (2012) Sacred Ecology. 3rd edn. New York: Routledge.

[161] Sen, A. (1999) Development as Freedom. Oxford: Oxford University Press.

[162] Raworth, K. (2017) Doughnut Economics: Seven Ways to Think Like a 21st-Century Economist. London: Random House Business.

[163] Rockström, J. et al. (2009) 'A safe operating space for humanity', Nature, 461(7263), pp. 472–475.

[164] Lovelock, J. (1979) Gaia: A New Look at Life on Earth. Oxford: Oxford University Press.

[165] Ostrom, E. (1990) Governing the Commons: The Evolution of Institutions for Collective Action. Cambridge: Cambridge University Press.

[166] UNGA (United Nations General Assembly) (2007) United Nations Declaration on the Rights of Indigenous Peoples, A/RES/61/295 (13 September). New York: United Nations.

[167] Kukutai, T. and Taylor, J. (eds) (2016) Indigenous Data Sovereignty: Toward an Agenda. Canberra: ANU Press.

with reciprocity (systems that meet needs while absorbing shocks without exporting harm) and "wealth" as capabilities sustained across generations. It privileges institutions that the evidence shows to be effective: co-governance with clear boundaries and monitoring; layered tenure; community-defined indicators; benefit-sharing and data sovereignty; and finance that conditions capital on FPIC, restoration, and long-run stewardship.[168,169,170,171] Finally, SGE clarifies what "pluralism" must mean. The chapter's comparative work has emphasized pluriversal rationalities, many legitimate ways of knowing and governing economies.[172,173] Pluralism here is not relativism. It is a constitutional stance: multiple ontologies can co-govern so long as consent is secured, and planetary limits are honoured. That stance reconciles institutional diversity with universal ecological constraint. It also answers the most serious critique of earlier ideologies: that they either erase difference (by equation to a representative agent or historical teleology) or cannot articulate credible material constraints on desire and power. SGE does both, recognises difference and binds action to the Gaian envelope. This chapter therefore concludes with a programmatic claim. To understand Indigenous economies on their own terms, and to design viable futures in an era of polycrisis, we need a model that is empirically grounded, institutionally realistic, and ecologically literate. Symbiotic Gaian Economics is offered as that model: not a single blueprint, but a principled framework for co-creating economies that keep faith with kin, country, and the Earth that makes life possible.

[168] Ostrom, E. (1990) Governing the Commons: The Evolution of Institutions for Collective Action. Cambridge: Cambridge University Press.

[169] Corbera, E. and Schroeder, H. (2011) 'Governing and implementing REDD+', Environmental Science & Policy, 14(2), pp. 89–99.

[170] Fletcher, R., Dressler, W., Büscher, B. and Anderson, Z.R. (2016) 'Questioning REDD+ and the future of market-based' conservation', Conservation Biology, 30(3), pp. 673–675.

[171] Kukutai, T. and Taylor, J. (eds) (2016) Indigenous Data Sovereignty: Toward an Agenda. Canberra: ANU Press.

[172] De la Cadena, M. and Blaser, M. (eds) (2018) A World of Many Worlds. Durham, NC: Duke University Press.

[173] Escobar, A. (2018) Designs for the Pluriverse: Radical Interdependence, Autonomy, and the Making of Worlds. Durham, NC: Duke University Press.

References

Altieri, M.A. and Nicholls, C.I. (2017) 'Agroecology: A brief account of its origins and currents of thought in Latin America', Agroecology and Sustainable Food Systems, 41(3–4), pp. 231–237.

Aristotle. (1962). Politics (T. A. Sinclair, Trans.). Penguin Books. (Original work c. 4th century BCE).

Beckert, S. (2014). Empire of Cotton: A Global History. Knopf.

Berkes, F. (2012) Sacred Ecology. 3rd edn. New York: Routledge.

Bloom, I. (2009) Mencius. New York: Columbia University Press.

Bowles, S. and Gintis, H. (2011) A Cooperative Species: Human Reciprocity and Its Evolution. Princeton, NJ: Princeton University Press.

Corbera, E. and Schroeder, H. (2011) 'Governing and implementing REDD+', Environmental Science & Policy, 14(2), pp. 89–99.

D'Altroy, T.N. (2014) The Incas. 2nd edn. Malden, MA: Wiley-Blackwell.

de la Cadena, M. and Blaser, M. (eds) (2018) A World of Many Worlds. Durham, NC: Duke University Press.

Dikötter, F. (2010). Mao's Great Famine: The History of China's Most Devastating Catastrophe, 1958–1962. Walker & Company.

Durie, M. (1998) Te Mana, Te Kāwanatanga: The Politics of Māori Self-Determination. Auckland: Oxford University Press.

Elman, B.A. (2005) On Their Own Terms: Science in China, 1550–1900. Cambridge, MA: Harvard University Press.

Elman, B. A. (2005). Classicism, Politics, and Kinship: The Ch'ing Imperial Examinations. Cambridge University Press.

Escobar, A. (2018) Designs for the Pluriverse: Radical Interdependence, Autonomy, and the Making of Worlds. Durham, NC: Duke University Press.

Federici, S. (2004) Caliban and the Witch: Women, the Body and Primitive Accumulation. New York: Autonomedia.

Finley, M.I. (1973) The Ancient Economy. Berkeley, CA: University of California Press.

Fletcher, R., Dressler, W., Büscher, B. and Anderson, Z.R. (2016) 'Questioning REDD+ and the future of market-based conservation', Conservation Biology, 30(3), pp. 673–675.

Gammage, B. (2011). The Biggest Estate on Earth: How Aborigines Made Australia. Allen & Unwin.

Garnett, S. T., Burgess, N. D., Fa, J. E., Fernández-Llamazares, Á., Molnár, Z., Robinson, C. J., ... & Leiper, I. (2018). A spatial overview of the global importance of Indigenous lands for conservation. Nature Sustainability, 1(7), 369–374.

Graeber, D. (2011) Debt: The First 5,000 Years. Brooklyn, NY and London: Melville House.

Han Feizi. (2003). Han Feizi: Basic Writings (B. Watson, Trans.). Columbia University Press. (Original work c. 3rd century BCE).
Inikori, J.E. (2002) Africans and the Industrial Revolution in England: A Study in International Trade and Economic Development. Cambridge: Cambridge University Press.
IPBES. (2019). Summary for Policymakers of the Global Assessment Report on Biodiversity and Ecosystem Services. Intergovernmental Science-Policy Platform on Biodiversity and Ecosystem Services.
IPBES (2019) Global Assessment Report on Biodiversity and Ecosystem Services. Bonn: Intergovernmental Science-Policy Platform on Biodiversity and Ecosystem Services.
Johansen, B. E. (1982). Forgotten Founders: How the American Indian Helped Shape Democracy. The Harvard Common Press.
Kallis, G. (2018). Degrowth. Agenda Publishing.
Kautilya (1992) The Arthashastra. Translated with an introduction by L.N. Rangarajan. New Delhi: Penguin Books India.
Kimmerer, R.W. (2013) Braiding Sweetgrass: Indigenous Wisdom, Scientific Knowledge and the Teachings of Plants. Minneapolis, MN: Milkweed Editions.
Kukutai, T. and Taylor, J. (eds) (2016) Indigenous Data Sovereignty: Toward an Agenda. Canberra: ANU Press.
Liao, W.K. (trans.) (1939) The Complete Works of Han Fei Tzŭ: A Classic of Chinese Political Science. London: Arthur Probsthain.
Lovelock, J. (1979) Gaia: A New Look at Life on Earth. Oxford: Oxford University Press.
Ludden, D. (1999). An Agrarian History of South Asia. Cambridge University Press.
Marx, K. (1976) Capital: Volume 1. London: Penguin.
Murra, J.V. (1972) 'El "control vertical" de un máximo de pisos ecológicos en la economía de las sociedades andinas', in Murra, J.V. (ed.) Visita de la Provincia de León de Huánuco. Huánuco: Universidad Nacional Hermilio Valdizán, pp. 427–476.
Nadasdy, P. (2003) Hunters and Bureaucrats: Power, Knowledge, and Aboriginal-State Relations in the Southwest Yukon. Vancouver: UBC Press.
Niamir-Fuller, M. (1999) Managing Mobility in African Rangelands: The Legitimization of Transhumance. London: Intermediate Technology Publications.
North, D.C. (1990) Institutions, Institutional Change and Economic Performance. Cambridge: Cambridge University Press.
Olivelle, P. (2004). The Law Code of Manu. Oxford University Press.
Ostrom, E. (1990) Governing the Commons: The Evolution of Institutions for Collective Action. Cambridge: Cambridge University Press.

Ostrom, E. (2010) 'Polycentric systems for coping with collective action and global environmental change', Global Environmental Change, 20(4), pp. 550–557.

Ostrom, E. (2010). Beyond Markets and States: Polycentric Governance of Complex Economic Systems. American Economic Review, 100(3), 641–672.

Patterson, O. (1982) Slavery and Social Death. Cambridge, MA: Harvard University Press.

Polanyi, K. (1944) The Great Transformation: The Political and Economic Origins of Our Time. New York: Rinehart.

Rangarajan, L. N. (trans.) (1992) Kautilya: The Arthashastra. New Delhi: Penguin Books.

Raworth, K. (2017) Doughnut Economics: Seven Ways to Think Like a 21st-Century Economist. London: Random House Business.

Rockström, J. et al. (2009) 'A safe operating space for humanity', Nature, 461(7263), pp. 472–475.

Sahlins, M. (1972) Stone Age Economics. Chicago, IL: Aldine-Atherton.

Scoones, I. (1995) Living with Uncertainty: New Directions in Pastoral Development in Africa. London: Intermediate Technology Publications.

Scott, J.C. (1998) Seeing Like a State: How Certain Schemes to Improve the Human Condition Have Failed. New Haven, CT: Yale University Press.

Sen, A. (1999) Development as Freedom. Oxford: Oxford University Press.

Trautmann, T. R. (2012). Arthashastra: The Science of Wealth. Aleph Book Company.

United Nations General Assembly (UNGA). (2007). United Nations Declaration on the Rights of Indigenous Peoples. A/RES/61/295.

UNGA (United Nations General Assembly) (2007) United Nations Declaration on the Rights of Indigenous Peoples, A/RES/61/295 (13 September). New York: United Nations.

Waterfield, R. (ed./trans.) (1997) Conversations of Socrates (includes Oeconomicus). London: Penguin Classics.

Will, P. E., & Wong, R. B. (1991). Nourish the People: The State Civilian Granary System in China, 1650–1850. University of Michigan Center for Chinese Studies.

Xenophon. (1997). Oeconomicus (S. Waterfield, Trans.). Oxford University Press. (Original work c. 4th century BCE).

CHAPTER 3

Historical Context and the Rise of European Expansion

1 Introduction

The European expansion of the early modern period was not a spontaneous or purely exploratory venture; it was the product of deeply embedded ideological, religious, economic, and political forces that converged to produce a global order founded on colonial extraction, coercion, and systemic inequality. This chapter interrogates the structural conditions and intellectual frameworks that legitimized European colonization, with particular attention to how Indigenous peoples were dispossessed, subordinated, and integrated into imperial political economies. Central to this process were the interlocking roles of religious doctrine, mercantilist ambition, capitalist transformation, and state violence. Christian theology provided the moral scaffolding for conquest. Catholic empires invoked Papal Bulls, such as Inter Caetera (1493), to sanctify territorial claims and erase Indigenous sovereignty through the "Doctrine of Discovery".[1] Protestant empires, though ideologically distinct, reproduced similar logics by framing colonization as a divine

[1] Miller, R.J., Ruru, J., Behrendt, L. and Lindberg, T., 2010. Discovering Indigenous Lands: The Doctrine of Discovery in the English Colonies. Oxford: Oxford University Press.

S. Ramesh, *The Political Economy of the Indigenous Peoples of the World, Volume I*, https://doi.org/10.1007/978-3-032-24041-5_3

mandate for civilization and conversion.[2] These theological narratives, far from being abstract, justified military interventions, legal disenfranchisement, and cultural erasure across the Americas, Africa, and Asia. The Jesuit reducciones in South America and the residential schools in Canada exemplify how missionary infrastructures became instruments of both religious indoctrination and economic integration.[3,4]

Economically, the colonial expansion coincided with, and helped forge, the emergence of global capitalism. Silver mines in Zacatecas and Potosí fuelled European treasuries, enabling the rise of joint-stock companies like the Dutch East India Company and laying the foundations for international finance.[5,6] Marxist critiques argue that colonialism constituted the "primitive accumulation" that capitalism required, extracting labour, land, and resources through violence and law.[7,8] This stands in stark contrast to neoclassical economic narratives, which treat markets as natural and ahistorical, obscuring the systemic coercion and dispossession that underpinned wealth generation. Others, building on Marx, identified imperialism as the terminal phase of capitalist expansion, where state and corporate power converged to dominate peripheral economies and peoples.[9] Empirical case studies further illuminate these dynamics. In the

[2] Pagden, A., 1993. European Encounters with the New World: From Renaissance to Romanticism. New Haven: Yale University Press.

[3] Gruzinski, S., 2002. The Mestizo Mind: The Intellectual Dynamics of Colonization and Globalization. New York: Routledge.

[4] Truth and Reconciliation Commission of Canada, 2015. Final Report of the Truth and Reconciliation Commission of Canada, Volume One: Summary. Toronto: James Lorimer & Company.

[5] Bakewell, P., 1984. Silver Mining and Society in Colonial Mexico: Zacatecas 1546–1700. Cambridge: Cambridge University Press.

[6] Subrahmanyam, S., 1997. The Career and Legend of Vasco da Gama. Cambridge: Cambridge University Press.

[7] Marx, K., 2004. Capital: A Critique of Political Economy. Volume 1. London: Penguin Classics. [Original work published 1867].

[8] Perelman, M., 2000. The Invention of Capitalism: Classical Political Economy and the Secret History of Primitive Accumulation. Durham: Duke University Press.

[9] Lenin, V.I., 1917. Imperialism: The Highest Stage of Capitalism. New York: International Publishers.

Philippines, Spanish authorities tethered Christian conversion to compulsory labour through the polo y servicios system.[10] In the Atlantic world, enslaved Africans were commodified through the triangular trade, while Indigenous economies were forcibly reshaped to provide raw materials for European markets.[11] These processes were not incidental but central to the birth of the modern world system. The integration of Indigenous lands into global trade networks, combined with the ecological and epidemiological shocks of the Columbian Exchange, accelerated the transformation of local societies and environments. Crops like maize and potatoes radically altered European agriculture, while the introduction of livestock and monoculture farming disrupted Indigenous agroecological systems.[12] Communist and decolonial frameworks, in contrast to liberal economic theory, centre the agency of colonized peoples and the structural violence of empire. Thinkers have argued that underdevelopment in the Global South is not a natural condition but the result of deliberate extraction and racial capitalism.[13] In this view, colonialism was not a by-product of development but a condition for it. The European conquest cannot be disentangled from its long-term legacies: racial hierarchies, legal regimes of dispossession, environmental degradation, poverty and enduring economic inequality. These themes form the backbone of the chapter, which critically examines the instruments, ideologies, and impacts of European expansion from a political economy perspective, foregrounding the experiences and resistance of Indigenous peoples throughout.

This chapter builds upon the foundational themes explored in Chapters 1 and 2 by turning attention to the legal architectures, policy regimes, and historical precedents that have framed—and often constrained—the economic agency of Indigenous Peoples globally. Where Chapter 1 introduced the centrality of land and sovereignty to Indigenous economies, and Chapter 2 examined the philosophical and institutional divergence

[10] Rafael, V.L., 1988. Contracting Colonialism: Translation and Christian Conversion in Tagalog Society Under Early Spanish Rule. Ithaca: Cornell University Press.

[11] Williams, E., 1944. Capitalism and Slavery. Chapel Hill: University of North Carolina Press.

[12] Crosby, A.W., 1972. The Columbian Exchange: Biological and Cultural Consequences of 1492. Westport: Greenwood Press.

[13] Rodney, W., 1972. How Europe Underdeveloped Africa. London: Bogle-L'Ouverture Publications.

between Indigenous and Western economic models, this chapter narrows the lens to examine how Indigenous economic autonomy has been either undermined or shaped by external legal and political systems. In doing so, it highlights the enduring tension between imposed state structures and Indigenous self-determination, preparing the ground for the examination of institutional innovations and resistance movements detailed in Chapter 4.

2 Ideology, Religion, and the Justification of Empire

2.1 *The Role of Religion and Ideology in European Expansion*

European expansion during the early modern period was not merely a geopolitical or economic phenomenon; it was deeply rooted in ideological justifications that legitimized conquest, subjugation, and resource extraction. Religion, especially Christianity, functioned as a dominant ideological apparatus that rationalized imperial domination over Indigenous peoples. Both Catholic and Protestant empires framed their colonial missions as divinely ordained, drawing on theological doctrine to legitimize the dispossession of Indigenous land, the erosion of local governance structures, and the transformation of cultural and spiritual systems. Central to this was the Doctrine of Discovery, codified in papal bulls such as Inter Caetera (1493), which conferred divine authority on Spain and Portugal to claim dominion over non-Christian lands.[14] This doctrine laid the foundation for the legal marginalization of Indigenous sovereignty and became a recurring motif in European imperial charters. The Spanish deployment of the Requerimiento, a document read to Indigenous populations declaring their obligation to submit to Christian and Spanish authority, illustrates how religion functioned as both a juridical and spiritual weapon.[15] Protestant empires, though rejecting papal authority, continued to employ similar ideological frameworks. British colonists in North America, for instance, interpreted the land

[14] Miller, R.J., Ruru, J., Behrendt, L. and Lindberg, T., 2010. Discovering Indigenous Lands: The Doctrine of Discovery in the English Colonies. Oxford: Oxford University Press.

[15] Pagden, A., 1993. European Encounters with the New World: From Renaissance to Romanticism. New Haven: Yale University Press.

as a 'vacuum domicilium', an empty space devoid of civilization, thus morally justifying its occupation.[16] The Puritan mission in New England framed colonization as a sacred duty, with Indigenous resistance interpreted as satanic opposition to divine providence. This religious narrative masked the material motives underpinning land acquisition and labour exploitation. Missionary activity functioned as the soft arm of imperialism. Catholic Jesuit missions in South America, particularly in Paraguay and Brazil, established reducciones, planned settlements that imposed European norms, languages, and labour structures on Indigenous populations.[17] While offering some protection from settler violence, these missions also integrated Indigenous communities into mercantile and extractive economies. In the Philippines, Spanish missionary control was closely intertwined with colonial administration. Parishes operated as units of taxation and labour conscription under the polo y servicios system, reinforcing the fusion of spiritual conversion and economic subjugation.[18] These ideological tools were not peripheral; they were instrumental in securing the conditions necessary for capitalist accumulation. Neoclassical economics, which emerged during the Enlightenment and dominated nineteenth- and twentieth-century policy frameworks, tends to obscure this foundational violence. By assuming perfect information, voluntary exchange, and rational choice, neoclassical models depoliticize history and ignore the coercive mechanisms through which property and capital were first accumulated.[19] For instance, the enclosure of Indigenous land under Christian legal frameworks was critical to establishing private property regimes essential for capitalist agriculture. In contrast, Marxist and postcolonial critiques underscore the role of religion as part of the ideological superstructure that facilitated and masked primitive accumulation. It has been argued that Christianity was deployed to morally validate the expropriation of African labour and resources, presenting spiritual salvation as a

16 Seed, P., 1995. Ceremonies of Possession in Europe's Conquest of the New World, 1492–1640. Cambridge: Cambridge University Press.

17 Gruzinski, S., 2002. The Mestizo Mind: The Intellectual Dynamics of Colonization and Globalization. New York: Routledge.

18 Rafael, V.L., 1988. Contracting Colonialism: Translation and Christian Conversion in Tagalog Society Under Early Spanish Rule. Ithaca: Cornell University Press.

19 Perelman, M., 2000. The Invention of Capitalism: Classical Political Economy and the Secret History of Primitive Accumulation. Durham: Duke University Press.

justification for slavery and colonization.[20] Moreover, others have viewed imperialism as an inevitable extension of capitalism's internal contradictions, where ideological justifications, including religious ones, served to manage and legitimize expanding capital frontiers.[21] For example, Marxist theorists such as Lenin argued that as capital accumulated and domestic markets became saturated, capitalist powers were compelled to seek new territories for investment, resource extraction, and labour exploitation. This economic drive was often cloaked in civilizing missions, missionary activity, and the rhetoric of progress, portraying colonial expansion as benevolent or divinely ordained. In practice, such narratives helped to obscure the violence of expropriation, land dispossession, and racial hierarchy that underpinned imperial conquest. Empirical legacies of this ideological entanglement remain evident. In Canada, Christian missions were instrumental in operating residential schools that aimed to culturally assimilate Indigenous children and prepare them for wage labour in settler economies.[22] These schools not only destroyed Indigenous languages and traditions but also reinforced class stratification under a colonial-capitalist order. Ideology thus functioned not only to legitimize conquest but to remake Indigenous life to fit the demands of an expanding global economy. Thus, religion and ideology were not external to European expansion; they were its core rationalizing agents. Whether through papal decrees, Protestant sermons, or missionary settlements, religious doctrine was used to moralize dispossession, justify forced labour, and facilitate the insertion of Indigenous societies into colonial economies. Understanding this intersection is crucial to any political economy of colonization and its enduring global consequences.

2.2 *Papal Authority and the Doctrine of Discovery*

The consolidation of European imperial expansion during the late 15th and early sixteenth centuries was deeply shaped by religious authority,

[20] Rodney, W., 1972. How Europe Underdeveloped Africa. London: Bogle-L'Ouverture Publications.

[21] Lenin, V.I., 1917. Imperialism: The Highest Stage of Capitalism. New York: International Publishers.

[22] Truth and Reconciliation Commission of Canada, 2015. Final Report of the Truth and Reconciliation Commission of Canada, Volume One: Summary. Toronto: James Lorimer & Company.

particularly the Catholic Church's claim to moral jurisdiction over global territories. The Papal Bull Inter Caetera (1493), issued by Pope Alexander VI, is emblematic of this fusion of theology and geopolitics. It provided Spain and Portugal with divine sanction to conquer and convert non-Christian lands, effectively creating a theological-legal framework for global colonization. This edict institutionalized the Doctrine of Discovery, which held that Christian monarchs had the exclusive right to claim sovereignty over territories deemed terra nullius, lands without Christian rulers, even when those lands were occupied by Indigenous peoples.[23] The Doctrine of Discovery thus operated not only as an ecclesiastical claim but as a geopolitical mechanism, granting legitimacy to imperial violence and dispossession. In political-economic terms, it served as a form of ideological infrastructure for early capitalism, enabling the appropriation of resources, labour, and land under the guise of spiritual salvation. From a neoclassical economics perspective, such Papal endorsements are largely omitted or depoliticized. The neoclassical framework assumes property rights as pre-existing or naturally evolving from rational contracts, ignoring how imperial legal doctrines violently constructed those rights through forced conversion, land seizure, and legal fiction.[24] In contrast, Marxist and postcolonial theorists expose the Doctrine's function as a superstructural tool that facilitated primitive accumulation, the expropriation of land and labour foundational to capitalist development.[25,26] A case study of Spanish colonization in the Americas reveals how the Papal Bulls translated into concrete statecraft. The Requerimiento, read to Indigenous populations in Spanish, a language they did not understand, demanded submission to Christian and royal authority or justified enslavement and slaughter. This legal ritual, while farcical,

[23] Miller, R.J., Ruru, J., Behrendt, L. and Lindberg, T., 2010. Discovering Indigenous Lands: The Doctrine of Discovery in the English Colonies. Oxford: Oxford University Press.

[24] Perelman, M., 2000. The Invention of Capitalism: Classical Political Economy and the Secret History of Primitive Accumulation. Durham: Duke University Press.

[25] Marx, K., 1867. Capital: A Critique of Political Economy, Vol. 1. London: Penguin Classics (2004 ed.).

[26] Rodney, W., 1972. How Europe Underdeveloped Africa. London: Bogle-L'Ouverture Publications.

was central to maintaining the ideological illusion of lawful conquest.[27] In Mexico and Peru, lands seized under the authority of the Doctrine of Discovery were redistributed to encomenderos (given the right to collect tribute and labour from Indigenous people in a particular area), who exploited Indigenous labour in mines and plantations. These acts of dispossession were rationalized not just through military might, but through Papal blessing. The global reach of this doctrine extended far beyond Iberian empires. Its principles were later adopted by Protestant colonial powers, Britain, the Netherlands, and France, albeit in secularized forms. For instance, British colonial law in North America invoked discovery doctrines to override Indigenous land claims, leading to widespread displacements and legal marginalization.[28] In settler colonial states such as Canada, Australia, and the United States, the Doctrine of Discovery remains embedded in legal precedent, used to deny Indigenous sovereignty to this day. Communist critiques of this history interpret Papal authority and the Doctrine of Discovery as ideological expressions of class domination and imperialism. It has been argued that colonialism was not merely a byproduct of religious fervour or cultural arrogance but a structural necessity for capitalism's survival, requiring new markets, cheap labour, and raw materials.[29] Religious justification, in this view, masked economic motives that were materially determinative. Ultimately, the Doctrine of Discovery should be understood as a legal-ideological apparatus that enabled the economic transformation of global societies under the hegemony of European capital. It facilitated the mapping, claiming, and commodification of lands in ways that laid the foundation for modern property regimes and state sovereignty, while marginalizing Indigenous epistemologies, legal systems, and land relationships.

[27] Seed, P., 1995. Ceremonies of Possession in Europe's Conquest of the New World, 1492–1640. Cambridge: Cambridge University Press.

[28] Miller, R.J., Ruru, J., Behrendt, L. and Lindberg, T., 2010. Discovering Indigenous Lands: The Doctrine of Discovery in the English Colonies. Oxford: Oxford University Press.

[29] Lenin, V.I., 1917. Imperialism: The Highest Stage of Capitalism. New York: International Publishers.

2.3 *Protestantism, Moral Geography, and Imperial Purpose*

The fragmentation of Catholic hegemony during the Protestant Reformation did not dismantle the imperial logic that underpinned European expansion but rather provided a parallel theological justification for conquest and economic domination. Protestant states, particularly England and the Netherlands, adapted Christian narratives to align with their own geopolitical ambitions. Protestantism's emphasis on individual moral rectitude, work ethic, and predestined salvation reinforced emerging capitalist ideologies by portraying economic success as a sign of divine favour. This belief system, closely aligned with Max Weber's thesis on the "Protestant ethic", gave religious sanction to accumulation and colonial expansion under the guise of civilizing non-Christian peoples.[30] In British North America, Puritan settlers conceptualized the land as both physically and morally vacant, a "wilderness" devoid of legitimate ownership and culture. Indigenous societies were often perceived as spiritually and morally deficient, thereby legitimizing the usurpation of their lands and the imposition of Protestant norms. This narrative of moral geography facilitated the expropriation of land through legal constructs such as terra nullius, which denied Indigenous sovereignty by portraying their lifeways as incompatible with European conceptions of civilization and property.[31,32] These ideological constructs were intertwined with the material imperatives of early capitalism. The English colonial enterprise in North America, bolstered by joint-stock companies like the Virginia Company, relied on settler colonialism to establish agricultural and extractive economies. Neoclassical economics later depoliticized these historical processes, interpreting land enclosures and forced labour as the natural outcomes of market efficiency and property rights.[33] In contrast, Marxist critiques argue that colonial expropriation was an essential phase of "primitive accumulation", in which violence and ideology were instrumental in

[30] Weber, M., 1930. The Protestant Ethic and the Spirit of Capitalism. London: Allen and Unwin.

[31] Pagden, A., 1993. European Encounters with the New World: From Renaissance to Romanticism. New Haven: Yale University Press.

[32] Benton, L., 2010. A Search for Sovereignty: Law and Geography in European Empires, 1400–1900. Cambridge: Cambridge University Press.

[33] Perelman, M., 2000. The Invention of Capitalism: Classical Political Economy and the Secret History of Primitive Accumulation. Durham: Duke University Press.

converting communal lands into capitalist assets.[34,35] One clear example is the imposition of English property laws in Ireland and later in the Thirteen Colonies, where Protestant settlers were granted legal titles to land inhabited by Indigenous or Catholic populations. This dispossession was justified not only through racial hierarchies but through religious binaries: Protestant industriousness versus the presumed idleness or paganism of the colonized.[36] Moreover, Protestant missions were frequently aligned with commercial interests. The London Missionary Society, active in Africa and the Pacific, often collaborated with British traders and colonial administrators to facilitate resource extraction and impose cultural hegemony.

Communist critiques of imperialism similarly frame Protestant expansion as part of a larger system of capitalist penetration, where ideology served as a tool to naturalise exploitation.[37] Religious missions were not merely spiritual endeavours but agents of political and economic transformation, operating under the moral veil of salvation while reordering land, labour, and life to serve imperial capital. Thus, Protestantism's contribution to European expansion lay not in altering the objectives of empire, but in refining and legitimizing them through a different theological lens, deeply enmeshed with emergent capitalist logics.

2.4 *Missions as Ideological and Economic Instruments*

Missionary activity during European expansion was not merely spiritual; it functioned as a core mechanism of colonial governance, economic extraction, and ideological control. Missions were frequently deployed to pacify Indigenous populations, erode pre-colonial socio-economic systems, and embed capitalist discipline through cultural assimilation. The Jesuit reducciones in Paraguay exemplify this duality. Although they offered relative

[34] Marx, K., 1867. Capital: A Critique of Political Economy, Vol. 1. London: Penguin Classics, 2004 ed.

[35] Rodney, W., 1972. How Europe Underdeveloped Africa. London: Bogle-L'Ouverture Publications.

[36] Seed, P., 1995. Ceremonies of Possession in Europe's Conquest of the New World, 1492–1640. Cambridge: Cambridge University Press.

[37] Lenin, V.I., 1917. Imperialism: The Highest Stage of Capitalism. New York: International Publishers.

protection from encomienda systems and settler violence, they simultaneously restructured Indigenous life into regimented, European-style settlements that facilitated surveillance and labour mobilization for colonial production.[38] The reducciones became microcosms of a nascent colonial capitalist order, where land, labour, and time were strictly managed to produce surplus value for imperial interests. In the Philippines, Spanish religious conversion efforts were intimately tied to the polo y servicios system, which required Indigenous males to provide forced labour for colonial infrastructure and agricultural projects. Tagalog translations of Catholic catechisms enabled deeper ideological penetration while naturalizing coercive systems of taxation and labour extraction.[39] The theological promise of salvation was weaponized to instil obedience and justify economic subjugation. Similarly, in colonial Canada, missionary-run residential schools played a strategic role in the destruction of Indigenous cultures and the imposition of Euro-Christian norms, which were tightly interwoven with capitalist logics. The residential school system functioned not only to Christianise but also to assimilate Indigenous children into an industrial capitalist economy by severing kinship ties, suppressing traditional knowledge systems, and promoting Eurocentric labour discipline.[40] These missionary projects reflect a broader convergence between religious ideology and economic rationality, a convergence that parallels the assumptions of neoclassical economics, particularly the emphasis on individual rationality, utility maximization, and integration into formal markets. For instance, Jesuit missions in South America, particularly in Paraguay, organized Indigenous Guaraní communities into structured settlements (reducciones) that operated as collective economies under missionary supervision. While nominally protecting Indigenous peoples from enslavement, these missions also trained them in European agricultural techniques, imposed fixed working hours, and channelled their labour into export-oriented production systems, mirroring capitalist principles of labour discipline and productivity. In contrast, Marxist and

[38] Gruzinski, S. (2002). The Mestizo Mind: The Intellectual Dynamics of Colonization and Globalization. New York: Routledge.

[39] Rafael, V.L. (1988). Contracting Colonialism: Translation and Christian Conversion in Tagalog Society Under Early Spanish Rule. Ithaca: Cornell University Press.

[40] Truth and Reconciliation Commission of Canada. (2015). Final Report of the Truth and Reconciliation Commission of Canada, Volume One: Summary. Toronto: James Lorimer & Company.

communist critiques highlight how missions functioned as ideological state apparatuses masking the coercive appropriation of land and labour behind a humanitarian and spiritual façade.[41] The missionary encounter was, therefore, an early expression of capitalist expansion wrapped in theological rhetoric, prefiguring later development models that also sought to "uplift" Indigenous populations into participation within extractive and exploitative economies. This ideological-economic nexus finds contemporary parallels in structural adjustment programs and foreign aid conditionalities, where modern institutions, often secular but equally hegemonic, promote assimilation into global market systems. The historical trajectory of missions illustrates how ideological justification and material exploitation have long been co-constitutive in projects of Indigenous dispossession.

2.5 *Religion and Political Economy: A Theoretical Perspective*

Throughout the early modern period, religion played a pivotal role in shaping the ideological underpinnings of global economic expansion. Rather than functioning solely as a spiritual domain, religion helped legitimise conquest, dispossession, and labour exploitation. In the Spanish and Portuguese empires, Catholic doctrine provided theological sanction for colonization, such as through the concept of "just war" and the civilizing imperative to convert Indigenous peoples. These religious rationales served to moralise otherwise violent and extractive practices by framing them as benevolent missions. Jesuit reductions in South America, for example, were both spiritual sanctuaries and mechanisms of economic control that channelled Indigenous labour and loyalty towards colonial ends.[42] From a theoretical standpoint, neoclassical economics has often abstracted away these historical processes, privileging models of individual rationality and efficient markets while occluding the coercive foundations of wealth accumulation. In contrast, Marxist and postcolonial scholars have foregrounded the role of ideology, including religion, as a material force in shaping historical trajectories. Christianity provided moral cover for slavery, resource extraction, and systemic violence, effectively

[41] Althusser, L. (1971). Ideology and Ideological State Apparatuses. In Lenin and Philosophy and Other Essays. London: Monthly Review Press.

[42] Gruzinski, S. (2002). The Mestizo Mind: The Intellectual Dynamics of Colonization and Globalization. New York: Routledge.

integrating colonialism into the global capitalist system.[43] Similarly, religious discourse was central to the creation and legitimation of early capitalist institutions, particularly through the naturalization of inequality and the sanctification of private property. In Christian theological traditions, especially those shaped by Protestant Reformation ideologies, wealth accumulation and industriousness were increasingly interpreted as signs of divine favour. Calvinist doctrines, which emphasized predestination and worldly asceticism, encouraged believers to pursue disciplined, rational labour and reinvestment of profits, behaviours that aligned closely with capitalist enterprise.[44] Religious narratives also provided a moral justification for private property. The idea that land ownership was a God-given right and a reward for stewardship enabled colonial powers to dispossess Indigenous peoples while framing such expropriation as both lawful and divinely sanctioned. Papal bulls such as Inter Caetera (1493) granted Christian rulers the authority to claim non-Christian lands, establishing a theological basis for colonial property regimes that excluded Indigenous sovereignty. Moreover, inequality, both within Europe and in colonial societies, was often justified through religious hierarchies. The poor were seen not as victims of systemic exploitation but as part of a divinely ordained social order in which suffering could have spiritual merit. Wealth, on the other hand, was portrayed as a sign of moral virtue and discipline. This moral framing suppressed challenges to exploitative structures and reinforced economic stratification as natural and righteous.

These religious underpinnings helped solidify capitalist institutions such as wage labour, land enclosures, and commercial credit systems. They gave legitimacy to laws protecting private capital and marginalized communal forms of ownership or redistribution rooted in non-Western or Indigenous traditions. In doing so, religious discourse played a foundational role in embedding capitalist norms into both law and culture, turning historical and political processes into moral imperatives. On the other hand, Communist and socialist regimes, while rejecting religion as a tool of capitalist ideology, often substituted their own legitimizing frameworks, typically class struggle and scientific materialism. Yet even here, quasi-religious language of redemption, sacrifice, and historical

[43] Rodney, W. (1972). How Europe Underdeveloped Africa. London: Bogle-L'Ouverture Publications.

[44] Weber, M., 1930. The Protestant Ethic and the Spirit of Capitalism. London: Allen & Unwin.

destiny was deployed to justify the forced transformation of Indigenous economies, as seen in collectivization campaigns among minority populations in the Soviet Union or the restructuring of peasant communities in Maoist China. Both capitalist and communist systems, despite their ideological antagonism, employed overarching narratives that subordinated Indigenous social formations to broader political-economic logics. The persistence of inequality and dispossession in the postcolonial era underscores the need to critically reassess the ideological foundations of global political economy. Religious justifications were not mere epiphenomena of expansion but structurally embedded in the machinery of conquest and capital formation. Recognizing this allows for a deeper interrogation of contemporary economic discourse, whether neoliberal, developmentalist, or socialist, that continues to depoliticise or universalise what are, in essence, historically contingent and ideologically mediated processes.

3 Trade, Capitalism, and the Restructuring of Indigenous Economies

3.1 *The Impact of European Trade Networks on Indigenous Societies*

The expansion of European trade networks during the early modern period profoundly altered the economic, social, and political dynamics of Indigenous societies. Driven by European demand for commodities such as spices, silver, furs, and tobacco, Indigenous territories were drawn into global capitalist circuits. In many cases, this integration was neither voluntary nor benign; it entailed the displacement of Indigenous systems of reciprocity and barter with extractive market logics geared towards surplus accumulation and commodification. In North America, the fur trade exemplifies how Indigenous economies were restructured under European pressures. French and British traders, seeking beaver pelts for the booming European hat industry, engaged with Indigenous nations such as the Huron, Cree, and Algonquin, transforming their subsistence patterns into fur-dependent economies. This trade introduced cycles of dependency and environmental depletion, undermining Indigenous autonomy.[45] Likewise, in South America, Spanish extraction

[45] Cronon, W., 1983. Changes in the Land: Indians, Colonists, and the Ecology of New England. New York: Hill and Wang.

of silver in Potosí relied on systems like the mita, a colonial reinvention of Incan rotational labour, that funnelled Indigenous labour into the imperial economy.[46] These transformations reflected deeper ideological currents aligned with emerging capitalist rationality. Trade was not merely economic but civilizational, often framed in religious and moral language that portrayed Indigenous societies as primitive and in need of integration into the so-called civilized global order. Neoclassical economic models retrospectively abstract these processes as the rational expansion of markets and comparative advantage, ignoring the violent asymmetries of power and coercion involved in their formation. Marxist critiques, in contrast, have long emphasized "primitive accumulation" as a necessary phase for capitalist development, where non-capitalist modes of production are destroyed or subsumed to enable capital expansion,[47,48] The Soviet critique of colonial trade systems similarly underscored how global trade served imperial centres at the expense of peripheral Indigenous communities. Under communism, trade relationships were ideologically framed as exploitative linkages embedded in imperialism, an argument notably advanced in the context of the analysis of capitalist expansion.[49] Empirically, the impact of these trade networks was devastating in many regions. In Central America, the collapse of Indigenous agricultural systems and artisanal production under Spanish rule led to chronic underdevelopment that persists today.[50] The global hunger for silver led to currency inflation in Ming China, creating fiscal crises and contributing to state decline.[51] These examples show how Indigenous societies were not merely affected by trade, but fundamentally transformed—and in many cases destabilized, by their incorporation into European-dominated global

[46] Bakewell, P., 1984. Silver Mining and Society in Colonial Mexico: Zacatecas 1546–1700. Cambridge: Cambridge. University Press.

[47] Perelman, M., 2000. The Invention of Capitalism: Classical Political Economy and the Secret History of Primitive Accumulation. Durham: Duke University Press.

[48] Marx, K., 1867. Capital: A Critique of Political Economy, Volume I. London: Penguin Classics, 2004 ed.

[49] Lenin, V.I., 1917. Imperialism: The Highest Stage of Capitalism. New York: International Publishers.

[50] Rodney, W., 1972. How Europe Underdeveloped Africa. London: Bogle-L'Ouverture Publications.

[51] Flynn, D.O. and Giráldez, A., 1995. Born with a "Silver Spoon": The Origin of World Trade in 1571. Journal of World History, 6(2), pp. 201–221.

markets. Ultimately, the imposition of capitalist trade logics disrupted Indigenous political economies, stripped economic activities of their social embeddedness, and intensified inequalities between core and periphery. This reordering of Indigenous life under global capitalism continues to shape contemporary Indigenous struggles over sovereignty, land, and economic justice.

3.2 *The Triangular Trade and Its Implications*

The triangular trade system was central to the development of global capitalism and profoundly restructured Indigenous economies in Africa and the Americas. This transoceanic economic mechanism connected Europe, West Africa, and the Americas in a three-pronged circuit of commodities, labour, and capital. European powers exported manufactured goods, such as textiles, firearms, and alcohol, to Africa, where they were exchanged for enslaved persons. These captives were then transported to the Americas via the Middle Passage and forced to labour on plantations producing sugar, cotton, and tobacco, which were then shipped back to Europe. The plantation system, based on coerced African labour, operated on land seized from Indigenous populations, thus doubly dispossessing native societies of both people and territory.[52,53] The commodification of Indigenous lands and people was not incidental but structural to the logic of European mercantilism and early capitalist accumulation. In the Americas, Indigenous agricultural systems, spiritual economies, and communal land ownership models were displaced by monoculture plantations and private property regimes. For instance, in the Caribbean, the imposition of sugar plantations led to widespread deforestation, environmental degradation, and the collapse of local subsistence economies. This transformation aligns with Karl Marx's notion of "primitive accumulation", whereby capital is birthed through violence, dispossession,

[52] Williams, E., 1944. Capitalism and Slavery. Chapel Hill: University of North Carolina Press.

[53] Rodney, W., 1972. How Europe Underdeveloped Africa. London: Bogle-L'Ouverture Publications.

and state-enforced property regimes.[54,55] The triangular trade's monopolistic character, enabled by European chartered companies like the Royal African Company and the Dutch West India Company, prevented the development of Indigenous commercial institutions and local industrialization. These companies often functioned as arms of imperial states, distorting local markets by enforcing exclusive trade privileges, price controls, and violent suppression of competition. This colonial economic infrastructure left a legacy of structural dependency and underdevelopment, particularly in West Africa, where pre-colonial trade networks and artisanal production were systematically dismantled.[56,57] Neoclassical economic theory largely abstracts from these historical realities, assuming frictionless trade, voluntary exchange, and comparative advantage. Yet the triangular trade reveals how coercion and inequality shaped global trade flows. Capital accumulation was not driven by mutual gains but by unfree labour, violent extraction, and dispossession. By contrast, Marxist and dependency theorists have long emphasized the role of imperialist trade structures in perpetuating uneven development. For example, it has been argued that Africa's integration into the capitalist world-economy under the slave trade actively underdeveloped the continent, extracting value without allowing reciprocal investment or structural transformation.[58] Communist critiques further illuminated the ideological function of capitalist trade networks. The USSR's early economic historiography framed the slave trade and colonial economies as mechanisms of bourgeois expansionism, serving to entrench class hierarchies across racialized lines. While Soviet development strategies also displaced Indigenous communities, particularly in Central Asia and Siberia, they were often justified in anti-imperialist terms, revealing the ideological complexities of different

[54] Marx, K., 1867. Capital: A Critique of Political Economy, Volume I. London: Penguin Classics, 2004 ed.

[55] Perelman, M., 2000. The Invention of Capitalism: Classical Political Economy and the Secret History of Primitive Accumulation. Durham: Duke University Press.

[56] Amin, S., 1976. Unequal Development: An Essay on the Social Formations of Peripheral Capitalism. New York: Monthly Review Press.

[57] Inikori, J.E., 2002. Africans and the Industrial Revolution in England: A Study in International Trade and Economic Development. Cambridge: Cambridge University Press.

[58] Rodney, W., 1972. How Europe Underdeveloped Africa. London: Bogle-L'Ouverture Publications.

political-economic systems.[59] The lasting impact of the triangular trade is evident in the systemic inequalities between the global North and South. The concentration of capital in Europe was predicated on the devaluation of Indigenous and African lives, labour, and land. Recognizing this history is essential for understanding persistent global inequalities and rethinking development in more equitable and historically conscious ways.

3.3 Transformation of Indigenous Societies into Raw Material Zones

European expansion during the early modern period catalysed a profound and often violent transformation of Indigenous economies across the Americas and other colonized regions. These transformations were not merely incidental but were driven by the structural imperatives of capitalist expansion, in which colonial powers sought to reorganize native modes of production to extract and export raw materials for profit in European markets. As Marxist historian Immanuel Wallerstein observed, the incorporation of peripheral regions into the capitalist world-economy depended on their restructuring as sites of cheap labour and raw material production.[60] This transformation displaced Indigenous economic systems, which were typically diverse, localized, and grounded in subsistence production, reciprocity, and ecological stewardship. In the Americas, Spanish colonization restructured Indigenous economies to extract precious metals, particularly silver. The mining town of Zacatecas in present-day Mexico exemplifies this transformation. Indigenous labour, often coerced through systems such as encomienda and repartimiento, were redirected towards silver mining, primarily for export to Europe and Asia.[61] The exploitation of Andean Indigenous populations in Potosí's silver mines under the mita system, an adaptation of pre-colonial labour tribute, further illustrates the subjugation of local economies to global capitalist demands.[62] Between 1550 and 1800, Potosí alone is estimated

[59] Davis, M., 2003. *Late Victorian Holocausts: El Niño Famines and the Making of the Third World*. London: Verso.

[60] Wallerstein, I. (1974). The Modern World-System I: Capitalist Agriculture and the Origins of the European World-Economy in the Sixteenth Century. Academic Press.

[61] Bakewell, P. (1984). Miners of the Red Mountain: Indian Labour in Potosí, 1545–1650. University of New Mexico Press.

[62] Tandeter, E. (1993). Coercion and Market: Silver Mining in Colonial Potosí, 1692–1826. University of New Mexico Press.

to have produced over 40,000 metric tons of silver, feeding Spanish mercantile accumulation while impoverishing Indigenous communities.[63] In contrast to the mineral economies of Latin America, Indigenous economies in North America were redirected towards the fur trade. In what is now Canada, Indigenous groups such as the Huron-Wendat, Cree, and Inuit were drawn into extensive fur trading networks operated by French and later British colonial powers. These communities shifted from subsistence hunting to intensive trapping of beavers and other fur-bearing animals to meet European demand, particularly during the height of the fur trade in the seventeenth and eighteenth centuries.[64] This commodification of nature disrupted ecological balances, intensified inter-tribal conflict over trading privileges, and undermined traditional food systems. The logic of restructuring Indigenous economies for raw material extraction can be compared to the prescriptions of neoclassical economics, which emphasizes efficiency, comparative advantage, and market integration. However, neoclassical models often ignore historical inequalities in initial endowments and the coercive mechanisms used to incorporate Indigenous societies into global markets. The colonial restructuring of Indigenous economies did not result from voluntary market exchanges but from dispossession, violence, and institutionalized coercion. While neoclassical theory assumes rational agents in competitive markets, colonial capitalism imposed new property regimes, destroyed communal landholding systems, and eliminated Indigenous agency in economic decisions.[65] Conversely, communist economic planning in twentieth-century socialist states, such as the USSR or Maoist China, also involved restructuring traditional economies, but with ideological goals of collectivization and state ownership rather than profit maximization In some post-colonial contexts like Nicaragua or Bolivia, leftist regimes have attempted to revive or protect Indigenous economic forms as alternatives to extractive capitalism, though often with limited success.[66] These cases suggest

[63] Seed, P. (2001). American Pentimento: The Invention of Indians and the Pursuit of Riches. University of Minnesota Press.

[64] Carlos, A. M., & Lewis, F. D. (2010). Commerce by a Frozen Sea: Native Americans and the European Fur Trade. University of Pennsylvania Press.

[65] Polanyi, K. (1944). The Great Transformation: The Political and Economic Origins of Our Time. Beacon Press.

[66] Hale, C. (2006). Más que un indio (More Than an Indian): Racial Ambivalence and Neoliberal Multiculturalism in Guatemala. School of American Research Press.

that neither capitalism nor state socialism has adequately addressed the autonomy and sustainability of Indigenous economies. A comparative data point can be drawn from the silver export figures: between 1500 and 1800, Spanish America exported an estimated 150,000 metric tons of silver, accounting for 80% of world production.[67] In contrast, Indigenous communities before colonization operated economies that were largely non-monetized and oriented towards local social reproduction, not global trade. The transformation of Indigenous societies into raw material zones was not a natural or efficient economic progression, but a deliberate and exploitative restructuring underpinned by colonial capitalist imperatives. The legacy of this transformation persists today in the form of economic marginalization, environmental degradation, and disrupted cultural practices in many Indigenous communities.

4 Military Superiority and the Machinery of Conquest

4.1 *Technological Dominance and Tactical Advantage*

European conquest of Indigenous societies was not solely a function of economic ambition but was undergirded by a machinery of military dominance that combined technological innovation with ruthless tactical application. European armies of the early modern era deployed gunpowder-based weapons, arquebuses, muskets, and cannons that were virtually unknown to Indigenous populations in the Americas, Africa, and parts of Asia. The psychological and physical impact of these weapons—particularly when combined with steel-edged swords and heavily armoured cavalry—often shattered Indigenous resistance, despite superior knowledge of local terrains and initial numerical advantages.[68,69] The conquistadors in Mexico and Peru, for instance, defeated the Aztec and Inca Empires not only through alliances and strategic deceit but also due to their military hardware. The Battle of Cajamarca in 1532, where a few hundred Spaniards captured the Incan emperor Atahualpa, is emblematic.

[67] Barrett, W. (1990). World bullion flows, 1450–1800. In J.D. Tracy (Ed.), The Rise of Merchant Empires (pp. 224–254). Cambridge University Press.

[68] Restall, M. (2003). Seven Myths of the Spanish Conquest. Oxford University Press.

[69] Mann, C. C. (2005). 1491: New Revelations of the Americas Before Columbus. Alfred A. Knopf.

Firearms and cavalry, unfamiliar and terrifying to Inca troops, contributed decisively to the Spanish victory despite the overwhelming numerical superiority of the Inca forces.[70] While these technologies were rudimentary by later European standards, they imposed shock and awe in societies that had not developed metal weaponry beyond bronze or copper.[71] This technological asymmetry can be examined through the lens of neoclassical economics, which assumes rational agents responding to incentives and constraints. In neoclassical terms, Europeans had a comparative advantage in military capital and logistical networks, enabling them to extract surplus value from Indigenous economies by coercion rather than competition. Indigenous societies, lacking the means to accumulate or replicate such military capital, were structurally disadvantaged. The military dimension thus created a distortion in what could otherwise be seen as economic exchange, skewing any potential market equilibrium in favour of imperial actors. Communist interpretations provide a counterpoint, emphasizing how military conquest functioned as the enforcer of capitalist imperialism. It has been argued that imperial expansion was the highest stage of capitalism, requiring military coercion to open new markets and extract labour and resources.[72] The "machinery of conquest" thus ensured the penetration of capitalist relations into non-capitalist spaces. European firearms and ships were not neutral tools but instruments of class violence and accumulation by dispossession.[73] In the process, they transformed communal Indigenous land tenure systems into commodified assets for export-oriented production. Moreover, European maritime superiority, reinforced by innovations like the caravel, galleon, and advanced navigation tools such as the astrolabe, enabled long-distance invasions and sustained colonial presence. These vessels were floating armouries, capable of enforcing blockades, supporting amphibious assaults, and controlling key trade routes. The Portuguese conquests in the Indian Ocean and the Spanish expansion across the Atlantic attest to the strategic

[70] Hemming, J. (1970). *The Conquest of the Incas*. Harcourt Brace Jovanovich.

[71] Diamond, J. (1997). Guns, Germs, and Steel: The Fates of Human Societies. W. W. Norton & Company.

[72] Lenin, V. I. (1917). Imperialism: The Highest Stage of Capitalism. International Publishers.

[73] Harvey, D. (2003). The New Imperialism. Oxford University Press.

advantage conferred by naval technology.[74] Maritime supremacy was not merely a matter of exploration; it was the logistical infrastructure of empire. In effect, the military-technological superiority of European forces was foundational to the broader capitalist transformation of Indigenous economies. This was not a peaceful integration into global trade but a forcible restructuring of life, land, and labour. The very presence of European arms and fleets undermined any possibility of sovereign Indigenous development, inserting these societies into the global periphery through conquest. The logic of the musket, the sword, and the ship established the conditions for extractive colonialism and set the stage for centuries of economic dependency.

4.2 *Psychological and Cultural Impacts of Military Defeat*

Military conquest not only resulted in territorial subjugation but also triggered profound psychological and cultural trauma among Indigenous populations. The loss of sovereignty, sacred sites, and ancestral lands disrupted cosmologies that had bound communities to spiritual and ecological worlds for generations. The defeat of Indigenous armies by European forces wielding unfamiliar technologies, firearms, cavalry, and steel weapons was often interpreted not simply as a loss of power but as a cosmic collapse. In many Indigenous societies, military defeat called into question the legitimacy of local rulers, the efficacy of traditional rituals, and even the protection of gods or spirits. This disorientation contributed to a rapid erosion of Indigenous authority structures and opened the space for colonial ideologies and Christian proselytization to take root.[75,76] In Mesoamerica, the Spanish conquest of the Aztec Empire devastated not only the polity but also the religious and cultural institutions. The capture and execution of Moctezuma II, followed by the destruction of Tenochtitlan, symbolized a rupture in the sacred order. Nahua scribes recorded laments reflecting spiritual despair and a

[74] Subrahmanyam, S. (1997). The Career and Legend of Vasco da Gama. Cambridge University Press.

[75] Pagden, A. (1993). European Encounters with the New World: From Renaissance to Romanticism. Yale University Press.

[76] Clendinnen, I. (2003). Ambivalent Conquests: Maya and Spaniard in Yucatan, 1517–1570. Cambridge University Press.

loss of cosmic balance.[77] Spanish friars exploited this cultural vacuum, promoting the superiority of Christian cosmology while denigrating Indigenous beliefs as diabolical. A similar pattern emerged in the Andes, where the death of Atahualpa and the fall of the Inca Empire dismantled the state religion centred on sun worship. Quechua cultural expressions were repressed or reconfigured through the syncretic practices of Catholicism.[78] The psychological shock of conquest also induced fragmentation. Kin-based governance structures weakened under colonial impositions such as reducciones in Spanish America, which reorganized Indigenous populations into grid-like settlements to facilitate taxation, surveillance, and evangelization. The forced relocation and imposition of European legal frameworks undermined collective identities, encouraging competition for colonial favour and generating internal divisions.[79] These policies served the broader economic aims of empire, facilitating the extraction of labour and resources while neutralizing Indigenous resistance. From a neoclassical economic perspective, this breakdown of Indigenous institutional coherence can be interpreted as a distortion of incentive structures. With the collapse of endogenous governance and cultural norms, individuals were compelled to respond to new colonial signals, monetary taxation, forced labour quotas, and Christian conversion, as rational economic agents. However, this framing omits the coercive context in which these decisions were made. It assumes atomized utility maximization, ignoring how spiritual disintegration and social dislocation fundamentally altered agency and choice. A Marxist or communist analysis, by contrast, situates the psychological and cultural impact of conquest within the broader framework of ideological domination. Military conquest was not simply a prelude to economic exploitation; it was a necessary ideological act to dismantle pre-capitalist worldviews that might obstruct commodification. As Gramsci's theory of cultural hegemony suggests, domination requires consent, often secured through symbolic systems. The eradication or absorption of Indigenous cosmologies thus enabled the insertion of capitalist relations of production under the guise of civilizing missions

[77] León-Portilla, M. (1992). The Broken Spears: The Aztec Account of the Conquest of Mexico. Beacon Press.

[78] Mills, K. (1997). Idolatry and Its Enemies: Colonial Andean Religion and Extirpation, 1640–1750. Princeton University Press.

[79] Gruzinski, S. (1993). The Conquest of Mexico: The Incorporation of Indian Societies into the Western World, 16th–18th Centuries. Polity Press.

and Christian salvation.[80,81] The long-term impact of this psychological violence is measurable. Scholars have linked historic cultural disruption to present-day socio-economic outcomes among Indigenous populations, including lower levels of trust in formal institutions, intergenerational trauma, and diminished political cohesion.[82,83] The trauma of conquest continues to reverberate, embedded in language loss, disrupted transmission of knowledge, and the ongoing marginalization of Indigenous voices in national narratives.

5 Disease, Demographic Collapse, and Societal Disruption

5.1 *Disease and Demographic Catastrophe*

The introduction of Old-World diseases into the Americas catalysed one of the most severe demographic collapses in human history. Pathogens such as smallpox, measles, typhus, and influenza spread rapidly among Indigenous populations, whose immunological isolation had left them biologically unprepared. Mortality rates ranged from 50% to 90% in many areas, decimating communities before they even encountered European soldiers or missionaries.[84,85] In central Mexico, for example, the population is estimated to have declined from approximately 25 million in 1519 to just over 1 million by 1600.[86] The catastrophic loss of life not only undermined Indigenous resistance to conquest but also dismantled

[80] Gramsci, A. (1971). Selections from the Prison Notebooks. (Q. Hoare & G. N. Smith, Eds. and Trans.). International Publishers.

[81] Wolf, E. R. (1982). Europe and the People Without History. University of California Press.

[82] Gone, J. P. (2013). Redressing First Nations historical trauma: Theorizing mechanisms for Indigenous culture as mental health treatment. Transcultural Psychiatry, 50(5), 683–706.

[83] Kirmayer, L. J., Gone, J. P., & Moses, J. (2007). Rethinking historical trauma. Transcultural Psychiatry, 44(2), 112–136.

[84] Crosby, A. W. (1972). The Columbian Exchange: Biological and Cultural Consequences of 1492. Greenwood Press.

[85] Mann, C. C. (2005). 1491: New Revelations of the Americas Before Columbus. Alfred A. Knopf.

[86] Cook, S. F., & Borah, W. (1979). Essays in Population History: Mexico and the Caribbean. University of California Press.

the social cohesion necessary for sustaining political autonomy, spiritual practices, and subsistence economies. This demographic collapse had distinct economic consequences. From a neoclassical perspective, the massive decline in labour supply in the Americas should have increased wages and reduced output. However, in the colonial context, the opposite occurred. Colonial powers intensified coercive institutions such as the encomienda and repartimiento systems to extract labour from the remnants of Indigenous populations. Rather than allowing market forces to equilibrate supply and demand, colonial capitalism operated through forced labour regimes, enabling accumulation for imperial centres at the expense of demographic catastrophe.[87,88] In contrast, communist analyses interpret this biological devastation not as a random epidemiological tragedy, but as part of a larger process of primitive accumulation, in which land, labour, and bodies were violently appropriated to establish capitalist modes of production. Depopulation created the structural conditions for settler colonialism, emptying territories for resource extraction and plantation agriculture under systems of racialized control.[89] Case studies in North America underscore the interplay of disease and policy. The spread of smallpox through Indigenous trade networks in the Great Plains, prior to direct colonial occupation, fundamentally destabilized regional power structures and economic systems.[90] From a neoclassical economics standpoint, this disruption can be interpreted as a catastrophic supply-side shock. The decimation of labour (i.e., human capital) reduced productive capacity, inhibited trade efficiency, and led to a breakdown of market coordination within and between Indigenous economies. The epidemic effectively distorted the optimal allocation of resources, creating disequilibrium long before formal colonial markets were imposed. In contrast, from a Marxist perspective, the spread of disease functioned as an instrument of primitive accumulation, the violent precondition for capitalist expansion. The weakening of Indigenous populations through smallpox

87 Wolf, E. R. (1982). Europe and the People Without History. University of California Press.

88 Wallerstein, I. (1974). The Modern World-System I: Capitalist Agriculture and the Origins of the European World-Economy in the Sixteenth Century. Academic Press.

89 Engels, F. (1876). The Part Played by Labour in the Transition from Ape to Man. Retrieved from Marxists Internet Archive.

90 Daschuk, J. W. (2013). *Clearing the Plains: Disease, Politics of Starvation, and the Loss of Aboriginal Life*. University of Regina Press.

epidemics prefigured the forcible expropriation of land and destruction of communal modes of production. Disease thus acted as a tool of structural dispossession, softening resistance and enabling capitalist penetration without direct military confrontation. This aligns with analysis that the epidemic was not merely a biological event, but part of a broader settler colonial project aimed at clearing Indigenous people from economically strategic territories.[91] In the Andes, successive epidemics not only reduced population but also facilitated the Spanish mita labour draft by undermining Indigenous leadership.[92] Meanwhile, the decimation of the Taino in the Caribbean within a few decades of Columbus's arrival erased cultural memory and made way for the Atlantic slave trade as a labour substitute, shifting demographic catastrophe from one population to another.[93] Overall, disease was not merely a biological event but a political-economic process. Its impact accelerated the erosion of Indigenous sovereignty, facilitated capitalist expansion, and cemented a legacy of extractive development. The enduring effects of colonial-era biological devastation, manifested through mass depopulation, cultural disintegration, and entrenched structural inequality, continue to shape the lived realities of Indigenous communities today. From a neoclassical perspective, the collapse of Indigenous populations disrupted traditional labour markets and allowed colonial powers to reallocate land and labour in ways that maximized perceived economic efficiency. For example, the demographic decline in North America due to smallpox allowed settlers to acquire land at low cost, transforming subsistence economies into commercial agriculture with minimal resistance. In the Andes, Spanish colonists filled labour shortages created by disease through coercive systems like the mita, channelling Indigenous labour into silver mining at Potosí, which became a cornerstone of Spanish imperial wealth.[94] In contrast, Marxist theory interprets these processes as central to the

[91] Daschuk, J. W. (2013). Clearing the Plains: Disease, Politics of Starvation, and the Loss of Aboriginal Life. University of Regina Press.

[92] Tandeter, E. (1993). Coercion and Market: Silver Mining in Colonial Potosí, 1692–1826. University of New Mexico Press.

[93] Green, T. A. (2019). *The Rise of the Trans-Atlantic Slave Trade in Western Africa, 1300–1589*. Cambridge University Press.

[94] Bakewell, P. (1984) Miners of the Red Mountain: Indian Labour in Potosí, 1545–1650. Albuquerque: University of New Mexico Press.

development of primitive accumulation, the expropriation of Indigenous lands and destruction of communal social relations necessary for capitalist expansion.[95,96] The biological collapse served as a de facto enabler of capitalist imperialism, clearing Indigenous populations from valuable territories and disembodying pre-capitalist systems. Disease was not merely incidental but functioned as a structural instrument aligned with capitalist goals: weaken resistance, fragment societies, and transform people and resources into exploitable commodities. Today, these historical dynamics are visible in the persistent economic marginalization of Indigenous peoples. In Canada, life expectancy among Indigenous populations is up to ten years lower than the national average,[97] and poverty rates remain disproportionately high. In Brazil, Indigenous communities in the Amazon continue to face displacement driven by agribusiness and resource extraction, as well as facing disproportionate poverty and reduced access to healthcare.[98] These are not isolated outcomes but long-term consequences of a global system that weaponized biology and economy to entrench colonial dominance and facilitate capital accumulation.

5.2 *Consequences of Depopulation*

The demographic catastrophe inflicted upon Indigenous populations by European-introduced diseases like smallpox, measles, and influenza not only devastated communities biologically, but also triggered profound social and economic disintegration. In some regions of the Americas, such as central Mexico, population levels declined by as much as 90% within a century of first contact, largely due to smallpox, measles, and

[95] Marx, K. (1867) Capital: A Critique of Political Economy. Volume I. Translated by B. Fowkes. London: Penguin Classics, 1990.

[96] Wallerstein, I. (1974) The Modern World-System I: Capitalist Agriculture and the Origins of the European World-Economy in the Sixteenth Century. New York: Academic Press.

[97] Statistics Canada (2023) Life expectancy and mortality. [Online] Available at: https://www150.statcan.gc.ca/n1/en/subject/life_expectancy_and_mortality [Accessed 8 Jul. 2025].

[98] Instituto Brasileiro de Geografia e Estatística (IBGE) (2022) Indicadores Sociais dos Povos Indígenas no Brasil [Online]. Available at: https://www.ibge.gov.br [Accessed 8 Jul. 2025].

influenza introduced by Europeans.[99,100] This demographic catastrophe destabilized traditional economic systems that were essential to Indigenous societies. In central Mexico, the calpulli system, which organized communal landholding, rotational farming, and reciprocal labour sharing among the Nahua people, was disrupted as deaths eroded the collective capacity to cultivate land and fulfil tribute obligations.[101] Likewise, in the Andes, the ayllu, a kinship-based economic unit foundational to Inka and Quechua societies, coordinated shared agricultural labour (minka), resource redistribution, and social security through communal granaries. The collapse of these structures under the pressure of disease and colonial forced labour regimes such as the mit'a fractured their resilience.[102] In North America, Plains societies such as the Mandan and Hidatsa operated seasonal economies built around maize agriculture, bison hunting, and extensive trade networks along the Missouri River. These economies depended on inter-village alliances and division of labour, which were weakened by epidemics and the resulting loss of leadership and skilled labour.[103] In the Pacific Northwest, potlatch-based redistribution systems structured around clan hierarchy and gift exchange among the Tlingit, Haida, and Kwakwaka'wakw peoples began to erode under population loss and missionary pressure, breaking down mechanisms of social welfare and ceremonial cohesion.[104] The destruction of these systems did not merely represent economic collapse but also the breakdown of cultural identity, political autonomy, and spiritual order, components inseparable from Indigenous economic life. In

[99] Cook, S. F., & Borah, W. (1979). Essays in Population History: Mexico and the Caribbean. University of California Press.

[100] Crosby, A.W. (1972) The Columbian Exchange: Biological and Cultural Consequences of 1492. Westport: Greenwood Press.

[101] Lockhart, J. (1992) The Nahuas After the Conquest: A Social and Cultural History of the Indians of Central Mexico Sixteenth Through Eighteenth Centuries. Stanford: Stanford University Press.

[102] Murra, J.V. (1980) The Economic Organization of the Inka State. Greenwich: JAI Press.

[103] Daschuk, J.W. (2013) Clearing the Plains: Disease, Politics of Starvation, and the Loss of Aboriginal Life. Regina: University of Regina Press.

[104] Codere, H. (1950) Fighting with Property: A Study of Kwakiutl Potlatching and Warfare, 1792–1930. New York: J.J. Augustin.

their place, colonial regimes imposed extractive labour systems, taxation, and market integration, further marginalizing surviving Indigenous communities. From a neoclassical economic perspective, labour shortages might suggest a rise in individual bargaining power or wage levels. However, within colonial systems, these shortages were often met not with market-based adjustments but with coercive responses, such as forced labour systems, slavery, and the repartimiento, as seen in Peru and New Spain.[105,106] The repartimiento was a Spanish colonial labour system that emerged as a formalized replacement for the earlier and even more coercive encomienda system. The encomienda granted Spanish settlers the right to extract labour and tribute from Indigenous communities, ostensibly in exchange for protection and Christian instruction. In practice, it functioned as a form of forced labour akin to slavery, resulting in extreme exploitation and demographic collapse. As criticism of the encomienda grew, particularly from religious reformers such as Bartolomé de las Casas, the Spanish Crown introduced the repartimiento system in the mid-sixteenth century to project a more regulated and ostensibly humanitarian alternative. Under repartimiento (literally "distribution" in Spanish), Indigenous communities in colonial territories such as Peru and New Spain (now Mexico) were legally obliged to provide rotating cohorts of labourers to work for Spanish colonial authorities or private enterprises. These stints, often lasting weeks or months, were formally temporary and compensated with minimal wages, distinguishing them from outright slavery. However, despite the veneer of legality and payment, the repartimiento was deeply exploitative, functioning through state enforcement and enforced by colonial officials or church agents. The repartimiento system, instituted by the Spanish colonial state, was deeply exploitative due to the coercive labour obligations it imposed on Indigenous communities, despite its official framing as a legal and compensated institution. While labourers were nominally free and were supposed to receive wages, in practice, they had little or no autonomy over their participation. Indigenous men were conscripted into rotational labour cycles that were physically demanding, particularly in extractive sectors such as the silver mines of Potosí, where mortality rates were notoriously high

[105] Tandeter, E. (1993). Coercion and Market: Silver Mining in Colonial Potosí, 1692–1826. University of New Mexico Press.

[106] Wallerstein, I. (1974). The Modern World-System I: Capitalist Agriculture and the Origins of the European World-Economy in the Sixteenth Century. Academic Press.

due to harsh conditions, overwork, and exposure to mercury and other toxins.[107] Wages were minimal and often withheld or offset by deductions for food, lodging, and transport, leaving many labourers effectively unpaid.[108] These labour obligations also destabilized Indigenous communities by removing able-bodied men from agricultural production and family life, thereby disrupting subsistence cycles and kinship networks.[109] Additionally, although the system was state-administered, local elites and colonial officials frequently abused their authority, manipulating labour quotas and extending service durations for private gain, while oversight was weak or complicit.[110] Ultimately, the repartimiento operated under the guise of legal reform but functioned as a tool of systemic exploitation and socio-economic disintegration for Indigenous populations. In Peru, the system was most notoriously implemented in Potosí, where thousands of Indigenous men from the Andean highlands were conscripted under the mita, a local variant of the repartimiento, to extract silver under brutal conditions.[111] In New Spain, Indigenous labour was distributed to support Spanish agricultural estates, obrajes (textile workshops), and colonial infrastructure projects, all critical to the colonial economy. Despite its supposed reforms, the repartimiento caused lasting damage to Indigenous societies. Communities were disrupted, displaced, and subjected to gruelling work conditions that led to population decline, cultural disintegration, and economic dependency. The system illustrates how colonial capitalism masked coerced Indigenous labour behind bureaucratic structures, legitimizing exploitation under the guise of state oversight and economic necessity. Far from alleviating suffering, repartimiento institutionalized a form of colonial extraction that reshaped Indigenous life and left enduring legacies of inequality.

[107] Bakewell, P. (1984) Miners of the Red Mountain: Indian Labour in Potosí, 1545–1650. Albuquerque: University of New Mexico Press.

[108] Tandeter, E. (1993). Coercion and Market: Silver Mining in Colonial Potosí, 1692–1826. University of New Mexico Press.

[109] Wallerstein, I. (1974) The Modern World-System I: Capitalist Agriculture and the Origins of the European World-Economy in the Sixteenth Century. New York: Academic Press.

[110] Wolf, E.R. (1982) Europe and the People Without History. Berkeley: University of California Press.

[111] Bakewell, P. (1984) Miners of the Red Mountain: Indian Labour in Potosí, 1545–1650. Albuquerque: University of New Mexico Press.

The assumption that markets efficiently allocate labour fails to hold in such exploitative contexts where Indigenous labour was not a freely moving factor but a resource to be captured. In contrast, communist economic theory might interpret the communal reorganization of Indigenous societies during this era as a form of resilient social production, relying less on hierarchical accumulation and more on kinship-based redistribution. In many Andean communities, ayllu structures endured through demographic trauma, enabling the reconstitution of political life and local autonomy even under Spanish domination. Ayllu[112] structures were the foundational socio-economic units of Indigenous Andean societies, particularly among the Quechua and Aymara peoples. These structures persisted before and during the Inca Empire and were integral to organizing kinship, land tenure, labour, and governance.[113] An ayllu was composed of extended kin groups claiming descent from a common ancestor, often mythologized, and its members were tied to specific ecological zones, facilitating a highly localized sense of identity and community.[114] Land was held communally, with no concept of private property. Individual families cultivated allocated plots, but these were inalienable and could not be sold or inherited outside the ayllu. The land was subdivided into sections for family use, state tribute (mit'a), and religious offerings. Labour obligations were organized around reciprocal systems rather than wage labour: ayni referred to mutual aid among neighbours; minka involved community labour for collective projects; and mit'a was a rotational labour service for the state.[115,116] These systems embedded work within a moral economy of reciprocity and redistribution. Economically, the ayllu system was highly adaptive. Many communities employed a "vertical archipelago" model, maintaining agricultural plots across multiple altitudes to maximize productivity, potatoes in the

[112] Wolf, E. R. (1982). Europe and the People Without History. University of California Press.

[113] Murra, J.V. (1980) The Economic Organization of the Inka State. Greenwich: JAI Press.

[114] Wachtel, N. (1977) The Vision of the Vanquished: The Spanish Conquest of Peru through Indian Eyes. New York: Harvester Press.

[115] Murra, J.V. (1980) The Economic Organization of the Inka State. Greenwich: JAI Press.

[116] Rostworowski, M. (1999) History of the Inca Realm. Cambridge: Cambridge University Press.

highlands and maize in the lower valleys, for instance.[117] This system minimized risk and ensured subsistence across environmental zones. Politically, ayllus were overseen by kurakas (local chiefs), who administered labour obligations, adjudicated disputes, and conducted religious rites centred on sacred sites (wak'as), reinforcing cosmological and territorial cohesion.[118] Colonialism disrupted but did not entirely dismantle the ayllu. The Spanish co-opted mit'a labour for silver mining, especially at Potosí, transforming reciprocal service into exploitative forced labour. Tribute systems were intensified, and land privatization gradually eroded communal landholdings. While the ayllu persisted in form, its function shifted under colonial pressures towards facilitating extraction rather than sustaining Indigenous lifeways.[119] Similarly, Indigenous groups in North America, such as the Haudenosaunee Confederacy, reorganized politically and militarily in response to depopulation and external threats, illustrating a remarkable adaptability.[120] The psychological and institutional damage of depopulation also affected intergenerational knowledge transmission, agricultural practices, and cultural memory. However, responses were not merely passive. Communities frequently restructured by forming new kinship bonds, integrating remnants of disbanded groups, and reviving ceremonial practices to reaffirm cosmological coherence.[121] For example, in the aftermath of demographic collapse caused by disease and colonial violence, many Andean ayllus, traditional kin-based communities, absorbed survivors from neighbouring, decimated groups. These integrations often transcended lineage boundaries, allowing for broader coalitions to maintain agricultural systems and political representation under colonial rule.[122] In North America, some Indigenous nations like

[117] Murra, J.V. (1980) The Economic Organization of the Inka State. Greenwich: JAI Press.

[118] Wachtel, N. (1977) The Vision of the Vanquished: The Spanish Conquest of Peru through Indian Eyes. New York: Harvester Press.

[119] Platt, T. (1982) 'The Andean Experience of Bolivian Liberalism, 1825–1900', in State and Peasant in Latin America.

[120] Mann, C. C. (2005). 1491: New Revelations of the Americas Before Columbus. Alfred A. Knopf.

[121] Kirmayer, L.J., Gone, J.P., & Moses, J. (2007) 'Rethinking Historical Trauma', Transcultural Psychiatry, 44(2), pp. 112–138.

[122] Murra, J.V. (1980) The Economic Organization of the Inka State. Greenwich: JAI Press.

the Haudenosaunee (Iroquois Confederacy) offered sanctuary to war refugees and disease survivors from other tribes, incorporating them through formal adoption rituals and clan realignment, thereby strengthening their confederation despite population losses.[123] Similarly, among the Pueblo peoples of the American Southwest, revitalization movements emerged that blended ancestral cosmologies with new ceremonial cycles, such as the reemergence of kachina dances, as a way to heal communal trauma and reinforce identity in the face of Spanish suppression.[124] These adaptive strategies served not only to replenish population and labour capacity but also to reaffirm ontological frameworks, allowing communities to symbolically re-anchor themselves within their sacred landscapes, thereby resisting cultural erasure. These adaptations challenge deterministic economic models that view Indigenous societies as permanently debilitated by population loss. Importantly, depopulation increased Indigenous vulnerability to conquest and colonization. With fewer people to resist encroachment, European powers could impose territorial claims and resource extraction regimes with greater ease. Yet, in the Canadian context, disease and starvation were often weaponized as tools of state policy, not just unintended consequences.[125] This underscores how demographic collapse was not merely a backdrop to imperial expansion but an instrument of it, embedded within the broader political economy of colonial capitalism (Table 1).

6 The Columbian Exchange and Environmental Transformation

6.1 Bi-directional Transfer of Species and Practices

The Columbian Exchange initiated one of the most transformative ecological and economic revolutions in global history, with far-reaching consequences for Indigenous societies, European economies, and the planetary environment. At its core, the Exchange involved a bi-directional

[123] Richter, D.K. (2001) Facing East from Indian Country: A Native History of Early America. Cambridge, MA: Harvard University Press.

[124] Schaafsma, P. (2001) Pueblo Cultures and Resistance in the Southwest. Santa Fe: School of American Research Press.

[125] Daschuk, J. W. (2013). Clearing the Plains: Disease, Politics of Starvation, and the Loss of Aboriginal Life. University of Regina Press.

Table 1 Neoclassical economics, Marxian economics, and traditional indigenous economics systems

Dimension	*Neoclassical economics*	*Marxian economics*	*Traditional indigenous economic systems*
Core assumption	Rational individuals maximize utility; markets allocate resources efficiently	Historical materialism; economic structures shaped by class struggle and exploitation	Reciprocity, kinship, and cosmological balance guide production and distribution
Labour	A factor of production priced by supply and demand; scarcity increases wages	Exploited through systems of coerced labour; key to capitalist primitive accumulation	Organized through communal obligations (*ayni*, *minka*, *mit'a*); labour embedded in kinship and ritual systems
Response to depopulation	Predicts labour scarcity increases bargaining power and reduces output	Depopulation facilitates land appropriation and forced labour regimes (e.g., *encomienda*, *mita*)	Communities adapt via kinship reconstruction, ceremonial renewal, and integrating remnants of other groups (e.g., Andean *ayllus*, Haudenosaunee Confederacy)
View on disease impact	Seen as a supply-side shock disrupting labour markets and productive capacity	Viewed as a structural tool of colonial domination enabling accumulation and dispossession	Disrupts subsistence and social order, but also triggers cultural and social resilience through ritual and reorganization
Land ownership	Private ownership maximizes efficiency and incentivizes use	Land seized and commodified for capitalist production (e.g., plantations, mining)	Land held communally (e.g., *calpulli* in Mesoamerica, *ayllu* in the Andes); linked to spirituality and sustainability

Dimension	*Neoclassical economics*	*Marxian economics*	*Traditional indigenous economic systems*
Economic rationality	Efficiency, utility-maximization, and equilibrium drive decisions	Driven by class interests, surplus extraction, and capital accumulation	Economic life embedded in moral and spiritual obligations; emphasis on balance, reciprocity, and stewardship
Labour systems under colonialism	Forced labour distorts efficient markets (e.g., *repartimiento*, *mit'a*)	Forced labour is central to capitalist expansion via primitive accumulation	Original reciprocal systems co-opted into coercive labour regimes (e.g., *mit'a* turned into mining conscription in Potosí)
Adaptation to collapse	Assumes reallocation of labour and capital restores equilibrium	Collapse of Indigenous society facilitates capitalist expansion and settler colonialism	Adaptive strategies include spiritual revival (e.g., kachina dances), clan realignment, and absorption of refugees (e.g., Pueblo peoples, Haudenosaunee adoption practices)
Impact of depopulation	Loss of human capital reduces productivity and weakens markets	Creates structural conditions for dispossession, labour control, and racialized inequality	Disrupts economies and cultures but also triggers reorganization and resistance strategies rooted in collective memory and ceremony

Source Author

flow of species, diseases, crops, animals, and agricultural practices between the Old and New Worlds following 1492. The introduction of European livestock, especially horses, cattle, pigs, and sheep, into the Americas profoundly altered Indigenous ecologies and subsistence strategies. Horses reconfigured the mobility and warfare capabilities of Plains societies such as the Comanche and Lakota, enabling expanded territorial control but also intensifying intertribal conflict and dependency on bison economies.[126] Meanwhile, cattle and pigs devastated native flora through overgrazing, disrupted traditional land-use systems, and facilitated settler colonial agriculture by displacing Indigenous food systems.[127] This radically altered both ecological and cultural landscapes. These non-native animals overgrazed and trampled native plants, destroying traditional foraging grounds and disrupting the ecological balance essential to Indigenous hunting, gathering, and small-scale cultivation. The resulting degradation of native flora changed soil composition, encouraged the spread of invasive species, and reduced biodiversity, making it difficult for many edible and medicinal plants to regenerate. This ecological upheaval directly removed key resources from Indigenous diets and traditional healing practices. Additionally, settler expansion disrupted established Indigenous land-use systems, such as controlled burning, seasonal harvesting, and crop rotation, which were either suppressed or replaced by colonial land management practices. These practices prioritized fenced grazing lands and monocultural farming over sustainable, place-based methods. Place-based methods refer to ecological and cultural practices specifically adapted to the local environment, climate, and ecosystem in which a community lives. Rooted in generations of observation, experience, and interaction with the land, these methods are central to Indigenous knowledge systems. They are ecologically tailored to soil types, rainfall patterns, seasonal cycles, and biodiversity. For instance, Indigenous communities in arid regions have developed drought-resistant cropping and water-harvesting techniques, while those in forested areas practice agroforestry suited to dense vegetation. There are many distinctive examples of place-based methods. Aboriginal Australians have long used controlled burning to manage bushland, reduce wildfire risk, and promote

[126] Hämäläinen, P. (2008) *The Comanche Empire*. New Haven: Yale University Press.

[127] Crosby, A.W. (1972) The Columbian Exchange: Biological and Cultural Consequences of 1492. Westport: Greenwood Press.

biodiversity. The Aztecs developed chinampas, or floating gardens, to cultivate crops in shallow lakebeds, demonstrating sophisticated water and land management in wetland environments. In the Andes, Indigenous farmers built terraced fields into steep mountain slopes to prevent erosion and control water flow. Along the Pacific Northwest coast, communities practiced rotational harvesting and hunting aligned with seasonal cycles to avoid resource depletion. These methods are not merely technical or ecological, they are also cultural, spiritual, and relational. They reflect a worldview in which the land is seen as kin or ancestor rather than a commodity, emphasizing reciprocity and stewardship. Because they are deeply adapted to specific environments, place-based methods tend to be sustainable over long timeframes, maintaining ecological balance and ensuring the survival of both ecosystems and human communities across generations. However, in settler colonial contexts, these systems were often disregarded, criminalized, or displaced by industrial agriculture, which introduced standardized methods unsuited to local conditions. This led to ecological degradation, the erosion of biodiversity, and the suppression of Indigenous cultural practices and land-based knowledge. The introduction of livestock facilitated settler colonial agriculture and enabled the imposition of private land ownership, ultimately marginalizing Indigenous knowledge systems and displacing their food sovereignty. Conversely, American crops such as maize, potatoes, cassava, and tomatoes were transported to Europe, Asia, and Africa, where they dramatically enhanced caloric intake and population growth. The potato, for example, became a dietary staple in Ireland, Germany, and Russia, contributing to a near doubling of Europe's population between 1500 and 1800.[128] From a neoclassical economic perspective, these transfers represent significant positive supply shocks that expanded agricultural productivity and diversified consumption preferences. Yet this framing overlooks the uneven distribution of gains, and the social costs imposed on Indigenous communities. The transfer of livestock and plantation crops often facilitated land expropriation and labour exploitation in the Americas, particularly through the expansion of settler economies and coerced labour systems like the encomienda and transatlantic slavery. On the other hand, Marxist interpretations view the Columbian Exchange

[128] Nunn, N. and Qian, N. (2011) 'The Potato's Contribution to Population and Urbanization: Evidence from a Historical Experiment', Quarterly Journal of Economics, 126(2), pp. 593–650.

not as a neutral ecological process, but as a mechanism of primitive accumulation that violently restructured global production. The global movement of species, especially cash crops like sugar and tobacco, supported the development of a capitalist world-economy rooted in slavery, dispossession, and ecological degradation.[129,130] Crops introduced to Europe enabled surplus extraction and urbanization, while the ecological disruption in the Americas facilitated the erasure of Indigenous agricultural knowledge and subsistence autonomy. The commodification of land, plants, and animals was central to this process, transforming nature into an instrument of colonial profit. In ecological terms, the Columbian Exchange triggered widespread biotic homogenization. Invasive European weeds and domesticated animals displaced native species and degraded soils, while monoculture farming practices replaced biodiverse Indigenous methods. This ecological restructuring intensified under capitalist modes of production, privileging yield over sustainability. Yet Indigenous societies often resisted or selectively integrated new species into their existing agroecological frameworks. The Andean highlands, for example, saw the incorporation of sheep alongside continued use of traditional camelids (llamas and alpacas), preserving elements of pre-colonial resilience.[131] Thus, the Columbian Exchange was not merely a biological event, but a politically and economically mediated transformation that reshaped global demography, ecology, and labour. While it contributed to increased productivity and global integration, its benefits were asymmetrically distributed and often came at the cost of Indigenous displacement and environmental degradation.

6.2 *Environmental and Cultural Consequences*

The environmental repercussions of the Columbian Exchange extended far beyond the introduction of new species. European agricultural practices, imposed through colonial expansion, fundamentally displaced

[129] Moore, J.W. (2010) 'The End of the Road? Agricultural Revolutions in the Capitalist World-Ecology, 1450–2010', Journal of Agrarian Change, 10(3), pp. 389–413.

[130] Wallerstein, I. (1974) The Modern World-System I: Capitalist Agriculture and the Origins of the European World-Economy in the Sixteenth Century. New York: Academic Press.

[131] Murra, J.V. (1980) The Economic Organization of the Inka State. Greenwich: JAI Press.

Indigenous agroecological systems that had been adapted to diverse local environments over millennia. Practices such as monoculture, deforestation, and overgrazing not only degraded ecosystems but also undermined cultural knowledge systems rooted in sustainable land use. In regions like Brazil and the Caribbean, the plantation economy prioritized sugar, tobacco, and cotton for export, transforming biodiverse landscapes into monocultural estates.[132] This transition drastically reduced soil fertility and increased dependency on imported food, eroding local food sovereignty. From a neoclassical economic standpoint, these changes were framed as rational reallocations of land and labour towards 'comparative advantage' in global trade. However, such models neglect the social and ecological externalities, including biodiversity loss, declining water quality, and soil exhaustion. For example, the expansion of cattle ranching in the Argentine Pampas and northern Mexico, driven by European demand, contributed to massive deforestation and erosion of native grasslands.[133] In contrast, Indigenous agroecological systems such as the Andean waru waru (raised field agriculture) or Mesoamerican milpa (polyculture of maize, beans, and squash) maintained ecological resilience and soil fertility through crop rotation, fallowing, and reciprocal labour systems.[134] From a Marxian perspective, the environmental degradation following European colonization is understood as part of the metabolic rift: a disruption of the organic relationship between humans and nature under capitalist accumulation.[135] The imposition of plantation monoculture and extractive agriculture alienated Indigenous communities from their means of subsistence and transformed land into a commodity. In this sense, environmental degradation was not accidental but integral to the process of primitive accumulation, stripping Indigenous people of land, autonomy, and ecological knowledge. The replacement of Indigenous land management with extractive colonial regimes also had profound cultural consequences. Sacred groves, rotational forest gardens, and

[132] Moore, J.W. (2010) 'The End of the Road? Agricultural Revolutions in the Capitalist World-Ecology, 1450–2010', Journal of Agrarian Change, 10(3), pp. 389–413.

[133] Hämäläinen, P. (2008) The Comanche Empire. New Haven: Yale University Press.

[134] Murra, J.V. (1980) The Economic Organization of the Inka State. Greenwich: JAI Press.

[135] Foster, J.B. (2000) Marx's Ecology: Materialism and Nature. New York: Monthly Review Press.

ceremonial landscapes were cleared to make way for commercial agriculture. European livestock, especially pigs and cattle, roamed freely, destroying Indigenous fields and polluting water sources. This not only disrupted ecological systems but also desecrated cosmological geographies and rituals tied to land. For many Indigenous cultures, specific rivers, mountains, and forests are not just natural resources but sacred entities embedded with ancestral presence, spiritual meaning, and ceremonial function. The destruction of these landscapes through mining, dam construction, or deforestation severed relationships between people and place, making it difficult to carry out rites of passage, seasonal ceremonies, or offerings that maintain balance in both the material and spiritual world. For instance, the flooding of traditional territories due to hydroelectric projects in Canada submerged burial grounds and sacred sites, erasing centuries of cultural continuity and violating Indigenous legal and moral frameworks. Across North America, the buffalo herds were decimated not just for hides and meat but as a military strategy to destroy Indigenous economies based on hunting and mobility, further entrenching settler colonial control.[136] Ultimately, the environmental transformation catalysed by the Columbian Exchange represents more than ecological change; it marks the systematic dismantling of Indigenous knowledge systems in favour of extractive and unsustainable modes of production. These processes are not historical footnotes but remain embedded in contemporary land inequality, food insecurity, and ecological crises across the Indigenous world.

7 Capitalism, Imperialism, and the Global Expansion Drive

7.1 The Role of Early Capitalism in Driving European Expansion

The emergence of early capitalism in Europe during the 15th to seventeenth centuries provided the structural foundations for global imperial expansion. Central to this transformation were the rise of new financial institutions, such as public banks and bills of exchange, and the creation of joint-stock companies like the Dutch East India Company (VOC) and

[136] Wallerstein, I. (1974) *The Modern World-System I: Capitalist Agriculture and the Origins of the European World-Economy in the Sixteenth Century*. New York: Academic Press.

the British East India Company. These entities pooled investor capital, reduced individual risk, and offered the logistical coordination necessary for long-distance trade and conquest. Mercantilist policies, grounded in the idea that national wealth depended on a favourable balance of trade and accumulation of precious metals, incentivized overseas expansion as European powers competed to control colonies and trade routes. Such institutions were deeply embedded in state-building and militarization, with joint-stock companies often operating as quasi-sovereign powers, raising armies, minting currency, and signing treaties.[137] From a neoclassical economic perspective, these developments can be interpreted as institutional innovations that reduced transaction costs and information asymmetries, enabling more efficient capital allocation and global market integration. However, this analysis often overlooks the violence, dispossession, and coercive labour systems required to sustain such efficiency. For example, the VOC's operations in Indonesia involved forced monopolies on spices, brutal suppression of local resistance, and the destruction of native production systems that conflicted with Dutch commercial aims.[138] The Spanish silver galleon trade linking Potosí, Manila, and Seville exemplified how state-backed capital accumulation operated through extraction, not voluntary exchange. By contrast, Marxist economic theory views early capitalist expansion as the historical phase of "primitive accumulation", wherein capital was amassed through expropriation rather than production.[139] This included the plundering of the Americas, the slave trade, and the violent restructuring of global labour systems. The Atlantic triangle trade and plantation economies were not market-neutral developments, but deliberately racialized structures of accumulation that transformed enslaved Africans and colonized Indigenous peoples into sources of surplus value. These patterns marked the transition into a capitalist world-economy based on a core-periphery dynamic, where European cores extracted value from colonial peripheries

[137] Subrahmanyam, S. (1997) The Career and Legend of Vasco da Gama. Cambridge: Cambridge University Press.

[138] Boxer, C.R. (1965) The Dutch Seaborne Empire, 1600–1800. London: Hutchinson.

[139] Marx, K. (1867) Capital: A Critique of Political Economy. Volume I. Translated by B. Fowkes. London: Penguin Classics, 1990.

through asymmetrical trade and coercion.[140] For example, raw materials like cotton from India, sugar from the Caribbean, and rubber from the Congo were exported under exploitative conditions to fuel industrial production in Britain, France, and other European powers. Manufactured goods were then sold back to colonized regions at inflated prices, reinforcing dependency. In the Americas, enslaved Africans were forced to labour on plantations producing commodities for European markets, generating immense wealth for the core while impoverishing the peripheries. This unequal system was maintained through military conquest, colonial administration, and trade monopolies such as those operated by the British and Dutch East India Companies. Ultimately, the early capitalist impulse for global expansion was not merely commercial but systemic. It depended on the fusion of state power and private capital, with imperialism functioning as capitalism's military and logistical arm. The expansion of European empires was not the byproduct of competitive markets alone, but the result of deliberate policy to subordinate foreign territories, resources, and peoples to the logic of capital accumulation.

7.2 Profit-Driven Exploitation of Land and Labour

The expansion of European capitalism during the colonial period was inseparable from the violent expropriation of Indigenous land and the systematic exploitation of Indigenous labour. The logic of profit maximization, central to emerging capitalist systems, incentivized aggressive resource extraction and coerced labour practices. In contrast to the normative assumptions of neoclassical economics, which frame markets as neutral, self-correcting mechanisms that efficiently allocate resources, this process was neither peaceful nor equitable. Neoclassical models largely overlook the role of coercion and dispossession, instead portraying expansion through the lens of comparative advantage or capital accumulation. However, Marxist and anti-colonial theorists argued that imperialism represented capitalism's final and most exploitative stage, where capital sought new frontiers for surplus extraction via militarized expansion

[140] Wallerstein, I. (1974) The Modern World-System I: Capitalist Agriculture and the Origins of the European World-Economy in the Sixteenth Century. New York: Academic Press.

and domination.[141,142] In the Americas, this was exemplified through forced labour systems such as the encomienda and repartimiento, which converted Indigenous workers into a coerced labour force to support colonial agricultural and mining economies.[143,144] Silver extraction from Potosí in the Andean highlands illustrates how Indigenous bodies were commodified under colonial capitalism; conscripted miners were overworked and underpaid, and mortality rates were devastating.[145] In North America, settler colonialism and plantation slavery institutionalized the capitalist imperative of land accumulation and labour discipline. This is evident in the rise of plantation economies in the American South and Caribbean, which replaced depopulated Indigenous societies with enslaved African labour.[146] From a neoclassical perspective, these labour reallocations might appear as rational responses to resource scarcities or demographic shifts. But this framing erases the systemic violence and structural coercion underpinning colonial economic systems. Marxist analysis, in contrast, interprets these events through the lens of primitive accumulation, wherein land, bodies, and social systems were forcibly restructured to facilitate capitalist relations of production.[147,148] This process not only disrupted Indigenous economic sovereignty but also laid the foundations for the global capitalist order by transforming colonized regions into resource frontiers for European markets. Moreover, environmental exploitation was integral to capitalist expansion. European powers deforested vast areas, introduced monocultures, and depleted

[141] Williams, E. (1944) Capitalism and Slavery. Chapel Hill: University of North Carolina Press.

[142] Lenin, V.I. (1917) Imperialism: The Highest Stage of Capitalism. New York: International Publishers.

[143] Bakewell, P. (1984) Miners of the Red Mountain: Indian Labour in Potosí, 1545–1650. Albuquerque: University of New Mexico Press.

[144] Tandeter, E. (1993) Coercion and Market: Silver Mining in Colonial Potosí, 1692–1826. Albuquerque: University of New Mexico Press.

[145] Wallerstein, I. (1974) The Modern World-System I: Capitalist Agriculture and the Origins of the European World-Economy in the Sixteenth Century. New York: Academic Press.

[146] Beckert, S. (2014) Empire of Cotton: A Global History. New York: Knopf.

[147] Marx, K. (1867) Capital: A Critique of Political Economy. Volume I. Translated by B. Fowkes. London: Penguin Classics, 1990.

[148] Federici, S. (2004) Caliban and the Witch: Women, the Body and Primitive Accumulation. New York: Autonomedia.

Indigenous-managed ecosystems to maximize profits.[149,150] Such practices were embedded within a global imperial apparatus supported by institutions like the Dutch and British East India Companies, which leveraged state and military power to secure profitable trade monopolies and suppress Indigenous resistance.[151,152] In this way, capitalist imperialism constructed a world-system wherein Indigenous land and labour were systematically appropriated to fuel capital accumulation at the metropole.

8 Resistance, Adaptation, and Cultural Survival

8.1 Indigenous Resistance Movements

Throughout the era of European expansion, Indigenous peoples across the world mounted sustained and multifaceted resistance to imperial domination. These efforts took the form of military conflict, diplomatic negotiation, strategic alliances, and cultural resilience. The Pueblo Revolt of 1680 in the American Southwest stands as one of the most successful uprisings against colonial rule. Led by Popé, Pueblo communities united across linguistic and regional lines to expel Spanish forces from present-day New Mexico for over a decade.[153] Similarly, the Mapuche of southern Chile resisted Spanish, and later Chilean and Argentinian, incursions for over 300 years through guerrilla warfare and mobile pastoral strategies that undermined settler encroachment.[154] In Africa, Queen Nzinga of Ndongo and Matamba in present-day Angola employed a combination of military resistance and diplomacy to counter Portuguese colonialism and slave raids. Her use of shifting alliances with the Dutch, her adaptation of Christian iconography for political legitimacy, and her tactical

[149] Crosby, A.W. (1972) The Columbian Exchange: Biological and Cultural Consequences of 1492. Westport: Greenwood Press.

[150] Moore, J.W. (2010) 'The End of the Road? Agricultural Revolutions in the Capitalist World-Ecology, 1450–2010', Journal of Agrarian Change, 10(3), pp. 389–413.

[151] Boxer, C.R. (1965) The Dutch Seaborne Empire, 1600–1800. London: Hutchinson.

[152] Subrahmanyam, S. (1997) The Career and Legend of Vasco da Gama. Cambridge: Cambridge University Press.

[153] Knaut, A.L. (1995) *The Pueblo Revolt of 1680: Conquest and Resistance in Seventeenth-Century New Mexico*. Norman: University of Oklahoma Press.

[154] Bengoa, J. (2000) *Historia del pueblo mapuche: Siglos XIX y XX*. Santiago: LOM Ediciones.

relocations illustrate how Indigenous leaders manipulated imperial divisions to prolong autonomy.[155] These resistance movements were not merely reactions to military conquest but also challenges to the political economy of colonialism. From a Marxist perspective, Indigenous uprisings can be interpreted as struggles against primitive accumulation, where resistance was aimed not only at preserving sovereignty but also at protecting communal land tenure and labour systems from commodification.[156,157] Neoclassical economic theory, which assumes rational actors within efficient markets, fails to account for such resistance. It tends to obscure how colonial expansion disrupted existing non-market institutions and relied on coercion rather than voluntary exchange. For instance, Indigenous resistance often erupted when colonial regimes imposed tribute systems, expropriated land for monoculture, or conscripted labour into mines and plantations—conditions that were framed as "development" under mercantilist logic but in fact represented extraction and violence. Despite extreme depopulation, technological disadvantage, and strategic marginalization, Indigenous groups adapted through flexible leadership structures, spiritual revitalization, and intertribal confederations. The Iroquois Confederacy (Haudenosaunee), for example, maintained a sophisticated system of federal governance and diplomatic engagement with both British and French empires during the seventeenth and eighteenth centuries, preserving autonomy through balance-of-power politics.[158] These resistance movements reveal that far from being passive victims of colonialism, Indigenous peoples actively contested imperial expansion with strategies rooted in historical memory, cultural continuity, and political innovation.

[155] Heywood, L.M. (2017) *Njinga of Angola: Africa's Warrior Queen*. Cambridge, MA: Harvard University Press.

[156] Federici, S. (2004) *Caliban and the Witch: Women, the Body and Primitive Accumulation*. New York: Autonomedia.

[157] Marx, K. (1867) *Capital: A Critique of Political Economy. Volume I*. Translated by B. Fowkes. London: Penguin Classics, 1990.

[158] Richter, D.K. (2001) *Facing East from Indian Country: A Native History of Early America*. Cambridge, MA: Harvard University Press.

8.2 *Cultural Adaptation and Syncretism*

Despite the catastrophic upheavals triggered by colonial expansion, many Indigenous societies developed resilient strategies of cultural adaptation and syncretism. Rather than being passive recipients of European domination, Indigenous peoples selectively appropriated elements of colonial material culture, such as metal tools, horses, firearms, and writing systems, while simultaneously safeguarding and reconfiguring their spiritual beliefs, oral histories, and systems of governance. This cultural hybridity did not signal assimilation but represented an active, creative response to structural violence. For example, in the Andes, Quechua communities integrated Catholic saints into existing cosmologies, identifying them with traditional deities and incorporating them into local festivals and rituals.[159] Churches were often built atop sacred wak'as (ancestral shrines), symbolizing both domination and continuity. Similarly, the Virgin of Copacabana in Bolivia became a central figure of Indigenous devotion, embodying both Marian and Andean spiritual attributes.[160] In North America, Pueblo peoples, after the suppression of the 1680 revolt, continued to practice kachina ceremonies under the guise of Christian ritual, ensuring the survival of their cosmological frameworks.[161] This syncretism was not merely spiritual but political. Clan systems, councils, and forms of consensus-based governance persisted under colonial rule, even when Indigenous nations formally adopted European-style constitutions, as seen with the Haudenosaunee Confederacy's influence on the U.S. Constitution.[162] The Haudenosaunee Confederacy, also known as the Iroquois Confederacy or the Six Nations, played an indirect but significant role in influencing democratic thought in colonial North America, particularly in relation to federalism, unity, and constitutional design. Formed around 1142 CE, it is considered one of the oldest participatory democracies in the world. The Confederacy originally

[159] Wachtel, N. (1977) The Vision of the Vanquished: The Spanish Conquest of Peru through Indian Eyes. New York: Harvester Press.

[160] Rostworowski, M. (1999) History of the Inca Realm. Cambridge: Cambridge University Press.

[161] Knaut, A.L. (1995) The Pueblo Revolt of 1680: Conquest and Resistance in Seventeenth-Century New Mexico. Norman: University of Oklahoma Press.

[162] Richter, D.K. (2001) Facing East from Indian Country: A Native History of Early America. Cambridge, MA: Harvard University Press.

united five, and later six, Indigenous nations in the northeastern woodlands: Mohawk, Oneida, Onondaga, Cayuga, Seneca, and Tuscarora. Its governance was structured under the Great Law of Peace, an oral constitution that emphasized consensus, division of powers, and the responsibilities and accountability of leadership. This system provided a real-life model of a union of autonomous nations operating under a shared framework, like the federal structure eventually adopted by the United States, which sought to balance power between individual states and a central authority. Council procedures within the Confederacy emphasized deliberation and consensus, with distinct roles allocated to clan mothers (who selected chiefs), peace chiefs, and war chiefs, demonstrating early practices of checks and balances and institutional accountability. During the eighteenth century, colonial figures such as Benjamin Franklin, Thomas Jefferson, and John Adams interacted with Haudenosaunee leaders. Franklin expressed admiration for their political unity, rhetorically asking whether the American colonies should not be able to form a union if six "nations of ignorant savages" had done so. Indigenous political structures were not merely observed by colonists but actively engaged with and, in some cases, emulated.[163] The Continental Congress received Haudenosaunee diplomats, and the use of wampum belts and traditional diplomatic protocols shaped treaty-making practices. Nevertheless, scholars differ on the degree of influence the Confederacy had on the U.S. Constitution. Some suggest its impact was largely symbolic or rhetorical, while others argue it formed part of the broader intellectual environment that helped shape American republicanism, even though Indigenous peoples were ultimately excluded from the constitutional process itself. Even if not formally acknowledged, the Haudenosaunee Confederacy contributed a functioning and longstanding model of confederated governance, which left a mark on the political thinking of early American leaders searching for democratic models in a new world. Nevertheless, from a neoclassical economic perspective, these adaptations can be interpreted as rational utility-maximizing responses to new constraints and opportunities, strategies to optimize survival and cultural coherence in disrupted economic environments. However, this perspective often ignores the symbolic, spiritual, and collective dimensions of Indigenous decision-making, reducing adaptation to market logic.

[163] Richter, D.K. (2001) Facing East from Indian Country: A Native History of Early America. Cambridge, MA: Harvard University Press.

In contrast, a Marxist analysis sees syncretism as part of the broader dialectic of resistance under domination: a cultural "counter-hegemony" that preserved non-capitalist worldviews in the face of primitive accumulation.[164,165] Cultural adaptation served as a form of subaltern agency that undermined total colonial control and laid the foundation for long-term resilience. Even in regions where colonial regimes imposed forced labour systems like the repartimiento or slavery, Indigenous languages, kinship structures, and performative traditions endured. The survival of Nahuatl as a lingua franca in colonial Mexico, or Mapudungun among the Mapuche in Chile, highlights how oral traditions served as repositories of communal memory and resistance.[166,167] These forms of cultural continuity enabled Indigenous societies to adapt not by erasure, but through synthesis, safeguarding their ontologies and collective identities while navigating colonial impositions.

9 Gendered Impacts of Colonization

9.1 *Disruption of Indigenous Gender Roles*

Colonialism fundamentally restructured Indigenous gender relations, replacing diverse and often egalitarian systems with patriarchal norms rooted in European legal, religious, and economic ideologies. In many Indigenous societies, gender roles were fluid and often complementary, with women holding political, spiritual, and economic authority. For instance, among the Haudenosaunee (Iroquois), clan mothers wielded considerable influence in political decisions and selected male chiefs.[168] Similarly, Inca society institutionalized dual-gender roles within its state administration, reflecting a broader Andean cosmology that valued gender

[164] Gramsci, A. (1971) Selections from the Prison Notebooks. Edited by Q. Hoare and G.N. Smith. New York: International Publishers.

[165] Federici, S. (2004) Caliban and the Witch: Women, the Body and Primitive Accumulation. New York: Autonomedia.

[166] Bengoa, J. (2000) Historia del pueblo mapuche: Siglos XIX y XX. Santiago: LOM Ediciones.

[167] Lockhart, J. (1992) *The Nahuas After the Conquest: A Social and Cultural History of the Indians of Central Mexico, Sixteenth Through Eighteenth Centuries*. Stanford: Stanford University Press.

[168] Allen, P.G. (1992) The Sacred Hoop: Recovering the Feminine in American Indian Traditions. Boston: Beacon Press.

complementarity rather than hierarchy. Men and women held parallel but distinct offices at every level of governance, ensuring that both masculine and feminine domains were represented in political, economic, and religious life. One key example was the aclla system, in which selected women, known as acllas or "chosen women", were removed from their communities and trained in state-run institutions. These women performed vital religious functions, such as preparing ritual offerings and maintaining sacred fires, while also engaging in high-status economic production, including the creation of fine textiles and chicha (corn beer) used in state ceremonies. The acllas operated under female leadership, often mirroring the authority of male priests and bureaucrats, and their labour supported both imperial rituals and redistribution systems. This system exemplified how gender roles in the Inca Empire were not merely symbolic but structurally embedded in governance, production, and ideology, affirming a political economy that recognized and institutionalized gendered forms of power.[169] However, the imposition of colonial patriarchy, undergirded by Christian doctrine and European legal frameworks, led to the erosion of these roles. The Spanish colonial state marginalized Andean women by dissolving traditional communal landholding practices that had secured their economic autonomy. Institutions like the encomienda and repartimiento systems conscripted male labour, further displacing women's roles in agriculture and governance.[170] Missionary conversion campaigns targeted matrilineal traditions and spiritual leadership among women, replacing them with rigid nuclear family models and male-centric religious hierarchies.[171] From a neoclassical economic perspective, colonial economic systems interpreted labour through rigid gender binaries that aligned with the theory's assumptions about productivity, utility, and market value. Neoclassical economics, which privileges quantifiable labour, individual rational choice, and market exchange, categorized only wage-earning, commodified labour as "productive". Within this framework, colonial administrations and capitalist enterprises systematically constructed women's labour, particularly in

[169] Silverblatt, I. (1987) Moon, Sun, and Witches: Gender Ideologies and Class in Inca and Colonial Peru. Princeton: Princeton University Press.

[170] Federici, S. (2004) Caliban and the Witch: Women, the Body and Primitive Accumulation. New York: Autonomedia.

[171] Oyěwùmí, O. (1997) The Invention of Women: Making an African Sense of Western Gender Discourses. Minneapolis: University of Minnesota Press.

Indigenous, African, and colonized societies, as non-productive or outside the formal economy. Women were relegated to reproductive roles, such as childbearing, domestic maintenance, food preparation, and care work, all of which were essential for social reproduction but excluded from wage systems, market valuation, and statistical accounting like GDP. In contrast, men were positioned as economic agents, suitable for incorporation into formal labour markets, as miners, plantation workers, soldiers, or porters, whose labour was commodified, taxed, and measured. This dichotomy justified differential access to wages, land rights, and legal personhood. For example, in settler colonies across Africa and the Americas, colonial labour codes restricted land ownership or contract rights to men while criminalizing women's economic autonomy outside the household. This gendered division of labour also enabled the colonial state and capitalist firms to externalize the costs of reproduction, housing, health, food, and education onto women's unpaid labour, sustaining the male workforce without state or corporate expense. Colonial and capitalist systems deliberately structured labour in a way that relied on women's unpaid work to support the broader economy without having to pay for it. In economic terms, "reproduction" doesn't just mean having children; it refers to the ongoing daily and generational maintenance of the labour force. This includes preparing food, cleaning, raising children, caring for the sick and elderly, and providing emotional support, tasks overwhelmingly assigned to women, especially in colonized and working-class communities. By assigning these roles to women and classifying them as "private" or "natural" duties rather than "real work", colonial governments and capitalist enterprises were able to externalize costs. This means they avoided having to pay for essential services, like housing, healthcare, food preparation, or child-rearing, because women were expected to perform them without wages. In turn, this system allowed male workers (who were considered the primary breadwinners) to arrive at plantations, factories, or mines fed, clothed, and cared for, ready to be productive, without employers or the state having to provide for their well-being off the clock. This setup significantly reduced labour reproduction costs for colonial economies and global capitalism. It also reinforced the idea that only wage labour counts as economic activity, erasing women's contributions from formal economic analysis, while extracting real value from their unpaid efforts. The result was a gendered and racialized system of exploitation in which entire economies were built on invisible labour performed by women in the domestic sphere.

Ultimately, this ideological separation between "productive" male labour and "reproductive" female labour was not natural or universal; it was a colonial construction grounded in neoclassical assumptions and used to justify economic exploitation, racial hierarchy, and gender subordination. This segmentation devalued women's productive roles within subsistence economies and erased the labour value of cultural reproduction. In contrast, Marxist and feminist scholars argue that colonialism enacted a form of "primitive accumulation" that depended on the simultaneous expropriation of land and subjugation of women, reproducing gendered divisions of labour foundational to capitalist expansion.[172,173] In Africa, Queen Nzinga's resistance to Portuguese incursion in Angola reveals how colonialism actively sought to dismantle female political authority. Nzinga's military and diplomatic leadership was exceptional precisely because it stood in opposition to the emerging colonial gender order.[174] Across the Americas, the transformation of gender systems was not incidental but instrumental in consolidating colonial power. Indigenous women's loss of land rights, leadership roles, and ritual authority facilitated both economic exploitation and cultural assimilation. These changes contributed to a long-standing legacy of gendered dispossession, still visible today in disparities in land ownership, political representation, and exposure to violence within Indigenous communities.

9.2 Indigenous Women and Resistance

Despite facing systemic exploitation under colonial rule, Indigenous women across the Americas, Africa, and beyond were not passive victims but active agents of cultural preservation, resistance, and negotiation. Colonization disrupted traditional gender roles, disempowering women economically, politically, and spiritually, but Indigenous women adapted by becoming key custodians of oral traditions, ritual knowledge, and intergenerational education. For example, among the Andean communities, women maintained ayllu-based agricultural cycles and ceremonial life

[172] Federici, S. (2004) Caliban and the Witch: Women, the Body and Primitive Accumulation. New York: Autonomedia.

[173] Mies, M. (1986) Patriarchy and Accumulation on a World Scale: Women in the International Division of Labour London: Zed Books.

[174] Heywood, L.M. (2017) Njinga of Angola: Africa's Warrior Queen. Cambridge, MA: Harvard University Press.

even as male labour was conscripted into the colonial mita system.[175] In North America, Haudenosaunee (Iroquois) women retained matrilineal authority and exercised influence over diplomatic affairs, including during treaty negotiations with colonial powers.[176] Similarly, in West Africa, Queen Njinga of Ndongo and Matamba resisted Portuguese colonization through military strategy and alliance-building, defying European gender norms and asserting sovereignty.[177] From a neoclassical perspective, these roles are often rendered invisible because such frameworks privilege market-based labour and undervalue subsistence economies and reproductive labour, domains where Indigenous women historically exerted power. In contrast, Marxist and feminist theorists interpret women's resistance as part of a broader struggle against the gendered processes of primitive accumulation, where female bodies were appropriated to reproduce labour and enforce colonial order.[178,179] For instance, spiritual leaders like María Caxuxa in the Pueblo Revolt of 1680 helped mobilize resistance by reasserting Indigenous cosmology in defiance of missionary conversion.[180] In the face of cultural erasure, Indigenous women also resisted through syncretism, infusing imposed Christian practices with Indigenous meaning, and by reviving suppressed traditions, such as kachina dances among the Hopi or menstrual rites in Andean villages.[181] These actions ensured the survival of Indigenous worldviews and challenged the colonial state's cultural hegemony. In many societies, women mediated between Indigenous and colonial systems, acting as translators, cultural brokers, or even legal advocates, blurring the binary

[175] Silverblatt, I. (1987) Moon, Sun, and Witches: Gender Ideologies and Class in Inca and Colonial Peru. Princeton: Princeton University Press.

[176] Richter, D.K. (2001) Facing East from Indian Country: A Native History of Early America. Cambridge, MA: Harvard.
University Press.

[177] Heywood, L.M. (2017) Njinga of Angola: Africa's Warrior Queen. Cambridge, MA: Harvard University Press.

[178] Mies, M. (1986) Patriarchy and Accumulation on a World Scale: Women in the International Division of Labour. London: Zed Books.

[179] Federici, S. (2004) Caliban and the Witch: Women, the Body and Primitive Accumulation. New York: Autonomedia.

[180] Knaut, A.L. (1995) The Pueblo Revolt of 1680: Conquest and Resistance in Seventeenth-Century New Mexico. Norman: University of Oklahoma Press.

[181] Allen, P.G. (1992) The Sacred Hoop: Recovering the Feminine in American Indian Traditions. Boston: Beacon Press.

of resistance and accommodation. Their contributions underline how Indigenous resistance was not solely military but deeply embedded in cultural, spiritual, and domestic spheres. Recognizing these roles complicates linear narratives of colonization and foregrounds Indigenous women as central agents in the survival and transformation of their societies.

10 Environmental Imperialism and Ecological Reordering

10.1 The Ecological Impact of European Expansion

The European expansion into Indigenous territories was not only an economic and political project but an ecological one that transformed landscapes and disrupted biodiverse systems. Colonial agriculture introduced monocultures like sugar, coffee, and cotton, replacing complex Indigenous agroecology. The Spanish encomienda and plantation economies in the Americas cleared vast tracts of forest for cash crops, leading to soil degradation and long-term ecological instability.[182,183] In Brazil, the Atlantic Forest was heavily deforested for sugar plantations, destroying endemic ecosystems and displacing Indigenous communities whose land management practices were more ecologically sustainable.[184] Mining, especially for silver and gold, intensified environmental degradation. In Potosí, Bolivia, the Spanish extracted vast quantities of silver using forced Indigenous labour under the mit'a system. This led to widespread deforestation for fuel and construction, mercury contamination from refining processes, and erosion of mountain ecosystems.[185,186] These extractive activities, driven by early capitalist logics of profit maximization, ignored ecological limits and externalized environmental

[182] Crosby, A.W. (1972) The Columbian Exchange: Biological and Cultural Consequences of 1492. Westport: Greenwood Press.

[183] Grove, R.H. (1995) Green Imperialism: Colonial Expansion, Tropical Island Edens and the Origins of Environmentalism, 1600–1860. Cambridge: Cambridge University Press.

[184] Dean, W. (1995) With Broadax and Firebrand: The Destruction of the Brazilian Atlantic Forest. Berkeley: University of California Press.

[185] Robins, N.A. (2011) Mercury, Mining, and Empire: The Human and Ecological Cost of Colonial Silver Mining in the Andes. Bloomington: Indiana University Press..

[186] Tandeter, E. (1993) Coercion and Market: Silver Mining in Colonial Potosí, 1692–1826. Albuquerque: University of New Mexico Press.

costs, an approach justified under neoclassical economic frameworks that viewed nature as a passive input into production rather than a co-constitutive system.[187] From a Marxist perspective, this transformation is interpreted as ecological primitive accumulation: the violent separation of people from land and the commodification of nature for capital expansion.[188,189] The environment, like Indigenous labour, became a resource to be extracted, stripped of its relational and spiritual meanings embedded in Indigenous cosmologies. In the Andes, communal land systems (ayllus) that maintained environmental balance through rotational agriculture and ecological zoning were systematically undermined to prioritise export-oriented production. The consequences were global. European consumption of colonial crops accelerated urban growth and industrialization in the metropoles, while the colonies suffered biodiversity loss, altered water cycles, and disrupted food systems.[190] These ecological imbalances endure. Contemporary deforestation patterns in the Amazon, for instance, trace their roots to the colonial plantation economy and its extractive orientation. Indigenous stewardship, sidelined by imperial land tenure regimes, remains more effective in preserving biodiversity than state or market-led conservation models.[191]

10.2 Long-Term Effects on Indigenous Livelihoods

The long-term effects of settler colonial agriculture and land expropriation profoundly undermined Indigenous economic systems by dismantling their ecological foundations and forcibly integrating their economies into colonial market structures. Prior to European expansion, Indigenous

[187] Moore, J.W. (2010) 'The End of the Road? Agricultural Revolutions in the Capitalist World-Ecology, 1450–2010', Journal of Agrarian Change, 10(3), pp. 389–413.

[188] Foster, J.B. (2000) Marx's Ecology: Materialism and Nature. New York: Monthly Review Press.

[189] Federici, S. (2004) Caliban and the Witch: Women, the Body and Primitive Accumulation. New York: Autonomedia.

[190] Nunn, N. and Qian, N. (2011) 'The Potato's Contribution to Population and Urbanization: Evidence from a Historical Experiment', Quarterly Journal of Economics, 126(2), pp. 593–650.

[191] Garnett, S.T., Burgess, N.D., Fa, J.E., Fernández-Llamazares, Á., Molnár, Z., Robinson, C.J., Watson, J.E.M., Zander, K.K., Austin, B., Brondizio, E.S. and Collier, N.F. (2018) 'A spatial overview of the global importance of Indigenous lands for conservation', Nature Sustainability, 1(7), pp. 369–374.

livelihoods were largely embedded in sustainable agroecological practices, such as the milpa system in Mesoamerica, the vertical archipelago model of Andean agriculture, or the seasonal bison-hunting economies of the North American Plains.[192,193] These systems were disrupted as colonizers imposed monoculture plantations, fenced property regimes, and extractive industries that exhausted the land and displaced Indigenous populations from their ancestral territories. From a neoclassical economic standpoint, the integration of Indigenous communities into colonial markets is framed as development through increased productivity and trade specialization. However, this narrative masks the coercive context of dispossession, unequal exchange, and dependency formation. For example, the replacement of subsistence agriculture with export-oriented cash crops, such as sugar in the Caribbean or rubber in the Amazon, did not result from free market competition but from land grabs and forced labour regimes.[194,195]. Indigenous communities were pushed onto marginal lands or coerced into labour on colonial estates, which drastically reduced their food sovereignty and subjected them to price volatility and external supply chains. Marxist and dependency theorists interpret this transformation as a textbook case of primitive accumulation, the violent precondition for capitalist expansion. Land expropriation, coupled with ecological degradation, eliminated Indigenous systems of self-reproduction and forced a proletarianization of Indigenous labour. The loss of communal landownership not only impoverished communities but also broke down systems of reciprocity and redistribution foundational to Indigenous social economies.[196] In regions such as southern Africa, Indigenous groups were often compelled to become migrant labourers in settler mines and farms, creating patterns of dependence and

[192] Murra, J.V. (1980) The Economic Organization of the Inka State. Greenwich: JAI Press.

[193] Dean, W. (1995) With Broadax and Firebrand: The Destruction of the Brazilian Atlantic Forest. Berkeley: University of California Press.

[194] Federici, S. (2004) *Caliban and the Witch: Women, the Body and Primitive Accumulation*. New York: Autonomedia.

[195] Moore, J.W. (2010) 'The End of the Road? Agricultural Revolutions in the Capitalist World-Ecology, 1450–2010', *Journal of Agrarian Change*, 10(3), pp. 389–413.

[196] Wallerstein, I. (1974) *The Modern World-System I: Capitalist Agriculture and the Origins of the European World-Economy in the Sixteenth Century*. New York: Academic Press.

dislocation that persist into the present. These disruptions had enduring consequences. In Canada, the transformation of Indigenous territories into agricultural and resource frontiers led to chronic poverty and food insecurity in Indigenous communities, exacerbated by colonial policies such as the Indian Act and residential school system.[197,198] These policies restricted Indigenous peoples to small reserves, undermining their traditional economies, food systems, and governance structures. The Indian Act imposed federal control over land, mobility, and political organization, while residential schools forcibly removed children from their families, eroding intergenerational knowledge about land stewardship and subsistence practices. Simultaneously, settler agriculture, logging, and mining displaced Indigenous communities from ecologically rich areas, further severing their access to hunting, fishing, and foraging grounds that had sustained them for generations. In the Amazon, industrial agriculture and extractive projects continue to displace Indigenous populations, who now rely on wage labour or state subsidies, weakening traditional economies and intergenerational knowledge transmission.[199,200] Rather than facilitating equitable development, colonial economic integration has entrenched dependency and ecological precarity. Indigenous resistance to these legacies has focused on land reclamation, food sovereignty, and ecological restoration as strategies of decolonization and survival.

11 Comparative Colonial Regimes and Their Legacies

11.1 Spanish, British, and French Colonial Models

The colonial strategies adopted by Spain, Britain, and France shaped the divergent political economies that Indigenous societies experienced across the Americas and Africa. Each empire employed structurally different

[197] Robins, N.A. (2011) *Mercury, Mining, and Empire: The Human and Ecological Cost of Colonial Silver Mining in the Andes*. Bloomington: Indiana University Press.

[198] Garnett, S.T. et al. (2018) 'A spatial overview of the global importance of Indigenous lands for conservation', *Nature Sustainability*, 1(7), pp. 369–374.

[199] Dean, W. (1995) *With Broadax and Firebrand: The Destruction of the Brazilian Atlantic Forest*. Berkeley: University of California Press.

[200] Crosby, A.W. (1972) *The Columbian Exchange: Biological and Cultural Consequences of 1492*. Westport: Greenwood Press.

economic logics and institutional models rooted in their political ideologies and economic interests. The Spanish Empire relied heavily on the encomienda system, a form of tribute labour whereby conquistadors were granted rights to Indigenous labour in exchange for religious instruction and protection.[201,202] This extractive model facilitated the accumulation of wealth through forced labour in agriculture and mining, most notoriously in the silver mines of Potosí. Neoclassical models might interpret this as a misallocation of labour due to the lack of free-market conditions; however, from a Marxist perspective, the encomienda exemplifies primitive accumulation, the violent separation of people from their means of production.[203,204] In contrast, British colonialism emphasized settler expansion and land expropriation. Settler colonialism operated through the logic of elimination rather than incorporation,[205] displacing Indigenous populations to make way for privately owned farms and plantations. The British focused less on integrating Indigenous labour into formal extractive systems and more on removing Indigenous peoples from productive land. The development of capitalist markets in the colonies was closely tied to private property and liberal economic thought. However, labour was coerced in other ways: indentured servitude, slavery and, later, wage labour regimes underpinned the settler economy.[206,207] The French Empire, especially in Canada and West Africa, often pursued a trade alliance model that relied more on cooperation than conquest, at least initially. French colonial agents built alliances with Indigenous nations like the Huron-Wendat, often mediated through missionaries and the fur

[201] Bakewell, P. (1984) *Miners of the Red Mountain: Indian Labour in Potosí, 1545–1650*. Albuquerque: University of New Mexico Press.

[202] Silverblatt, I. (1987) *Moon, Sun, and Witches: Gender Ideologies and Class in Inca and Colonial Peru*. Princeton: Princeton University Press.

[203] Marx, K. (1867) Capital: A Critique of Political Economy. Volume I. Translated by B. Fowkes. London: Penguin Classics, 1990.

[204] Federici, S. (2004) Caliban and the Witch: Women, the Body and Primitive Accumulation. New York: Autonomedia.

[205] Wolfe, P. (2006) 'Settler Colonialism and the Elimination of the Native', Journal of Genocide Research, 8(4), pp. 387–409. https://doi.org/10.1080/14623520601056240.

[206] Beckert, S. (2014) *Empire of Cotton: A Global History*. New York: Knopf.

[207] Williams, E. (1944) *Capitalism and Slavery*. Chapel Hill: University of North Carolina Press.

trade.[208] Unlike the Spanish or British, the French lacked the manpower and infrastructure to impose large-scale settler or extractive systems, so their economic model cantered on integrating Indigenous societies into commercial networks. This method appears to resonate more closely with neoclassical notions of voluntary exchange, though power imbalances and dependency were still prevalent. Communist and anti-colonial theorists argue that all three models, despite surface differences, functioned as tools of imperialist expansion, transforming Indigenous land and labour into capital.[209,210] What varied was the method: the Spanish via forced tribute, the British via elimination and commodification, and the French via incorporation into external markets. The legacies of these regimes remain visible today in land tenure systems, legal structures, and the socio-economic marginalization of Indigenous populations.

11.2 Institutional Legacies in Post-colonial States

The institutional legacies of European colonial regimes continue to shape post-colonial governance, land rights, and Indigenous autonomy across the globe. Spanish colonialism, characterized by centralized bureaucratic governance and extractive labour systems such as the encomienda and repartimiento, laid the foundation for post-independence Latin American states that inherited hierarchical state structures and weak protections for communal landholding.[211,212] In contrast, British settler colonialism, particularly in North America and Australia, fostered legal systems that dispossessed Indigenous peoples through treaties and private property regimes, often underpinned by doctrines like terra nullius.

[208] Richter, D.K. (2001) Facing East from Indian Country: A Native History of Early America. Cambridge, MA: Harvard University Press.

[209] Lenin, V.I. (1917) Imperialism: The Highest Stage of Capitalism. New York: International Publishers.

[210] Wallerstein, I. (1974) The Modern World-System I: Capitalist Agriculture and the Origins of the European World-Economy in the Sixteenth Century. New York: Academic Press.

[211] Bakewell, P. (1984) Miners of the Red Mountain: Indian Labour in Potosí, 1545–1650. Albuquerque: University of New Mexico Press.

[212] Silverblatt, I. (1987) Moon, Sun, and Witches: Gender Ideologies and Class in Inca and Colonial Peru. Princeton: Princeton University Press.

These legal mechanisms facilitated the transfer of vast Indigenous territories to settler control, embedding racialized property systems and state-sanctioned inequality.[213,214] French colonialism, notably in West Africa and parts of the Americas, emphasized assimilationist policies that centralized authority in metropolitan France while maintaining indirect control through Indigenous intermediaries, producing mixed legacies of legal pluralism and contested citizenship.[215] Neoclassical economists often describe colonialism's legacy as a distortion of institutional efficiency, arguing that insecure property rights, rent-seeking elites, and underdeveloped markets persist due to colonial-era path dependencies.[216] From this view, colonialism disrupted optimal economic development by entrenching extractive institutions rather than inclusive ones. However, Marxian economists and world-systems theorists contend that these institutions were not aberrations but intentional features of capitalist expansion. For them, post-colonial governance systems continue to serve as mechanisms of primitive accumulation, facilitating the ongoing expropriation of land and labour from Indigenous communities for global capital.[217,218,219] For example, in Bolivia, Indigenous communities such as the Aymara and Quechua have fought to regain land rights in the wake of neoliberal reforms that prioritized private mining concessions,

[213] Wolfe, P. (2006) 'Settler Colonialism and the Elimination of the Native', Journal of Genocide Research, 8(4), pp. 387–409. https://doi.org/10.1080/14623520601056240.

[214] Williams, E. (1944) Capitalism and Slavery. Chapel Hill: University of North Carolina Press.

[215] Wallerstein, I. (1974) The Modern World-System I: Capitalist Agriculture and the Origins of the European World-Economy in the Sixteenth Century. New York: Academic Press.

[216] Acemoglu, D., Johnson, S. and Robinson, J.A. (2001) 'The Colonial Origins of Comparative Development: An Empirical Investigation', American Economic Review, 91(5), pp. 1369–1401.

[217] Federici, S. (2004) Caliban and the Witch: Women, the Body and Primitive Accumulation. New York: Autonomedia.

[218] Lenin, V.I. (1917) Imperialism: The Highest Stage of Capitalism. New York: International Publishers.

[219] Wallerstein, I. (1974) The Modern World-System I: Capitalist Agriculture and the Origins of the European World-Economy in the Sixteenth Century. New York: Academic Press.

echoing colonial exploitation patterns.[220] In Canada, the Indian Act continues to regulate Indigenous governance and land use, a direct legacy of British colonial control that limits self-determination despite constitutional recognition of Indigenous rights.[221] In contrast, the 1988 Brazilian Constitution formally recognizes Indigenous land rights, yet agribusiness-driven policies and enforcement gaps reflect the enduring power of settler capitalist interests rooted in colonial plantation systems.[222] These divergent institutional outcomes reflect not only historical colonial strategies but also the ongoing global dynamics of capitalism, development, and resistance. While neoclassical models advocate institutional reform to align with liberal market norms, Marxist and Indigenous critiques emphasize decolonization, land restitution, and the resurgence of communal governance as pathways to justice and autonomy.

12 Maritime Technology, Navigation, and Indigenous Knowledge

12.1 Innovations in European Navigation

European maritime expansion from the fifteenth century onwards was underpinned by significant technological advancements in navigation. Instruments such as the astrolabe, adopted and refined from earlier Islamic and Hellenistic models, allowed sailors to determine latitude by measuring the altitude of celestial bodies. The magnetic compass, introduced to Europe via China through Arab intermediaries, enabled more consistent orientation during voyages, particularly in open waters where landmarks were absent. The sextant, which came into use in the eighteenth century, further enhanced navigational accuracy by measuring the angle between celestial bodies and the horizon, crucial for determining

220 Postero, N.G. (2007) Now We Are Citizens: Indigenous Politics in Postmulticultural Bolivia. Stanford: Stanford University Press.

221 Richter, D.K. (2001) Facing East from Indian Country: A Native History of Early America. Cambridge, MA: Harvard University Press.

222 Dean, W. (1995) With Broadax and Firebrand: The Destruction of the Brazilian Atlantic Forest. Berkeley: University of California Press.

longitude in conjunction with increasingly precise marine chronometers.[223] Determining a ship's position at sea historically posed a significant challenge, particularly regarding longitude. While latitude (the north–south position) could be calculated relatively easily using the sun or stars, especially with instruments like the sextant, longitude (the east–west position) proved far more difficult to establish with accuracy. The sextant played a crucial role by allowing navigators to measure the angle between a celestial object and the horizon. This measurement enabled them not only to determine their latitude but also to calculate the local solar time at their position. The introduction of the marine chronometer transformed this process. As a highly accurate clock set to the time at a reference point, usually Greenwich Mean Time, the chronometer allowed sailors to compare their local time (measured using the sextant) to the fixed time of their home port. The difference between these two times revealed the ship's longitude, since the Earth rotates 15 degrees per hour. This combination of technologies was revolutionary. Prior to the availability of reliable chronometers, miscalculations in longitude frequently led to maritime disasters, including shipwrecks and loss of cargo or life. With the sextant providing angular measurements and the chronometer offering precise reference time, navigators could finally determine both latitude and longitude with confidence. This advance dramatically increased the accuracy and safety of oceanic travel, laying the groundwork for modern global navigation, trade expansion, and colonial exploration. Together, the sextant and chronometer solved what was once known as the longitude problem, a breakthrough that reshaped maritime history. These innovations allowed European empires to conduct transoceanic exploration with increasing efficiency and precision, facilitating the establishment of colonial trade routes, military dominance at sea, and resource extraction from colonized territories. From a neoclassical economic perspective, these tools can be understood as technological inputs that reduced transaction and transportation costs, increased market access, and enhanced the efficiency of capital investment in global trade. Maritime innovations helped expand the spatial scale of economic activity, enabling European states and merchants to integrate distant regions into a global division of labour. This perspective emphasizes the role of innovation and entrepreneurship in facilitating

[223] Waters, D.W. (1978) The Art of Navigation in England in Elizabethan and Early Stuart Times. London: Hollis & Carter.

expansion and capital accumulation, but it often abstracts away from the coercive structures, such as slavery, dispossession, and forced labour, that underpinned colonial maritime economies. In contrast, Marxist and world-systems theorists argue that maritime technologies were instrumental to processes of primitive accumulation. By enabling the projection of military and commercial power across oceans, navigation tools became instruments of imperial conquest. Technological advancement did not operate in a political vacuum but was embedded in a broader mode of capitalist expansion that entailed the violent incorporation of peripheral societies into exploitative trade relations.[224,225] For instance, the Portuguese caravel, a ship design optimized for speed and cargo, was vital in facilitating the Atlantic slave trade, a cornerstone of capitalist development in the early modern period. While European navigation was lauded for its scientific advancement, it often stood on the shoulders of Indigenous and non-European knowledge. Polynesian navigators, for example, used sophisticated systems based on wave patterns, star paths, and bird flight to traverse thousands of miles of open ocean long before European seafarers ventured beyond coastal waters.[226] Arab sailors had long employed monsoon wind patterns in the Indian Ocean trade. These alternative epistemologies were largely erased or appropriated in colonial narratives, which portrayed maritime superiority as a purely European achievement. The material impact of navigational technology was profound: it enabled the triangular trade, the rapid movement of bullion from the Americas to Europe, and the subjugation of Indigenous coastal societies. It also had long-term consequences for Indigenous economies, which were disrupted by the influx of foreign ships, diseases, and extractive economic models. The illusion of neutral progress obscures the fact that maritime innovation functioned as an enabling force for colonial capitalism, shaping the structure of global inequality that persists to this day.

[224] Wallerstein, I. (1974) The Modern World-System I: Capitalist Agriculture and the Origins of the European World-Economy in the Sixteenth Century. New York: Academic Press.

[225] Blaut, J.M. (1993) The Colonizer's Model of the World: Geographical Diffusionism and Eurocentric History. New York: Guilford Press.

[226] Finney, B. (1994). Voyage of Rediscovery: A Cultural Odyssey through Polynesia. Honolulu: Bishop Museum Press.

12.2 Indigenous Contributions to Maritime Knowledge

While European imperial expansion often celebrated technological advancements like the astrolabe and sextant, Indigenous navigational systems profoundly shaped early transoceanic exploration and inland mobility. Polynesian navigation demonstrated sophisticated oceanic expertise long before European arrival. Polynesian way finders used stellar constellations, wave patterns, cloud formations, and bird flight paths to navigate thousands of miles of open ocean across the Pacific. These skills, encoded in oral traditions and embodied through intensive training, enabled Polynesian expansion from Samoa and Tonga to Hawai 'i, Rapa Nui (Easter Island), and Aotearoa (New Zealand).[227] This Indigenous expertise was not isolated. Spanish and Portuguese explorers in the Pacific and Southeast Asia often relied on Indigenous pilots (pilotos) to chart unfamiliar waters. In Mesoamerica and the Andes, overland and riverine trade routes also influenced colonial logistics. The Inca Empire's vast road network, extending over 40,000 km across difficult terrain, facilitated rapid communication and troop movement via relay runners (chasquis) and llama caravans. These roads later became critical corridors for Spanish military and economic control.[228] Similarly, riverine systems in both the Amazon and Mississippi basins played a foundational role in enabling complex pre-colonial trade networks, political organization, and cultural integration across vast regions. In the Amazon basin, large, navigable rivers such as the Solimões, Negro, and Madeira allowed for the long-distance movement of goods, people, and cultural practices between highly organized pre-Columbian settlements. Archaeological research has revealed complex societies connected by these waterways, evidenced by the widespread presence of earthworks, ceramics, and terra preta soils.[229] In particular, the Upper Xingu region demonstrates elaborate regional planning, including walled villages, road systems, and

[227] Finney, B. (1994) Voyage of Rediscovery: A Cultural Odyssey through Polynesia. Berkeley: University of California Press.

[228] Murra, J.V. (1980) The Economic Organization of the Inka State. Greenwich: JAI Press.

[229] De Souza, J.G., Schaan, D., Robinson, M., Barbosa, C.P., Antunes, A.P., Guapindaia, V., Alves, D.S. and Ranzi, A., 2018. Pre-Columbian earth-builders of the Amazon: Geoglyphs and forest islands as testimony of complex societies. Nature Communications, 9(1), Article 112. https://doi.org/10.1038/s41467-017-02015-9.

coordinated resource management, suggesting a decentralized but coordinated political structure dependent on riverine access.[230,231] Similarly, the Mississippi River system supported the emergence of Mississippian culture, most prominently represented by Cahokia, a massive urban and ceremonial centre that thrived between the ninth and fourteenth centuries CE. River connectivity enabled Cahokia to serve as a hub for the exchange of goods such as copper from the Great Lakes, marine shells from the Gulf Coast, and chert from the Ozarks, material evidence of long-distance interaction.[232] The North Plaza of Cahokia also appears to have served as a diplomatic space for ritual and political gatherings involving elites from distant regions, reinforcing the integrative role of riverine corridors in social and ceremonial life.[233] Indigenous knowledge of seasonal flows, canoe routes, and hydrological cycles was indispensable to colonial fur trade and mission settlement strategies.[234] Unlike neoclassical frameworks that view technological diffusion as unidirectional, from Europe to the rest of the world, the real history reveals multidirectional exchanges rooted in Indigenous ingenuity. Neoclassical economics often reduces innovation to capital-labour dynamics, missing how knowledge is embedded in cultural, ecological, and cosmological systems. In contrast, Marxist theorists acknowledge that the world-economy emerged through uneven exchanges that incorporated peripheral knowledge into core capitalist structures, albeit under coercive terms.[235] Thus, Indigenous systems

[230] Heckenberger, M.J., 2005. The Ecology of Power: Culture, Place, and Personhood in the Southern Amazon, AD 1000–2000. New York: Routledge.

[231] Heckenberger, M.J., Russell, J.C., Toney, J.R. and Schmidt, M.J., 2008. The legacy of cultural landscapes in the Brazilian Amazon: implications for biodiversity. Philosophical Transactions of the Royal Society B: Biological Sciences, 362(1478), pp. 197–208. https://doi.org/10.1098/rstb.2006.1987.

[232] Pauketat, T.R., 2004. Ancient Cahokia and the Mississippians. Cambridge: Cambridge University Press.

[233] Emerson, T.E., Hargrave, E.A. and Hedman, K.M., 2017. Death and diplomacy: The evidence for Cahokia's north plaza as an arena of interregional interaction. Journal of Anthropological Archaeology, 45, pp. 84–103. https://doi.org/10.1016/j.jaa.2016.11.004.

[234] Gómez, P. (2017) The Experiential Caribbean: Creating Knowledge and Healing in the Early Modern Atlantic. Chapel Hill: University of North Carolina Press.

[235] Wallerstein, I. (1974) The Modern World-System I: Capitalist Agriculture and the Origins of the European World-Economy in the Sixteenth Century. New York: Academic Press.

not only contributed to European expansion but also challenge Eurocentric assumptions of technological superiority. The appropriation of Indigenous maritime and terrestrial infrastructure illustrates a recurring dynamic: colonialism's dependency on the very knowledge systems it sought to marginalize.

13 The Long-Term Legacy of European Expansion

13.1 Global Trade Patterns and the Atlantic World

The expansion of European powers from the fifteenth century onwards fundamentally reshaped global trade patterns, laying the institutional and material foundations of modern capitalism. European maritime empires, particularly those of Spain, Portugal, Britain, France, and the Netherlands, constructed a transatlantic system that integrated diverse regions into a single economic network. Through the Atlantic slave trade, Indigenous dispossession, and plantation economies, European states and merchant capitalists orchestrated a triangular exchange of African labour, American raw materials, and European manufactured goods.[236] This structure fostered colonial dependency, extracting surplus from the periphery to enrich the metropole while systematically under developing colonized societies.[237] From a neoclassical perspective, this expansion could be mischaracterized as the global spread of comparative advantage and market efficiency. However, such models obscure the coercive underpinnings of colonial trade, where labour was not mobile but enslaved or conscripted, and markets were neither free nor competitive but shaped by monopoly charters, tariffs, and gunboat diplomacy.[238] The rise of joint-stock companies such as the Dutch and British East India Companies exemplifies how private capital was underwritten by state violence to control trade routes and extract colonial profit.[239] Marxist theorists,

[236] Williams, E. (1944) Capitalism and Slavery. Chapel Hill: University of North Carolina Press.

[237] Rodney, W. (1972) How Europe Underdeveloped Africa. London: Bogle-L'Ouverture Publications.

[238] Acemoglu, D., Johnson, S. and Robinson, J.A. (2001) 'The Colonial Origins of Comparative Development: An Empirical Investigation', American Economic Review, 91(5), pp. 1369–1401.

[239] Subrahmanyam, S. (1997) The Career and Legend of Vasco da Gama. Cambridge: Cambridge University Press.

in contrast, interpret European expansion as the vehicle for primitive accumulation, the violent expropriation of land, labour, and resources that set the stage for capitalist development. Karl Marx identified this in the dispossession of peasants and the transatlantic slave trade, while Immanuel Wallerstein's world-systems theory framed colonial trade as a core-periphery dynamic in which wealth flowed from Indigenous and colonized labour to capitalist centres.[240,241] The legacy of this system is visible in contemporary trade imbalances, structural inequalities, and the persistence of racialized labour hierarchies across the Global South. The Atlantic World also codified racial hierarchies that justified exploitation. Legal systems in colonies institutionalized racial slavery, while pseudoscientific theories later provided ideological support for economic inequality.[242] The interlinkage between capitalism and racial ideologies remains evident in post-colonial economies, where former colonies often remain dependent on primary exports and external capital, locked into unequal terms of trade.[243] Thus, the long-term legacy of European expansion was not merely increased trade or economic integration, but a reordering of global power structures through racialized capitalism, extractive institutions, and enduring colonial dependency. Indigenous societies bore the brunt of this transformation, experiencing land expropriation, demographic collapse, and incorporation into a world economy built on coerced labour and structural inequality.

13.2 Persistent Inequalities and the Coloniality of Power

The legacies of European expansion are not confined to historical conquest but persist structurally in the form of global economic disparities, cultural erasure, and the ongoing dispossession of Indigenous lands. The concept of coloniality of power, developed by Aníbal Quijano,

[240] Marx, K. (1867) Capital: A Critique of Political Economy. Volume I. Translated by B. Fowkes. London: Penguin Classics, 1990.

[241] Wallerstein, I. (1974) The Modern World-System I: Capitalist Agriculture and the Origins of the European World-Economy in the Sixteenth Century. New York: Academic Press.

[242] Federici, S. (2004) Caliban and the Witch: Women, the Body and Primitive Accumulation. New York: Autonomedia.

[243] Frank, A.G. (1967) Capitalism and Underdevelopment in Latin America. New York: Monthly Review Press.

captures how colonial structures of domination continue to shape global hierarchies long after formal colonialism ended. Through racialized labour systems, epistemic suppression, and legal dispossession, European colonial regimes institutionalized inequalities that have proven remarkably durable. For instance, Latin American Indigenous populations, while often nominally included in modern nation-states, remain disproportionately impoverished and landless, particularly in Bolivia, Peru, and Guatemala.[244,245] From a neoclassical perspective, these disparities are often framed as "market failures" or deficits in human capital, overlooking the historical processes that systematically undermined Indigenous economic autonomy. In contrast, Marxist and dependency theorists contend that underdevelopment was actively produced through capital accumulation mechanisms rooted in the exploitation of Indigenous and enslaved labour.[246,247] Land dispossession remains central. In countries like Brazil, deforestation and agribusiness expansion continue to encroach on Indigenous territories, exacerbating inequality while erasing ecologically sustainable livelihoods.[248,249] Cultural erasure, too, endures via assimilationist education policies, the criminalization of Indigenous languages and rituals, and the valorization of European epistemologies over Indigenous knowledge systems.[250,251] The imposition of private property regimes over communal landholdings further entrenched dispossession and exclusion, often legitimized by liberal legal frameworks. This dynamic contradicts the neoclassical model, which assumes voluntary

[244] Postero, N.G. (2007) Now We Are Citizens: Indigenous Politics in Postmulticultural Bolivia. Stanford: Stanford University Press.

[245] Quijano, A. (2000) 'Coloniality of Power and Eurocentrism in Latin America', International Sociology, 15(2), pp. 215–232.

[246] Frank, A.G. (1967) Capitalism and Underdevelopment in Latin America. New York: Monthly Review Press.

[247] Williams, E. (1944) Capitalism and Slavery. Chapel Hill: University of North Carolina Press.

[248] Dean, W. (1995) With Broadax and Firebrand: The Destruction of the Brazilian Atlantic Forest. Berkeley: University of California Press.

[249] Garnett, S.T. et al. (2018) 'A spatial overview of the global importance of Indigenous lands for conservation', Nature Sustainability, 1(7), pp. 369–374.

[250] Federici, S. (2004) Caliban and the Witch: Women, the Body and Primitive Accumulation. New York: Autonomedia.

[251] Mignolo, W.D. (2011) The Darker Side of Western Modernity: Global Futures, Decolonial Options. Durham, NC: Duke University Press.

exchange and legal neutrality, and instead supports critiques that capitalism, especially in its colonial form, requires unequal access to land and labour.[252,253] Contemporary inequalities in life expectancy, access to education, health services, and political representation illustrate that the coloniality of power is not simply a legacy, but a structuring principle of the modern world-system. Indigenous women are particularly marginalized, bearing the compounded burdens of race, gender, and class oppression, often excluded from both market participation and land rights.[254,255] (Allen, 1992; Mies, 1986). In sum, the current global order continues to reflect the hierarchies inaugurated by European expansion, underscoring the need for decolonial approaches to economic justice, cultural revitalization, and land restitution.

14 Conclusion

The historical rise of European expansion was neither a neutral voyage of discovery nor an inevitable step in the progress of human civilization. It was, rather, a structured and violent reordering of global power relations, an intentional system of domination rooted in the political economy of emerging capitalism. This reordering was neither accidental nor secondary to the development of the modern world; it was the engine that drove it. From the outset, European colonial regimes did not merely seek to trade, they sought to expropriate. Through the encomienda and repartimiento systems in Spanish America, the plantation slavery complex of the Caribbean, and the settler colonialism that displaced and decimated Indigenous societies in North America, Africa, and Oceania, empire enabled the mass extraction of land, labour, and surplus value. This process was fundamental to what Marx would call primitive accumulation, the theft of resources and the genocide of millions of lives that

[252] Wallerstein, I. (1974) The Modern World-System I: Capitalist Agriculture and the Origins of the European World-Economy in the Sixteenth Century. New York: Academic Press.

[253] Rodney, W. (1972) How Europe Underdeveloped Africa. London: Bogle-L'Ouverture Publications.

[254] Allen, P.G. (1992) The Sacred Hoop: Recovering the Feminine in American Indian Traditions. Boston: Beacon Press.

[255] Mies, M. (1986) Patriarchy and Accumulation on a World Scale: Women in the International Division of Labour. London: Zed Books.

preceded and enabled capital accumulation on a world scale. Colonialism functioned not only as a system of resource extraction but as a mode of epistemic warfare. Indigenous economies, rooted in reciprocity, collective stewardship, and embedded knowledge of ecology, were systematically dismantled and recoded as "backward" or "unproductive". Colonial administrators, missionaries, and later economists imposed linear notions of time, extractivist logics of land use, and racialized hierarchies of knowledge. As decolonial theorists argue, this epistemological violence did not end with the retreat of formal empire; it continues to shape institutions of knowledge, property, and development today. Indeed, the discipline of economics itself, especially in its neoclassical form, remains implicated in this legacy. Its methodological individualism, emphasis on rational utility maximizers, and idealized models of market equilibrium obscure the historical reality of coercion, conquest, and commodification that laid the groundwork for global capitalism. In contrast, Marxist and world-systems theorists expose imperialism not as an anomaly but as a structural necessity of capitalist expansion. Imperialism resolves crises of overaccumulation by opening new frontiers of exploitation, what scholars term as accumulation by dispossession. Decolonial thinkers extend this critique by foregrounding the coloniality of power (Quijano), which persists beyond formal colonial rule through racialized labour markets, extractive trade regimes, and epistemic exclusion. Against this backdrop, Indigenous resistance must be recognized not as peripheral or reactive, but as foundational to world-historical struggle. From the Pueblo Revolt of 1680 to the enduring sovereignty of the Mapuche, and from cultural revitalization movements to land back campaigns, Indigenous peoples have generated alternative systems of governance, economics, and cosmology. These systems prioritize interdependence over accumulation, place-based knowledge over abstraction, and relationality over exploitation.

Today, the legacies of these colonial systems are not confined to the past. They manifest in enduring patterns of land dispossession, ecological collapse, racial capitalism, and epistemic marginalization. The global South remains structurally subordinated in systems of finance, trade, and knowledge production, while Indigenous communities face extractive violence under the guise of "development" and "sustainability". Recognizing this history is not merely an act of recovery—it is a political imperative. To confront the crises of our time, climate breakdown, widening inequality, and cultural erasure, we must dismantle the enduring architectures of imperial capitalism and affirm epistemologies rooted in sovereignty, justice, and regeneration. This is not simply about "inclusion" into existing structures but about reconfiguring the foundations of political economy itself. Only by reckoning with the true origins of the modern world can we begin to imagine futures that centre Indigenous autonomy, ecological balance, and collective emancipation as the basis for global transformation. These complex legal, political, and administrative dynamics are not merely historical artefacts; they are actively shaping the present and future of Indigenous economies. As such, Chapter 4 turns from critique to construction, investigating how Indigenous communities have developed alternative institutional frameworks and governance models that affirm cultural identity while asserting economic self-determination. By examining real-world examples of Indigenous-led development strategies and community-owned enterprises, the next chapter deepens our understanding of the ways Indigenous Peoples are actively redefining sovereignty and economic sustainability on their own terms.

References

Acemoglu, D., Johnson, S. and Robinson, J.A. (2001) 'The Colonial Origins of Comparative Development: An Empirical Investigation', American Economic Review, 91(5), pp. 1369–1401.

Allen, P.G. (1992) The Sacred Hoop: Recovering the Feminine in American Indian Traditions. Boston: Beacon Press.

Althusser, L. (1971). Ideology and Ideological State Apparatuses. In Lenin and Philosophy and Other Essays. London: Monthly Review Press.

Amin, S., 1976. Unequal Development: An Essay on the Social Formations of Peripheral Capitalism. New York: Monthly Review Press.

Bakewell, P., 1984. Silver Mining and Society in Colonial Mexico: Zacatecas 1546–1700. Cambridge: Cambridge University Press.

Bakewell, P. (1984). Miners of the Red Mountain: Indian Labour in Potosí, 1545–1650. University of New Mexico Press.

Barrett, W. (1990). World bullion flows, 1450–1800. In J.D. Tracy (Ed.), The Rise of Merchant Empires (pp. 224–254). Cambridge University Press

Beckert, S. (2014) Empire of Cotton: A Global History. New York: Knopf.

Bengoa, J. (2000) Historia del pueblo mapuche: Siglos XIX y XX. Santiago: LOM Ediciones.

Benton, L., 2010. A Search for Sovereignty: Law and Geography in European Empires, 1400–1900. Cambridge: Cambridge University Press.

Blaut, J.M. (1993) The Colonizer's Model of the World: Geographical Diffusionism and Eurocentric History. New York: Guilford Press.

Boxer, C.R. (1965) The Dutch Seaborne Empire, 1600–1800. London: Hutchinson.

Carlos, A. M., & Lewis, F. D. (2010). Commerce by a Frozen Sea: Native Americans and the European Fur Trade. University of Pennsylvania Press.

Clendinnen, I. (2003). Ambivalent Conquests: Maya and Spaniard in Yucatan, 1517–1570. Cambridge University Press.

Cook, S. F., & Borah, W. (1979). Essays in Population History: Mexico and the Caribbean. University of California Press.

Codere, H. (1950) Fighting with Property: A Study of Kwakiutl Potlatching and Warfare, 1792–1930. New York: J.J. Augustin.

Cronon, W. (1983). Changes in the Land: Indians, Colonists, and the Ecology of New England. New York: Hill and Wang.

Crosby, A.W. (1972). The Columbian Exchange: Biological and Cultural Consequences of 1492. Westport: Greenwood Press.

Daschuk, J. W. (2013). Clearing the Plains: Disease, Politics of Starvation, and the Loss of Aboriginal Life. University of Regina Press.

Davis, M. (2003). Late Victorian Holocausts: El Niño Famines and the Making of the Third World. London: Verso.

Dean, W. (1995) With Broadax and Firebrand: The Destruction of the Brazilian Atlantic Forest. Berkeley: University of California Press.

De Souza, J.G., Schaan, D., Robinson, M., Barbosa, C.P., Antunes, A.P., Guapindaia, V., Alves, D.S. and Ranzi, A. (2018). Pre-Columbian earth-builders of the Amazon: Geoglyphs and forest islands as testimony of complex societies. Nature Communications, 9(1), Article 112. https://doi.org/10.1038/s41467-017-02015-9

Diamond, J. (1997). *Guns, Germs, and Steel: The Fates of Human Societies*. W. W. Norton & Company.

Emerson, T.E., Hargrave, E.A. and Hedman, K.M. (2017). Death and diplomacy: The evidence for Cahokia's north plaza as an arena of interregional interaction. Journal of Anthropological Archaeology, 45, pp. 84–103. https://doi.org/10.1016/j.jaa.2016.11.004

Engels, F. (1876). The Part Played by Labour in the Transition from Ape to Man. Retrieved from Marxists Internet Archive.

Federici, S. (2004) Caliban and the Witch: Women, the Body and Primitive Accumulation. New York: Autonomedia.

Finney, B. (1994). Voyage of Rediscovery: A Cultural Odyssey through Polynesia. Honolulu: Bishop Museum Press.

Flynn, D.O. and Giráldez, A. (1995). Born with a "silver spoon": The origin of world trade in 1571. Journal of World History, 6(2), pp. 201–221.

Foster, J.B. (2000) Marx's Ecology: Materialism and Nature. New York: Monthly Review Press.
Frank, A.G. (1967) Capitalism and Underdevelopment in Latin America. New York: Monthly Review Press.
Garnett, S.T., Burgess, N.D., Fa, J.E., Fernández-Llamazares, Á., Molnár, Z., Robinson, C.J., Watson, J.E.M., Zander, K.K., Austin, B., Brondizio, E.S. and Collier, N.F. (2018) 'A spatial overview of the global importance of Indigenous lands for conservation', Nature Sustainability, 1(7), pp. 369–374.
Gómez, P. (2017) The Experiential Caribbean: Creating Knowledge and Healing in the Early Modern Atlantic. Chapel Hill: University of North Carolina Press.
Gone, J. P. (2013). Redressing First Nations historical trauma: Theorizing mechanisms for Indigenous culture as mental health treatment. Transcultural Psychiatry, 50(5), 683–706.
Gramsci, A. (1971). Selections from the Prison Notebooks. (Q. Hoare & G. N. Smith, Eds. and Trans.). International Publishers.
Green, T. A. (2019). The Rise of the Trans-Atlantic Slave Trade in Western Africa, 1300–1589. Cambridge University Press.
Grove, R.H. (1995) Green Imperialism: Colonial Expansion, Tropical Island Edens and the Origins of Environmentalism, 1600–1860. Cambridge: Cambridge University Press.
Gruzinski, S. (1993). The Conquest of Mexico: The Incorporation of Indian Societies into the Western World, 16th–18th Centuries. Polity Press
Gruzinski, S. (2002). The Mestizo Mind: The Intellectual Dynamics of Colonization and Globalization. New York: Routledge.
Hale, C. (2006). Más que un indio (More Than an Indian): Racial Ambivalence and Neoliberal Multiculturalism in Guatemala. School of American Research Press.
Hämäläinen, P. (2008) The Comanche Empire. New Haven: Yale University Press.
Harvey, D. (2003). *The New Imperialism*. Oxford University Press.
Heckenberger, M.J. (2005). The Ecology of Power: Culture, Place, and Personhood in the Southern Amazon, AD 1000–2000. New York: Routledge.
Heckenberger, M.J., Russell, J.C., Toney, J.R. and Schmidt, M.J. (2008). The legacy of cultural landscapes in the Brazilian Amazon: implications for biodiversity. Philosophical Transactions of the Royal Society B: Biological Sciences, 362(1478), pp. 197–208. https://doi.org/10.1098/rstb.2006.1987
Hemming, J. (1970). The Conquest of the Incas. Harcourt Brace Jovanovich.
Heywood, L.M. (2017) *Njinga of Angola: Africa's Warrior Queen*. Cambridge, MA: Harvard University Press
Inikori, J.E. (2002). Africans and the Industrial Revolution in England: A Study in International Trade and Economic Development. Cambridge: Cambridge University Press.

Instituto Brasileiro de Geografia e Estatística (IBGE) (2022) Indicadores Sociais dos Povos Indígenas no Brasil. [Online] Available at: https://www.ibge.gov.br [Accessed 8 Jul. 2025].

Kirmayer, L. J., Gone, J. P., & Moses, J. (2007). Rethinking historical trauma. Transcultural Psychiatry, 44(2), 112–136.

Knaut, A.L. (1995) The Pueblo Revolt of 1680: Conquest and Resistance in Seventeenth-Century New Mexico. Norman: University of Oklahoma Press.

Lenin, V.I. (1917). Imperialism: The Highest Stage of Capitalism. New York: International Publishers.

León-Portilla, M. (1992). *The Broken Spears: The Aztec Account of the Conquest of Mexico*. Beacon Press.

Lockhart, J. (1992) The Nahuas After the Conquest: A Social and Cultural History of the Indians of Central Mexico, Sixteenth Through Eighteenth Centuries. Stanford: Stanford University Press.

Mann, C. C. (2005). 1491: New Revelations of the Americas Before Columbus. Alfred A. Knopf.

Marx, K. (1867). Capital: A Critique of Political Economy, Vol. 1. London: Penguin Classics, 2004 ed.

Marx, K. (2004). Capital: A Critique of Political Economy. Volume 1. London: Penguin Classics. [Original work published 1867]

Mies, M. (1986) Patriarchy and Accumulation on a World Scale: Women in the International Division of Labour. London: Zed Books.

Mignolo, W.D. (2011) The Darker Side of Western Modernity: Global Futures, Decolonial Options. Durham, NC: Duke University Press.

Miller, R.J., Ruru, J., Behrendt, L. and Lindberg, T. (2010). Discovering Indigenous Lands: The Doctrine of Discovery in the English Colonies. Oxford: Oxford University Press.

Mills, K. (1997). Idolatry and Its Enemies: Colonial Andean Religion and Extirpation, 1640–1750. Princeton University Press.

Moore, J.W. (2010) 'The End of the Road? Agricultural Revolutions in the Capitalist World-Ecology, 1450–2010', *Journal of Agrarian Change*, 10(3), pp. 389–413.

Murra, J.V. (1980) The Economic Organization of the Inka State. Greenwich: JAI Press.

Nunn, N. and Qian, N. (2011) 'The Potato's Contribution to Population and Urbanization: Evidence from a Historical Experiment', Quarterly Journal of Economics, 126(2), pp. 593–650.

Oyěwùmí, O. (1997) The Invention of Women: Making an African Sense of Western Gender Discourses. Minneapolis: University of Minnesota Press.

Pagden, A. (1993). European Encounters with the New World: From Renaissance to Romanticism. New Haven: Yale University Press.

Pauketat, T.R. (2004). Ancient Cahokia and the Mississippians. Cambridge: Cambridge University Press.

Perelman, M. (2000). The Invention of Capitalism: Classical Political Economy and the Secret History of Primitive Accumulation. Durham: Duke University Press.

Platt, T. (1982) 'The Andean Experience of Bolivian Liberalism, 1825–1900', in Wolf, E.R. (ed.) State and Peasant in Latin America. New York: JAI Press, pp. 289–314.

Polanyi, K. (1944). The Great Transformation: The Political and Economic Origins of Our Time. Beacon Press.

Postero, N.G. (2007) Now We Are Citizens: Indigenous Politics in Postmulticultural Bolivia. Stanford: Stanford University Press.

Quijano, A. (2000) 'Coloniality of Power and Eurocentrism in Latin America', International Sociology, 15(2), pp. 215–232.

Rafael, V.L. (1988). Contracting Colonialism: Translation and Christian Conversion in Tagalog Society Under Early Spanish Rule. Ithaca: Cornell University Press.

Restall, M. (2003). Seven Myths of the Spanish Conquest. Oxford University Press.

Richter, D.K. (2001) Facing East from Indian Country: A Native History of Early America. Cambridge, MA: Harvard University Press.

Robins, N.A. (2011) Mercury, Mining, and Empire: The Human and Ecological Cost of Colonial Silver Mining in the Andes. Bloomington: Indiana University Press.

Rodney, W. (1972). How Europe Underdeveloped Africa. London: Bogle-L'Ouverture Publications.

Rostworowski, M. (1999) History of the Inca Realm. Cambridge: Cambridge University Press.

Schaafsma, P. (2001) Pueblo Cultures and Resistance in the Southwest. Santa Fe: School of American Research Press.

Seed, P. (1995). Ceremonies of Possession in Europe's Conquest of the New World, 1492–1640. Cambridge: Cambridge University Press.

Seed, P. (2001). American Pentimento: The Invention of Indians and the Pursuit of Riches. University of Minnesota Press.

Silverblatt, I. (1987) Moon, Sun, and Witches: Gender Ideologies and Class in Inca and Colonial Peru. Princeton: Princeton University Press.

Statistics Canada (2023) Life expectancy and mortality. [Online] Available at: https://www150.statcan.gc.ca/n1/en/subject/life_expectancy_and_mortality [Accessed 8 Jul. 2025].

Subrahmanyam, S. (1997). The Career and Legend of Vasco da Gama. Cambridge: Cambridge University Press.

Tandeter, E. (1993). Coercion and Market: Silver Mining in Colonial Potosí, 1692–1826. University of New Mexico Press.
Truth and Reconciliation Commission of Canada, 2015. Final Report of the Truth and Reconciliation Commission of Canada, Volume One: Summary. Toronto: James Lorimer & Company.
Wachtel, N. (1977) The Vision of the Vanquished: The Spanish Conquest of Peru through Indian Eyes. New York: Harvester Press.
Wallerstein, I. (1974). The Modern World-System I: Capitalist Agriculture and the Origins of the European World-Economy in the Sixteenth Century. Academic Press.
Waters, D.W. (1978) The Art of Navigation in England in Elizabethan and Early Stuart Times. London: Hollis & Carter.
Weber, M. (1930). The Protestant Ethic and the Spirit of Capitalism. London: Allen and Unwin.
Williams, E. (1944). Capitalism and Slavery. Chapel Hill: University of North Carolina Press.
Wolf, E. R. (1982). Europe and the People Without History. University of California Press.
Wolfe, P. (2006) 'Settler Colonialism and the Elimination of the Native', *Journal of Genocide Research*, 8(4), pp. 387–409.

CHAPTER 4

Technological and Strategic Superiority: An Analysis

1 Introduction

The rise of European global dominance between the fifteenth and nineteenth centuries cannot be understood without a rigorous examination of the technological and strategic systems that underpinned it. Unlike the often-deterministic narratives of inherent civilizational superiority, this chapter contends that a confluence of maritime, military, agricultural, and institutional innovations allowed Europe to project unprecedented power across the globe. The successful colonization of vast territories in the Americas, Australia, and New Zealand, areas that would become settler colonial states, was not merely the result of superior ideology or intent, but of technical and logistical advantages embedded within European societies. These innovations facilitated not only long-distance navigation and conquest but also the sustained control and transformation of foreign environments and populations. Maritime technologies such as the caravel and galleon, refined through centuries of Mediterranean and Atlantic navigation, provided the structural means for intercontinental voyages.[1] European navigators, empowered by instruments such as the astrolabe and magnetic compass, were able to exploit global wind patterns like the trade winds and westerlies to reliably traverse oceans, thereby

[1] Fernández-Armesto, F., 2006. Pathfinders: A Global History of Exploration. New York: W.W. Norton & Company.

S. Ramesh, *The Political Economy of the Indigenous Peoples of the World, Volume I*, https://doi.org/10.1007/978-3-032-24041-5_4

enabling the logistical backbone of empire.[2] The military edge of European empires lay not only in the possession of gunpowder weaponry, muskets, cannons, and naval artillery, but in the systemic application of battlefield discipline, combined arms tactics, and the strategic use of cavalry and steel.[3] These tools were decisive in conflicts such as the Spanish conquest of the Inca Empire, where technological asymmetry converted small expeditionary forces into agents of overwhelming dominance.[4] Simultaneously, the ability to sustain large imperial ventures rested on profound agricultural transformation: improved crop rotation, the domestication of livestock, and the global transplantation of staple crops and animals allowed for demographic expansion and economic surplus.[5] These systems directly displaced and restructured Indigenous ecologies and food systems, enabling settler consolidation. Crucially, European technological ascendancy did not emerge in isolation. The diffusion of knowledge from Islamic, Indian, and Chinese civilizations, particularly via the Silk Roads and the Mediterranean, fuelled European advances in mathematics, metallurgy, and navigation.[6,7] However, Europe differed in its institutional responses to knowledge, the Scientific Revolution, the rise of capitalism, and the entrenchment of state-backed exploration efforts catalysed a feedback loop between discovery, wealth generation, and technological refinement.[8] Joint-stock companies like the Dutch and British East India Companies exemplified this synthesis, embedding innovation within a system of commercial imperialism.[9] In

[2] Parry, J.H., 1963. The Age of Reconnaissance: Discovery, Exploration and Settlement, 1450 to 1650. London: Weidenfeld & Nicolson.

[3] Black, J., 2002. European Warfare, 1494–1660. London: Routledge.

[4] Restall, M., 2003. Seven Myths of the Spanish Conquest. Oxford: Oxford University Press.

[5] Crosby, A.W., 1972. The Columbian Exchange: Biological and Cultural Consequences of 1492. Westport: Greenwood Press.

[6] Needham, J., 1954. Science and Civilisation in China, Vol. 1. Cambridge: Cambridge University Press.

[7] Hobson, J.M., 2004. The Eastern Origins of Western Civilisation. Cambridge: Cambridge University Press.

[8] Mokyr, J., 2009. The Enlightened Economy: An Economic History of Britain 1700–1850. New Haven: Yale University Press.

[9] Braudel, F., 1982. The Wheels of Commerce: Civilization and Capitalism 15th–18th Century, Vol. 2. New York: Harper & Row.

contrast, advanced civilizations such as China and the Indian subcontinent, despite their long histories of innovation, oceanic navigation, and political centralization, did not pursue overseas empire-building on the same scale. The Ming dynasty's early maritime expeditions under Zheng He were abruptly ended due to internal political shifts and Confucian bureaucratic suspicion of merchant-military ventures.[10] In India, fragmented political authority, combined with a land-oriented economy and lack of naval investment, curtailed similar expansionist trajectories.[11] Moreover, both China and India lacked the external pressures and intra-European competition that drove states like Spain, Portugal, and England to continuously innovate, expand, and militarize their economies. The geopolitical configuration of Europe, with its decentralized states vying for dominance, created a unique Darwinian environment for strategic and technological evolution.[12] What distinguishes European expansion is not an absolute superiority in invention but the integration of innovations into systems of conquest, colonization, and economic exploitation. Indigenous peoples across the globe possessed rich technologies suited to their environments, Polynesian navigators traversed the Pacific with sophisticated knowledge of stars and currents; Andean civilizations engineered complex terracing and irrigation systems; and North American nations practiced sustainable agroforestry.[13] These achievements, however, were frequently overwhelmed not by lack of ingenuity, but by the systemic advantages of European imperial structures: concentrated violence, extractive economies, and global logistics chains. The legacy of these asymmetries continues to shape the modern world, making it essential to scrutinize the historical technologies that enabled them, not merely as artefacts of progress, but as instruments of power.

This chapter builds upon the theoretical foundations established in Chapters 1 and 2 by closely examining the contested terrain of Indigenous land rights and resource management. Chapter 1 introduced the

[10] Levathes, L., 1994. When China Ruled the Seas: The Treasure Fleet of the Dragon Throne, 1405–1433. Oxford: Oxford University Press.

[11] Bayly, C.A., 1988. Indian Society and the Making of the British Empire. Cambridge: Cambridge University Press.

[12] Kennedy, P., 1987. The Rise and Fall of the Great Powers: Economic Change and Military Conflict from 1500 to 2000. New York: Random House.

[13] Mann, C.C., 2005. 1491: New Revelations of the Americas Before Columbus. New York: Vintage.

central concepts of sovereignty, colonial dispossession, and the spiritual and ecological relationships that underpin Indigenous economies, while Chapter 2 detailed the philosophical divergences between Indigenous, neoclassical, and communist approaches to land and governance. This chapter expands this analysis through historical and comparative case studies of specific Indigenous communities confronting settler expansion, legal marginalization, and extractive resource economies. These examples provide a grounded context for understanding the persistent structural inequalities faced by Indigenous peoples, as well as the strategies of resistance and adaptation that continue to shape their political economies. By drawing these links, this chapter serves as a bridge between the conceptual framework and the empirical realities of Indigenous dispossession and resistance, setting the stage for deeper explorations of land-based movements, Indigenous legal traditions, and restorative justice initiatives in the chapters that follow.

2 Examination of Key Technologies That Enabled European Expansion

2.1 *Maritime Technologies: The Backbone of Expansion*

The maritime expansion of Europe between the fifteenth and eighteenth centuries marked a pivotal transformation in global political economy. The development of advanced seafaring technologies did not occur in a vacuum but emerged from a complex interplay of material needs, state patronage, competitive pressures, and evolving systems of production. Central to this expansion was the invention and refinement of ocean-going vessels, particularly the caravel and later the galleon. The caravel, developed by the Portuguese in the fifteenth century, was lightweight, highly manoeuvrable, and capable of sailing windward due to its lateen sails, an adaptation that allowed navigation along the West African coast and, eventually, across the Atlantic.[14] The galleon, emerging in the sixteenth century, further exemplified technological evolution by integrating firepower and cargo capacity, thus functioning as both a

[14] Parry, J.H., 1963. The Age of Reconnaissance: Discovery, Exploration and Settlement, 1450 to 1650. London: Weidenfeld & Nicolson.

warship and merchant vessel.[15] These ships became instruments not only of commerce but of colonization and domination, enabling European powers to project force and extract wealth across continents. Innovations in navigation were equally transformative. The adoption of the magnetic compass from Chinese sources and the astrolabe from the Islamic world provided European sailors with tools for determining direction and latitude, critical for long-distance voyages.[16,17] By the seventeenth century, the sextant replaced the astrolabe with greater accuracy, enabling transoceanic navigation with minimal land-based reference points. Portolan charts, highly detailed coastal maps developed in the Mediterranean, provided mariners with unprecedented navigational precision and facilitated the planning of maritime routes and the claiming of strategic harbours.[18] These tools not only revolutionized travel but served as mechanisms of enclosure, allowing European empires to assert territorial claims and map geographies in their own economic and strategic image. The strategic exploitation of ocean currents and wind systems, such as the trade winds and the westerlies, provided advantage. Portuguese and Spanish navigators learned to exploit the Volta do Mar, a navigational technique using circular wind currents in the Atlantic, to return from the African coast or the Americas to Europe more efficiently.[19] Such mastery converted environmental knowledge into imperial logistics, lowering transaction costs, reducing risk, and enhancing the predictability of transoceanic trade. Naval dominance was not merely the result of isolated technical achievements but was embedded in broader politico-economic structures. Advanced shipbuilding techniques, standardized hull construction, modular design, and improvements in ballast

[15] Rodger, N.A.M., 2004. The Command of the Ocean: A Naval History of Britain, 1649–1815. London: Penguin.

[16] Needham, J., 1971. Science and Civilisation in China, Volume 4: Physics and Physical Technology, Part 3: Civil Engineering and Nautics. Cambridge: Cambridge University Press.

[17] Burnett, C., 2001. The Coherence of the Arabic-Latin Translation Program in Toledo in the Twelfth Century. Science in Context, 14(1–2), pp.249–288.

[18] Campbell, T., 1987. Portolan Charts from the Late Thirteenth Century to 1500. In: J.B. Harley and D. Woodward (eds.) The History of Cartography, Volume 1: Cartography in Prehistoric, Ancient, and Medieval Europe and the Mediterranean. Chicago: University of Chicago Press, pp. 371–463.

[19] Boxer, C.R., 1969. The Portuguese Seaborne Empire 1415–1825. London: Hutchinson.

and keel structure enabled European states to mass-produce and maintain fleets, establishing military supremacy at sea.[20] Naval capacity was also closely linked to the rise of proto-capitalist states. In neoclassical economic terms, these maritime advancements can be interpreted as increases in capital efficiency and mobility, reducing spatial transaction costs and generating comparative advantages in global trade.[21] State-sponsored fleets, such as the Portuguese armada or the English Royal Navy, functioned as public goods with high positive externalities for mercantile classes and imperial bureaucracies. Comparatively, under communist or command economies, such coordinated technological and logistical investments have often faced limits due to rigid central planning and lack of market incentives. For instance, the Soviet Union's attempts in the twentieth century to develop blue-water naval capabilities were technologically sophisticated but economically burdensome and inefficiently allocated relative to returns.[22] By contrast, early capitalist Europe used both public and private investment (e.g., through joint-stock companies like the Dutch East India Company) to fund maritime expansion, creating dynamic feedback loops between state, capital, and innovation.[23] The strategic use of ports and harbours was essential to sustaining imperial expansion. Cities such as Lisbon, Seville, and later Amsterdam and London were not only centres of commerce but nodes in a global logistical network. These ports became supply hubs, data collection points, and military outposts. The economic rationale was clear: controlling maritime chokepoints and harbour infrastructure allowed for monopolistic control of trade routes and resource flows. In the colonial Americas and Asia, the establishment of ports like Manila and Calcutta functioned as extensions of European state power, directly facilitating capital extraction, resource transfer, and the insertion of Indigenous societies into global

[20] Unger, R.W., 1978. Dutch Shipbuilding Before 1800: Ships and Guilds. Assen: Van Gorcum.

[21] North, D.C., 1990. Institutions, Institutional Change and Economic Performance. Cambridge: Cambridge University Press.

[22] Holloway, D., 1982. The Soviet Union and the Arms Race. New Haven: Yale University Press.

[23] Glete, J., 1993. Navies and Nations: Warships, Navies and State Building in Europe and America, 1500–1860. Stockholm: Almqvist & Wiksell International.

commodity circuits.[24] In totality, the technological foundation of European maritime expansion was inseparable from the political economy of the time. Innovations were not simply matters of engineering; they were political technologies, tools for creating empires, disciplining labour, and enclosing space. Indigenous peoples encountered these technologies not as neutral instruments but as instruments of transformation, disruption, and often destruction. The asymmetry in maritime capability was thus not an accident of geography or culture, but the outcome of systemic investments in technology, finance, and coercion that allowed Europe to navigate, conquer, and reorder much of the world.

2.2 Military Technologies: Tools of Conquest

European expansion during the early modern period was underpinned by the strategic application of military technologies that decisively tilted the balance of power in confrontations with Indigenous peoples. Gunpowder weapons played a transformative role in conquest and colonization. Muskets, cannons, and naval artillery offered a devastating advantage over Indigenous societies, many of whom were unfamiliar with projectile warfare at such a scale. The Spanish conquest of the Inca Empire exemplifies this asymmetry. At the Battle of Cajamarca in 1532, Francisco Pizarro's force of fewer than 200 men captured Atahualpa, the Inca emperor, using surprise tactics, steel swords, cavalry, and a few small cannons, despite facing thousands of Inca warriors.[25] The psychological impact of firearms, combined with their auditory and destructive force, was often as significant as their material effects.[26] The integration of gunpowder weaponry with tactical discipline and formations like the pike-and-shot method allowed small European units to exert force disproportionate to their size. These formations, common in European warfare from the sixteenth century, enabled simultaneous offensive and defensive operations, especially against large, loosely organized Indigenous forces. It has been noted that these tactics reflected a broader military revolution

[24] Curtin, P.D., 1984. Cross-Cultural Trade in World History. Cambridge: Cambridge University Press.

[25] Restall, M., 2003. Seven Myths of the Spanish Conquest. Oxford: Oxford University Press.

[26] Crosby, A.W., 1972. The Columbian Exchange: Biological and Cultural Consequences of 1492. Westport: Greenwood Press.

that prioritized coordinated firepower and drilled infantry over heroic or chaotic battle styles, common in some Indigenous warfare traditions.[27] Meanwhile, European steel weaponry, refined through centuries of metallurgical experimentation, far surpassed the obsidian or wooden arms used by many Indigenous groups in the Americas and Africa.[28] Protective armour, though gradually phased out, offered early protection that could turn skirmishes decisively. Crucially, the horse revolutionized European campaigns. The mobility, shock power, and command elevation offered by cavalry units proved decisive, especially in the Americas, where horses had been extinct for millennia. Indigenous societies such as the Mapuche and Plains tribes of North America eventually adapted to equestrian warfare, but by then the strategic initiative had already shifted.[29] The role of horses at Cajamarca, for example, was both tactical and psychological; the Inca had never encountered mounted warriors and were unprepared for the agility and terror induced by cavalry charges.[30] The effectiveness of military technology was not merely material. It was embedded in economic systems that supported innovation and deployment. Neoclassical economics attributes European military supremacy in part to rational allocation of resources towards military R&D, incentivized through state support, colonial profit, and capitalist enterprise.[31] By contrast, centrally planned economies such as those inspired by communist ideology often struggled with the decentralized innovation required for tactical adaptability. In the colonial context, however, Indigenous economies, whether communal or hierarchical, lacked the institutional capacity for rapid militarization or technological absorption. This does not reflect technological inferiority per se, but rather the absence of an extractive-capitalist structure that could fund standing armies, metallurgy industries, or

[27] Black, J., 2002. European Warfare, 1494–1660. London: Routledge.

[28] Parry, J.H., 1963. The Age of Reconnaissance: Discovery, Exploration and Settlement, 1450 to 1650. London: Weidenfeld & Nicolson.

[29] Kennedy, P., 1987. The Rise and Fall of the Great Powers: Economic Change and Military Conflict from 1500 to 2000. New York: Random House.

[30] Restall, M., 2003. Seven Myths of the Spanish Conquest. Oxford: Oxford University Press.

[31] North, D.C., 1990. Institutions, Institutional Change and Economic Performance. Cambridge: Cambridge University Press.

transoceanic arsenals.[32] Comparatively, the Soviet military buildup in the twentieth century under communism demonstrates that state-directed economies can produce formidable military forces, though often at high social cost and inefficiencies.[33] Yet this historical analogy highlights what many Indigenous societies lacked: a bureaucratic-military complex capable of sustaining long-term armament and innovation. The European military model, while violent and exploitative, was integrated into a broader system of maritime capitalism, mercantilism, and imperial competition.[34] This structural synergy amplified the impact of each weapon and tactic in the field. Thus, the military technologies enabled European expansion not just because they were more advanced, but because they were part of a wider political economy rooted in competition, technological diffusion, and strategic accumulation. Indigenous resistance was often brave and creative, but ultimately overmatched by a system designed to produce conquest.

2.3 Agricultural Innovations: Sustaining Empires

European expansion during the early modern period was not solely driven by guns and ships; it was equally sustained by agricultural innovations that supported demographic growth, military provisioning, and the establishment of settler colonies. Advances in ploughing technology, such as the heavy wheeled plough with an iron ploughshare, allowed European farmers to cultivate more challenging soils, especially in Northern and Central Europe. This efficiency was further enhanced by the three-field crop rotation system, which reduced soil exhaustion and allowed for higher yields over time.[35] These techniques were exported to colonial territories, fundamentally altering local ecosystems and food production systems. Domesticated livestock played a central role in both agricultural and military logistics. Horses, oxen, and cattle were used not only

[32] Hobson, J.M., 2004. The Eastern Origins of Western Civilisation. Cambridge: Cambridge University Press.

[33] Holloway, D., 1982. The Soviet Union and the Arms Race. New Haven: Yale University Press.

[34] Braudel, F., 1982. The Wheels of Commerce: Civilization and Capitalism 15th–18th Century, Vol. 2. New York: Harper & Row.

[35] Braudel, F., 1982. The Wheels of Commerce: Civilization and Capitalism 15th–18th Century, Vol. 2. New York: Harper & Row.

for ploughing and transportation but also as mobile sources of food and wealth. The Columbian Exchange facilitated the introduction of these animals into the Americas, transforming Indigenous landscapes and economies. In many regions of the Americas, Indigenous populations had not domesticated large animals suitable for ploughing or transport, making European livestock a disruptive force. For example, in the Pampas of Argentina and the Great Plains of North America, the introduction of the horse restructured Indigenous economies and warfare, but only after initial European control had been secured.[36] Similarly, European settlers introduced new crops such as wheat, barley, oats, and rye, which often displaced Indigenous staples like maize, quinoa, or millet. These cereals were not simply dietary preferences; they reflected European ecological imperialism, wherein colonial environments were forcibly reshaped to resemble European agricultural regimes.[37] The result was not only a transformation of local diets but also a reconfiguration of land use, labour, and settlement patterns. The widespread establishment of plantation economies in the Caribbean and parts of Latin America further exemplifies how agriculture was harnessed for imperial gain, often through coercive labour systems such as slavery or encomienda.[38] Irrigation and drainage systems were also introduced or intensified in colonized regions to increase productivity. European engineers implemented hydraulic infrastructure in places like India and Egypt, transforming arid or flood-prone areas into agriculturally productive zones.[39] In British India, for example, large-scale canal systems such as the Upper Ganges Canal (completed in 1854) and the Punjab Canal Colonies were developed to irrigate millions of acres in the northwestern provinces, particularly in Punjab and Uttar Pradesh. These projects dramatically increased agricultural yields of cash crops like wheat, cotton, and sugarcane, serving imperial economic interests. Similarly, in Egypt under British control, the construction of the Aswan Low Dam in 1902 enabled greater control of

[36] Crosby, A.W., 1972. The Columbian Exchange: Biological and Cultural Consequences of 1492. Westport: Greenwood Press.

[37] Mann, C.C., 2005. 1491: New Revelations of the Americas Before Columbus. New York: Vintage.

[38] Parry, J.H., 1963. The Age of Reconnaissance: Discovery, Exploration and Settlement, 1450 to 1650. London: Weidenfeld & Nicolson.

[39] Bayly, C.A., 1988. Indian Society and the Making of the British Empire. Cambridge: Cambridge University Press.

the Nile's annual floods and extended cultivation into previously barren lands. These interventions were not neutral technological feats; they often disrupted traditional water-sharing practices, displaced local knowledge systems, and restructured agrarian societies to prioritise imperial extraction and export-oriented agriculture. While this boosted imperial revenues, it also undermined Indigenous ecological balances. In the Indian subcontinent, British-imposed canal irrigation systems disrupted traditional water management practices and, in some cases, contributed to salinization and ecological degradation.[40] The environmental consequences of these transformations were profound. The displacement of native crops, the spread of invasive European species (both flora and fauna), and changes in soil use all contributed to biodiversity loss and ecological instability. Moreover, the imposition of European agricultural systems often ignored the sustainability of Indigenous methods, such as intercropping, agroforestry, and shifting cultivation, which were better adapted to local environmental conditions.[41,42] From a neoclassical economic perspective, these innovations are viewed as rational responses to scarcity and productivity challenges and as mechanisms to maximise output and enable trade. However, this framing omits the coercive and extractive dimensions of imperial agriculture. The capitalist logic driving agricultural intensification often prioritized export production over local subsistence, leading to food insecurity and land alienation in colonized regions.[43] In contrast, communist regimes, such as the Soviet Union and Maoist China, also prioritized agricultural transformation but through centralized collectivization, often resulting in massive inefficiencies, famines, and ecological destruction, evident in cases like Stalin's Ukraine or China's Great Leap Forward.[44] These divergent models

[40] Gilmartin, D., 1994. Scientific Empire and Imperial Science: Colonialism and Irrigation Technology in the Indus Basin. The Journal of Asian Studies, 53(4), pp.1127–1149.

[41] Mann, C.C., 2005. 1491: New Revelations of the Americas Before Columbus. New York: Vintage.

[42] Hobson, J.M., 2004. The Eastern Origins of Western Civilisation. Cambridge: Cambridge University Press.

[43] North, D.C., 1990. Institutions, Institutional Change and Economic Performance. Cambridge: Cambridge University Press.

[44] Holloway, D., 1982. The Soviet Union and the Arms Race. New Haven: Yale University Press.

underscore the complex relationships between state systems, ideology, and ecological outcomes. Ultimately, agricultural innovation under European empires cannot be viewed in isolation from the political economy of colonization. It was a key instrument of territorial control, population settlement, and economic extraction—one that reshaped Indigenous landscapes and livelihoods in enduring ways.

3 Social and Economic Factors That Fostered European Innovation

3.1 *The Role of Trade Networks in Knowledge Exchange*

European participation in long-distance trade networks, particularly the Silk Road, played a decisive role in the diffusion of technological and scientific knowledge that underpinned Europe's later industrial and strategic superiority. The overland and maritime Silk Roads facilitated the transfer of innovations such as gunpowder, paper-making techniques, and the magnetic compass from China to Europe via Central Asia and the Islamic world.[45] During the Crusades (1096–1291), contact with Islamic states exposed Europeans to advanced medical, astronomical, and mathematical knowledge preserved and expanded upon by scholars in Baghdad, Damascus, and Cordoba.[46] Mediterranean hubs such as Venice and Genoa became vital nodes where Eastern and Western innovations intersected, blending technological imports with local experimentation.[47] From a neoclassical economics perspective, these exchanges reduced transaction costs and expanded the technological production possibility frontier (PPF) by enhancing factor productivity. Access to better navigational tools and cartographic knowledge, for example, reduced the marginal cost of long-distance shipping, enabling European merchants to exploit comparative advantages in high-value commodities such as spices, silk, and precious metals. Historical trade data indicate that by the late fifteenth century, Venetian spice imports from the Levant accounted for

[45] Needham, J. (1981). Science in traditional China: A comparative perspective. Harvard University Press.

[46] Saliba, G. (2007). *Islamic science and the making of the European Renaissance*. MIT Press.

[47] Chaudhuri, K. N. (1985). Trade and civilisation in the Indian Ocean: An economic history from the rise of Islam to 1750. Cambridge University Press.

over 60% of its merchant fleet's cargo value, directly funding further voyages and exploratory ventures.[48] This self-reinforcing cycle of trade profits funding innovation aligns with the endogenous growth theory in economics, where knowledge spillovers fuel sustained technological advancement.[49] In contrast, communist economic systems, as historically implemented in the twentieth century, adopted a more centralized and planned approach to technological diffusion. While central planning could direct large-scale scientific projects (as in Soviet space and military technology), the lack of decentralized trade networks often limited the diversity and rapidity of technological imports from abroad.[50] The European early modern experience shows the opposite dynamic: decentralized, competitive polities like the Dutch Republic leveraged global trade to acquire and adapt foreign innovations quickly. The Dutch East India Company (VOC), for instance, established direct maritime links with Asian producers, bypassing intermediaries and reinvesting profits into shipbuilding and navigational research, an iterative feedback loop largely absent in command economies with restricted international market engagement. The circulation of inventions through international trade was not merely a passive transfer but involved active adaptation. The printing press, introduced to Europe in the mid-fifteenth century via knowledge of movable type from East Asia,[51] rapidly spread along major trade routes. By 1500, over 20 million books had been printed in Europe, significantly accelerating literacy, scientific discourse, and commercial record-keeping.[52] The diffusion of gunpowder weapons, initially a Chinese invention, transformed European warfare by the sixteenth century, with the adoption of cannons and firearms reshaping

[48] Braudel, F. (1972). The Mediterranean and the Mediterranean world in the age of Philip II. Harper & Row.

[49] Romer, P. M. (1990). Endogenous technological change. Journal of Political Economy, 98(5, Part 2), S71–S102.

[50] Allen, R. C. (2003). Farm to factory: A reinterpretation of the Soviet industrial revolution. Princeton University Press.

[51] Eisenstein, E. L. (1980). The printing press as an agent of change. Cambridge University Press.

[52] Pettegree, A. (2010). The book in the Renaissance. Yale University Press.

both military tactics and state formation.[53] These technological adoptions were sustained through robust capital accumulation from colonial and intercontinental trade, particularly the extraction of silver from the Americas, which provided liquidity to finance imports from Asia via the Manila Galleons.[54] Ultimately, Europe's intertwined trade and innovation systems created a feedback mechanism: exploration generated profits, profits financed innovation, and innovation reduced the cost and risk of further exploration. This process, while explicable through neoclassical models of capital accumulation and knowledge spillovers, also highlights how the competitive political economy of Europe differed from centralized communist systems, in which political control often constrained the international exchange of ideas. Historical evidence suggests that the openness and plurality of European trade networks during the early modern period accelerated technological convergence with, and eventual divergence from, other regions, laying the foundation for industrial and imperial dominance.

3.2 Knowledge Exchange and the Scientific Revolution

The European Scientific Revolution was not an isolated intellectual eruption but the product of centuries of knowledge exchange that transcended geographical and cultural boundaries. The Renaissance provided a fertile cultural environment for inquiry, curiosity, and systematic observation, driven in part by the revival of classical Greek and Roman learning through the reintroduction of ancient texts preserved by Islamic scholars.[55] The adoption of Arabic numerals and the development of algebra, both imported through contact with the Islamic world, replaced cumbersome Roman numerals and facilitated more sophisticated

[53] Parker, G. (1996). The military revolution: Military innovation and the rise of the West, 1500–1800. Cambridge University Press.

[54] Flynn, D. O., & Giráldez, A. (1995). Born with a 'silver spoon': The origin of world trade in 1571. Journal of World History, 6(2), 201–221.

[55] Saliba, G. (2007). *Islamic science and the making of the European Renaissance*. MIT Press.

calculation, accounting, and engineering design.[56,57] These imported concepts were critical for navigation and astronomy, which underpinned Europe's Age of Exploration. Techniques such as latitude calculation using the astrolabe and the refinement of celestial navigation were adapted from Islamic and earlier Hellenistic sources. European mariners began using these tools to determine their position at sea with greater accuracy, reducing the risks of long voyages. Improvements in astronomical tables—many based on Arabic translations and innovations—allowed for more precise predictions of planetary positions and eclipses, which were essential for timekeeping and route planning. Without these cross-cultural transfers of knowledge, the expansive maritime ventures of powers like Portugal, Spain, and the Dutch Republic would have been far more perilous and less economically viable. Institutions such as universities and academies became hubs for intellectual debate and experimentation, institutionalizing research and learning. The University of Padua and the Royal Society of London exemplify this role, fostering structured peer review and the accumulation of empirical evidence.[58,59] These institutions not only transmitted existing knowledge but also enabled the generation of new ideas through collaborative inquiry, reducing informational asymmetries and creating a form of knowledge commons, an idea resonant with both neoclassical and communist perspectives. From a neoclassical standpoint, universities reduced transaction costs in knowledge production and diffusion, enhancing innovation efficiency.[60] From a communist perspective, they represented collective ownership of intellectual resources, prioritizing social benefit over private profit, albeit within a European socio-political structure that still valued competition for prestige and patronage. The printing press transformed the velocity and breadth of information dissemination. Between 1450 and 1500, over 20 million books were printed in Europe, dramatically reducing the marginal

[56] Needham, J. (1981). Science in traditional China: A comparative perspective. Harvard University Press.

[57] Chaudhuri, K. N. (1985). *Trade and civilisation in the Indian Ocean: An economic history from the rise of Islam to 1750*. Cambridge University Press.

[58] Eisenstein, E. L. (1980). The printing press as an agent of change: Communications and cultural transformations in early-modern Europe. Cambridge University Press.

[59] Pettegree, A. (2010). The book in the Renaissance. Yale University Press.

[60] Romer, P. M. (1990). Endogenous technological change. Journal of Political Economy, 98(5, Part 2), S71–S102.

cost of reproducing knowledge.[61] This rapid spread of scientific treatises enabled a more competitive intellectual environment, akin to neoclassical models of market competition, where ideas competed for acceptance based on merit and evidence. Yet, in practice, the printing press also created centralized control points in the form of licensing and censorship regimes, echoing communist concerns about the suppression of dissenting ideas. The link between scientific discovery and practical application was particularly evident in exploration technologies. Advances in cartography, ship design, and navigation, facilitated by knowledge from Islamic, Chinese, and Polynesian sources, were instrumental in European expansion.[62,63] Empirical data on maritime innovation suggest that Portuguese and Spanish voyages between 1500 and 1600 reduced average Atlantic crossing times by nearly 40%, an increase in productivity that translated directly into economic gains through faster trade and lower costs per unit of transported goods.[64] Ultimately, the Scientific Revolution can be interpreted as an emergent property of cross-cultural exchange embedded within particular political-economic structures. The neoclassical lens highlights the efficiency gains from reduced information costs and improved human capital, while the communist lens emphasizes the collective dimension of knowledge and the risks posed by private monopolization of information. Europe's advantage lay not solely in endogenous creativity, but in its ability to integrate and institutionalize global knowledge flows into sustained technological and economic development.

3.3 Capitalism and State Patronage as Drivers of Innovation

The interplay between capitalism and state patronage in early modern Europe created an unprecedented environment for sustained technological innovation. The emergence of joint-stock companies such as the Dutch East India Company (VOC) and the English East India Company

[61] Eisenstein, E. L. (1980). The printing press as an agent of change: Communications and cultural transformations in early-modern Europe. Cambridge University Press.

[62] Needham, J. (1981). Science in traditional China: A comparative perspective. Harvard University Press.

[63] Flynn, D. O., & Giráldez, A. (1995). Born with a 'silver spoon': The origin of world trade in 1571. *Journal of World History, 6*(2), 201–221.

[64] Allen, R. C. (2003). *Farm to factory: A reinterpretation of the Soviet industrial revolution.* Princeton University Press.

exemplified how private capital could be mobilized to fund exploration, technological advancement, and large-scale commercial operations. These companies operated as quasi-sovereign entities, possessing the capacity to raise capital from a wide investor base, spread risks, and finance innovations in ship design, navigation, and armaments.[65] State patronage reinforced these capitalist initiatives. Maritime powers such as Portugal and Spain actively subsidized exploration, military technology, and knowledge infrastructure. Prince Henry the Navigator's sponsorship of the Sagres School of Navigation in Portugal during the fifteenth century exemplified the role of state-led investment in building technological capacity, integrating cartographic advances from Islamic and Chinese sources with European shipbuilding techniques.[66] Similarly, the Spanish Crown's financing of Christopher Columbus's transatlantic voyages in 1492 reflected a deliberate state strategy to secure new trade routes, resources, and geopolitical influence.[67] From a neoclassical economics perspective, these developments can be understood through the lens of capital accumulation, market expansion, and comparative advantage. The joint-stock model reduced transaction costs and facilitated economies of scale, aligning private profit motives with broader societal gains through spillover effects in technology and infrastructure.[68] Estimates suggest that between 1500 and 1820, Western Europe's GDP per capita rose from approximately $771 to $1202 (1990 international dollars), outpacing most other world regions due to expanding trade networks and innovation.[69] By contrast, a centrally planned communist model, as seen in the Soviet Union from 1928 onwards, substituted state monopoly for private competition, directing resources into heavy industry and military research without reliance on capital markets. Soviet industrial output grew at an

[65] Carlos, A. M., & Neal, L. (2011). Commerce and conflict: The East India Company and the rise of British dominance in Asia, 1600–1800. Cambridge University Press.

[66] Diffie, B. W., & Winius, G. D. (1977). Foundations of the Portuguese empire, 1415–1580. University of Minnesota Press.

[67] Fernández-Armesto, F. (2007). Pathfinders: A global history of exploration. Oxford University Press.

[68] North, D. C., & Weingast, B. R. (1989). Constitutions and commitment: The evolution of institutions governing public choice in seventeenth-century England. The Journal of Economic History, 49(4), 803–832.

[69] Maddison, A., 2001. The world economy: A millennial perspective. Paris: OECD, p. 264.

average annual rate of 5.8% between 1928 and 1940, compared to less than 3% in many capitalist economies during the Great Depression.[70] However, Soviet innovation was heavily concentrated in military and industrial applications, with weaker spillover into consumer goods and services compared to capitalist economies. Economic competition among European powers, particularly during the Age of Discovery, further reinforced innovation incentives. Rivalries between Spain, Portugal, England, and the Netherlands created an arms race in shipbuilding, navigation, and weaponry, like modern technological competition in aerospace and digital industries. Trade volume estimates indicate that by 1700, the Dutch Republic controlled over 50% of European shipping in Asia[71] and by 1750, Britain's share of world trade had grown to 20%.[72] The wealth generated from colonial trade and resource extraction was frequently reinvested into further expeditions, scientific research, and military development. The VOC, for instance, dedicated significant funds to improving maritime charts and logistical systems, enabling more efficient trade routes and higher profitability. The company invested in the development of detailed hydrographic maps, particularly of the Indian Ocean, Southeast Asian archipelagos, and the treacherous waters around the Cape of Good Hope. It also maintained a centralized information system in Amsterdam, where returning captains were required to submit logs and updated charts, which were then revised and redistributed. This systematic approach allowed the VOC to shorten voyage times, avoid hazards, and establish more reliable shipping schedules. Furthermore, the VOC built and maintained strategic supply stations—such as the Cape Colony (modern-day Cape Town)—to refuel and resupply its fleets, contributing to the longevity and profitability of its trade routes between Europe and Asia. These innovations were often the result of a hybrid system, where private investment and public sponsorship combined to create a self-reinforcing cycle of technological progress. Such a framework contrasts with both the purely profit-maximizing assumptions of neoclassical theory and the centrally directed innovation model of communist economies, highlighting a historically contingent balance that proved particularly

[70] Allen, R. C. (2003). Farm to factory: A reinterpretation of the Soviet industrial revolution. Princeton University Press.

[71] Boxer, C. R. (1965). The Dutch seaborne empire, 1600–1800. Hutchinson.

[72] Maddison, A., 2001. The world economy: A millennial perspective. Paris: OECD, p. 264.

effective in early modern Europe. While communism demonstrated the capacity for rapid industrial mobilization under state planning, capitalist Europe's competitive, decentralized model allowed for more diversified innovation and sustained technological diffusion.

4 Comparisons with Indigenous Technological Practices and Innovations

4.1 Indigenous Maritime and Navigation Practices

Indigenous maritime technologies were not primitive precursors to "modern" craft but highly optimized solutions to distinct ecological and economic constraints. In Polynesia, double-hulled voyaging canoes and outrigger configurations produced seaworthy, fast, and repairable vessels capable of blue-water crossings measured in thousands of nautical miles. Navigators employed star paths, swell refraction, cloud and bird cues, and mental cartographies rather than instruments.[73,74] Experimental voyages have demonstrated the technical sufficiency of this knowledge: the Hōkūle'a sailed roughly 2,500 nautical miles from Hawai'i to Tahiti in 34 days without modern navigation, validating oral and embodied techniques that once enabled the settlement of Remote Oceania.[75,76,77] Governance of nearshore resources likewise reflected sophisticated institutional design. Practices such as rāhui, temporary closures or spatial restrictions, allocated harvesting rights and synchronized effort with ecological cycles, producing predictable yields without heavy capital inputs.[78] Viewed through a neoclassical lens, the point is simply that

[73] Lewis, David. 1972. We, the Navigators: The Ancient Art of Landfinding in the Pacific. Honolulu: University of Hawai 'i Press.

[74] Gladwin, Thomas. 1970. East Is a Big Bird: Navigation and Logic on Puluwat Atoll. Cambridge, MA: Harvard University Press.

[75] Finney, Ben. 1994. Voyage of Rediscovery: A Cultural Odyssey Through Polynesia. Berkeley: University of California Press.

[76] Irwin, Geoffrey. 1992. The Prehistoric Exploration and Colonization of the Pacific. Cambridge: Cambridge University Press.

[77] Kirch, Patrick Vinton. 2017. On the Road of the Winds: An Archaeological History of the Pacific Islands before European Contact. Revised and Expanded Edition. Berkeley: University of California Press.

[78] Johannes, R. E. 1978. "Traditional Marine Conservation Methods in Oceania and Their Demise." Annual Review of Ecology and Systematics 9: 349–364.

people minimize total costs, including risk, given their "factor endowments" (what is abundant versus scarce). In pre-contact Polynesia, skilled labour and organic materials (timber, fibre, shell) were abundant, while metal fasteners and precision instruments were scarce or absent. Builders and navigators therefore substituted what they had (labour, skill, locally generated information) for what they lacked (iron hardware, compasses, sextants) in ways that lowered the effective cost of safe movement across open ocean.[79] This logic shows up first in boatbuilding. Canoe makers invested many skilled hours to produce lightweight hulls, thin planks or finely worked dugouts that accelerate quickly, surf well, and can be beached or hauled, so each mile requires fewer person-hours per kilogram moved. In economic terms, they chose a production technique with high labour (L) and very low capital (K) in metal and tooling because the implicit price of labour (w) was relatively low while the price of capital (r) for scarce metal was extremely high; in the simple cost function $C = w \cdot L + r \cdot K$, a labour-heavy, capital-light design minimizes C under those prices.[80] Joinery followed the same substitution rule: modular lashings of sennit (coconut-fibre cord) replaced metal nails and bolts. Lashings flex under load, are repairable at sea with local materials, and reduce catastrophic failure in heavy swell, which lowers expected maintenance, downtime, and loss—hidden components of the "risk cost" per voyage mile. Navigation completed the substitution. Rather than instruments, way finders relied on star paths, swell refraction, bird and cloud cues, and mental charts, an information-rich system built on training, practice, and shared mnemonics. This is human capital standing in for physical capital: better information reduces the variance of landfall times and the probability of getting lost, thereby cutting expected risk costs and lowering the unit cost of mobility.[81] Social rules were built to fit how the maritime technology actually worked, so the community could use canoes and fisheries efficiently without depleting them or fighting about access. Take rāhui: a chief or guardian could temporarily close a reef, lagoon, or species during spawning or after a death. That's a

[79] Irwin, Geoffrey. 1992. The Prehistoric Exploration and Colonization of the Pacific. Cambridge: Cambridge University Press.

[80] Irwin, Geoffrey. 1992. The Prehistoric Exploration and Colonization of the Pacific. Cambridge: Cambridge University Press.

[81] Irwin, Geoffrey. 1992. The Prehistoric Exploration and Colonization of the Pacific. Cambridge: Cambridge University Press.

rule tuned to the ecology and the boat economy; by pausing harvest where light, fast canoes could otherwise overexploit a spot, rāhui protects future yields and reduces conflict over "who gets to fish now". Sea-territory norms (often called customary marine tenure) did similar work. Reefs, channels, and nearshore patches were recognized as belonging to specific kin groups or villages, with named boundaries marked by landmarks or known waypoints. Because those boundaries were widely understood, crews knew where they could land, fish, or anchor, which cut down on costly disputes during voyages. Role specialization, distinct responsibilities for navigators, captains, fishers, and steersmen, matched the technical demands of blue water sailing and nearshore harvesting. Training and authority were concentrated where errors are most expensive (e.g., navigation decisions), which improves safety and coordination. This package lines up with Elinor Ostrom's design principles for successful commons. Clear boundaries: named reef sections or lagoons and acknowledged rights-holders make it obvious who may use what. Congruent rules: rāhui durations, gear limits, and seasonal closures fit local conditions (tides, spawning runs, storm seasons), so the costs and benefits of rules make sense to users. Local monitoring: fishers, guardians, or appointed wardens can see who is on "their" water and whether they follow the rules, no expensive bureaucracy needed. Graduated sanctions: first a warning, then a fine, then gear confiscation or exclusion, punishment scales with the offense, keeping enforcement credible without blowing up relationships. Low-cost conflict resolution: disagreements can be settled quickly by elders, councils, or chiefs at the beach or meeting house, avoiding long, disruptive disputes. Often, two further principles also applied: collective-choice arrangements (users help make or revise the rules, so compliance rises) and nesting (village rules sit within island- or archipelago-level protocols for inter-community travel). In short, governance "matched the tech" by lowering the real costs of coordination, enforcement, and ecological uncertainty that come with fast, portable boats operating across patchy, sensitive marine environments. These institutions reduce transaction costs (less conflict over landing sites or fishing grounds, smoother provisioning and layovers) and stabilize ecological yields, which lowers total costs across voyages and seasons.[82] Taken together, lightweight hulls, lashing-based modularity, information-dense

[82] Ostrom, Elinor. 1990. Governing the Commons: The Evolution of Institutions for Collective Action. Cambridge: Cambridge University Press.

wayfinding, and locally designed rules form an efficient bundle for an oceanic frontier: labour and information substitute for scarce metal and instruments, while governance trims maintenance, delay, and loss. That is exactly what neoclassical theory predicts when relative scarcities look like Polynesia's, and why these systems delivered low cost per payload-mile at lower risk than "primitive vs. modern" stereotypes suggest.[83,84] By contrast, communist and other high-modernist programs that attempted to standardize fisheries or resettle coastal populations often suppressed such fine-grained local knowledge systems; the broader pattern, visible in state-socialist campaigns elsewhere, is that standardized designs underperform when they cannot "see" local ecologies and tacit skills.[85] On continental waterways, North American Indigenous peoples developed a distinct technological superiority for mixed river–lake transport. The birchbark canoe combined ultra-light hulls with high payload-to-weight ratios and portability, minimizing the transaction costs of traversing watersheds segmented by rapids and short overland carries.[86] The ensuing political economy of the fur trade depended on Indigenous designs: French and later British traders adopted the canot du maître and canot du nord, scaling the throughput of furs and trade goods across the Saint Lawrence–Great Lakes–Athabasca corridors.[87,88] Here, technology and institutions were co-produced: fish weirs, reef-net complexes, clam gardens, and tenure-like arrangements along rivers and shores channelled

[83] Irwin, Geoffrey. 1992. The Prehistoric Exploration and Colonization of the Pacific. Cambridge: Cambridge University Press.

[84] Ostrom, Elinor. 1990. Governing the Commons: The Evolution of Institutions for Collective Action. Cambridge: Cambridge University Press.

[85] Scott, James C. 1998. Seeing Like a State: How Certain Schemes to Improve the Human Condition Have Failed. New Haven: Yale University Press.

[86] Adney, Edwin Tappan, and Howard I. Chapelle. 1964. The Bark Canoes and Skin Boats of North America. Washington, DC: Smithsonian Institution Press.

[87] Innis, Harold A. 1956. The Fur Trade in Canada: An Introduction to Canadian Economic History. Toronto: University of Toronto Press.

[88] White, Richard. 1991. The Middle Ground: Indians, Empires, and Republics in the Great Lakes Region, 1650–1815. Cambridge: Cambridge University Press.

effort, stabilized returns, and internalized ecological feedbacks.[89,90] The result, in neoclassical terms, was a reduction in search, monitoring, and transport costs at every margin, vessel design, route choice, and access rules, yielding high total factor productivity without large fixed capital.[91,92] In communist analogues, most clearly in the Soviet North, state efforts to collectivize production and replace "archaic" boats and routes with standardized equipment often ignored the contingent efficiencies of Indigenous craft and mobility. Policies that relocated small peoples of the North and reoriented subsistence and trade curtailed the agility of canoe, kayak, and umiak systems evolved for ice, wind, and river regimes, with predictable losses in efficiency and resilience.[93,94] African cases illustrate both long-distance and localized variants. Along the Niger and its tributaries, large dugout canoes sustained interregional trade, as recorded in medieval Arabic sources describing extensive river transport within the Sahelian empires.[95] On the Swahili coast, sewn boats (including the mtepe) and regionally adapted rigs integrated monsoon knowledge with coastal and archipelagic exchange, linking micro-scale fishing to macro-scale commerce.[96] The technological logics parallel those seen in Polynesia and North America: hull forms, joinery, and sail plans economized on locally available materials and the variance of wind, wave, and current, while social institutions governed access and seasonal labour allocation. From a neoclassical perspective, these systems

[89] Lepofsky, Dana, et al. 2015. "Ancient Mariculture on the Northwest Coast of North America." PLoS ONE 10(2): e0115345.

[90] Deur, Douglas, and Adam Dick, eds., with Dana Lepofsky, Kristin Rowell, and Anne K. Salomon. 2015. Clam Gardens: Aboriginal Mariculture on Canada's West Coast. Vancouver: UBC Press.

[91] Demsetz, Harold. 1967. "Toward a Theory of Property Rights." American Economic Review 57(2): 347–359.

[92] Ostrom, Elinor. 1990. Governing the Commons: The Evolution of Institutions for Collective Action. Cambridge: Cambridge University Press.

[93] Slezkine, Yuri. 1994. Arctic Mirrors: Russia and the Small Peoples of the North. Ithaca: Cornell University Press.

[94] Scott, James C. 1998. Seeing Like a State: How Certain Schemes to Improve the Human Condition Have Failed. New Haven: Yale University Press.

[95] Levtzion, Nehemia, and J. F. P. Hopkins, eds. 2000. Corpus of Early Arabic Sources for West African History. Princeton: Markus Wiener Publishers.

[96] Horton, Mark, and John Middleton. 2000. The Swahili: The Social Landscape of a Mercantile Society. Oxford: Blackwell.

optimized under local scarcity and uncertainty, using design diversity and flexible property regimes to lower risk-adjusted costs. Under centrally planned development, however, attempts to homogenize craft or reorganize coastal settlement, exemplars of "seeing like a state", tended to raise hidden costs (maintenance, fuel, downtime, ecological mismatch) by stripping out locally tuned design and tenure.[97] The contrast between long-distance and localized maritime technologies clarifies that "superiority" is contextual. Polynesian blue-water canoes were superior for inter-archipelagic voyaging, high freeboard, redundancy of double hulls, and navigational logics that convert sky and sea signals into positional estimates.[98,99] Riverine and lacustrine technologies in North America and Africa were superior for shallow-draft access, rapid portage, and high-frequency, low-batch transport, precisely the conditions of interior trade and subsistence.[100,101,102] Europeans adapted these technologies where they lowered costs: voyageurs wore moccasins, paddled Indigenous canoes, and followed Indigenous route knowledge because those choices dominated alternatives on efficiency grounds.[103,104] In modern policy terms, Indigenous maritime complexes look less like "traditional" survivals and more like coherent technological–institutional equilibria. They align with commons theory, credible local monitoring, calibrated

[97] Scott, James C. 1998. Seeing Like a State: How Certain Schemes to Improve the Human Condition Have Failed. New Haven: Yale University Press.

[98] Lewis, David. 1972. We, the Navigators: The Ancient Art of Landfinding in the Pacific. Honolulu: University of Hawai ʻi Press.

[99] Finney, Ben. 1994. Voyage of Rediscovery: A Cultural Odyssey Through Polynesia. Berkeley: University of California Press.

[100] Adney, Edwin Tappan, and Howard I. Chapelle. 1964. The Bark Canoes and Skin Boats of North America. Washington, DC: Smithsonian Institution Press.

[101] Innis, Harold A. 1956. The Fur Trade in Canada: An Introduction to Canadian Economic History. Toronto: University of Toronto Press.

[102] Levtzion, Nehemia, and J. F. P. Hopkins, eds. 2000. Corpus of Early Arabic Sources for West African History. Princeton: Markus Wiener Publishers.

[103] White, Richard. 1991. The Middle Ground: Indians, Empires, and Republics in the Great Lakes Region, 1650–1815. Cambridge: Cambridge University Press.

[104] Adney, Edwin Tappan, and Howard I. Chapelle. 1964. The Bark Canoes and Skin Boats of North America. Washington, DC: Smithsonian Institution Press.

sanctions, and rules matched to ecological conditions[105] and they challenge both naïve neoclassical assumptions of frictionless substitution and communist assumptions that technical standardization can supplant place-based know-how without productivity loss. Empirically, experimental voyaging and ecological studies reinforce the point: non-instrument navigation can deliver reliable blue-water performance[106,107] and engineered seascapes such as clam gardens measurably increase shellfish density and growth compared to unmodified beaches.[108,109] The strategic lesson for contemporary development is not to romanticize indigeneity but to recognize when technological variety and local governance minimize real costs and ecological risk better than standardized, capital-heavy alternatives.

4.2 *Indigenous Agricultural Practices*

Indigenous agricultural systems were not "preludes" to modern farming but finely tuned responses to local ecologies and relative scarcities, and they often achieved high productivity with low external inputs. Consider the Haudenosaunee "Three Sisters" intercropping of maize, beans, and squash. Agronomically, maize provides a living trellis, beans fix atmospheric nitrogen and lift protein quality, and squash shades soil to conserve moisture and suppress weeds. Experimental and meta-analytic evidence shows that such cereal–legume–cucurbit intercrops commonly deliver land equivalent ratios (LER) greater than 1, often in the 1.2–1.6 range, meaning the mixture produces 20–60% more total output than the

[105] Ostrom, Elinor. 1990. Governing the Commons: The Evolution of Institutions for Collective Action. Cambridge: Cambridge University Press.

[106] Finney, Ben. 1994. Voyage of Rediscovery: A Cultural Odyssey Through Polynesia. Berkeley: University of California Press.

[107] Gladwin, Thomas. 1970. East Is a Big Bird: Navigation and Logic on Puluwat Atoll. Cambridge, MA: Harvard University Press.

[108] Groesbeck, Amy S., Kristin Rowell, Dana Lepofsky, and Anne K. Salomon. 2014. "Ancient Clam Gardens Increased Shellfish Production: Adaptive Strategies from the Past Can Inform Sustainable Management Today." PLoS ONE 9(3): e91235.

[109] Lepofsky, Dana, et al. 2015. "Ancient Mariculture on the Northwest Coast of North America." PLoS ONE 10(2): e0115345.

component monocultures grown on the same combined area.[110,111] In a neoclassical frame, this is rational factor substitution and risk management: where labour and ecological knowledge are relatively abundant but fertilizers and machinery are scarce or costly, farmers choose labour- and knowledge-intensive techniques that raise output per unit land while stabilizing yields through functional diversity. By contrast, nineteenth–twentieth century settler agriculture in North America reoriented production towards the plough, single-species fields, and external inputs, a shift that made sense under different prices (abundant land, cheap iron, later cheap nitrogen) but frequently dismantled Indigenous polycultures that internalized fertility and weed control.[112,113] In the Andes, Inca and pre-Inca farmers engineered entire mountainsides through terracing and irrigation, and in some basins created raised fields (waru-waru) with water-filled canals that buffer frost and improve soil structure. Archaeological and agronomic studies document the biophysical gains: canal water stores daytime heat and releases it at night, mitigating cold snaps by several degrees and reducing crop losses at high elevation; carefully built terrace soils increase moisture retention and reduce erosion, supporting reliable harvests on steep slopes.[114,115,116] The economic logic mirrors

[110] Mt. Pleasant, Jane. 2006. "The Science behind the Three Sisters Mound System: An Agronomic Assessment of an Indigenous Agricultural System in the Northeast." In Histories of Maize: Multidisciplinary Approaches to the Prehistory, Linguistics, Biogeography, Domestication, and Evolution of Maize, edited by John E. Staller, Robert H. Tykot, and Bruce F. Benz, 529–537. Amsterdam: Elsevier.

[111] Martin-Guay, Marie-Ève, Alain-G. Paquette, Judy Dupras, and Rachelle Leroux. 2018. "Intercropping Systems Sustain Crop Yields and the Ecological Services in Arable Land." Agronomy for Sustainable Development 38: 69.

[112] Cronon, William. 1983. Changes in the Land: Indians, Colonists, and the Ecology of New England. New York: Hill and Wang.

[113] Hayami, Yujiro, and Vernon W. Ruttan. 1985. Agricultural Development: An International Perspective. Rev. and expanded ed. Baltimore: Johns Hopkins University Press.

[114] Ortloff, Charles R., and Alan L. Kolata. 1993. "Climate and Collapse: Agro-Ecological Perspectives on the Decline of the Tiwanaku State." Journal of Archaeological Science 20(2): 195–221.

[115] Denevan, William M. 2001. Cultivated Landscapes of Native Amazonia and the Andes: Triumph over the Soil. Oxford: Oxford University Press.

[116] Netting, Robert McC. 1993. Smallholders, Householders: Farm Families and the Ecology of Intensive, Sustainable Agriculture. Stanford, CA: Stanford University Press.

induced-innovation theory: with land scarcity in valley bottoms and abundant communal labour, high-fixed-cost landscape investments (terraces, canals) become efficient because their payoffs are durable, shared, and compound over time in the form of stabilized yields and reduced variance.[117,118] Under communist or high-modernist programs that sought to standardize production, these locally adapted technologies have often been neglected or dismantled, not because they were inefficient, but because they were illegible to centralized planners and hard to manage from a distance. The broader pattern, seen in numerous collectivization and resettlement campaigns, is that uniform field designs and top-down labour organization can raise apparent short-run control while increasing hidden costs (maintenance, ecological mismatch, yield risk) once local knowledge and incentives are displaced.[119] Andean case studies of terrace abandonment under state-led modernization illustrate these trade-offs: when communal labour arrangements and fine-grained water management were disrupted, terraces degraded and variability in harvests rose.[120,121] "Sustainable" practices such as long-fallow swidden, agroforestry, and rotational mosaics were likewise calibrated to ecological constraints rather than signs of backwardness. These systems were engineered to fit local ecologies and constraints, nutrient-poor soils, seasonal rainfall, pests, frost risk, so they could produce reliably with minimal external inputs. They look "simple" only if you miss how timing, species mixes, and rules are tuned to place.

Take long-fallow swidden (a.k.a. shifting cultivation). Among the Hanunóo in the Philippines, farmers cleared small patches, cropped them briefly, then let them revert to forest for well over a decade before returning. The long fallow lets secondary forest rebuild soil organic

[117] Hayami, Yujiro, and Vernon W. Ruttan. 1985. Agricultural Development: An International Perspective. Rev. and expanded ed. Baltimore: Johns Hopkins University Press.

[118] Netting, Robert McC. 1993. Smallholders, Householders: Farm Families and the Ecology of Intensive, Sustainable Agriculture. Stanford, CA: Stanford University Press.

[119] Scott, James C. 1998. Seeing Like a State: How Certain Schemes to Improve the Human Condition Have Failed. New Haven: Yale University Press.

[120] Guillet, David. 1987. "Terracing and Irrigation in the Peruvian Highlands." Human Ecology 15(4): 431–447.

[121] Denevan, William M. 2001. Cultivated Landscapes of Native Amazonia and the Andes: Triumph over the Soil. Oxford: Oxford University Press.

matter and nutrients in biomass; burning that regrowth releases a short pulse of fertility for the next cropping cycle. Because tropical nutrients are stored mostly in vegetation rather than in inherently leached soils, the "moving field" is the rational way to keep nutrients cycling without purchased fertilizer.[122] Where fallows remain long (often 10–20 years), studies show these systems maintain soil fertility and biodiversity and meet local food needs; they tip into degradation mainly when population or policy shortens fallows below ecological thresholds (e.g., < 5–7 years), which is why regional reviews warn that "swidden is not the problem, short fallow is".[123] Agroforestry illustrates the same calibration. In West African Sahelian "parklands", farmers deliberately maintain scattered Faidherbia albida trees over millet or sorghum. The species leaf's out in the dry season and drops leaves during the rains ("reverse phenology"), so it fixes nitrogen and adds leaf litter without shading crops when they need light. Result: cooler soils, more nitrogen, and better moisture, often translating into markedly higher grain yields under the canopy compared with open fields, achieved without synthetic fertilizer because the tree supplies nutrients and microclimate services. In Amazonia, Indigenous home gardens and forest "islands" (e.g., Kayapó apêtê) combine perennial crops like peach palm and cacao with annuals and medicinals in layered canopies. That structure spreads risk across species and seasons, dampens pest outbreaks, and maintains production during drought years, again, a rational substitution of knowledge and labour for cash inputs.[124] Rotational mosaics scale this logic to whole landscapes. Instead of every plot doing the same thing every year, communities maintain a patchwork of fields and fallows at different ages: new clearings, 1–3-year fields, mid-successional fallows, and old secondary forest. In Mesoamerica's milpa regions, for example, maize–bean–squash plots cycle back into tree-rich fallow, while neighbouring patches are at other stages. The mosaic

[122] Conklin, Harold C. 1957. Hanunóo Agriculture: A Report on an Integral System of Shifting Cultivation. Rome: Food and Agriculture Organization of the United Nations.

[123] Mertz, Ole, Christine Padoch, Jefferson Fox, R. A. Cramb, Stephen J. Leisz, N. T. Lam, and Tran Duc Vien. 2009. "Trends in Shifting Cultivation and the REDD Policy." Trends in Ecology & Evolution 24(12).

[124] Clement, Charles R., William M. Denevan, Michael J. Heckenberger, André B. Junqueira, Eduardo G. Neves, William G. Teixeira, and William I. Woods. 2015. "The Domestication of Amazonia before European Conquest." Proceedings of the Royal Society B 282: 20150813.

suppresses pests (they can't spread as easily across discontinuous hosts), evens labour demand over the year, and buffers against localized crop failure, if storms flatten one cohort, others elsewhere in the cycle still produce. Where water is the binding constraint, Andean communities paired such spatial rotation with terracing and canal schedules to manage frost and runoff, stabilizing yields on steep, erosion-prone slopes.[125,126] In all three cases, what looks "backward" from a distance is actually optimization under local prices and risks: when cash, fertilizer, and machinery are scarce, but skilled labour and ecological knowledge are relatively abundant, it's efficient to invest in timing, diversity, trees, and rotation rather than steel and synthetic nitrogen. These practices conserve soil, spread risk, and keep yields reliable, until external pressures (population growth, bans on swidden, enclosure) force cycles that are shorter or simpler than the ecology will sustain. Classic ethnography and contemporary ecology show that shifting cultivation, where fallow periods are sufficiently long, can maintain soil fertility, conserve biodiversity, and yield competitively for staple needs without external inputs; swidden systems fail not inherently, but when demographic or political pressures truncate fallows.[127,128] Amazonian agroforestry and anthropogenic forests, replete with managed stands of tree crops like Brazil nut, peach palm, and cacao, demonstrate intentional domestication across landscapes that Western agronomy long misread as "wild", with archaeobotanical and genetic evidence indicating extensive pre-Columbian enhancement of useful species.[129] In neoclassical terms, these systems economize on scarce cash and purchased

[125] Guillet, David. 1987. "Terracing and Irrigation in the Peruvian Highlands." Human Ecology 15(4): 431–447.

[126] Ortloff, Charles R., and Alan L. Kolata. 1993. "Climate and Collapse: Agro-Ecological Perspectives on the Decline of the Tiwanaku State." Journal of Archaeological Science 20(2): 195–221.

[127] Conklin, Harold C. 1957. Hanunóo Agriculture: A Report on an Integral System of Shifting Cultivation. Rome: Food and Agriculture Organization of the United Nations.

[128] Mertz, Ole, Christine Padoch, Jefferson Fox, R. A. Cramb, Stephen J. Leisz, N. T. Lam, and Tran Duc Vien. 2009. "Trends in Shifting Cultivation and the REDD Policy." Trends in Ecology & Evolution 24(12).

[129] Clement, Charles R., William M. Denevan, Michael J. Heckenberger, André B. Junqueira, Eduardo G. Neves, William G. Teixeira, and William I. Woods. 2015. "The Domestication of Amazonia before European Conquest." Proceedings of the Royal Society B 282: 20150813.

inputs by substituting portfolio diversity, labour timing, and local information; they minimize variance (a cost) through ecological redundancy and spatial spread. Under communist planning, similar environments were often subjected to simplified, large-scale schemes that prioritized uniformity and ease of measurement over resilience, a trade that tended to increase long-run costs when variability in rainfall, soils, and pests asserted itself.[130] Crop domestication and preservation decisions also reveal Indigenous priorities at the intersection of nutrition, storage, and climate risk. Maize, domesticated from teosinte in southwestern Mexico, spread as a remarkably plastic staple across the Americas, supporting both intensive and extensive systems and underpinning complex polities.[131,132] In the Andean highlands, quinoa was domesticated and maintained not for calories alone but for nutrient density and stress tolerance: it typically contains ~ 14–18% protein with an amino acid profile that complements cereals, along with minerals and saponins that deter pests, traits that lower input requirements and make cropping portfolios more resilient to drought and frost.[133,134] Read through either neoclassical or communist lenses, these choices make sense: where insurance markets are thin or absent, risk is managed through crop portfolios; where a state allocates inputs, discounting local nutritional and agronomic knowledge can undermine the very food security such programs aim to enhance. European and later colonial agricultural interventions often disrupted these equilibria by reconfiguring land tenure, insisting on the plough

[130] Scott, James C. 1998. Seeing Like a State: How Certain Schemes to Improve the Human Condition Have Failed. New Haven: Yale University Press.

[131] Matsuoka, Yoshihiro, Yves Vigouroux, Major M. Goodman, Jesus Sanchez, Edward Buckler, and John Doebley. 2002. "A Single Domestication for Maize Shown by Multilocus Microsatellite Genotyping." Proceedings of the National Academy of Sciences 99(9): 6080–6084.

[132] Staller, John E., Robert H. Tykot, and Bruce F. Benz, eds. 2006. Histories of Maize: Multidisciplinary Approaches to the Prehistory, Linguistics, Biogeography, Domestication, and Evolution of Maize. Amsterdam: Elsevier.

[133] Vega-Gálvez, Antonio, Maria Miranda, Jorge Vergara, Eduardo Uribe, Luis Puente, and Enrique A. Martínez. 2010. "Nutrition Facts and Functional Potential of Quinoa (Chenopodium quinoa Willd.), an Ancient Andean Grain: A Review." Journal of the Science of Food and Agriculture 90(15): 2541–2547.

[134] Repo-Carrasco-Valencia, R., and L. A. Serna. 2011. "Quinoa (Chenopodium quinoa Willd.) as a Source of Dietary Fiber and Other Functional Components." Food Science and Technology (Campinas) 31(1): 225–230.

and fixed-field monocultures, and criminalizing or devaluing rotational and communal practices. In North America, enclosure and property-law transformations replaced polycultural commons with individual freeholds optimized for market staples, eroding intercropping and fallow-based fertility regimes that had minimized external input costs.[135] In the Andes, market and state pressures to adopt standardized cropping calendars and privatized water rights undermined communal irrigation and terrace maintenance, raising erosion and yield variance once the labour institutions that sustained those infrastructures were weakened.[136,137] The comparative lesson is not that Indigenous systems were uniformly superior, but that, under their own price and risk structures, they achieved low-cost, low-variance production by aligning technology and governance with place. Neoclassical economics explains much of this as efficient adaptation to relative prices and constraints; the communist record, as analysed by critics of high-modernist planning, shows how ignoring local information and incentives in favour of standardization often raises real costs over time.[138,139]

4.3 Military Practices and Innovations Among Indigenous Peoples

Indigenous military systems were not ad hoc reactions to European invasion, but coherent strategic packages tuned to place, logistics, and political economy. Viewed through a neoclassical lens, communities with scarce capital (firearms, artillery, transport animals, industrial supply) but abundant information and local networks economized by substituting mobility, concealment, and terrain mastery for firepower. Guerrilla warfare, distributed command, and alliance-making reduced the unit cost

[135] Cronon, William. 1983. Changes in the Land: Indians, Colonists, and the Ecology of New England. New York: Hill and Wang.

[136] Guillet, David. 1987. "Terracing and Irrigation in the Peruvian Highlands." Human Ecology 15(4): 431–447.

[137] Denevan, William M. 2001. Cultivated Landscapes of Native Amazonia and the Andes: Triumph over the Soil. Oxford: Oxford University Press.

[138] Hayami, Yujiro, and Vernon W. Ruttan. 1985. Agricultural Development: An International Perspective. Rev. and expanded ed. Baltimore: Johns Hopkins University Press.

[139] Scott, James C. 1998. Seeing Like a State: How Certain Schemes to Improve the Human Condition Have Failed. New Haven: Yale University Press.

of coercion in forests, mountains, and riverine mosaics where conventional formations were expensive and brittle. A communist lens provides a revealing counterpoint: later Marxist–Leninist doctrines codified irregular warfare (e.g., Mao's and Giáp's "people's war"), but they also centralized political control and standardized tactics; where planning ignored local ecologies and indigenous social institutions, costs rose, and effectiveness declined.[140,141,142] In the woodlands of northeastern North America, Indigenous forces leveraged dense cover, broken sightlines, and knowledge of trails and waterways to favour ambush, dispersed movement, and decisive strikes against supply lines and small detachments. Haudenosaunee polities combined such tactics with a diplomatic economy of alliance, neutrality, and "mourning war" that replenished populations through captive adoption while managing conflict externalities.[143] Europeans adapted. Frontier units such as ranger companies abandoned linear drill for skirmishing and scouting, integrating Native guides and tactics; over time, "the first way of war" in North America fused Indigenous methods with colonial objectives.[144,145] Weapon choices reflected rational substitution: before mass access to reliable firearms, bows offered far higher rates of fire in close cover, while Indigenous adoption and strategic control of gun markets later shifted power in the northeast and Great Lakes.[146] These were not "primitive" expedients but cost-minimizing responses to forests where visibility, logistics, and morale, rather than parade-ground firepower, determined outcomes. On the Great Plains and in the Southwest, equestrian peoples converted grass

[140] Mao, Zedong. 1961. On Guerrilla Warfare. Translated by Samuel B. Griffith. Urbana: University of Illinois Press.

[141] Giáp, Võ Nguyên. 1962. People's War, People's Army: The Viet Cong Insurrection Manual for Underdeveloped Countries. New York: Praeger.

[142] Scott, James C. 1998. Seeing Like a State: How Certain Schemes to Improve the Human Condition Have Failed. New Haven: Yale University Press.

[143] Richter, Daniel K. 1992. The Ordeal of the Longhouse: The Peoples of the Iroquois League in the Era of European Colonization. Chapel Hill: University of North Carolina Press.

[144] Grenier, John. 2005. The First Way of War: American War Making on the Frontier, 1607–1814. Cambridge: Cambridge University Press.

[145] White, Richard. 1991. The Middle Ground: Indians, Empires, and Republics in the Great Lakes Region, 1650–1815. Cambridge: Cambridge University Press.

[146] Silverman, David J. 2016. Thundersticks: Firearms and the Violent Transformation of Native America. Cambridge, MA: Harvard University Press.

into military mobility, extending operational reach and tactical shock. The Comanche in particular built a regional hegemon by combining superior horsemanship, mounted archery, and a flexible raiding–trading economy that projected force deep into northern Mexico and redirected flows of livestock, captives, and goods across the Southern Plains.[147] From a neoclassical standpoint, horses and dispersed kin networks lowered transport and information costs across vast distances; raids targeted the opponent's scarce capital (herds, caravans, settlements) rather than their massed formations. European and later American forces learned to counter only by altering the production function, fortifying lines of communication, concentrating firepower at nodes, and deploying mounted rifles to match speed. Indigenous engineering often neutralized European technological advantage. In the New Zealand Wars, Māori developed the "gunfighter pā", a suite of earthwork forts with traversed trenches, anti-ricochet angles, and layered firing positions that absorbed artillery and blunted infantry assaults. These forts were rapidly built, sometimes abandoned after serving their operational purpose, and reconstituted elsewhere, an agile, modular defence that forced British commanders into expensive stalemates or pyrrhic attacks.[148] In economic terms, Māori substituted engineering knowledge, labour, and deception (feints, decoy pā) for artillery and mass, pushing the British into an unfavourable cost curve where each incremental yard demanded disproportionate shells and lives. Analogous dynamics appeared in South America. The Mapuche of southern Chile transformed the balance with rapid horse adoption, flexible command under toqui war leaders, and shifting coalitions that countered Spanish and later Chilean pushes. Combined-arms tactics, lances, shields, and mobile formations adapted to forest–plain ecotones, paired with a durable diplomacy of parlamentos (formal negotiations) that managed war–peace cycles on Mapuche terms for centuries.[149] Here too, political institutions, assemblies, ritual legitimations, and inter-village federations, were "technologies" that economized on information and enforcement under frontier conditions, sustaining autonomy against states

[147] Hämäläinen, Pekka. 2008. The Comanche Empire. New Haven: Yale University Press.

[148] Belich, James. 1986. The New Zealand Wars and the Victorian Interpretation of Racial Conflict. Auckland: Auckland University Press / Oxford: Oxford University Press.

[149] Dillehay, Tom D. 2007. Monuments, Empires, and Resistance: The Araucanian Polity and Ritual Narratives. Cambridge: Cambridge University Press.

that enjoyed gunpowder superiority but suffered from overextended supply chains. African cases further underscore terrain-based optimization. Zulu commanders employed the "horns of the buffalo" to encircle and overwhelm in close combat, integrating age-grade regiments, speed, and intelligence networks. At Isandlwana (1879), Zulu forces exploited reconnaissance failures and dispersed British formations to achieve a major victory, after which the British adapted with fortified laagers, more scouts, and concentrated volleys and artillery at Rorke's Drift and beyond.[150] The episode illustrates both the effectiveness and the limits of indigenous tactics: when European forces reorganized to protect their scarce capital (ammunition, wagons) and maximized their comparative advantage (sustained firepower, fortified camps), the Zulu cost curve steepened. Cultural and symbolic practices were strategically functional, not decorative. Among Iroquoian peoples, "mourning wars" were not aimless raiding but a demographic and political institution for repairing losses from battle, disease, or accidents. When a death occurred, kin had a social obligation to "cover" the loss; war parties sought captives who could be ritually adopted to "requicken" the deceased's lineage. Women, especially matrons of clans, often decided whether a captive was adopted, enslaved, or executed, and the condolence ceremony formalized that incorporation. In the seventeenth century, when epidemic mortality surged, the Haudenosaunee (Iroquois League) intensified captive-taking from neighbours such as the Huron-Wendat, Erie, and Susquehannock; many captives became full members, marrying into clans and swelling the League's villages.[151] Strategically, this system sustained manpower without the chronic costs of coercive conscription. It also lowered "transaction costs" of state-like recruitment and assimilation: rules and rituals made integration predictable, reduced internal disputes over newcomers, and turned raiding into a demographically rational, if often brutal, mechanism for maintaining fighting strength and household labour. On the North American Plains, the practice of "counting coup" created a finely graded economy of honour that rewarded close-quarter audacity, touching an enemy with the hand or coup stick, seizing a weapon, or

[150] Knight, Ian. 2010. Zulu Rising: The Epic Story of iSandlwana and Rorke's Drift. London: Macmillan.

[151] Richter, Daniel K. 1992. The Ordeal of the Longhouse: The Peoples of the Iroquois League in the Era of European Colonization. Chapel Hill: University of North Carolina Press.

stealing horses, often without killing. Warrior societies (e.g., Cheyenne Dog Soldiers, Lakota akíčhita, Blackfoot societies) kept ledgers and coup sticks recording these feats; status translated into leadership credibility, marriage prospects, and influence in council. Because honours scaled with risk and proximity, small units trained to move fast, scout well, and strike surgically, tactics that economized on scarce ammunition (once firearms arrived), protected limited horse herds, and avoided pitched battles that could bleed a band white. The reputational effects shaped deterrence, too: communities facing warriors known for successful coup and horse raids adjusted travel, corrals, and camp layouts to avoid surprise, which is exactly how a reputation system disciplines adversaries without constant large-scale fighting. In economic terms, counting coup substituted information and incentives for matériel—producing highly effective light infantry at low sustained cost. For Māori in nineteenth-century Aotearoa/New Zealand, ritual leadership and engineering combined to mobilize quickly and negotiate effectively. Rangatira (chiefs) legitimated taua (expeditions) through hui (assemblies) and kawa (ritual protocols), embedding decisions in concepts of mana (authority), tapu (sacred restriction), and utu (reciprocity). During the New Zealand Wars, this authority underwrote rapid labour mobilization to build and man the "gunfighter pā": earthwork fortifications with traversed trenches and anti-ricochet angles that blunted British artillery and infantry, often leading imperial commanders into costly, indecisive assaults.[152] The same ritualized governance lowered bargaining costs, leaders could credibly call truces, exchange prisoners, or shift from offense to defence without splintering coalition cohesion, because followers recognized the legitimacy of public decision-making and sanctioning. A parallel logic appears among the Mapuche of south-central Chile. In times of war, lof (local communities) selected a toqui (war leader) in council; ritual performances and symbols (including the rehue and collective ceremonies) authorized rapid musters for malón (raids) and, equally, the suspension of operations to hold parlamentos (formal negotiations) with Spanish and later Chilean authorities. These parlamentos, like Quilín (1641) and many subsequent treaties, were not empty theatre: they encoded boundaries, tribute, and safe-conduct rules that reduced uncertainty and

[152] Belich, James. 1986. The New Zealand Wars and the Victorian Interpretation of Racial Conflict. Auckland: Auckland University Press / Oxford: Oxford University Press.

transaction costs of war and peace over centuries.[153] In both Māori and Mapuche cases, ritual leadership acted as governance "infrastructure", turning costly coordination and conflict resolution into routinized, low-friction processes that made indigenous coalitions resilient against materially stronger states. Put together, these institutions, mourning-war adoption, coup-based honour systems, and ritualized leadership, were strategic technologies. They converted culture into capacity: replenishing people without bureaucratic apparatus (Iroquoian adoption), producing disciplined, high-initiative light forces without standing armies (Plains coup), and enabling fast mobilization and credible de-escalation under stress (Māori and Mapuche ritual authority). That is why they mattered in war: they minimized the everyday costs of mustering, motivating, policing, and negotiating, exactly the frictions that so often undo small polities facing larger, richer adversaries.[154,155.156] These norms created credible commitments and swift dispute resolution, features that Elinor Ostrom identified as pillars of effective commons governance and that, in war, translate into reliable coordination under stress.[157] The hard constraint, however, was the gunpowder–fortification complex. European advantage did not rest on muskets alone but on the entire industrial and institutional ecology that sustained them: standardized calibres, deep magazines, artillery trains, fortified depots, and states capable of taxing, provisioning, and replacing losses at scale. Where Indigenous forces could fragment supply, canalize columns into unfavourable ground, or engineer defences that wasted enemy munitions, they equalized costs; where they faced concentrated artillery, disciplined volley fire, and fortified logistics,

[153] Dillehay, Tom D. 2007. Monuments, Empires, and Resistance: The Araucanian Polity and Ritual Narratives. Cambridge: Cambridge University Press.

[154] Richter, Daniel K. 1992. The Ordeal of the Longhouse: The Peoples of the Iroquois League in the Era of European Colonization. Chapel Hill: University of North Carolina Press.

[155] Belich, James. 1986. The New Zealand Wars and the Victorian Interpretation of Racial Conflict. Auckland: Auckland University Press / Oxford: Oxford University Press.

[156] Dillehay, Tom D. 2007. Monuments, Empires, and Resistance: The Araucanian Polity and Ritual Narratives. Cambridge: Cambridge University Press.

[157] Scott, James C. 1998. Seeing Like a State: How Certain Schemes to Improve the Human Condition Have Failed. New Haven: Yale University Press.

the return on guerrilla shock declined.[158,159,160] Communist theorists studying anti-colonial war recognized many of these lessons, emphasizing terrain, mobility, and political work to erode the enemy's logistics and will. When doctrine and organization fit the social and physical landscape, foodways, paths, seasons, soils, cover, forces conserve lives and accrue legitimacy; when they don't, losses mount and communities withdraw cooperation. Mao and Giáp encode "fit" as a first principle for insurgency; Scott generalizes the warning to state schemes. Indigenous polities had long practiced that matching, tailoring war parties, fortifications, logistics, and peace-making to their ecologies, which is why they so often made stronger powers pay steep prices when those powers arrived with a template instead of a map.[161,162,163]

5 Strategic Superiority and Its Broader Implications

5.1 *Logistics and Resource Mobilization*

European empires achieved a form of strategic superiority by building long, resilient supply chains that converted distant resources into sustained coercive capacity. In a neoclassical frame, they lowered the unit cost of campaigning by combining capital-intensive shipping, fiscal institutions, and credible property rights to mobilize provisions at scale and on schedule. The British state's eighteenth-century "fiscal-military" apparatus, excise systems, funded national debt, centralized victualling, kept fleets and armies in the field for years at a time, most visibly in the Seven Years' War when sea-borne logistics enabled simultaneous

158 Parker, Geoffrey. 1988. The Military Revolution: Military Innovation and the Rise of the West, 1500–1800. Cambridge: Cambridge University Press.

159 Knight, Ian. 2010. Zulu Rising: The Epic Story of iSandlwana and Rorke's Drift. London: Macmillan.

160 Silverman, David J. 2016. Thundersticks: Firearms and the Violent Transformation of Native America. Cambridge, MA: Harvard University Press.

161 Mao, Zedong. 1961. On Guerrilla Warfare. Translated by Samuel B. Griffith. New York: Praeger.

162 Giáp, Võ Nguyên. 1962. People's War, People's Army: The Vietcong Insurrection Manual for Underdeveloped Countries. New York: Praeger.

163 Scott, James C. 1998. Seeing Like a State: How Certain Schemes to Improve the Human Condition Have Failed. New Haven: Yale University Press.

expeditions against Louisburg and Quebec.[164,165,166] Joint-stock trading companies amplified this reach; the VOC and the East India Company coordinated multi-year convoys, warehouses, and credit networks that integrated Asia–Europe circuits into the provisioning of imperial garrisons and fleets.[167,168,169] By contrast, many Indigenous polities optimized for local fit, shorter supply lines, dispersed storage, and fast decision cycles keyed to terrain and the natural environment, excellent for mobility and resilience but less suited to protracted siege-and-supply warfare. Haudenosaunee canoe logistics linked lakes and portages with light craft and cached maize stores, creating high payload-to-weight transport for raiding and alliance diplomacy rather than maintaining distant, fortified posts.[170] Plains equestrian economies such as the Comanche used horsepower to project raids and trade over vast distances, but deliberately avoided the fixed costs of garrisons and siege trains that European armies could afford.[171] In short, Europeans economized through scale and capital, while Indigenous systems economized through information, ecology, and agility. Moreover, Imperial supply chains were underwritten by colonial extraction, which provided the bulk commodities and fiscal surpluses that made long campaigns cheaper on the margin. Silver from Potosí and other Andean mines, routed via Atlantic and Pacific circuits, underwrote European and Asian purchases and lubricated military finance; the Spanish Crown's capacity to tax this flow, the quinto and related levies, illustrates how bullion revenues became

[164] Brewer, J. (1989) The Sinews of Power: War, Money and the English State, 1688–1783. Cambridge, MA: Harvard University Press.

[165] Rodger, N.A.M. (2004) The Command of the Ocean: A Naval History of Britain, 1649–1815. London: Allen Lane.

[166] Parker, G. (1988) The Military Revolution: Military Innovation and the Rise of the West, 1500–1800. Cambridge: Cambridge University Press.

[167] De Vries, J. and van der Woude, A. (1997) The First Modern Economy: Success, Failure, and Perseverance of the Dutch Economy, 1500–1815. Cambridge: Cambridge University Press.

[168] Bowen, H.V. (2006) The Business of Empire: The East India Company and Imperial Britain, 1756–1833. Cambridge: Cambridge University Press.

[169] Stern, P.J. (2011) The Company-State: Corporate Sovereignty and the Early Modern Foundations of the British Empire in India. New York: Oxford University Press.

[170] White, R. (1991) The Middle Ground: Indians, Empires, and Republics in the Great Lakes Region, 1650–1815. Cambridge: Cambridge University Press.

[171] Hämäläinen, P. (2008) The Comanche Empire. New Haven: Yale University Press.

state capacity.[172,173] Plantation zones in the Caribbean and Brazil converted enslaved labour, land, and capital equipment (mills, boilers) into sugar and by-products that fed metropolitan treasuries and credit markets.[174,175] The scale is stark: across the transatlantic trade, roughly 12.5 million African captives embarked for the Americas, and about 10.7 million survived the Middle Passage and disembarked. These individuals formed an enormous, coerced labour pool that sustained plantation economies and naval victualling across the Atlantic world. The majority were delivered to just a few key regions, approximately 4.9 million were taken to Brazil, around 4.8 million to the Caribbean (including British, French, Spanish, and Dutch colonies), and about 388,000 were taken to North America (mainly the British colonies that would become the United States). This dispersal shaped the demographic, economic, and cultural landscapes of the Americas for centuries.[176,177] In neoclassical economic terms, empires reweighted the global production function by reallocating key factors of production, labour, land, and capital, through coercion and asymmetric institutional design. Most notably, the transatlantic slave trade provided a vast supply of forcibly mobilized labour, enabling plantation economies in the Caribbean and Brazil to produce high-value export commodities like sugar and cotton at exceptionally low marginal costs.[178] These coerced labour flows, sustained over centuries, allowed imperial centres to benefit from productivity gains without incurring the costs of domestic wage labour. Empires also externalized ecological and demographic risks to their colonies. Plantation monocultures

[172] Flynn, D.O. and Giráldez, A. (1995) 'Born with a "Silver Spoon": The Origin of World Trade in 1571', Journal of World History, 6(2), pp. 201–221.

[173] Bakewell, P. (1984) Miners of the Red Mountain: Indian Labour in Potosí, 1545–1650. Albuquerque: University of New Mexico Press.

[174] Mintz, S.W. (1985) Sweetness and Power: The Place of Sugar in Modern History. New York: Viking.

[175] Inikori, J.E. (2002) Africans and the Industrial Revolution in England: A Study in International Trade and Economic Development. Cambridge: Cambridge University Press.

[176] Eltis, D., & Richardson, D. (2010). Atlas of the Transatlantic Slave Trade. Yale University Press.

[177] Slave Voyages. (2024). Trans-Atlantic Slave Trade Database. Retrieved from https://www.slavevoyages.org

[178] Eltis, D., & Engerman, S. L. (2000). The importance of slavery and the slave trade to industrializing Britain. Journal of Economic History, 60(1), 123–144.

depleted soil and accelerated deforestation, while slave mortality rates in colonies like Jamaica routinely exceeded replacement levels, making continuous imports of enslaved labour necessary.[179,180] These burdens were borne by colonial environments and populations, shielding imperial metropolitan societies from their consequences. In parallel, imperial states developed financial mechanisms to distribute and mitigate economic shocks across their global holdings. The British Empire used institutions such as the Bank of England and marine insurance markets at Lloyd's of London to manage commercial risk and underwrite long-distance trade.[181] Companies like the East India Company issued bonds to fund military and commercial expansion, backed by state guarantees and legal privileges that socialized private risk.[182] These innovations enabled empires to project power over vast distances and timeframes while maintaining capital discipline and fiscal resilience at the centre. By orchestrating flows of coerced labour, displacing ecological risk, and leveraging financial tools to buffer volatility, empires achieved structurally lower marginal costs of force projection. This allowed imperial metropolitan economies to enjoy relative macroeconomic stability while outsourcing volatility and exploitation to colonial peripheries. Indigenous economies, in contrast, typically drew on smallholder production, commons regimes, and seasonal labour obligations, systems that were efficient and sustainable in place, but which lacked the coercive leverage and capital intensity to field and feed massed forces far from home for extended periods. Comparisons with communist political economies sharpen the point about logistics and fit. Central planning can mobilize resources at scale, but doing so with rigid templates in diverse geographies raises hidden costs, attrition in the field and legitimacy losses among civilians who supply food, labour, and information.[183] State power depends not just on coercion but on legitimacy, civilians'

[179] Williams, E. (1944). Capitalism and Slavery. University of North Carolina Press.

[180] Beckles, H. (1989). Natural Rebels: A Social History of Enslaved Black Women in Barbados. Rutgers University Press.

[181] Neal, L. (1990). The Rise of Financial Capitalism: International Capital Markets in the Age of Reason. Cambridge University Press.

[182] Arrighi, G. (1994). The Long Twentieth Century: Money, Power and the Origins of Our Times. Verso.

[183] Scott, J.C. (1998) Seeing Like a State: How Certain Schemes to Improve the Human Condition Have Failed. New Haven: Yale University Press.

willingness to provide vital support such as food, labour, and information. When legitimacy erodes, as in British India during the 1943 Bengal Famine or in South Vietnam during the war, civilians may withhold cooperation, disrupt supply chains and enable insurgents. Similarly, in French Algeria, the withdrawal of local intelligence crippled colonial control. Scott terms these quiet refusals "everyday forms of resistance", showing how legitimacy loss can strategically undermine state authority without overt rebellion. The Soviet Union's World War II experience shows both sides: extraordinary, centralized throughput, railway prioritization, standardized munitions, and command over grain sustained armies across vast theatres, albeit at immense human cost and with heavy reliance on locally adapted tactics by front line commanders to reconcile plan with ground truth.[184] Vietnam offers a different communist-era configuration, Giáp's logistics emphasized decentralization, camouflage, redundancy, and terrain-fit along the Hồ Chí Minh Trail, exploiting mountains and forests to move men and material under the enemy's surveillance umbrella, an Indigenous-style solution embedded in a state-led war effort.[185] Read against European imperial practice, the lesson is consistent with neoclassical and institutional theory: large coercive projects are cheapest when organizational form matches environment and when states can transform distant resources into predictable supplies. Where planners impose standardized designs that ignore local ecologies and social institutions, costs rise rapidly; where logistics and labour systems are tailored to place, whether in Haudenosaunee canoe networks, Comanche horse pastoralism, or Giáp's trail system, smaller polities can punch above their material weight, but they generally cannot substitute indefinitely for the imperial combination of scale, capital, and colonial extraction.[186,187,188]

[184] Harrison, M. (ed.) (1998) The Economics of World War II: Six Great Powers in International Comparison. Cambridge: Cambridge University Press.

[185] Giáp, V.N. (1962) People's War, People's Army: The Vietcong Insurrection Manual for Underdeveloped Countries. New York: Praeger.

[186] Pomeranz, K. (2000) The Great Divergence: China, Europe, and the Making of the Modern World Economy. Princeton: Princeton University Press.

[187] Parker, G. (1988) The Military Revolution: Military Innovation and the Rise of the West, 1500–1800. Cambridge: Cambridge University Press.

[188] Scott, J.C. (1998) Seeing Like a State: How Certain Schemes to Improve the Human Condition Have Failed. New Haven: Yale University Press.

5.2 *Psychological and Diplomatic Strategies*

European powers paired coercion with psychology and diplomacy to lower the cost of conquest and governance. In a neoclassical frame, "divide-and-rule" is a cost-minimizing strategy: rather than bearing the full expense of continuous warfare, empires bought information, allies, and legitimacy on the cheap by exploiting existing fissures and creating new ones. The Spanish conquest of central Mexico hinged on alliances with Indigenous rivals of the Mexica, above all the Tlaxcalans, who provided guides, porters, and large fighting contingents in return for exemption and privileges in the new order.[189,190] In northeastern North America, the English and French refined this logic into a durable diplomatic economy, the "play-off system", in which Haudenosaunee and other nations leveraged inter-imperial rivalry while colonizers recruited native allies and neutralities to seize footholds without paying the full price of occupation.[191,192,193] From a transaction-cost perspective, treaties and clientele arrangements substituted local enforcement and knowledge for expensive garrisons; Europeans essentially rented pre-existing political networks to project power at lower marginal cost. Treaties and alliances also worked as credible-commitment technologies. In the Great Lakes and Ohio Country, wampum diplomacy and treaty councils bound parties to shared protocols that controlled violence, exchange, and passage. Europeans learned to perform these rituals and to weave written treaties into Indigenous diplomatic forms, securing safe conduct and provisioning in zones they could neither conquer outright

[189] Restall, M. (2003) Seven Myths of the Spanish Conquest. Oxford: Oxford University Press.

[190] Hassig, R. (1988) Aztec Warfare: Imperial Expansion and Political Control. Norman: University of Oklahoma Press.

[191] Jennings, F. (1984) The Ambiguous Iroquois Empire: The Covenant Chain Confederation of Indian Tribes with English Colonies from Its Beginnings to the Lancaster Treaty of 1744. New York: W.W. Norton.

[192] White, R. (1991) The Middle Ground: Indians, Empires, and Republics in the Great Lakes Region, 1650–1815. Cambridge: Cambridge University Press.

[193] Richter, D.K. (1992) The Ordeal of the Longhouse: The Peoples of the Iroquois League in the Era of European Colonization. Chapel Hill: University of North Carolina Press.

nor supply cheaply.[194,195] In southern Chile, the Spanish and, later, Chilean states held parlamentos with the Mapuche, formal negotiations that acknowledged boundaries, tribute, and trade in order to reduce uncertainty on a frontier where fort-building was costly and columns were vulnerable.[196] In comparison to both neoclassical and institutional theory, diplomacy lowered monitoring and enforcement costs by turning rivals into partners and by translating imperial aims into locally legible rules. The psychological wage of technology amplified these bargains. Early firearms and artillery had outsized signalling effects even when tactically inferior to bows at close range: the sound, smoke, and armour-piercing potential of "thunder sticks" reshaped reputations, markets, and battlefield expectations.[197,198] Horses similarly altered perceptions and payoffs. Once Plains nations adopted the horse, they converted grass into military mobility and raiding range; when Europeans arrived at equestrian frontiers, they faced opponents who could strike far and fast, forcing colonizers to negotiate, fortify, and co-opt rather than simply overrun.[199] Conversely, where Indigenous communities first encountered mounted or gun-armed Europeans without comparable platforms, the demonstration effect magnified diplomatic leverage: a few volleys or cavalry displays could compel food, guides, and treaties, economizing on direct violence even when logistical depth was thin.[200,201] Missionaries and Christianity functioned as tools of persuasion, social reorganization, and surveillance.

[194] White, R. (1991) The Middle Ground: Indians, Empires, and Republics in the Great Lakes Region, 1650–1815. Cambridge: Cambridge University Press.

[195] Richter, D.K. (1992) The Ordeal of the Longhouse: The Peoples of the Iroquois League in the Era of European Colonization. Chapel Hill: University of North Carolina Press.

[196] Dillehay, T.D. (2007) Monuments, Empires, and Resistance: The Araucanian Polity and Ritual Narratives. Cambridge: Cambridge University Press.

[197] Silverman, D.J. (2016) Thundersticks: Firearms and the Violent Transformation of Native America. Cambridge, MA: Harvard University Press.

[198] Parker, G. (1988) The Military Revolution: Military Innovation and the Rise of the West, 1500–1800. Cambridge: Cambridge University Press.

[199] Hämäläinen, P. (2008) The Comanche Empire. New Haven: Yale University Press.

[200] Parker, G. (1988) The Military Revolution: Military Innovation and the Rise of the West, 1500–1800. Cambridge: Cambridge University Press.

[201] Crosby, A.W. (2004) Ecological Imperialism: The Biological Expansion of Europe, 900–1900. 2nd edn. Cambridge: Cambridge University Press.

Missions translated imperial authority into vernacular moral orders, reorganized settlement into nucleated towns, and redefined labour and gender roles in ways that lowered the state's future costs of rule. In southern Africa, mission Christianity carried a "civilizing" program that recoded time, work, and authority, making colonial extraction and discipline cheaper by embedding them in congregational life.[202,203] In Spanish America, ritual claims of possession and the legal-theological argument for conversion legitimated appropriation while missions and reducciones concentrated populations into governable nodes.[204,205] In neoclassical terms, evangelization and legal ceremony created legitimacy and information flows that reduced enforcement costs; they substituted ideology and local intermediaries for raw coercion. Comparisons with communist strategy highlight both convergence and warning. Revolutionary theorists insisted that political work, fronts, united-front diplomacy, and psychological operations were the main effort and combat the supporting arm. Mao and Giáp prioritized splitting adversaries, aligning with "middle forces", and tailoring appeals to local grievances, because legitimacy and intelligence are the cheapest inputs into victory.[206,207] Where movements or states abandoned fit and imposed rigid templates, costs rose. An analysis of high-modernist schemes shows how standardized doctrines that ignore local knowledge bleed legitimacy and escalate attrition, precisely what European empires often avoided in their early phases by flexibly matching diplomacy, spectacle, and missionary work to place.[208] The

[202] Comaroff, J. and Comaroff, J. (1991) Of Revelation and Revolution, Volume 1: Christianity, Colonialism, and Consciousness in South Africa. Chicago: University of Chicago Press.

[203] Comaroff, J. and Comaroff, J. (1997) Of Revelation and Revolution, Volume 2: The Dialectics of Modernity on a South African Frontier. Chicago: University of Chicago Press.

[204] Seed, P. (1995) Ceremonies of Possession in Europe's Conquest of the New World, 1492–1640. Cambridge: Cambridge University Press.

[205] Pagden, A. (1993) European Encounters with the New World: From Renaissance to Romanticism. New Haven: Yale University Press.

[206] Mao, Z. (1961) On Guerrilla Warfare. Translated by S.B. Griffith. New York: Praeger.

[207] Giáp, V.N. (1962) People's War, People's Army: The Vietcong Insurrection Manual for Underdeveloped Countries. New York: Praeger.

[208] Scott, J.C. (1998) Seeing Like a State: How Certain Schemes to Improve the Human Condition Have Failed. New Haven: Yale University Press.

contrast with Indigenous polities is instructive: communities such as the Haudenosaunee or Mapuche had long minimized the costs of war and peace by aligning organization with ecology and culture; Europeans achieved strategic superiority not because they always fought better, but because they added scalable logistics to an already sophisticated repertoire of psychological and diplomatic leverage.

6 The Legacy of Technological Superiority

6.1 Environmental and Social Transformations

European technological "superiority" mattered not only in battle but in the long-run reshaping of environments and societies. In a neoclassical frame, colonizers lowered their unit costs of extraction and supply by deploying capital-intensive technologies (iron ploughs, mills, pumps, ocean shipping) and by scaling production through property-rights regimes that facilitated investment and trade. Those choices also externalized costs, soil exhaustion, deforestation, toxics, to Indigenous lands and waters. Caribbean sugar offers a stark early case, wind- and animal-powered mills, later steam, converted land and enslaved labour into high-value exports, but did so by stripping forests for fuel and cane fields, eroding soils, and simplifying ecologies into monocultures.[209,210,211] In the Andes, silver mining at Potosí and mercury-amalgamation at Huancavelica generated bullion flows that underwrote imperial finance; they also emitted large quantities of mercury in to air, soils, and rivers, with documented legacies in sediments and biota.[212,213] According to induced-innovation theory, these outcomes were predictable: where land was abundant for Europeans and coerced labour could be procured,

[209] Mintz, S.W. (1985) Sweetness and Power: The Place of Sugar in Modern History. New York: Viking.

[210] Dunn, R.S. (1972) Sugar and Slaves: The Rise of the Planter Class in the English West Indies, 1624–1713. Chapel Hill: University of North Carolina Press.

[211] Richards, J.F. (2003) The Unending Frontier: An Environmental History of the Early Modern World. Berkeley: University of California Press.

[212] Bakewell, P. (1984) Miners of the Red Mountain: Indian Labour in Potosí, 1545–1650. Albuquerque: University of New Mexico Press.

[213] Nriagu, J.O. (1994) 'Mercury Pollution from the Past Mining of Gold and Silver in the Americas', Science of the Total Environment, 149(3), pp. 167–181.

capital deepening in mills, drainage, and transport was profit-maximizing even as environmental costs were pushed onto colonial commons.[214,215]

Environmental transformation entailed social transformation. In New England, English property law and market production reconfigured Indigenous subsistence landscapes, fencing commons, introducing livestock that compacted soils and browsed understory, and privileging fixed-field grain over rotational mosaics, thereby reducing access to wild foods and game and pushing Native communities towards wage labour and dependency.[216] In the northeast interior, the fur trade's demand, channelled through European credit and forts, drove regional beaver depletion, remade river economies, and reoriented diplomacy and conflict; Indigenous nations adapted with alliance systems and middle-ground diplomacy, but the ecological base thinned as local natural stocks declined.[217,218] On the Great Plains, industrial hides markets and U.S. state policy enabled the near-extirpation of bison, dropping from tens of millions to just a few hundred by the 1880s, collapsing a keystone of Plains political economy and forcing rapid social reorganization under external pressures driven by market demand and rail-borne logistics.[219] Deprived of their primary resource base, many Plains tribes, such as the Lakota and Comanche, were compelled to abandon mobile buffalo-hunting lifeways and adapt to reservation systems, government-issued rations, Christian mission schools, and wage labour. These shifts included changes in gender roles, as male hunting declined and women's roles in subsistence and domestic economies were redefined, along with the breakdown of traditional warrior societies and the imposition of new

214 Hayami, Y. and Ruttan, V.W. (1985) Agricultural Development: An International Perspective. Rev. and expanded ed. Baltimore: Johns Hopkins University Press.

215 Engerman, S.L. and Sokoloff, K.L. (1997) 'Factor Endowments, Institutions, and Differential Paths of Growth among New World Economies', in S. Haber (ed.) How Latin America Fell Behind: Essays on the Economic Histories of Brazil and Mexico, 1800–1914. Stanford, CA: Stanford University Press, pp. 260–304.

216 Cronon, W. (1983) Changes in the Land: Indians, Colonists, and the Ecology of New England. New York: Hill and Wang.

217 Innis, H.A. (1956) The Fur Trade in Canada: An Introduction to Canadian Economic History. Toronto: University of Toronto Press.

218 White, R. (1991) The Middle Ground: Indians, Empires, and Republics in the Great Lakes Region, 1650–1815. Cambridge: Cambridge University Press.

219 Isenberg, A.C. (2000) The Destruction of the Bison: An Environmental History, 1750–1920. Cambridge: Cambridge University Press.

political hierarchies mediated by U.S. Indian agents. These cases illustrate how European technologies and markets lowered metropolitan costs while raising local variance and risk, classic externalities in neoclassical terms. Furthermore, the mining sector illustrates the same logic of cost efficiency at scale. Amalgamation technology linked Andean silver ores to global finance, relying on mercury sourced from Huancavelica and later from Almadén to process vast quantities of silver. The resulting bullion, funnelled through imperial hubs like Seville and Acapulco, financed Spanish military and administrative operations while also fuelling long-distance commerce across the Pacific. Silver was the linchpin of the Manila Galleon trade, where it was exchanged for Chinese silk, porcelain, and spices, part of a broader set of Asian trades that integrated Spanish America into early modern global markets.[220,221] These flows highlight how colonial extraction underwrote both European statecraft and transoceanic commercial circuits. Science and engineering solved transport and drainage problems, adits—type of entrance used in underground mining, pumps, mule-trains, so mines could run year-round, but at the price of toxic releases and coerced draft labour (mita), whose demographic and social costs were borne by Andean communities rather than by mine owners.[222,223] In a comparative perspective, communist polities reproduced the extraction-at-scale logic with different instruments: five-year plans could mobilize rails, chemicals, and labour quotas quickly, but rigid targets and weak local feedback often magnified environmental damages and social dislocation. The Aral Sea disaster, surface area collapse after massive canalization for cotton, is a canonical case where centralized irrigation plans achieved high gross output while imposing catastrophic, unpriced externalities on fisheries, health,

[220] Bakewell, P. (1984) Miners of the Red Mountain: Indian Labour in Potosí, 1545–1650. Albuquerque: University of New Mexico Press.

[221] Flynn, D.O. and Giráldez, A. (1995) 'Born with a "Silver Spoon": The Origin of World Trade in 1571', Journal of World History, 6(2), pp. 201–221.

[222] Bakewell, P. (1984) Miners of the Red Mountain: Indian Labour in Potosí, 1545–1650. Albuquerque: University of New Mexico Press.

[223] Nriagu, J.O. (1994) 'Mercury Pollution from the Past Mining of Gold and Silver in the Americas', Science of the Total Environment, 149(3), pp. 167–181.

and climate.[224,225] The mechanism, standardization without local ecological fit, echoes colonial plantation and mining frontiers, underscoring that organizational form, not ideology alone, drives whether environmental costs are internalized. Global trade was transformed as European empires stitched distant ecologies into a single Atlantic (and Pacific) economy. Silver flows from Potosí and Mexico, especially after the Manila galleon routes solidified in 1571, lubricated Eurasian exchange; historians estimate that American bullion became critical to Asian trade balances, making the Atlantic a hinge in early globalization.[226,227] At the same time, the forced migration of roughly 12.5 million Africans, with about 10.7 million disembarking alive, created plantation labour regimes that mass-produced sugar, tobacco, and cotton for European markets and fiscal-military states.[228,229] Price and volume data show a significant post-1500 boom in Europe's overseas trade, driven by falling transport costs and institutional innovations such as royal charters and joint-stock companies. These changes reallocated global factor rewards, for example, increasing returns to European capital and Atlantic-facing ports while reducing the relative value of inland agriculture and non-coercive labour systems elsewhere. Urbanization patterns shifted accordingly, cities like Amsterdam, London, and Lisbon expanded rapidly as commercial hubs, while colonial port cities such as Veracruz, Batavia, and Manila

[224] Micklin, P. (2007) 'The Aral Sea Disaster', Annual Review of Earth and Planetary Sciences, 35, pp. 47–72.

[225] Scott, J.C. (1998) Seeing Like a State: How Certain Schemes to Improve the Human Condition Have Failed. New Haven: Yale University Press.

[226] Flynn, D.O. and Giráldez, A. (1995) 'Born with a "Silver Spoon": The Origin of World Trade in 1571', Journal of World History, 6(2), pp. 201–221.

[227] Pomeranz, K. (2000) The Great Divergence: China, Europe, and the Making of the Modern World Economy. Princeton: Princeton University Press.

[228] Eltis, D. and Richardson, D. (2010) Atlas of the Transatlantic Slave Trade. New Haven: Yale University Press.

[229] Brewer, J. (1989) The Sinews of Power: War, Money and the English State, 1688–1783. Cambridge, MA: Harvard University Press.

emerged as nodes in global trade networks.[230,231] This global redistribution of economic activity reinforced core-periphery dynamics and intensified the concentration of wealth and labour in strategic urban centres. The Columbian Exchange's biological side intensified these linkages: American crops such as maize and potatoes diffused across the Old World, raising caloric yields per hectare and contributing to population growth and urbanization, even as plantation commodities and pathogens restructured ecologies and demographics in the Americas.[232,233,234] In short, European technological and institutional packages lowered their own marginal costs of distance and coercion while exporting environmental and social risks to peripheries. A comparative glance at communist development highlights both convergences and contrasts. Central planning could, in moments of existential war, marshal resources to sustain logistics on continental scales, but peacetime campaigns that standardized production across diverse ecologies often produced familiar pathologies: soil degradation from rushed collectivization, desiccation from over-irrigation, forest loss from "planned" overharvest, costs undercounted because plans prioritized gross output and ideological metrics over local signals.[235,236] Where both imperial and communist projects succeeded was in building institutions that kept supply chains predictable; where they failed was in pricing environmental services and Indigenous knowledge. Indigenous systems, by contrast, often matched organization to place,

[230] O'Rourke, K.H. and Williamson, J.G. (2002) 'After Columbus: Explaining Europe's Overseas Trade Boom, 1500–1800', Journal of Economic History, 62(2), pp. 417–456.

[231] De Vries, J. and van der Woude, A. (1997) The First Modern Economy: Success, Failure, and Perseverance of the Dutch Economy, 1500–1815. Cambridge: Cambridge University Press.

[232] Crosby, A.W. (2004) Ecological Imperialism: The Biological Expansion of Europe, 900–1900. 2nd edn. Cambridge: Cambridge University Press.

[233] Nunn, N. and Qian, N. (2011) 'The Potato's Contribution to Population and Urbanization: Evidence from a Historical Experiment', Quarterly Journal of Economics, 126(2), pp. 593–650.

[234] McCann, J.C. (2005) Maize and Grace: Africa's Encounter with a New World Crop, 1500–2000. Cambridge, MA: Harvard University Press.

[235] Harrison, M. (ed.) (1998) The Economics of World War II: Six Great Powers in International Comparison. Cambridge: Cambridge University Press.

[236] Scott, J.C. (1998) Seeing Like a State: How Certain Schemes to Improve the Human Condition Have Failed. New Haven: Yale University Press.

agroforestry, rotational mosaics, commons governance, minimizing variance even at smaller scales. Those were not technologically inferior so much as differently optimized under local prices and risks; the tragedy came when they were displaced by systems that could outperform on cash yield while hiding their true environmental and social costs.

6.2 *The Myth of Technological Superiority*

European "technological superiority" was as much a story told as a fact on the ground. From the late eighteenth century, imperial writers equated steam, steel, and scientific instruments with civilizational worth, casting non-European systems as static or "pre-mechanical". This rhetoric naturalized conquest by making it seem the inevitable triumph of better tools.[237,238] In practice, Europeans won durable advantages where their technologies fit the logistics, epidemiology, and institutions of empire, ocean shipping, gunpowder, fiscal-military states, not because every European device outperformed local alternatives in all contexts.[239,240] A neoclassical reading clarifies why such narratives stuck: if metropolitan capital and global scale lowered Europeans' average costs of violence and extraction, elites had incentives to attribute success to inherent "superiority" rather than to contingent matches between technology, institutions, and environment. Communist modernizers later echoed similar claims about standardization and scientific planning, often replicating the same blind spots: when rigid templates ignored local ecologies and vernacular know-how, implementation costs rose and outcomes deteriorated. For example, during Mao's Great Leap Forward, state-driven agricultural schemes imposed uniform planting techniques and close cropping densities across diverse ecological zones, leading to massive crop failures

[237] Adas, M. (1989) Machines as the Measure of Men: Science, Technology, and Ideologies of Western Dominance. Ithaca, NY: Cornell University Press.

[238] Headrick, D.R. (1981) The Tools of Empire: Technology and European Imperialism in the Nineteenth Century. New York: Oxford University Press.

[239] Parker, G. (1988) The Military Revolution: Military Innovation and the Rise of the West, 1500–1800. Cambridge: Cambridge University Press.

[240] Brewer, J. (1989) The Sinews of Power: War, Money and the English State, 1688–1783. Cambridge, MA: Harvard University Press.

and contributing to one of the deadliest famines in human history.[241] Across domains, Indigenous technologies rivalled or surpassed European ones because they were optimized for local scarcities, risks, and information. In deep-ocean voyaging, Polynesian double-hulled and outrigger canoes paired light, repairable composite hulls with information-rich navigation, star paths, swell refraction, bird and cloud cues to achieve reliable blue-water passages of thousands of nautical miles without instruments; experimental voyages like Hōkūle'a's Hawai'i–Tahiti run demonstrated the technical sufficiency of this system.[242,243,244,245] In the boreal interior of North America, birchbark canoe design dominated mixed river-lake transport: the canot du maître carried ton-scale cargoes yet could be portaged, minimizing the transaction costs of traversing watersheds fractured by rapids and short carries, so compelling that French and British traders adopted Indigenous hulls, routes, and operating practices wholesale.[246,247,248] Coastal peoples on the Northwest Coast engineered clam gardens, rock-walled, intertidal terraces that flattened beach gradient and created optimal habitat, measurably increasing clam

[241] Scott, J.C. (1998) Seeing Like a State: How Certain Schemes to Improve the Human Condition Have Failed. New Haven: Yale University Press.

[242] Lewis, D. (1972) We, the Navigators: The Ancient Art of Landfinding in the Pacific. Honolulu: University of Hawai'i Press.

[243] Irwin, G. (1992) The Prehistoric Exploration and Colonization of the Pacific. Cambridge: Cambridge University Press.

[244] Finney, B. (1994) Voyage of Rediscovery: A Cultural Odyssey Through Polynesia. Berkeley: University of California Press.

[245] Kirch, P.V. (2017) On the Road of the Winds: An Archaeological History of the Pacific Islands before European Contact. Rev. and expanded edn. Berkeley: University of California Press.

[246] Adney, E.T. and Chapelle, H.I. (1964) The Bark Canoes and Skin Boats of North America. Washington, DC: Smithsonian Institution Press.

[247] Innis, H.A. (1956) The Fur Trade in Canada: An Introduction to Canadian Economic History. Toronto: University of Toronto Press.

[248] White, R. (1991) The Middle Ground: Indians, Empires, and Republics in the Great Lakes Region, 1650–1815. Cambridge: Cambridge University Press.

densities and growth versus unmodified shores, a clear case of preindustrial mariculture that outperformed "natural" baselines.[249,250,251] In highland Andes, terracing, raised fields, and canal systems buffered frost, conserved moisture, and stabilized yields on steep slopes, landscape engineering whose performance in marginal climates often exceeded that of transplanted European field systems.[252] In warfare, Māori "gunfighter pā" incorporated traversed trenches and anti-ricochet angles that absorbed artillery and blunted infantry assaults, forcing British commanders into stalemates or pyrrhic victories, an engineering response that inverted the imperial cost curve.[253] And in the early gun age of northeastern North America, Native control over firearms markets and tactics meant that "thundersticks" were integrated on Indigenous terms; at close range and in broken cover, high rates of fire with bows and ambush methods often outperformed early muskets until logistics and training shifted the balance.[254,255] These cases generalize: Indigenous systems substituted skilled labour, ecological knowledge, and modular design for scarce capital goods, thereby reducing unit costs under local price structures, exactly what neoclassical theory predicts efficient actors will do. Where European or later communist planners imposed standardized packages that mismatched place (e.g., fixed-field plough regimes in New England commons, or centrally planned irrigation that ignored

[249] Groesbeck, A.S., Rowell, K., Lepofsky, D. and Salomon, A.K. (2014) 'Ancient Clam Gardens Increased Shellfish Production: Adaptive Strategies from the Past Can Inform Sustainable Management Today', PLoS ONE, 9(3), e91235.

[250] Lepofsky, D., Smith, N.F., Cardinal, N., Harper, J., Morris, M., White, E. and Salomon, A.K. (2015) 'Ancient Mariculture on the Northwest Coast of North America', PLoS ONE, 10(2), e0115345.

[251] Deur, D. (ed.) (2015) Clam Gardens: Aboriginal Mariculture on Canada's West Coast. Vancouver: UBC Press.

[252] Denevan, W.M. (2001) Cultivated Landscapes of Native Amazonia and the Andes: Triumph over the Soil. Oxford: Oxford University Press.

[253] Belich, J. (1986) The New Zealand Wars and the Victorian Interpretation of Racial Conflict. Auckland: Auckland University Press / Oxford: Oxford University Press.

[254] Silverman, D.J. (2016) Thundersticks: Firearms and the Violent Transformation of Native America. Cambridge, MA: Harvard University Press.

[255] Parker, G. (1988) The Military Revolution: Military Innovation and the Rise of the West, 1500–1800. Cambridge: Cambridge University Press.

regional hydrology), the result was ecological damage and higher variance, costs hidden by ideology or distant accounting.[256,257] Just as important, Indigenous contributions quietly shaped global technology itself. Europeans learned, copied, or profited from Indigenous innovations, canoe and snowshoe mobility, parkas, kayaks and umiaks for Arctic travel;[258] agronomic complexes like milpa intercropping later validated by modern yield metrics[259]; high-productivity urban agricultures such as chinampas in the Basin of Mexico that inspired contemporary "wetland farming" revivals[260]; Amazonian terra preta (anthropogenic dark earths), now studied as a carbon-negative soil technology[261], refers to fertile soils created by pre-Columbian Indigenous populations through the controlled addition of charcoal, organic waste, and pottery shards. These soils retain nutrients far better than surrounding tropical soils and support long-term agricultural productivity, challenging earlier assumptions that the Amazon was too poor for sustained settlement.

Global commodity revolutions leaned on Indigenous biotechnologies and knowledge transfer: Amerindian latex processing underwrote the nineteenth-century rubber economy; Andean cinchona knowledge enabled quinine extraction, reshaping tropical medicine and imperial reach.[262,263] The Atlantic and Pacific economies did not spread European technology into a vacuum; they braided Indigenous devices, crops,

256 Cronon, W. (1983) Changes in the Land: Indians, Colonists, and the Ecology of New England. New York: Hill and Wang.

257 Scott, J.C. (1998) Seeing Like a State: How Certain Schemes to Improve the Human Condition Have Failed. New Haven: Yale University Press.

258 Adney, E.T. and Chapelle, H.I. (1964) The Bark Canoes and Skin Boats of North America. Washington, DC: Smithsonian Institution Press.

259 Mt. Pleasant, J. (2006) 'The Science behind the Three Sisters Mound System: An Agronomic Assessment of an Indigenous Agricultural System in the Northeast', in Staller, J.E., Tykot, R.H. and Benz, B.F. (eds) Histories of Maize. Amsterdam: Elsevier, pp. 529–537.

260 Denevan, W.M. (2001) Cultivated Landscapes of Native Amazonia and the Andes: Triumph over the Soil. Oxford: Oxford University Press.

261 Lehmann, J., Kern, D.C., Glaser, B. and Woods, W.I. (eds) (2003) Amazonian Dark Earths: Origin, Properties, Management. Dordrecht: Kluwer Academic Publishers.

262 Dean, W. (1987) Brazil and the Struggle for Rubber: A Study in Environmental History. Cambridge: Cambridge University Press.

263 Schiebinger, L. (2004) Plants and Empire: Colonial Bioprospecting in the Atlantic World. Cambridge, MA: Harvard University Press.

and know-how into world systems that magnified European power while masking its dependencies.[264,265,266] Recognizing the myth matters analytically. It shifts explanation from putative civilizational hierarchies to fit who matched organization and technology to environment, and who could scale that fit through institutions and finance. European states won where oceanic shipping, gunpowder logistics, and fiscal systems converted distance into predictable supply; Indigenous polities won, or imposed high costs, when locally tailored technologies, transport, food systems, fortifications, and governance neutralized imperial advantages; for example, the Mapuche of southern Chile resisted Spanish conquest for over three centuries by adapting horseback mobility, decentralized leadership, and fortified riverine settlements to their terrain, effectively blunting the logistical and tactical superiority of colonial forces. Communist modernizers reproduced both outcomes: success when political and logistical systems were adapted to terrain and society, failure when high-modernist standardization displaced local competence. The historical record thus supports a more precise claim: technological superiority is rarely absolute; it is relational, ecological, and institutional, and Indigenous systems frequently met or exceeded European performance under the conditions that mattered most on their own ground.

7 Conclusion

The chapter has shown that Europe's global ascendancy between the fifteenth and nineteenth centuries is best explained not by an intrinsic civilizational "edge", but by the assembly of complementary technologies and institutions into scalable systems of power. Ocean-going hulls, instrumented navigation, and routinized exploitation of winds and currents turned distance into a solvable logistics problem; gunpowder, drill, and fortification made violence predictable; and fiscal–military states, credit, and joint-stock enterprise stitched these capabilities together into repeatable projects of conquest and rule. What Europe "had" was less a list

[264] Crosby, A.W. (2004) Ecological Imperialism: The Biological Expansion of Europe, 900–1900. 2nd edn. Cambridge: Cambridge University Press.

[265] Flynn, D.O. and Giráldez, A. (1995) 'Born with a "Silver Spoon": The Origin of World Trade in 1571', Journal of World History, 6(2), pp. 201–221.

[266] Pomeranz, K. (2000) The Great Divergence: China, Europe, and the Making of the Modern World Economy. Princeton: Princeton University Press.

of inventions than an ability to integrate, finance, and institutionalize them for imperial ends. Viewed through a neoclassical lens, these arrangements lowered transaction and risk costs at every margin. State navies and chartered companies acted as public–private complements that generated economies of scale and scope, convoys, depots, standardized hulls, and capital markets, allowing predictable resupply and extraction across oceans. The Dutch and English East India Companies exemplify this hybrid architecture: they invested in charts and logistics and then monetized the resulting reliability, reinforcing a feedback loop among technology, finance, and coercion. In this frame, Europe's comparative advantage lay in system design that turned knowledge and capital into lower average costs of distance, violence, and administration. Comparisons with communist planning sharpen the point that organizational "fit" is decisive. Centralized regimes could mobilize at continental scale (e.g., the Soviet wartime logistics machine), but standardized templates deployed without local adaptation raised hidden costs in peacetime—attrition, environmental damage, and legitimacy loss. Conversely, insurgent logistics under Giáp fused decentralization, camouflage, and terrain-fit to move men and material efficiently under surveillance—indigenous-style solutions packaged within a state project. Even at sea, twentieth-century blue-water ambitions under central planning proved technologically impressive yet economically brittle relative to early-modern Europe's competitive, investor-driven model. Crucially, the chapter demonstrated that Indigenous technologies often matched or exceeded European performance in the environments that mattered to them. Polynesian canoe complexes substituted skilled labour and information for scarce metals and instruments; modular lashings, lightweight hulls, and wayfinding systems produced low cost per safe mile, while rāhui and customary marine tenure lowered conflict and ecological variance, an efficient, Ostrom-consistent bundle of technology and governance rather than a "primitive" stopgap. In the boreal interior, birchbark canoes dominated mixed river–lake transport so convincingly that European traders adopted Indigenous craft, routes, and operating practices wholesale; on the Northwest Coast, clam gardens measurably increased shellfish yields, evidencing sophisticated mariculture; and in the Andes, terraces and canals stabilized production on steep, frost-prone slopes. These cases undercut simple narratives of European "superiority" and instead highlight a broader rule: performance is relational to ecology, risk, and information. Where Europeans did achieve strategic superiority was in logistics and resource mobilization at scale. The fiscal–military state kept fleets and armies in the field for years; joint-stock companies extended the state's reach; and colonial extraction, Potosí silver, Caribbean sugar, enslaved labour underwrote the marginal costs of long campaigns. The numbers are stark: approximately 12.5 million captives embarked from Africa, with ~ 10.7 million disembarking in the Americas, creating coerced labour pools that fed both plantation output and naval victualling.[267] Indigenous logistics, by contrast, optimized for agility and information: canoe corridors, cached maize, horse-powered mobility—excellent for raiding, deterrence, and alliance diplomacy but not designed to sustain distant siege-and-supply warfare against industrial magazines and deep treasuries. Psychology and diplomacy further lowered imperial costs. Divide-and-rule alliances, treaty forms that piggybacked on local diplomatic rituals, and missionary institutions that reorganized settlement and labour turned rivals into auxiliaries and subjects into congregants, replacing garrisons with information and legitimacy. From Tlaxcalan alliances in central Mexico to Haudenosaunee "play-off" diplomacy and Mapuche parlamentos, Europeans learned to rent local networks rather than pay the full price of occupation; early gun and horse spectacles amplified these bargains by reshaping reputations and expectations. The long-run environmental and social consequences of this package were profound. In New England, fences, livestock, and fixed-field grains reconfigured subsistence landscapes and labour; beaver depletion and the bison's near-extirpation illustrate how metropolitan market signals remade ecologies and economies; in the Andes, amalgamation married ore to mercury with durable toxic legacies; and globally, bullion flows, coerced migrations, and falling transport costs knit a new Atlantic economy with reallocated factor rewards and urbanization patterns, benefits centrally captured, costs locally externalized. Communist high-modernist analogues reiterate the mechanism: centralized schemes that ignored local ecologies achieved gross outputs while imposing catastrophic, unpriced externalities, underscoring that organizational form, not ideology alone, determines whether environmental costs are internalized. The chapter therefore replaces a civilizational hierarchy story with a precision claim: technological superiority is rarely absolute; it is relational, ecological, and institutional. Europeans prevailed where

[267] Eltis, D. and Richardson, D. (2010) Atlas of the Transatlantic Slave Trade. New Haven, CT: Yale University Press.

ocean shipping, gunpowder logistics, and fiscal systems converted distance into predictable supply; Indigenous polities prevailed, or imposed high prices, where locally tailored technologies and governance neutralized imperial advantages; communist modernizers reproduced both outcomes depending on fit. The analytic payoff is twofold. First, it clarifies why "myths of superiority" were constructed—success bred narratives that credited essence rather than system fit. Second, it yields a policy lesson with contemporary reach: durable, low-cost performance comes from matching organization and technology to place, pricing externalities, and recognizing the informational capital embedded in Indigenous and local systems.

The historical narratives and contemporary examples explored in this chapter underscore how Indigenous struggles over land are inseparable from broader issues of sovereignty, ecological sustainability, and cultural survival. These conflicts are not relics of the past but are central to present-day debates on economic justice, environmental policy, and decolonization. As Indigenous peoples worldwide continue to assert their rights in the face of ongoing threats—from extractive industries to climate change—the need for models grounded in Indigenous knowledge systems becomes ever more urgent. In the next chapter, we turn to examine how Indigenous communities are reclaiming their lands and shaping resource governance through legal activism, institutional reforms, and the revitalization of traditional ecological knowledge. Chapter 5 will explore the transformative potential of Indigenous-led frameworks in redefining sustainability and challenging dominant economic paradigms.

References

Adas, M. (1989) Machines as the Measure of Men: Science, Technology, and Ideologies of Western Dominance. Ithaca, NY: Cornell University Press.

Adney, Edwin Tappan, and Howard I. Chapelle. 1964. The Bark Canoes and Skin Boats of North America. Washington, DC: Smithsonian Institution Press.

Allen, R. C. (2003). Farm to factory: A reinterpretation of the Soviet industrial revolution. Princeton University Press.

Arrighi, G. (1994) The Long Twentieth Century: Money, Power and the Origins of Our Times. London: Verso.

Bakewell, P. (1984) Miners of the Red Mountain: Indian Labour in Potosí, 1545–1650. Albuquerque: University of New Mexico Press.

Bayly, C.A., 1988. Indian Society and the Making of the British Empire. Cambridge: Cambridge University Press.

Beckles, H. (1989) Natural Rebels: A Social History of Enslaved Black Women in Barbados. New Brunswick, NJ: Rutgers University Press.
Belich, James. 1986. The New Zealand Wars and the Victorian Interpretation of Racial Conflict. Auckland: Auckland University Press / Oxford: Oxford University Press.
Black, J., 2002. European Warfare, 1494–1660. London: Routledge.
Boserup, Ester. 1965. The Conditions of Agricultural Growth: The Economics of Agrarian Change under Population Pressure. Chicago: Aldine.
Boxer, C. R. (1965). The Dutch seaborne empire, 1600–1800. Hutchinson.
Boxer, C.R., 1969. The Portuguese Seaborne Empire 1415–1825. London: Hutchinson.
Braudel, F. (1972). The Mediterranean and the Mediterranean world in the age of Philip II. Harper & Row.
Braudel, F., 1982. The Wheels of Commerce: Civilization and Capitalism 15th–18th Century, Vol. 2. New York: Harper & Row.
Brewer, J. (1989) The Sinews of Power: War, Money and the English State, 1688–1783. Cambridge, MA: Harvard University Press.
Brewer, J. (1990) The Sinews of Power: War, Money and the English State, 1688–1783. London: Unwin Hyman.
Burnett, C., 1996. The Introduction of Arabic Learning into England. London: The British Library.
Campbell, T., 1987. Portolan Charts from the Late Thirteenth Century to 1500. In: J.B. Harley and D. Woodward (eds.) The History of Cartography, Volume 1: Cartography in Prehistoric, Ancient, and Medieval Europe and the Mediterranean. Chicago: University of Chicago Press, pp. 371–463.
Carlos, A. M., & Neal, L. (2011). Commerce and conflict: The East India Company and the rise of British dominance in Asia, 1600–1800. Cambridge University Press
Chaudhuri, K. N. (1985). Trade and civilisation in the Indian Ocean: An economic history from the rise of Islam to 1750. Cambridge University Press.
Clement, Charles R., William M. Denevan, Michael J. Heckenberger, André B. Junqueira, Eduardo G. Neves, William G. Teixeira, and William I. Woods. 2015. "The Domestication of Amazonia before European Conquest." Proceedings of the Royal Society B 282: 20150813.
Comaroff, J. and Comaroff, J. (1991) Of Revelation and Revolution, Volume 1: Christianity, Colonialism, and Consciousness in South Africa. Chicago: University of Chicago Press.
Comaroff, J. and Comaroff, J. (1997) Of Revelation and Revolution, Volume 2: The Dialectics of Modernity on a South African Frontier. Chicago: University of Chicago Press.

Conklin, Harold C. 1957. Hanunóo Agriculture: A Report on an Integral System of Shifting Cultivation. Rome: Food and Agriculture Organization of the United Nations.
Cronon, William. 1983. Changes in the Land: Indians, Colonists, and the Ecology of New England. New York: Hill and Wang.
Crosby, A.W., 1972. The Columbian Exchange: Biological and Cultural Consequences of 1492. Westport: Greenwood Press.
Crosby, A. W. (2004). Ecological Imperialism: The Biological Expansion of Europe, 900–1900 (2nd ed.). Cambridge: Cambridge University Press.
Curtin, P.D., 1984. Cross-Cultural Trade in World History. Cambridge: Cambridge University Press.
de Vries, J. and van der Woude, A. (1997) The First Modern Economy: Success, Failure, and Perseverance of the Dutch Economy, 1500–1815. Cambridge: Cambridge University Press.
Dean, W. (1987) Brazil and the Struggle for Rubber: A Study in Environmental History. Cambridge: Cambridge University Press.
Demsetz, Harold. 1967. "Toward a Theory of Property Rights." American Economic Review 57(2): 347–359.
Denevan, William M. 2001. Cultivated Landscapes of Native Amazonia and the Andes: Triumph over the Soil. Oxford: Oxford University Press.
Deur, Douglas, and Adam Dick, eds., with Dana Lepofsky, Kristin Rowell, and Anne K. Salomon. 2015. Clam Gardens: Aboriginal Mariculture on Canada's West Coast. Vancouver: UBC Press.
Diffie, B. W., & Winius, G. D. (1977). Foundations of the Portuguese empire, 1415–1580. University of Minnesota Press.
Dillehay, Tom D. 2007. Monuments, Empires, and Resistance: The Araucanian Polity and Ritual Narratives. Cambridge: Cambridge University Press.
Dunn, R.S. (1972) Sugar and Slaves: The Rise of the Planter Class in the English West Indies, 1624–1713. Chapel Hill: University of North Carolina Press.
Eisenstein, E. L. (1980). The printing press as an agent of change. Cambridge University Press.
Eltis, D. and Richardson, D. (2010) Atlas of the Transatlantic Slave Trade. New Haven, CT: Yale University Press.
Engerman, S.L. and Sokoloff, K.L. (1997) 'Factor Endowments, Institutions, and Differential Paths of Growth among New World Economies', in S. Haber (ed.) How Latin America Fell Behind: Essays on the Economic Histories of Brazil and Mexico, 1800–1914. Stanford, CA: Stanford University Press, pp. 260–304.
Ewers, J.C. (1955) The Horse in Blackfoot Indian Culture: With Comparative Material from Other Western Tribes. Washington, DC: Smithsonian Institution (Bureau of American Ethnology Bulletin 159).

Fernández-Armesto, F., 2006. Pathfinders: A Global History of Exploration. New York: W.W. Norton & Company.

Finney, Ben. 1994. Voyage of Rediscovery: A Cultural Odyssey Through Polynesia. Berkeley: University of California Press.

Flynn, D. O., & Giráldez, A. (1995). Born with a 'silver spoon': The origin of world trade in 1571. Journal of World History, 6(2), 201–221.

Flynn, D.O. and Giráldez, A. (2002) 'Cycles of Silver: Global Economic Unity through the Mid-Eighteenth Century', Journal of World History, 13(2), pp. 391–427.

Giáp, Võ Nguyên. 1962. People's War, People's Army: The Vietcong Insurrection Manual for Underdeveloped Countries. New York: Praeger.

Gilmartin, D., 1994. Scientific Empire and Imperial Science: Colonialism and Irrigation Technology in the Indus Basin. The Journal of Asian Studies, 53(4), pp.1127–1149.

Gladwin, Thomas. 1970. East Is a Big Bird: Navigation and Logic on Puluwat Atoll. Cambridge, MA: Harvard University Press.

Glete, J., 1993. Navies and Nations: Warships, Navies and State Building in Europe and America, 1500–1860. Stockholm: Almqvist & Wiksell International.

Grenier, John. 2005. The First Way of War: American War Making on the Frontier, 1607–1814. Cambridge: Cambridge University Press.

Groesbeck, Amy S., Kristin Rowell, Dana Lepofsky, and Anne K. Salomon. 2014. "Ancient Clam Gardens Increased Shellfish Production: Adaptive Strategies from the Past Can Inform Sustainable Management Today." PLoS ONE 9(3): e91235

Guillet, David. 1987. "Terracing and Irrigation in the Peruvian Highlands." Human Ecology 15(4): 431–447.

Hämäläinen, Pekka. 2008. The Comanche Empire. New Haven: Yale University Press.

Harrison, M. (ed.) (1998) The Economics of World War II: Six Great Powers in International Comparison. Cambridge: Cambridge University Press.

Harrison, M. (2002) Accounting for War: Soviet Production, Employment, and the Defence Burden, 1940–1945. Cambridge: Cambridge University Press.

Hassig, R. (1988). Aztec Warfare: Imperial Expansion and Political Control. Norman: University of Oklahoma Press.

Hayami, Yujiro, and Vernon W. Ruttan. 1985. Agricultural Development: An International Perspective. Rev. and expanded ed. Baltimore: Johns Hopkins University Press.

Headrick, D.R. (1981) The Tools of Empire: Technology and European Imperialism in the Nineteenth Century. New York: Oxford University Press.

Hobson, J.M., 2004. The Eastern Origins of Western Civilisation. Cambridge: Cambridge University Press.

Holloway, D., 1982. The Soviet Union and the Arms Race. New Haven: Yale University Press.
Horton, Mark, and John Middleton. 2000. The Swahili: The Social Landscape of a Mercantile Society. Oxford: Blackwell
Innis, Harold A. 1956. The Fur Trade in Canada: An Introduction to Canadian Economic History. Toronto: University of Toronto Press.
Irwin, Geoffrey. 1992. The Prehistoric Exploration and Colonization of the Pacific. Cambridge: Cambridge University Press.
Isenberg, A.C. (2000) The Destruction of the Bison: An Environmental History, 1750–1920. Cambridge: Cambridge University Press.
Jennings, F. (1984). The Ambiguous Iroquois Empire: The Covenant Chain Confederation of Indian Tribes with English Colonies from Its Beginnings to the Lancaster Treaty of 1744. New York: W. W. Norton.
Johannes, R. E. 1978. "Traditional Marine Conservation Methods in Oceania and Their Demise." Annual Review of Ecology and Systematics 9: 349–364.
Kennedy, P., 1987. The Rise and Fall of the Great Powers: Economic Change and Military Conflict from 1500 to 2000. New York: Random House.
Kirch, Patrick Vinton. 2017. On the Road of the Winds: An Archaeological History of the Pacific Islands before European Contact. Revised and Expanded Edition. Berkeley: University of California Press.
Knight, Ian. 2010. Zulu Rising: The Epic Story of iSandlwana and Rorke's Drift. London: Macmillan.
Lehmann, J., Kern, D.C., Glaser, B. and Woods, W.I. (eds) (2003) Amazonian Dark Earths: Origin, Properties, Management. Dordrecht: Kluwer Academic Publishers.
Lepofsky, Dana, et al. 2015. "Ancient Mariculture on the Northwest Coast of North America." PLoS ONE 10(2): e0115345.
Levathes, L., 1994. When China Ruled the Seas: The Treasure Fleet of the Dragon Throne, 1405–1433. Oxford: Oxford University Press.
Levtzion, Nehemia, and J. F. P. Hopkins, eds. 2000. Corpus of Early Arabic Sources for West African History. Princeton: Markus Wiener Publishers.
Lewis, David. 1972. We, the Navigators: The Ancient Art of Landfinding in the Pacific. Honolulu: University of Hawai'i Press.
Maddison, A. (2001). The world economy: A millennial perspective. OECD.
Mann, C.C., 2005. 1491: New Revelations of the Americas Before Columbus. New York: Vintage.
Mao, Zedong. 1961. On Guerrilla Warfare. Translated by Samuel B. Griffith. New York: Praeger.
Martin-Guay, Marie-Ève, Alain-G. Paquette, Judy Dupras, and Rachelle Leroux. 2018. "Intercropping Systems Sustain Crop Yields and the Ecological Services in Arable Land." Agronomy for Sustainable Development 38: 69.

Matsuoka, Yoshihiro, Yves Vigouroux, Major M. Goodman, Jesus Sanchez, Edward Buckler, and John Doebley. 2002. "A Single Domestication for Maize Shown by Multilocus Microsatellite Genotyping." Proceedings of the National Academy of Sciences 99(9): 6080–6084.

McCann, J.C. (2005) Maize and Grace: Africa's Encounter with a New World Crop, 1500–2000. Cambridge, MA: Harvard University Press.

Mertz, Ole, Christine Padoch, Jefferson Fox, R. A. Cramb, Stephen J. Leisz, N. T. Lam, and Tran Duc Vien. 2009. "Trends in Shifting Cultivation and the REDD Policy." Trends in Ecology & Evolution 24(12).

Micklin, P. (2007) 'The Aral Sea Disaster', Annual Review of Earth and Planetary Sciences, 35, pp. 47–72.

Mintz, S.W. (1985) Sweetness and Power: The Place of Sugar in Modern History. New York: Viking.

Mokyr, J., 2009. The Enlightened Economy: An Economic History of Britain 1700–1850. New Haven: Yale University Press.

Mt. Pleasant, Jane. 2006. "The Science behind the Three Sisters Mound System: An Agronomic Assessment of an Indigenous Agricultural System in the Northeast." In Histories of Maize: Multidisciplinary Approaches to the Prehistory, Linguistics, Biogeography, Domestication, and Evolution of Maize, edited by John E. Staller, Robert H. Tykot, and Bruce F. Benz, 529–537. Amsterdam: Elsevier.

Neal, L. (1990) The Rise of Financial Capitalism: International Capital Markets in the Age of Reason. Cambridge: Cambridge University Press.

Needham, J., 1954. Science and Civilisation in China, Vol. 1. Cambridge: Cambridge University Press.

Needham, J., 1971. Science and Civilisation in China, Volume 4: Physics and Physical Technology, Part 3: Civil Engineering and Nautics. Cambridge: Cambridge University Press.

Needham, J. (1981). Science in traditional China: A comparative perspective. Harvard University Press.

Netting, Robert McC. 1993. Smallholders, Householders: Farm Families and the Ecology of Intensive, Sustainable Agriculture. Stanford, CA: Stanford University Press

North, D. C., & Weingast, B. R. (1989). Constitutions and commitment: The evolution of institutions governing public choice in seventeenth-century England. The Journal of Economic History, 49(4), 803–832.

North, D.C., 1990. Institutions, Institutional Change and Economic Performance. Cambridge: Cambridge University Press.

Nriagu, J.O. (1994) 'Mercury Pollution from the Past Mining of Gold and Silver in the Americas', Science of the Total Environment, 149(3), pp. 167–181.

Nunn, N. and Qian, N. (2011) 'The Potato's Contribution to Population and Urbanization: Evidence from a Historical Experiment', Quarterly Journal of Economics, 126(2), pp. 593–650.

O'Rourke, K.H. and Williamson, J.G. (2002) 'After Columbus: Explaining Europe's Overseas Trade Boom, 1500–1800', Journal of Economic History, 62(2), pp. 417–456.

Ortloff, Charles R., and Alan L. Kolata. 1993. "Climate and Collapse: Agro-Ecological Perspectives on the Decline of the Tiwanaku State." Journal of Archaeological Science 20(2): 195–221.

Ostrom, Elinor. 1990. Governing the Commons: The Evolution of Institutions for Collective Action. Cambridge: Cambridge University Press.

Pagden, A. (1993). European Encounters with the New World: From Renaissance to Romanticism. New Haven: Yale University Press.

Parker, Geoffrey. 1988. The Military Revolution: Military Innovation and the Rise of the West, 1500–1800. Cambridge: Cambridge University Press.

Parker, G. (1996). The military revolution: Military innovation and the rise of the West, 1500–1800. Cambridge University Press.

Parry, J.H., 1963. The Age of Reconnaissance: Discovery, Exploration and Settlement, 1450 to 1650. London: Weidenfeld & Nicolson.

Pettegree, A. (2010). The book in the Renaissance. Yale University Press.

Pomeranz, K. (2000) The Great Divergence: China, Europe, and the Making of the Modern World Economy. Princeton: Princeton University Press.

Repo-Carrasco-Valencia, R., and L. A. Serna. 2011. "Quinoa (Chenopodium quinoa Willd.) as a Source of Dietary Fiber and Other Functional Components." Food Science and Technology (Campinas) 31(1): 225–230.

Restall, M., 2003. Seven Myths of the Spanish Conquest. Oxford: Oxford University Press.

Richards, J.F. (2003) The Unending Frontier: An Environmental History of the Early Modern World. Berkeley: University of California Press.

Richter, Daniel K. 1992. The Ordeal of the Longhouse: The Peoples of the Iroquois League in the Era of European Colonization. Chapel Hill: University of North Carolina Press.

Rodger, N.A.M., 2004. The Command of the Ocean: A Naval History of Britain, 1649–1815. London: Penguin.

Romer, P. M. (1990). Endogenous technological change. Journal of Political Economy, 98(5, Part 2), S71–S102.

Saliba, G. (2007). Islamic science and the making of the European Renaissance. MIT Press.

Schiebinger, L. (2004) Plants and Empire: Colonial Bioprospecting in the Atlantic World. Cambridge, MA: Harvard University Press.

Scott, James C. 1998. Seeing Like a State: How Certain Schemes to Improve the Human Condition Have Failed. New Haven: Yale University Press.

Seed, P. (1995). Ceremonies of Possession in Europe's Conquest of the New World, 1492–1640. Cambridge: Cambridge University Press.

Silverman, David J. 2016. Thundersticks: Firearms and the Violent Transformation of Native America. Cambridge, MA: Harvard University Press.

Slezkine, Yuri. 1994. Arctic Mirrors: Russia and the Small Peoples of the North. Ithaca: Cornell University Press.

Staller, John E., Robert H. Tykot, and Bruce F. Benz, eds. 2006. Histories of Maize: Multidisciplinary Approaches to the Prehistory, Linguistics, Biogeography, Domestication, and Evolution of Maize. Amsterdam: Elsevier.

Stern, P.J. (2011) The Company-State: Corporate Sovereignty and the Early Modern Foundations of the British Empire in India. Oxford: Oxford University Press.

Tandeter, E. (1993) 'The Mining Industry', in Bethell, L. (ed.) Colonial Latin America. Cambridge: Cambridge University Press, pp. 144–182.

Tracy, J.D. (1990) The Rise of Merchant Empires: Long-Distance Trade in the Early Modern World, 1350–1750. Cambridge: Cambridge University Press.

Unger, R.W., 1978. Dutch Shipbuilding Before 1800: Ships and Guilds. Assen: Van Gorcum.

Vega-Gálvez, Antonio, Maria Miranda, Jorge Vergara, Eduardo Uribe, Luis Puente, and Enrique A. Martínez. 2010. "Nutrition Facts and Functional Potential of Quinoa (Chenopodium quinoa Willd.), an Ancient Andean Grain: A Review." Journal of the Science of Food and Agriculture 90(15): 2541–2547.

White, Richard. 1991. The Middle Ground: Indians, Empires, and Republics in the Great Lakes Region, 1650–1815. Cambridge: Cambridge University Press.

Williams, E. (1944) Capitalism and Slavery. Chapel Hill: University of North Carolina Press.

CHAPTER 5

Land Rights and Resource Management in Indigenous Societies

1 Introduction

Land is not merely a physical space for Indigenous peoples; it constitutes the foundation of their cultural, spiritual, economic, and political lives. Across diverse societies, from the Aboriginal nations of Australia to the First Nations of North America, the Sami of the Arctic, and the tribes of the Amazon, land embodies a living relationship between people, non-human species, and ecosystems.[1,2] This relationship is distinct from the dominant Western paradigm that has historically reduced land to a commodity for ownership, enclosure, and exploitation.[3] Instead, Indigenous worldviews understand land as sacred, communal, and deeply entwined with identity, kinship, and spirituality.[4] The significance of land and resources in Indigenous societies is reflected in stewardship practices that are inherently ecological and sustainable. Practices such as rotational farming, controlled burning, and agroforestry have ensured

[1] Watson, I. (2014) Aboriginal Peoples, Colonialism and International Law: Raw Law. Abingdon: Routledge.

[2] Alfred, T. (2009) Wasáse: Indigenous Pathways of Action and Freedom. Toronto: University of Toronto Press.

[3] Banner, S. (2005) How the Indians Lost Their Land: Law and Power on the Frontier. Cambridge, MA: Harvard University Press

[4] Wilson, S. (2008) Research is Ceremony: Indigenous Research Methods. Halifax: Fernwood Publishing.

S. Ramesh, *The Political Economy of the Indigenous Peoples of the World, Volume I*, https://doi.org/10.1007/978-3-032-24041-5_5

ecological balance for millennia.[5] These approaches are underpinned by Indigenous ecological knowledge (IEK), which emphasises harmony with natural cycles and interdependence between humans and ecosystems.[6] For example, the Zuni's water management systems, the Inca's terraced farming, and bison stewardship among the Plains tribes illustrate sophisticated models of environmental governance rooted in communal values rather than extractive imperatives.[7] However, Indigenous approaches to land have historically clashed with colonial and settler colonial ideologies of private property, resource commodification, and extractive development. European legal doctrines such as terra nullius and the Doctrine of Discovery systematically denied Indigenous sovereignty and facilitated widespread land dispossession.[8] These processes not only stripped Indigenous peoples of their territories but also disrupted ecological systems and cultural practices that had sustained communities for generations.[9] From the forced removals in North America to the displacement of Aboriginal Australians, the colonial encounter over land was both materially violent and epistemologically destructive.[10] The consequences of dispossession continue to reverberate in Indigenous communities. Loss of land has entrenched systemic poverty, undermined food sovereignty, and intensified vulnerabilities to climate change and resource exploitation.[11] At the same time, Indigenous resistance has persisted in diverse forms, legal challenges, advocacy, cultural revitalization, and ecological

[5] Berkes, F. (2018) Sacred Ecology. 4th edn. New York: Routledge.

[6] Kimmerer, R.W. (2013) Braiding Sweetgrass: Indigenous Wisdom, Scientific Knowledge, and the Teachings of Plants. Minneapolis: Milkweed Editions.

[7] Davidson-Hunt, I. & Berkes, F. (2003) 'Learning as you journey: Anishinaabe perception of social-ecological environments and adaptive learning', Conservation Ecology, 8(1), p. 5.

[8] Miller, R.J., Ruru, J., Behrendt, L. & Lindberg, T. (2010) Discovering Indigenous Lands: The Doctrine of Discovery in the English Colonies. Oxford: Oxford University Press.

[9] Coulthard, G.S. (2014) Red Skin, White Masks: Rejecting the Colonial Politics of Recognition. Minneapolis: University of Minnesota Press.

[10] Veracini, L. (2010) Settler Colonialism: A Theoretical Overview. Basingstoke: Palgrave Macmillan.

[11] Whyte, K.P. (2018) 'Indigenous science (fiction) for the Anthropocene: Ancestral dystopias and fantasies of climate change crises', Environment and Planning E: Nature and Space, 1(1–2), pp. 224–242.

restoration efforts.[12] Recent decades have witnessed important gains, such as the recognition of native title in Australia through the Mabo case, the implementation of co-management systems in Canada, and the adoption of the United Nations Declaration on the Rights of Indigenous Peoples (UNDRIP) as a global standard for Indigenous sovereignty.[13,14] This chapter explores Indigenous perspectives on land rights and resource management through a comparative and historical lens. Section 2 examines Indigenous philosophies of land stewardship, including the spiritual and cultural connections to land, communal ownership practices, and interdependence between people and ecosystems. Section 3 traces the early clashes between Indigenous and European land concepts, highlighting how legal frameworks and settler practices institutionalized dispossession. Section 4 offers comparative case studies from different regions, demonstrating the varied experiences of dispossession and resistance. Finally, Section 5 draws together broader themes and long-term implications, including the colonial roots of modern inequalities, Indigenous advocacy for land rights, and the integration of Indigenous ecological knowledge into contemporary conservation efforts. By situating Indigenous land rights within both historical processes and contemporary struggles, this chapter highlights the centrality of land to Indigenous survival, sovereignty, and ecological futures. It argues that addressing land rights is not only a matter of justice but also crucial for advancing sustainable and equitable responses to today's global environmental challenges.

Building on the foundational analyses in Chapters 3 and 4, which explored the relationship between land, labour, and the emergence of extractive colonial economies, Chapter 5 shifts focus towards the ideological and institutional scaffolding that legitimized dispossession and extraction: namely, the doctrine of terra nullius and its legal, theological, and economic underpinnings. While Chapter 3 traced the imposition of European economic rationalities onto Indigenous economies, and

[12] Niezen, R. (2003) The Origins of Indigenism: Human Rights and the Politics of Identity. Berkeley: University of California Press.

[13] Anaya, S.J. (2004) Indigenous Peoples in International Law. Oxford: Oxford University Press.

[14] United Nations (2007) United Nations Declaration on the Rights of Indigenous Peoples (UNDRIP). New York: United Nations.

Chapter 4 examined how religious missions facilitated these transformations, this chapter examines how the legal fiction of 'empty land' operated as a tool of both imperial domination and epistemological erasure. It sets the stage for a deeper understanding of the systemic denial of Indigenous sovereignty that will be examined further in Chapter 6 through the lens of governance and state-building.

2 Indigenous Perspectives on Land and Resource Stewardship

2.1 *The Spiritual and Cultural Connection to Land*

For Indigenous peoples, land is not a commodity to be owned, traded, or exploited for maximum profit; rather, it is a sacred living entity, central to identity, spirituality, and community survival. Indigenous cosmologies often position land as an ancestor or a relative, embodying both spiritual duty and ecological responsibility. For example, in Aboriginal Australia, the Dreaming tracks (or songlines) map ancestral journeys across the landscape, connecting individuals, clans, and species through sacred narratives inscribed in the land itself.[15] Similarly, among Native American nations such as the Hopi and Navajo, sacred mountains represent both physical landmarks and spiritual guardians of the people, with ceremonies designed to maintain harmony between humans and their environment.[16] In the Amazon, tribes such as the Kayapo view the rainforest as both a physical home and a spiritual source of life, where stewardship is a responsibility to future generations.[17] These connections demonstrate that Indigenous relationships to land are relational and reciprocal rather than extractive. This worldview stands in marked contrast to neoclassical economics, which frames land as one of the "factors of production" alongside labour and capital. In the neoclassical tradition, land is valued

[15] Rose, D.B. (1996) Nourishing Terrains: Australian Aboriginal Views of Landscape and Wilderness. Canberra: Australian
Heritage Commission.

[16] Yazzie, R. (2010) 'Indigenous Peoples and Sacred Lands: A Navajo Perspective', University of Colorado Law Review, 81(4), pp. 1031–1045.

[17] Turner, T. (1995) 'An Indigenous People's Struggle for Socially Equitable and Ecologically Sustainable Production: The Kayapo Revolt against Extractivism', Journal of Latin American Anthropology, 1(1), pp. 98–121.

according to its scarcity, productivity, and potential to generate rents.[18] The Indigenous perspective resists such abstraction, as it does not reduce land to market value but recognises it as inseparable from community well-being, spiritual continuity, and ecological balance. Case studies highlight the consequences of these contrasting worldviews. In Australia, the doctrine of terra nullius erased Indigenous understandings of sacred landscapes in favour of private property and capitalist exploitation, resulting in severe ecological disruption through overgrazing and deforestation.[19] Conversely, Indigenous land management through controlled burning (fire-stick farming) preserved biodiversity and reduced bushfire risks, practices that have only recently been reintegrated into Australian environmental policy.[20] Communist ideologies, although rejecting private property in favour of collective ownership, also clashed with Indigenous spiritual connections to land. In the Soviet Union, collectivization campaigns among Siberian Indigenous groups such as the Evenki imposed state-controlled land use regimes that disrupted reindeer herding practices and spiritual relationships to ancestral territories.[21] Similarly, in Maoist China, collectivization and state reclamation of minority lands often disregarded sacred landscapes and replaced Indigenous ecological knowledge with industrial agricultural schemes, leading to ecological degradation and loss of cultural continuity.[22] While communism aligns superficially with Indigenous communalism by rejecting private ownership, its instrumentalist view of land as a productive resource for the state still diverges fundamentally from Indigenous perspectives, which emphasise stewardship rooted in spiritual obligation and ecological reciprocity. Empirical evidence reinforces the sustainability embedded in Indigenous spiritual and cultural connections to land. Studies have shown that Indigenous-managed lands overlap significantly with areas of high biodiversity. A

[18] Ricardo, D. (1817/2001) On the Principles of Political Economy and Taxation. Kitchener: Batoche Books.

[19] Altman, J. & Kerins, S. (2012) People on Country: Vital Landscapes, Indigenous Futures. Sydney: Federation Press.

[20] Gammage, B. (2011) The Biggest Estate on Earth: How Aborigines Made Australia. Sydney: Allen & Unwin.

[21] Fondahl, G. (1998) Gaining Ground? Evenkis, Land, and Reform in Southeastern Siberia. Boston: Allyn & Bacon.

[22] Harrell, S. (2001) Perspectives on the Yi of Southwest China. Berkeley: University of California Press.

global analysis found that Indigenous territories cover about 38 million km^2, over a quarter of the Earth's terrestrial surface, and coincide with 40% of protected areas, illustrating how cultural and spiritual stewardship contributes directly to conservation outcomes.[23] By contrast, both capitalist and communist models of land use have often prioritized short-term productivity and resource extraction, leading to biodiversity loss, soil degradation, and long-term ecological vulnerability.[24] Therefore, the spiritual and cultural connection to land in Indigenous societies provides an alternative paradigm of resource management that cannot be reduced to property rights or state planning. Rather than treating land as a means of production, Indigenous peoples understand it as a living network of relations that sustains cultural identity, ecological resilience, and intergenerational survival. This perspective poses a direct challenge to both the commodification of land in neoclassical economics and the statist collectivism of communism, offering vital insights into sustainable stewardship in the face of global environmental crises.

2.2 Communal Land Ownership and Sustainable Practices

Indigenous perspectives on land and resource stewardship often emphasise collective forms of ownership and long-term ecological balance. For many Indigenous societies, land is not a commodity to be bought or sold but rather a communal resource, intertwined with cultural identity and spiritual significance. This worldview contrasts sharply with the neoclassical economic model, which treats land as a factor of production subject to market forces of supply and demand. In neoclassical economics, private ownership is assumed to generate efficiency by aligning individual incentives with resource use.[25] Although neoclassical economics

[23] Garnett, S.T., Burgess, N.D., Fa, J.E., Fernández-Llamazares, Á., Molnár, Z., Robinson, C.J., Watson, J.E.M., Zander, K.K., Austin, B., Brondizio, E.S., Collier, N.F., Duncan, T., Ellis, E., Geyle, H., Jackson, M.V., Jonas, H.D., Malmer, P., McGowan, B., Sivongxay, A. & Leiper, I. (2018) 'A spatial overview of the global importance of Indigenous lands for conservation', Nature Sustainability, 1(7), pp. 369–374.

[24] Foster, J.B. & Clark, B. (2009) 'The Paradox of Wealth: Capitalism and Ecological Destruction', Monthly Review, 61(6).

[25] Coase, R. (1960). The Problem of Social Cost. Journal of Law and Economics, 3, 1–44.

has long maintained that private ownership is the most efficient mechanism for allocating and conserving scarce resources, case studies of Indigenous communities demonstrate that collective stewardship can generate sustainability outcomes that undermine this orthodoxy. In neoclassical theory, the absence of private property rights is assumed to result in overuse and degradation, encapsulated in the "tragedy of the commons".[26] Yet ethnographic and ecological research reveals that Indigenous peoples often maintain complex communal governance systems that regulate access, monitor use, and sanction misuse in ways that prevent resource depletion. For example, the rotational farming and agroforestry practices of the Ifugao in the Philippines and the Kayapó in Brazil reflect sophisticated ecological knowledge systems that maintain soil fertility and biodiversity across generations.[27] Controlled burning by Indigenous Australians, often termed "fire-stick farming", is another instance of ecological stewardship, reducing wildfire risks while promoting new plant growth and sustaining animal populations.[28] These practices illustrate a model of communal management that prevents the tragedy of the commons in which common resources are over exploited in the absence of private property rights. Communal ownership also bears comparison with communist approaches to collective resource management, though the two are distinct. Whereas Marxist theory sought to abolish private ownership in favour of collective control mediated by the state.[29]However, Indigenous systems are typically decentralized and grounded in kinship, ritual, and customary law. For instance, in the Māori concept of whenua, land is an ancestral legacy held in trust for future generations, not the property of a centralized authority. Empirical evidence from New Zealand's Treaty of Waitangi settlements demonstrates how recognition of communal land rights has enhanced cultural continuity while also generating economic opportunities through tribal

[26] Hardin, G. (1968). The Tragedy of the Commons. Science, 162(3859), 1243–1248.

[27] Posey, D. (1985). Indigenous Management of Tropical Forest Ecosystems: The Case of the Kayapó Indians of the
Brazilian Amazon. Agroforestry Systems, 3(2), 139–158.

[28] Gammage, B. (2011). The Biggest Estate on Earth: How Aborigines Made Australia. Sydney: Allen & Unwin.

[29] Marx, K., & Engels, F. (1998). The Communist Manifesto (original work published 1848). London: Verso.

corporations.[30] By contrast, collectivization in the Soviet Union often undermined local knowledge, leading to ecological degradation such as soil depletion during the Virgin Lands campaign.[31] Quantitative data also suggest that Indigenous communal stewardship can outperform market-based systems in ecological terms. A study by the World Resources Institute found that deforestation rates within Indigenous-managed territories in the Amazon were two to three times lower than in adjacent non-Indigenous areas.[32] Similarly, comparative research in Canada shows that First Nations-managed forests exhibit higher biodiversity indices and lower rates of clear-cutting compared with privately managed lands.[33] Such findings question the assumption within neoclassical economics that efficiency is necessarily tied to private property regimes. Instead, they highlight how communal systems, when embedded in cultural and ecological knowledge, can achieve sustainability outcomes at scale. Modern environmentalism increasingly draws on these Indigenous practices, recognizing their relevance to contemporary challenges such as climate change and biodiversity loss. The Paris Agreement's emphasis on Indigenous knowledge systems reflects a growing acknowledgment that sustainability requires more than technological fixes or market instruments like carbon pricing. Indigenous stewardship offers a relational model where human societies are integrated into ecological systems rather than positioned above them. This comparative lens, juxtaposing Indigenous practices with both neoclassical economics and communist collectivization, demonstrates that communal land ownership is not merely a cultural artefact but a viable and empirically supported framework for resource sustainability in the twenty-first century.

[30] Durie, M. (1998). Te Mana, Te Kāwanatanga: The Politics of Māori Self-Determination. Auckland: Oxford University Press.

[31] Wegren, S. (1998). Agriculture and the State in Soviet and Post-Soviet Russia. Pittsburgh: University of Pittsburgh Press.

[32] Ricketts, T., Soares-Filho, B., da Fonseca, G., Nepstad, D., Pfaff, A., Petsonk, A., Kormos, C. (2010). Indigenous Lands, Protected Areas, and Slowing Climate Change. PLoS Biology, 8(3), e1000331.

[33] Natcher, D., & Hickey, C. (2002). Putting the Community Back into Community-Based Resource Management: A Criteria and Indicators Approach to Sustainability. Canadian Journal of Native Studies, 22(1), 1–26.

2.3 Interdependence between People and Ecosystems

Indigenous perspectives on land and resources are grounded in the philosophy of interdependence between people and ecosystems; whereby human activity is conceived as part of natural cycles rather than external to them. Unlike the neoclassical economic model, which views land, water, and biological resources as inputs into a production function to be optimized for utility or profit.[34] Indigenous systems emphasise reciprocal responsibility and balance. This worldview manifests in practices that both sustain livelihoods and preserve ecological integrity, often in ways that modern scientific approaches have only recently begun to recognise. For instance, the Zuni people of the American Southwest developed intricate water-harvesting systems to manage scarce desert resources. By building small stone dams and runoff diversions, they were able to regulate water distribution across communal fields, enhancing agricultural productivity while preserving aquifers.[35] In the Andes, the Inca constructed terraced farming systems that reduced soil erosion, maintained soil fertility, and allowed cultivation at high altitudes. These terraces remain productive today and are increasingly cited as models for climate-resilient agriculture.[36] Similarly, Plains tribes in North America developed rotational hunting practices and seasonal migration strategies to manage bison herds sustainably, ensuring that populations remained stable for centuries before colonial disruption.[37] These examples illustrate how Indigenous ecological knowledge (IEK) incorporates an understanding of ecosystems as dynamic systems requiring adaptive management. By contrast, both neoclassical economics and communism have often imposed extractive models that undermine such balances. Neoclassical frameworks tend to assume that efficient resource use derives from market allocation and private property rights, leading to policies that prioritise short-term

[34] Samuelson, P., & Nordhaus, W. (2009). Economics (19th ed.). New York: McGraw-Hill.

[35] Sandor, J. A., & Homburg, J. A. (2017). Zuni Agricultural History and Ecology: Resilience and Sustainability. Journal of Ethnobiology, 37(2), 195–216.

[36] Guillet, D. (1987). Terracing and Irrigation in the Peruvian Highlands. Current Anthropology, 28(4), 409–430.

[37] Isenberg, A. (2000). The Destruction of the Bison: An Environmental History, 1750–1920. Cambridge: Cambridge University Press.

maximization over long-term ecological balance.[38] Communist systems, meanwhile, replaced private ownership with state-directed collectivization, but often without integrating local ecological knowledge. The Soviet Union's collectivized agriculture, for example, led to over-irrigation and widespread salinization in Central Asia, contributing to the collapse of the Aral Sea ecosystem.[39] In both cases, the separation of people from ecosystems, either through commodification or bureaucratic abstraction, produced ecological degradation, in sharp contrast to Indigenous traditions that integrated human activity within ecological cycles. Empirical evidence reinforces the effectiveness of Indigenous approaches. Comparative studies show that biodiversity levels and ecosystem services are often highest in Indigenous-managed lands. It has been found that deforestation rates in Indigenous territories in the Amazon were up to three times lower than in surrounding areas under private or state control.[40] In New Mexico, Zuni water-management projects have demonstrated measurable improvements in soil moisture and crop yields while restoring watershed function.[41] These findings challenge the orthodox assumption that sustainability can only be achieved through market instruments or state control, highlighting instead the efficacy of communal systems rooted in ecological reciprocity. In this sense, Indigenous philosophies of harmony with natural cycles offer a powerful counterpoint to both neoclassical and communist models of resource management. Where the former prioritises efficiency and the latter equality, both often neglect the ecological context in which economic activity occurs. Indigenous stewardship, by contrast, situates human societies within ecosystems, offering not only a historically successful model of sustainability but also a vital framework for contemporary responses to climate change and biodiversity loss.

[38] Coase, R. (1960). The Problem of Social Cost. Journal of Law and Economics, 3, 1–44.

[39] Micklin, P. (2007). The Aral Sea Disaster. Annual Review of Earth and Planetary Sciences, 35, 47–72.

[40] Ricketts, T., Soares-Filho, B., da Fonseca, G., Nepstad, D., Pfaff, A., Petsonk, A., Kormos, C. (2010). Indigenous Lands, Protected Areas, and Slowing Climate Change. PLoS Biology, 8(3), e1000331.

[41] Homburg, J. A., Sandor, J. A., & Lightfoot, D. R. (2005). Agricultural Sustainability in Zuni Farming Systems. Journal of Ethnobiology, 25(2), 301–321.

2.4 Territorial Rights and Governance Structures

Indigenous societies have long developed intricate systems for allocating land, regulating its use, and resolving disputes in ways that embed social and ecological balance. Unlike the neoclassical economic framework, which privileges private property and assumes that clear, individual ownership maximises efficiency through market exchange.[42] Indeed, many Indigenous communities rely on customary tenure systems rooted in collective identity and kinship. These systems frequently employ councils of elders, clan leaders, or community assemblies to adjudicate land claims, ensure equitable access, and maintain social harmony. Oral traditions, myths, and ritual obligations often serve as binding frameworks for land governance, transmitting both ecological knowledge and social norms across generations.[43] Case studies from Africa illustrate the resilience of customary land tenure systems despite pressures from colonial and post-colonial states. In Ghana, for example, land is managed through stool or skin systems, whereby chiefs hold land in trust for their communities. These arrangements provide flexible mechanisms for dispute resolution and collective oversight, though they also face challenges from urbanization and land commodification.[44] Similarly, in Kenya, group ranches among the Maasai historically provided communal grazing rights, ensuring mobility and ecological balance in arid zones. The conversion of such lands into private parcels under state-led reform policies has often undermined sustainability, leading to overgrazing and conflict.[45] These cases highlight the tension between Indigenous governance systems and market-driven land reforms inspired by neoclassical efficiency arguments. In the Pacific Islands, clan-based systems of land rights illustrate another model of Indigenous governance. In Vanuatu, approximately 98% of land remains under customary ownership, with land allocated through lineage and administered by councils of chiefs. Disputes are mediated by elders

[42] Demsetz, H. (1967). Toward a Theory of Property Rights. American Economic Review, 57(2), 347–359.

[43] Boone, C. (2014). Property and Political Order in Africa: Land Rights and the Structure of Politics. Cambridge: Cambridge University Press.

[44] Ubink, J. (2008). In the Land of the Chiefs: Customary Law, Land Conflicts, and the Role of the State in Peri-Urban Ghana. Leiden: Leiden University Press.

[45] Mwangi, E. (2007). Subdividing the Commons: Distributional Conflict in the Transition from Collective to Individual Property Rights in Kenya's Maasailand. World Development, 35(5), 815–834.

using oral traditions and genealogical knowledge to determine legitimate claims.[46] These governance structures contrast with communist experiments in collectivization, where local institutions were often suppressed in favour of centralized state ownership. In the Soviet Union, collectivization replaced clan or village-based tenure with collective farms managed through bureaucratic authority, often disregarding local ecological and cultural practices. This imposed system produced significant inefficiencies and social dislocation, as evidenced by widespread resistance, food shortages, and environmental degradation during the 1930s.[47] Empirical evidence suggests that Indigenous territorial governance can support both social stability and ecological sustainability. It has been found that in sub-Saharan Africa, customary systems continue to govern up to 90 percent of land transactions in rural areas, providing legitimacy and local accountability in contexts where state institutions remain weak.[48] In Vanuatu, research indicates that customary land tenure correlates with stronger community cohesion and more effective management of forest resources compared to state-administered lands.[49] These findings challenge both the neoclassical assumption that individual titling ensures efficiency and the communist model of state ownership, demonstrating instead that Indigenous governance systems—anchored in social obligation and oral tradition—can effectively balance rights, responsibilities, and sustainability.

[46] Regenvanu, R. (2009). The Traditional Economy as Source of Resilience in Vanuatu. In S. Feeny & S. McDonald (Eds.), Pacific Island Countries: Growth, Welfare and Governance in the Twenty-First Century (pp. 91–106). Cheltenham: Edward Elgar.

[47] Wegren, S. (1998). Agriculture and the State in Soviet and Post-Soviet Russia. Pittsburgh: University of Pittsburgh Press.

[48] World Bank. (2010). Rising Global Interest in Farmland: Can It Yield Sustainable and Equitable Benefits? Washington, DC: World Bank.

[49] Anderson, T., & Lee, G. (2010). Land and Livelihoods in Melanesia: Customary Land Tenure and Poverty Reduction. Canberra: Australian National University, Crawford School of Economics and Government, Discussion Paper 2010/6.

3 Early Clashes over Land Ownership Concepts and Resource Use with European Settlers

3.1 *Diverging Concepts of Land Ownership*

The encounters between Indigenous peoples and European settlers were marked by profound misunderstandings over land ownership, rooted in fundamentally different worldviews. For Indigenous communities across the Americas, Africa, and the Pacific, land was not a commodity but a communal resource, tied to kinship, spirituality, and collective stewardship. Rights to land were embedded in social obligations and rotational use practices, where access was negotiated through clans, elders, or councils rather than through individual deeds. By contrast, European settlers imported legal traditions derived from Roman law and the emerging capitalist economy, where land was conceived as private property subject to demarcation, fencing, and exchange in markets.[50] This divergence created a structural basis for conflict, particularly as colonial authorities imposed treaties, surveys, and enclosure regimes that Indigenous peoples had interpreted through their own frameworks of reciprocity and shared custodianship. The Doctrine of Discovery exemplifies this clash. Developed in fifteenth-century papal bulls and later incorporated into European colonial law, it asserted that Christian nations could claim sovereignty over non-Christian lands. Indigenous occupancy was recognized only as "usufructuary", a right of use rather than of ownership.[51] The Treaty of Waitangi (1840) in New Zealand illustrates the consequences of these misunderstandings: Māori chiefs believed they were guaranteeing shared governance and protection of their lands, while the British Crown interpreted the treaty as cession of sovereignty and property rights. Such conflicting interpretations reflected the deep gulf between collective custodianship and private ownership models. From a theoretical standpoint, neoclassical economics posits that well-defined, individual property rights are essential to avoid overuse and achieve efficient allocation.[52] This logic underpinned European justifications for enclosure

[50] Banner, S. (2005). How the Indians Lost Their Land: Law and Power on the Frontier. Cambridge, MA: Harvard University Press.

[51] Miller, R. J. (2006/2010). Native America, Discovered and Conquered: Thomas Jefferson, Lewis & Clark, and Manifest Destiny. Lincoln: University of Nebraska Press.

[52] Demsetz, H. (1967). Toward a Theory of Property Rights. American Economic Review, 57(2), 347–359.

in both colonial and domestic contexts, such as the English Enclosure Acts that transformed communal commons into private plots. Yet Indigenous case studies suggest that communal systems could regulate access effectively through customary governance. For example, Native American tribes often managed hunting grounds collectively, imposing taboos and seasonal restrictions that sustained wildlife populations for centuries.[53] These practices contradict the "tragedy of the commons" argument by demonstrating how collective tenure, when embedded in cultural institutions, can prevent overexploitation.[54] Communist approaches to land tenure introduced another contrast. Like Indigenous systems, communism rejected private ownership, but it did so by centralizing control in the state rather than in local communities. The collectivization campaigns in the Soviet Union and China sought to abolish private property and communal traditions alike, replacing them with bureaucratic allocation systems.[55] Unlike Indigenous models, which were grounded in ecological reciprocity and decentralized governance, communist collectivization often ignored local knowledge and ecological constraints, leading to inefficiencies and ecological collapse, exemplified by the Dust Bowl-like effects of Soviet Virgin Lands schemes. Thus, while both Indigenous and communist systems opposed private ownership, their outcomes diverged sharply: one rooted in sustainability, the other in extractive centralism. Empirical research reinforces the sustainability of Indigenous governance relative to colonial and statist models. Studies of Indigenous land in Latin America reveal that territories under communal control show significantly lower rates of deforestation than adjacent lands.[56] In contrast, colonial enclosures in Africa frequently led to displacement, soil degradation, and social unrest, undermining both productivity and resilience.[57] These findings underscore that the imposition of European property

[53] Carlson, L. (1981). Indians, Bureaucrats, and Land: The Dawes Act and the Decline of Indian Farming. Westport, CT: Greenwood Press.

[54] Hardin, G. (1968). The Tragedy of the Commons. Science, 162(3859), 1243–1248.

[55] Wegren, S. (1998). Agriculture and the State in Soviet and Post-Soviet Russia. Pittsburgh: University of Pittsburgh Press.

[56] Ricketts, T., Soares-Filho, B., da Fonseca, G., Nepstad, D., Pfaff, A., Petsonk, A., Kormos, C. (2010). Indigenous Lands, Protected Areas, and Slowing Climate Change. PLoS Biology, 8(3), e1000331.

[57] Boone, C. (2014). Property and Political Order in Africa: Land Rights and the Structure of Politics. Cambridge: Cambridge University Press.

regimes was not simply a neutral economic reform but a fundamental restructuring of Indigenous political economies, with lasting ecological and social consequences.

3.2 *European Exploitation of Natural Resources*

The arrival of European settlers in Indigenous territories often marked the beginning of large-scale overextraction of natural resources, disrupting longstanding ecological balances maintained through Indigenous stewardship. Where Indigenous systems typically emphasized sustainable use through rotational hunting, communal management, and cultural restrictions, European settlers introduced extractive practices designed to maximise short-term output and profitability. This was consistent with the neoclassical economic logic of resource exploitation, which views natural resources as inputs to be extracted and commodified to meet demand.[58] The consequences of this shift were dramatic: ecosystems were destabilized, Indigenous subsistence economies were undermined, and many species faced rapid decline. One of the most striking examples is the overhunting of the North American buffalo (bison). For centuries, Plains tribes managed bison populations through seasonal hunting and spiritual practices that maintained herd sustainability. By the mid-nineteenth century, however, commercial hunting driven by European demand for hides, meat, and industrial uses accelerated to catastrophic levels. Between 1870 and 1883, an estimated 30–40 million bison were reduced to fewer than 1000 individuals.[59] This not only devastated the species but also dismantled Indigenous cultures reliant on the bison for food, clothing, shelter, and spiritual life. The collapse of the bison economy reflects the clash between communal stewardship and market-driven exploitation, as neoclassical incentives to harvest for profit ignored long-term ecological costs. Similar patterns of ecological disruption unfolded in the Amazon. European colonists and, later, multinational corporations initiated large-scale deforestation for timber, cattle ranching, and mining, often displacing Indigenous communities and undermining their resource cycles. In contrast to Indigenous agroforestry systems, which preserved

[58] Ricardo, D. (1996). Principles of Political Economy and Taxation. Amherst, NY: Prometheus Books. (Original work published 1817).

[59] Isenberg, A. (2000). The Destruction of the Bison: An Environmental History, 1750–1920. Cambridge: Cambridge University Press.

biodiversity through polycultures and shifting cultivation, colonial and capitalist models sought monocultures and extractive economies. Data from Brazil show that by 2005, nearly 20 percent of the Amazon rainforest had been cleared, with rates of deforestation two to three times lower in Indigenous territories compared with non-Indigenous lands.[60] These findings underscore the resilience of Indigenous management against the backdrop of extractive colonial economies. A comparison with communist approaches to resource use further highlights the distinctiveness of Indigenous systems. Communist regimes, like their capitalist counterparts, frequently adopted extractive models, but under state control. In the Soviet Union, large-scale timber extraction, collectivized agriculture, and mineral exploitation followed centralized production targets rather than ecological limits. For example, Siberian forests were harvested at unsustainable rates to fuel industrialization, with little regard for regeneration or Indigenous rights.[61] While communism rejected private ownership, it replaced it with bureaucratic exploitation, often disregarding both local ecological knowledge and the interdependence of human and natural systems. Empirical evidence consistently shows that Indigenous governance structures offer greater ecological sustainability. A global study found that deforestation rates in Indigenous-managed areas of the Amazon were significantly lower than in surrounding lands, with implications for biodiversity and carbon storage.[62] These contrasts demonstrate that European settler models of extraction, whether through capitalist or communist systems, were premised on short-term maximization of output, while Indigenous systems sustained resources for future generations through ecological reciprocity. The divergence underscores the political economy of dispossession, where Indigenous philosophies of stewardship were marginalized in favour of exploitative regimes that prioritized profit or production quotas over ecological balance.

[60] Nepstad, D., Schwartzman, S., Bamberger, B., Santilli, M., Ray, D., Schlesinger, P., Rolla, A. (2006). Inhibition of Amazon Deforestation and Fire by Parks and Indigenous Lands. Conservation Biology, 20(1), 65–73.

[61] Wegren, S. (1998). Agriculture and the State in Soviet and Post-Soviet Russia. Pittsburgh: University of Pittsburgh Press.

[62] Ricketts, T., Soares-Filho, B., da Fonseca, G., Nepstad, D., Pfaff, A., Petsonk, A., Kormos, C. (2010). Indigenous Lands, Protected Areas, and Slowing Climate Change. PLoS Biology, 8(3), e1000331.

3.3 Introduction of Market Economies and Commodification of Land

The imposition of European market economies profoundly altered Indigenous relationships to land and resources. Where Indigenous societies generally regarded land as a communal trust tied to kinship, spirituality, and ecological balance, European settlers introduced a cash-based economy in which land became a commodity to be bought, sold, or leased. This transformation was central to the colonial project, aligning with neoclassical economic principles that treat land as a factor of production whose efficient use is ensured through private ownership and market exchange.[63] The commodification of Indigenous territories was justified by legal doctrines such as terra nullius and the Doctrine of Discovery, which framed Indigenous lands as "empty" or insufficiently utilized unless enclosed and monetized. The expansion of resource-extractive industries accelerated this commodification process. Mining, oil drilling, and plantation agriculture displaced Indigenous communities and disrupted traditional livelihoods. In North America, the General Allotment (Dawes) Act of 1887 fragmented communally held Native American lands into individually owned plots, with "surplus" lands sold to non-Natives. Within fifty years, Native landholdings declined from 138 million acres to 48 million acres.[64] Simultaneously, fishing rights and access to water sources were eroded. The construction of dams along the Columbia and Colorado rivers decimated salmon populations, undermining the subsistence and cultural practices of tribes such as the Yakama and the Nez Perce.[65] These policies imposed a market economy on Indigenous peoples while depriving them of their ecological base, forcing participation in wage labour systems on terms determined by settlers. The logic underpinning these transformations resonates with neoclassical models, where efficiency is achieved through the reallocation of land from "underutilized" Indigenous use to supposedly higher-value

[63] Demsetz, H. (1967). Toward a Theory of Property Rights. American Economic Review, 57(2), 347–359.

[64] Carlson, L. (1981). Indians, Bureaucrats, and Land: The Dawes Act and the Decline of Indian Farming. Westport, CT: Greenwood Press.

[65] Hunn, E. (1990). Nch'i-Wána, "The Big River": Mid-Columbia Indians and Their Land. Seattle: University of Washington Press.

commercial use. Yet, case studies consistently show that Indigenous stewardship produced sustainable outcomes, while colonial commodification led to ecological degradation and social dislocation. For example, in the Amazon, Indigenous territories have maintained lower deforestation rates compared to areas opened to cattle ranching and logging for global markets.[66] By contrast, communist regimes also sought to eliminate communal tenure but replaced markets with state control. In the Soviet Union, collectivization abolished private property but still commodified land indirectly, treating it as an input for centralized industrial targets rather than a sacred trust. This bureaucratic form of commodification often ignored ecological cycles, resulting in soil erosion, over-irrigation, and the ecological catastrophe of the Aral Sea.[67] Empirical research demonstrates that Indigenous governance systems remain more sustainable than either capitalist or communist commodification. It has also been found that biodiversity and carbon storage in Indigenous-managed lands significantly exceed those in adjacent lands subject to market extraction or state exploitation.[68] These outcomes reveal the structural incompatibility between Indigenous communal frameworks and economic systems that commodify land, whether through the invisible hand of the market or the visible hand of the state.

3.4 Legal Frameworks Favouring Settlers

The imposition of European legal frameworks played a decisive role in dispossessing Indigenous peoples of their lands. Colonial authorities introduced doctrines such as terra nullius, the legal fiction that land not cultivated according to European standards was "empty" and available for appropriation, which erased Indigenous land tenure systems rooted in communal ownership, kinship, and stewardship. This doctrine underpinned British colonization in Australia, where Aboriginal sovereignty

[66] Nepstad, D., Schwartzman, S., Bamberger, B., Santilli, M., Ray, D., Schlesinger, P., Rolla, A. (2006). Inhibition of Amazon Deforestation and Fire by Parks and Indigenous Lands. Conservation Biology, 20(1), 65–73.

[67] Micklin, P. (2007). The Aral Sea Disaster. Annual Review of Earth and Planetary Sciences, 35, 47–72.

[68] Ricketts, T., Soares-Filho, B., da Fonseca, G., Nepstad, D., Pfaff, A., Petsonk, A., Kormos, C. (2010). Indigenous Lands, Protected Areas, and Slowing Climate Change. PLoS Biology, 8(3), e1000331.

was denied until the landmark Mabo v. Queensland (No. 2) (1992) decision overturned terra nullius and recognized native title.[69] Similarly, in North America, treaties were often imposed under coercive conditions and repeatedly violated. For example, the Treaty of Fort Laramie (1851) guaranteed Lakota control over the Black Hills, but following the discovery of gold in the 1870s, the U.S. government seized the territory, disregarding both treaty obligations and Indigenous rights.[70] These legal constructs reflected European economic rationalities aligned with neoclassical theories of property. In this framework, land is assumed to yield greater productivity and efficiency under private ownership, and thus colonial authorities justified dispossession as a reallocation of resources from "inefficient" communal use to "productive" capitalist enterprise.[71] Yet Indigenous systems demonstrated sustainable use, as seen in practices of rotational agriculture and regulated hunting. The displacement of these systems undermined ecological balance and led to resource depletion, contradicting the neoclassical claim of efficiency gains. Communist states also reconfigured Indigenous and peasant land rights but through centralized collectivization rather than private appropriation. In the Soviet Union, collectivization campaigns expropriated village lands, abolishing customary tenure and subordinating communities to state-controlled collective farms.[72] While communism rejected private ownership, it similarly denied Indigenous self-determination, replacing communal governance with bureaucratic authority. In both capitalist and communist contexts, Indigenous voices were excluded from legal decision-making, and land was commodified, whether for private markets or state production targets. Empirical evidence illustrates the long-term consequences of these legal frameworks. By 1934, following the U.S. General Allotment (Dawes) Act, Native American landholdings had declined by two-thirds,

[69] Banner, S. (2005). How the Indians Lost Their Land: Law and Power on the Frontier. Cambridge, MA: Harvard University Press.

[70] Wilkins, D. E., & Lomawaima, K. T. (2001). Uneven Ground: American Indian Sovereignty and Federal Law. Norman: University of Oklahoma Press.

[71] Demsetz, H. (1967). Toward a Theory of Property Rights. American Economic Review, 57(2), 347–359.

[72] Wegren, S. (1998). Agriculture and the State in Soviet and Post-Soviet Russia. Pittsburgh: University of Pittsburgh Press.

from 138 million acres to 48 million acres.[73] In Australia, Aboriginal peoples were excluded from land ownership until the 1976 Aboriginal Land Rights Act in the Northern Territory, which restored only limited areas of traditional land. These patterns reveal how legal systems designed for settler societies systematically alienated Indigenous peoples, legitimizing dispossession under the guise of law. In contrast, recognition of Indigenous governance, where it has been legally upheld, has been shown to strengthen ecological outcomes, with Indigenous-managed territories experiencing lower rates of deforestation and higher biodiversity than surrounding lands.[74] Thus, while legal frameworks in both capitalist and communist systems served as instruments of dispossession, Indigenous systems, based on collective stewardship and customary law, offered alternative models of governance. The political economy of Indigenous land rights highlights the enduring clash between imposed legal doctrines of property and Indigenous philosophies of reciprocity, revealing that dispossession was not a failure of law but rather its deliberate function in consolidating settler power.

3.5 *Environmental and Cultural Consequences of Settler Expansion*

Settler expansion into Indigenous territories was not only a process of political and legal dispossession but also one of ecological degradation with profound cultural consequences. European agricultural and industrial practices, grounded in extractive logics of monoculture farming, mining, and commercial forestry, disrupted ecosystems that Indigenous peoples had managed sustainably for centuries. Whereas Indigenous systems emphasized polycultures, rotational cycles, and ecological reciprocity, settler economies were oriented towards maximizing short-term yields for market exchange, consistent with neoclassical economic assumptions of efficiency through specialization.[75] The ecological result was

[73] Carlson, L. (1981). Indians, Bureaucrats, and Land: The Dawes Act and the Decline of Indian Farming. Westport, CT: Greenwood Press.

[74] Ricketts, T., Soares-Filho, B., da Fonseca, G., Nepstad, D., Pfaff, A., Petsonk, A., Kormos, C. (2010). Indigenous Lands, Protected Areas, and Slowing Climate Change. PLoS Biology, 8(3), e1000331.

[75] Ricardo, D. (1951). On the Principles of Political Economy and Taxation. Edited by Piero Sraffa with Maurice Dobb. Cambridge: Cambridge University Press. (Works and Correspondence of David Ricardo, Vol. 1).

declining soil fertility, erosion, and loss of biodiversity that had sustained Indigenous food systems, medicines, and spiritual practices. In Africa, colonial governments promoted cash crops such as cotton, cocoa, and groundnuts, often through coercive systems of taxation and forced labour. This shift undermined Indigenous subsistence farming and accelerated soil degradation. In colonial Kenya, for example, the emphasis on export-oriented coffee and maize displaced Indigenous mixed farming systems and contributed to severe soil erosion in the central highlands.[76] Similarly, in West Africa, cocoa monocultures led to widespread deforestation, with Ghana losing approximately 80% of its forest cover during the twentieth century.[77] These ecological transformations not only diminished biodiversity but also disrupted Indigenous cultural practices linked to land, forest spirits, and subsistence crops. In North America, the extermination of bison herds in the late nineteenth century not only eliminated a keystone species from the plains ecosystem but also dismantled the cultural, dietary, and spiritual practices of Plains tribes who relied on the animal for food, clothing, shelter, and ceremonial life.[78] In the Pacific Northwest, hydroelectric dams and river pollution decimated salmon runs that were central to Yakama and Nez Perce economies and ceremonies; the decline directly undermined the First Salmon rituals that reaffirmed reciprocal relationships between people and fish.[79] In West Africa, colonial conversion of forests to cocoa monocultures destroyed medicinal plant diversity and sacred groves, severing communities' connections to forest spirits and weakening Indigenous healing and ritual practices.[80,81] Similarly, in the

[76] Anderson, D. (2002). Eroding the Commons: The Politics of Ecology in Baringo, Kenya, 1890s–1963. Oxford: James Currey.

[77] Benhin, J., & Barbier, E. (2004). Structural Adjustment Programme, Deforestation and Biodiversity Loss in Ghana. Environmental and Resource Economics, 27(3), 337–366.

[78] Isenberg, A. (2000). The Destruction of the Bison: An Environmental History, 1750–1920. Cambridge: Cambridge
University Press.

[79] Hunn, E., & Selam, J. (1990). Nch'i-Wána: "The Big River": Mid-Columbia Indians and Their Land. Seattle: University of Washington Press.

[80] Benhin, J., & Barbier, E. (2004). Structural Adjustment Programme, Deforestation and Biodiversity Loss in Ghana. Environmental and Resource Economics, 27(3), 337–366.

[81] Sheridan, M., & Nyamweru, C. (2008). African Sacred Groves: Ecological Dynamics and Social Change. Oxford: James Currey.

Andes, the erosion of potato biodiversity under Spanish and later industrial agricultural systems disrupted Indigenous rituals tied to planting and harvest cycles of specific landraces.[82] These examples illustrate that biodiversity loss was not simply an ecological phenomenon but also a profound cultural rupture, as the disappearance of species and landscapes undermined the very practices, ceremonies, and identities that bound Indigenous communities to their environments. Furthermore, in North America, settler expansion brought intensive mining, dam building, and industrial agriculture, which polluted rivers and destroyed fisheries that were central to Indigenous economies and identities. Mercury contamination from 19th- and twentieth-century gold mining devastated fish populations in rivers across California, undermining Native Californian food systems.[83] Similarly, as mentioned previously, the construction of hydroelectric dams on the Columbia River in the Pacific Northwest eliminated salmon runs critical to the Yakama, Nez Perce, and other tribes, severing cultural and spiritual connections to the salmon as a "first food".[84] These examples highlight how settler economies disrupted not only ecosystems but also Indigenous cultural worlds grounded in reciprocal relationships with non-human beings. Communist states also oversaw ecological degradation through centralized extraction and monocultures, though in different institutional forms. In the Soviet Union, collectivized agriculture promoted extensive monocultures of wheat and cotton, which depleted soils and caused widespread environmental crises. The diversion of rivers for cotton irrigation in Central Asia resulted in the near-collapse of the Aral Sea, with catastrophic losses in fish species, biodiversity, and local livelihoods.[85] Although communism rejected private property, its productivity orientation treated land and water as inputs for state plans rather than as entities bound by ecological cycles and cultural

[82] Zimmerer, K. (1996). Changing Fortunes: Biodiversity and Peasant Livelihood in the Peruvian Andes. Berkeley: University of California Press.

[83] Alpers, C. N., Hunerlach, M. P., May, J. T., & Hothem, R. L. (2005). Mercury Contamination from Historic Gold Mining in California. Fact Sheet 2005–3014. U.S. Geological Survey.

[84] Hunn, E., & Selam, J. (1990). Nch'i-Wána: "The Big River": Mid-Columbia Indians and Their Land. Seattle: University of Washington Press.

[85] Micklin, P. (2007). The Aral Sea Disaster. Annual Review of Earth and Planetary Sciences, 35, 47–72.

significance, paralleling settler economies in their disregard for sustainability. In this case, empirical evidence suggests that Indigenous-managed lands continue to outperform both capitalist and communist systems in terms of biodiversity and ecological health. Global studies show that biodiversity levels in Indigenous territories are equal to or higher than in state-protected areas, and deforestation rates are significantly lower where Indigenous governance is legally recognized.[86] These findings challenge the neoclassical emphasis on efficiency through commodification and the communist reliance on centralized planning, revealing instead that ecological resilience is embedded in Indigenous practices of stewardship. The environmental and cultural consequences of settler expansion thus underscore the systemic incompatibility between Indigenous philosophies of reciprocity and extractive economic models imposed by both capitalist and communist regimes.

4 Case Studies on Dispossession and Resistance

4.1 North America: The Trail of Tears and Land Grabs

The dispossession of Indigenous nations in North America reached its most infamous expression in the forced removals sanctioned by the Indian Removal Act of 1830. Framed as a policy to "exchange" Indigenous lands east of the Mississippi for territories in the west, the Act in practice legitimized settler expansion and the mass displacement of Native peoples. The Cherokee, Muscogee (Creek), Chickasaw, Choctaw, and Seminole, known as the "Five Civilized Tribes", were compelled to leave their homelands despite existing treaties guaranteeing their rights. The Cherokee case exemplifies the contradiction between Indigenous sovereignty and settler law. In Worcester v. Georgia (1832), the U.S. Supreme Court recognized the Cherokee Nation as a distinct political community whose authority could not be unilaterally overridden by state governments.[87] Yet President Andrew Jackson and Congress ignored the ruling, and the subsequent forced march, the Trail of

[86] Ricketts, T., Soares-Filho, B., da Fonseca, G., Nepstad, D., Pfaff, A., Petsonk, A., Kormos, C. (2010). Indigenous Lands, Protected Areas, and Slowing Climate Change. PLoS Biology, 8(3), e1000331.

[87] Wilkins, D. E., & Lomawaima, K. T. (2001). Uneven Ground: American Indian Sovereignty and Federal Law. Norman: University of Oklahoma Press.

Tears, resulted in the deaths of approximately 4000 Cherokee out of 16,000 removed.[88] The dispossession was not merely political but also economic. Neoclassical economic rationales were used to justify land seizure, arguing that Indigenous lands were "underutilised" and that settlers, through private ownership, would allocate land more efficiently for farming and commerce.[89] In reality, Indigenous agricultural systems, including Cherokee mixed farming, were productive and sustainable, but they conflicted with settler visions of market-oriented monocultures. The logic of efficiency ignored the cultural embeddedness of Indigenous land, which encompassed kinship ties, burial grounds, and spiritual geographies that could not be commodified. The Trail of Tears thus demonstrates how neoclassical assumptions about property rights underpinned legal frameworks that facilitated large-scale expropriation. Communist systems also displaced Indigenous land tenure, albeit through centralization rather than privatization. In the Soviet Union, collectivization campaigns uprooted peasant and Indigenous communities, imposing collective farms managed according to state quotas.[90] Like the Indian Removal Act, these campaigns disregarded local institutions, severed people from ancestral lands, and caused widespread human suffering. Yet where the U.S. dispossessions were justified through markets and "efficiency", communist collectivization invoked equality and production targets, with equally destructive ecological and cultural consequences. Both illustrate how Indigenous land systems, rooted in collective governance and ecological reciprocity, were systematically undermined by external ideologies. Despite immense trauma, Indigenous nations resisted through legal, cultural, and political strategies. The Cherokee pursued legal remedies, as seen in Worcester v. Georgia, while others engaged in armed resistance, such as the Seminole Wars in Florida. Cultural survival strategies also emerged: displaced tribes preserved languages, oral traditions, and ceremonial practices in Indian Territory (modern-day Oklahoma). Today, Cherokee governance, education systems, and cultural revival initiatives

[88] Perdue, T., & Green, M. D. (2007). The Cherokee Nation and the Trail of Tears. New York: Penguin.

[89] Banner, S. (2005). How the Indians Lost Their Land: Law and Power on the Frontier. Cambridge, MA: Harvard University Press.

[90] Wegren, S. (1998). Agriculture and the State in Soviet and Post-Soviet Russia. Pittsburgh: University of Pittsburgh Press.

reflect long-term resilience despite historical dispossession.[91] These examples show that Indigenous resistance was not only immediate but also intergenerational, challenging both capitalist and communist models of land alienation by maintaining distinctive political economies of survival.

4.2 Australia: Land Rights and Dispossession of Aboriginal Peoples

The colonization of Australia was legally justified under the doctrine of terra nullius, the claim that the land belonged to no one because Aboriginal peoples did not practice agriculture in ways recognisable to European law. This fiction erased Indigenous tenure systems, which were highly sophisticated and grounded in spiritual, ecological, and kinship relations to Country. For more than two centuries, terra nullius legitimized widespread dispossession, the expansion of pastoral leases, and the denial of Aboriginal sovereignty. The consequences were not merely legal but cultural: sacred sites were destroyed, languages suppressed, and ceremonial practices tied to land curtailed.[92] Contemporary struggles for recognition culminated in the Mabo v. Queensland (No. 2) (1992) decision, in which the High Court overturned terra nullius and recognized native title for the Meriam people of the Torres Strait, led by Eddie Mabo. The subsequent Native Title Act of 1993 established mechanisms for Indigenous communities to reclaim land rights, though the burden of proof and complex legal requirements have often constrained its effectiveness.[93] Despite these limitations, the Mabo case marked a watershed in Indigenous–settler relations, challenging centuries of legal denial and creating avenues for cultural and economic renewal. The economic rationales behind Aboriginal dispossession echoed neoclassical assumptions that land was "wasted" if not enclosed and exploited for commercial use. European settlers applied an efficiency logic, prioritizing sheep grazing and agricultural expansion over Aboriginal land practices such as mosaic burning,

[91] Conley, R. J. (2005). The Cherokee Nation: A History. Albuquerque: University of New Mexico Press.

[92] Reynolds, H. (1996). Aboriginal Sovereignty: Reflections on Race, State and Nation. St. Leonards: Allen & Unwin.

[93] McRae, H., Nettheim, G., & Beacroft, L. (2009). Indigenous Legal Issues: Commentary and Materials (4th ed.). Sydney: Thomson Reuters.

rotational harvesting, and custodial management of biodiversity.[94] These practices, dismissed as primitive by colonisers, are now recognized as advanced ecological management systems that maintained fertile soils and reduced wildfire risks. In contrast, communist approaches also displaced Indigenous rights, though through collectivization rather than privatization. In the Soviet Union and Maoist China, collectivized agriculture erased customary tenures in favour of state-directed farms, subordinating local knowledge to centralized planning.[95] Both systems, capitalist and communist, marginalized Indigenous stewardship in the name of efficiency or equality, with ecological and cultural costs. Aboriginal resistance has taken many forms, from direct political advocacy to cultural expression. The Aboriginal Tent Embassy, established in 1972 on the lawns of Parliament House in Canberra, symbolized demands for land rights and sovereignty, while ongoing campaigns have used legal avenues to secure native title claims. Cultural resistance has also been expressed through art and ceremony. The Papunya Tula art movement of the 1970s translated sacred Dreaming stories into visual forms that gained global recognition, asserting cultural continuity while generating economic resources for Aboriginal communities.[96] Land management practices, such as the revival of fire-stick farming by Aboriginal ranger groups, represent both cultural renewal and ecological innovation, reducing wildfire risk while reaffirming custodial ties to Country.[97] These forms of resistance illustrate how Aboriginal peoples have adapted traditional practices to contemporary struggles, ensuring the survival of both culture and ecology despite centuries of dispossession.

[94] Gammage, B. (2011). The Biggest Estate on Earth: How Aborigines Made Australia. Sydney: Allen & Unwin.

[95] Wegren, S. (1998). Agriculture and the State in Soviet and Post-Soviet Russia. Pittsburgh: University of Pittsburgh Press.

[96] Myers, F. (2002). Painting Culture: The Making of an Aboriginal High Art. Durham: Duke University Press.

[97] Altman, J. (2012). People on Country as Alternative Development. In J. Altman & S. Kerins (Eds.), People on Country: Vital Landscapes, Indigenous Futures (pp. 1–25). Sydney: Federation Press.

4.3 *Latin America: Resource Exploitation and Indigenous Survival*

In Latin America, Indigenous peoples have faced centuries of dispossession through resource exploitation, with contemporary struggles often centred in the Amazon basin. Deforestation, oil extraction, and mining projects, framed by governments and corporations as engines of national development, have systematically undermined Indigenous livelihoods. In the Ecuadorian Amazon, the expansion of oil drilling since the 1970s has polluted rivers and soils, leading to high rates of cancer and declining fish stocks among Kichwa and Cofán communities.[98] Similarly, illegal gold mining in Peru and Brazil has destroyed thousands of hectares of rainforest, releasing mercury into waterways and threatening food systems central to Indigenous survival.[99] These ecological losses are not simply material but cultural, disrupting rituals, oral traditions, and spiritual practices that link Indigenous peoples to forests and rivers. Resistance to these incursions has taken both local and international forms. The Sarayaku Kichwa of Ecuador represent a prominent case. In the early 2000s, the Sarayaku successfully resisted oil exploration in their territory by combining traditional practices of spiritual defence with modern advocacy, bringing their case before the Inter-American Court of Human Rights. In its landmark 2012 judgment, the Court ruled that Ecuador had violated the community's right to prior consultation, affirming Indigenous sovereignty over resource decisions.[100] Similar movements across the Amazon, such as the coordination of Indigenous organizations in Brazil (COIAB), demonstrate how grassroots mobilizations challenge state and corporate narratives of development, asserting alternative models grounded in ecological reciprocity. From the perspective of neoclassical economics, natural resources are treated as factors of production, and efficiency is defined by extraction and integration into markets. Governments and corporations justify deforestation and mining

[98] Sawyer, S. (2004). Crude Chronicles: Indigenous Politics, Multinational Oil, and Neoliberalism in Ecuador. Durham: Duke University Press.

[99] Asner, G. P., Llactayo, W., Tupayachi, R., & Luna, E. R. (2013). Elevated Rates of Gold Mining in the Amazon Revealed through High-Resolution Monitoring. Proceedings of the National Academy of Sciences, 110(46), 18,454–18,459.

[100] Rodríguez-Garavito, C. (2011). Ethnicity.gov: Global Governance, Indigenous Peoples, and the Right to Prior Consultation in Social Minefields. Indiana Journal of Global Legal Studies, 18(1), 263–305.

as rational economic choices that maximize GDP, even as these activities externalize environmental and cultural costs. Indigenous stewardship, however, reveals an alternative logic in which biodiversity preservation sustains long-term social and ecological well-being. Comparative research shows that deforestation rates are significantly lower in Indigenous territories than in adjacent lands designated for commercial use.[101] Communist models have offered little relief: in countries such as Cuba and Nicaragua, state-led agricultural and forestry projects often disregarded Indigenous autonomy, treating resources as inputs for socialist development plans. While communist regimes replaced private corporations with state agencies, they shared with capitalist models a disregard for Indigenous governance and ecological interdependence. Yet Indigenous survival strategies have carved out spaces of autonomy and renewal. In Bolivia, land reforms under the 1996 INRA Law and the recognition of Tierras Comunitarias de Origen (TCOs) enabled Indigenous groups to reclaim millions of hectares, formalizing communal tenure over forests and grasslands.[102] In Brazil, the demarcation of Indigenous territories has preserved large tracts of the Amazon, providing measurable reductions in deforestation and carbon emissions.[103] These examples highlight not only resistance but also proactive governance, showing how Indigenous peoples assert political economies of survival that resist both neoliberal and statist models of exploitation.

4.4 *Africa: Customary Land Systems and Colonial Encroachment*

Across Africa, Indigenous and customary land systems were profoundly disrupted by European colonial expansion. Prior to colonization, communal tenure predominated, with land allocated by lineage, clan leaders, or councils of elders and governed through norms that ensured equitable access and ecological sustainability. Land was not viewed as

[101] Nepstad, D., Schwartzman, S., Bamberger, B., Santilli, M., Ray, D., Schlesinger, P., Rolla, A. (2006). Inhibition of Amazon Deforestation and Fire by Parks and Indigenous Lands. Conservation Biology, 20(1), 65–73.

[102] Assies, W. (2006). Land Tenure Legislation in a Pluri-cultural and Multi-ethnic Society: The Case of Bolivia. Journal of Peasant Studies, 33(4), 569–611.

[103] Ricketts, T., Soares-Filho, B., da Fonseca, G., Nepstad, D., Pfaff, A., Petsonk, A., Kormos, C. (2010). Indigenous Lands, Protected Areas, and Slowing Climate Change. PLoS Biology, 8(3), e1000331.

a commodity but as a collective trust linked to kinship, spirituality, and subsistence. Colonial administrations dismantled these frameworks, replacing them with European property regimes that introduced titling, enclosure, and alienation of land to settlers and colonial enterprises. In settler colonies such as Kenya, the establishment of the "White Highlands" in the early twentieth century displaced Kikuyu and Maasai communities from fertile lands, forcing them into reserves and labour migration.[104] These policies redefined land as private property, undermining Indigenous governance and ecological reciprocity. Resistance to colonial encroachment was widespread. The Mau Mau uprising in 1950s Kenya emerged as a direct response to land alienation and the confinement of Indigenous peoples in overcrowded reserves. Although often portrayed by colonial authorities as a law-and-order issue, the movement was fundamentally about land justice, demanding the restoration of Indigenous tenure systems and sovereignty.[105] Similar struggles were evident across the continent, from the Herero resistance against German land seizures in Namibia to anti-apartheid struggles over land dispossession in South Africa. These movements reveal how land was central not only to economic survival but also to cultural identity and political autonomy. From the perspective of neoclassical economics, colonial authorities justified dispossession on the grounds that communal land systems were "inefficient" and that private ownership would increase productivity. This argument mirrored the theory that property rights evolve to internalise externalities.[106] Yet empirical studies show that customary systems often allocate land flexibly and sustainably, adjusting to ecological variability in ways that private tenure could not.[107] In contrast, communist land reforms in post-colonial Africa also disrupted Indigenous systems, though by nationalizing or collectivizing land. In Ethiopia after 1975, the Derg regime abolished customary tenure, reallocating land through peasant associations that were subject to centralized control.

[104] Anderson, D. (2005). Histories of the Hanged: Britain's Dirty War in Kenya and the End of Empire. New York: W. W. Norton.

[105] Kanogo, T. (1987). Squatters and the Roots of Mau Mau, 1905–1963. London: James Currey.

[106] Demsetz, H. (1967). Toward a Theory of Property Rights. American Economic Review, 57(2), 347–359.

[107] Berry, S. (1993). No Condition is Permanent: The Social Dynamics of Agrarian Change in Sub-Saharan Africa. Madison: University of Wisconsin Press.

This system, like colonial private tenure, undermined local institutions, eroded accountability, and produced inefficiencies.[108] Thus, both capitalist and communist interventions subordinated Indigenous land systems to external ideologies of "efficiency" or "equality", with damaging social and ecological consequences. Post-colonial African states have struggled to reconcile customary rights with modern land administration. In Ghana, customary authorities still administer approximately 80 percent of land, yet pressures of urbanization and commercial agriculture have generated conflicts between chiefs, communities, and state authorities.[109] In South Africa, the persistence of racial land inequalities from apartheid continues to fuel debates about redistribution and restitution. Empirical evidence underscores the importance of customary land recognition. For example, a study found that tenure security in customary systems significantly enhances household investment and resilience.[110] These examples highlight the resilience of Indigenous systems and the enduring challenges of restoring land rights after decades of colonial and post-colonial disruption.

4.5 *The Arctic: Indigenous Rights in a Changing Climate*

In the Arctic, Indigenous peoples such as the Inuit in North America and Greenland, and the Sámi across northern Scandinavia and Russia, face complex challenges as their lands are subjected simultaneously to resource extraction and climate change. Since the mid-twentieth century, governments and corporations have targeted Arctic territories for oil, gas, and mineral development, often justifying extraction through discourses of national security and economic efficiency. In Alaska and northern Canada, large-scale oil projects such as the Prudhoe Bay oil field have generated state revenues but disrupted caribou migration routes, fish habitats,

[108] Rahmato, D. (1984). Agrarian Reform in Ethiopia. Uppsala: Scandinavian Institute of African Studies.

[109] Ubink, J. (2008). In the Land of the Chiefs: Customary Law, Land Conflicts, and the Role of the State in Peri-Urban Ghana. Leiden: Leiden University Press.

[110] World Bank. (2010). Rising Global Interest in Farmland: Can It Yield Sustainable and Equitable Benefits? Washington, DC: World Bank.

and the subsistence economies of Inuit and Gwich'in communities.[111] In Sámi territories, open-pit mining and hydroelectric dams imposed during the twentieth century have fragmented reindeer pastures, threatening the cultural and economic foundation of Sámi herding practices.[112] These developments exemplify the imposition of neoclassical economic logic, which treats land and resources as commodities to be maximized for national and global markets, disregarding Indigenous governance systems based on ecological reciprocity. Climate change compounds these pressures by accelerating land loss and cultural erosion. Arctic warming is occurring at nearly four times the global average, with profound consequences for sea ice, permafrost, and ecosystems.[113] Inuit hunting practices, which rely on stable ice routes for access to seals, whales, and polar bears, are increasingly precarious, undermining food security and intergenerational knowledge transmission.[114] Similarly, thawing permafrost threatens Sámi winter pastures, as ground ice melt leads to rain-on-snow events that encase vegetation in ice, preventing reindeer from feeding. These ecological disruptions erode not only material subsistence, but also ceremonial and spiritual traditions tied to land and seasonal cycles. For the Inuit in Canada and Greenland, the loss of stable sea ice due to climate change undermines subsistence hunting of seals and whales, threatening both food security and rituals of respect for animals that are integral to Inuit cultural identity. Between 1979 and 2018, Arctic sea ice declined by approximately 40% in late summer, making traditional ice routes for hunting increasingly dangerous.[115] Among the Sámi of northern Scandinavia, warming winters have increased rain-on-snow events that encase pastures in ice, reducing grazing access and causing reindeer starvation.

[111] Nuttall, M. (2000). Indigenous Peoples, Self-determination and the Arctic Environment. In M. Nuttall & T. Callaghan (Eds.), The Arctic: Environment, People, Policy (pp. 377–409). Amsterdam: Harwood Academic Publishers.

[112] Allard, C. (2018). The Nordic Countries' Sami Policy and Law from a Human Rights Perspective. Arctic Review on Law and Politics, 9, 40–62.

[113] AMAP (Arctic Monitoring and Assessment Programme). (2021). Arctic Climate Change Update 2021: Key Trends and Impacts. Oslo: AMAP.

[114] Ford, J. D., Clark, D. G., Pearce, T., Berrang-Ford, L., Copland, L., Dawson, J., McDowell, G. (2020). Changing Access to Ice, Land and Water in Arctic Communities. Nature Climate Change, 10(2), 135–142.

[115] Ford, J. D., Clark, D. G., Pearce, T., Berrang-Ford, L., Copland, L., Dawson, J., McDowell, G. (2020). Changing Access to Ice, Land and Water in Arctic Communities. Nature Climate Change, 10(2), 135–142.

A 2013–2014 event in northern Norway, for example, led to losses of up to 30% of local herds, directly undermining the economic base of herding and the joik songs, seasonal festivals, and spiritual practices tied to reindeer migration.[116] In the Pacific Northwest of North America, salmon populations have collapsed by more than 90% in some river systems since the late nineteenth century due to dam construction, overfishing, and pollution. This has not only removed a staple food source for tribes such as the Yakama and Nez Perce but also weakened the First Salmon ceremonies that honour salmon as a sacred "first food".[117] Similarly, in the Amazon, industrial deforestation and oil drilling have destroyed an estimated 20% of rainforest cover since the 1970s, diminishing access to hunting grounds, medicinal plants, and clean rivers while erasing sacred groves and waterways central to ritual offerings to forest spirits.[118] These cases demonstrate how ecological change produces a double erasure: the loss of material livelihoods and the erosion of cultural practices embedded in ecological rhythms. Comparisons with communist governance further illustrate the vulnerability of Indigenous rights to external ideologies. In the Soviet Union, Sámi and other Indigenous groups in the Kola Peninsula were collectivized into state farms, with reindeer herding reorganized under centralized bureaucratic plans. While framed as egalitarian reform, collectivization ignored Indigenous ecological knowledge, overburdened pastures, and eroded cultural autonomy.[119] Like capitalist exploitation, communist centralization commodified land and resources, whether for markets or production quotas, subordinating Indigenous sovereignty to external economic priorities. Despite these challenges, Indigenous-led solutions have demonstrated resilience and innovation. The Inuit Circumpolar Council (ICC), established in 1977, has become a leading transnational body advocating for Indigenous sovereignty, environmental protection, and climate justice. Similarly, Sámi parliaments in Norway,

[116] Allard, C. (2018). The Nordic Countries' Sami Policy and Law from a Human Rights Perspective. Arctic Review on Law and Politics, 9, 40–62.

[117] Hunn, E., & Selam, J. (1990). Nch'i-Wána: "The Big River": Mid-Columbia Indians and Their Land. Seattle: University of Washington Press.

[118] Sawyer, S. (2004). Crude Chronicles: Indigenous Politics, Multinational Oil, and Neoliberalism in Ecuador. Durham: Duke University Press.

[119] Stammler, F., & Wilson, E. (2006). Dialogue for Development: An Exploration of Relations between Oil and Gas Companies, Communities, and the State. Sibirica, 5(2), 1–42.

Sweden, and Finland provide political platforms for asserting land rights, even as they continue to face tensions with state development policies. Community-based monitoring systems, such as Inuit-led ice mapping projects, integrate Indigenous ecological knowledge with scientific data to adapt hunting practices to changing conditions.[120] For generations, Inuit hunters have relied on detailed understandings of snow texture, ice colour, wind patterns, and animal behaviour to assess the safety of sea ice and guide seasonal hunting practices. However, rapid climate change has made ice conditions increasingly unpredictable, challenging reliance on traditional indicators alone. In response, Inuit communities have developed participatory mapping projects that integrate hunters' observations of cracks, pressure ridges, and thin ice with GPS tracking, satellite imagery, and meteorological data. These maps, updated and shared within communities, allow hunters to adapt routes and timing to ensure safety while maintaining subsistence practices.[121] Beyond improving immediate safety, such projects exemplify the co-production of knowledge, demonstrating that Indigenous ecological knowledge is dynamic and compatible with scientific approaches. They also strengthen self-determination by placing Arctic communities at the centre of climate adaptation strategies, a priority emphasized by both the Arctic Monitoring and Assessment Program (2021) and the Inuit Circumpolar Council (2019), ensuring that cultural continuity and ecological stewardship remain embedded in responses to environmental change. These initiatives challenge both capitalist and communist models by centring Indigenous governance, demonstrating that ecological sustainability and cultural survival are best secured when Indigenous peoples control decisions over their lands.

[120] Ford, J. D., Clark, D. G., Pearce, T., Berrang-Ford, L., Copland, L., Dawson, J., McDowell, G. (2020). Changing Access to Ice, Land and Water in Arctic Communities. Nature Climate Change, 10(2), 135–142.

[121] Ford, J. D., Clark, D. G., Pearce, T., Berrang-Ford, L., Copland, L., Dawson, J., McDowell, G. (2020). Changing Access to Ice, Land and Water in Arctic Communities. Nature Climate Change, 10(2), 135–142.

5 Broader Themes and Long-Term Implications

5.1 The Role of Colonial Land Policies in Shaping Modern Inequalities

Colonial land policies played a foundational role in shaping the enduring inequalities that mark Indigenous societies today. Across North America, Australia, Africa, and Latin America, the systematic dispossession of Indigenous peoples through legal doctrines such as terra nullius, forced treaties, and reserve systems entrenched a structural divide between settler and Indigenous populations. In North America, the Dawes Act of 1887 fragmented tribal lands into individual allotments, with "surplus" lands sold to settlers, reducing Native American landholdings from 138 million acres in 1887 to just 48 million by 1934.[122] This created long-term poverty by severing Indigenous peoples from productive land bases, a legacy still visible in disproportionately high poverty rates and unemployment in many Native communities. In Australia, pastoral leases and land alienation policies dispossessed Aboriginal peoples of fertile lands, confining them to reserves and missions. The resulting exclusion from property rights produced stark disparities: Aboriginal Australians today experience household incomes 37% lower than non-Indigenous Australians and disproportionately high rates of homelessness and food insecurity.[123] From a neoclassical perspective, these policies were often justified as "efficient" reallocations of land from allegedly "underutilised" Indigenous tenure systems to settler farmers who were assumed to maximise productivity.[124] However, the ecological sustainability of Indigenous land management practices, including rotational agriculture and fire-stick farming, challenges this orthodoxy.[125] Instead of increasing efficiency, settler policies produced ecological degradation, entrenched inequalities, and dispossession that still limits Indigenous participation in

[122] Carlson, L. (1981). Indians, Bureaucrats, and Land: The Dawes Act and the Decline of Indian Farming. Westport, CT: Greenwood Press.

[123] Altman, J. (2012). People on Country as Alternative Development. In J. Altman & S. Kerins (Eds.), People on Country: Vital Landscapes, Indigenous Futures (pp. 1–25). Sydney: Federation Press.

[124] Demsetz, H. (1967). Toward a Theory of Property Rights. American Economic Review, 57(2), 347–359.

[125] Gammage, B. (2011). The Biggest Estate on Earth: How Aborigines Made Australia. Sydney: Allen & Unwin.

markets. Communist models likewise failed to protect Indigenous rights, though their mechanisms differed. In the Soviet Union, collectivization abolished customary tenures and subsumed Indigenous communities into state-controlled farms, denying self-determination while creating new inequalities between central authorities and local populations.[126] Both capitalist and communist frameworks therefore subordinated Indigenous systems to external ideologies, embedding inequality into economic and political structures. Today, land rights remain central to reconciliation and reparations efforts. In Canada, modern treaties and land claims, such as the Nunavut Land Claims Agreement of 1993, which created the largest Indigenous land settlement in the world, have enabled partial redress, though socio-economic gaps persist.[127] In South Africa, the legacy of colonial and apartheid-era land seizures remains evident in racialized patterns of property ownership, with Indigenous and Black South Africans disproportionately landless despite post-apartheid reforms.[128] Similarly, in Latin America, the recognition of Tierras Comunitarias de Origen in Bolivia has returned millions of hectares to Indigenous communities, but conflicts with extractive industries continue to undermine gains.[129] (Assies, 2006). These cases demonstrate that land rights are not only questions of historical justice but also foundational to addressing present-day inequalities, embedding Indigenous sovereignty within broader projects of reconciliation, reparations, and ecological sustainability.

5.2 *Indigenous Advocacy for Land Rights Today*

In recent decades, Indigenous peoples have mobilized globally to demand restitution, recognition, and sovereignty over their ancestral lands. Central to this advocacy has been the 2007 adoption of the United Nations Declaration on the Rights of Indigenous Peoples

[126] Wegren, S. (1998). Agriculture and the State in Soviet and Post-Soviet Russia. Pittsburgh: University of Pittsburgh Press.

[127] Abele, F. (2009). The State and the Northern Social Economy: Research Prospects. The Northern Review, 30, 37–56.

[128] World Bank. (2018). Overcoming Poverty and Inequality in South Africa: An Assessment of Drivers, Constraints and Opportunities. Washington, DC: World Bank.

[129] Assies, W. (2006). Land Tenure Legislation in a Pluri-cultural and Multi-ethnic Society: The Case of Bolivia. Journal of Peasant Studies, 33(4), 569–611.

(UNDRIP), which affirms Indigenous rights to land, resources, and self-determination. Although non-binding, UNDRIP has become a powerful tool in domestic legal and political arenas, cited by Indigenous leaders in Canada, Australia, and Latin America to strengthen land claims.[130] In Canada, the Truth and Reconciliation Commission (TRC) has explicitly linked reconciliation with the restoration of land and treaty rights, emphasizing that systemic poverty in Indigenous communities is inseparable from dispossession.[131] Legal victories such as the 2014 Tsilhqot'in Nation v. British Columbia decision, which recognized Aboriginal title over 1700 square kilometres of land, demonstrate how Indigenous advocacy has transformed jurisprudence by challenging colonial doctrines of terra nullius and Crown sovereignty.[132]

International organizations have also played a crucial role in supporting Indigenous land claims. The Inter-American Court of Human Rights has issued landmark rulings affirming Indigenous territorial rights, such as the 2001 Awas Tingni v. Nicaragua decision, which set a precedent for collective land ownership in Latin America.[133] Similarly, the International Labour Organization Convention 169 has provided a binding legal framework for Indigenous land rights in ratifying states, reinforcing claims to consultation and free, prior, and informed consent. These global instruments reflect a shift in international law from assimilative frameworks to recognition of Indigenous sovereignty. Contrasting these developments with neoclassical economics reveals ongoing tensions. Neoclassical theory prioritises efficiency and the commodification of land, often framing collective tenure as an obstacle to investment and market integration.[134] Yet empirical evidence suggests that lands managed under Indigenous governance have lower rates of deforestation and higher biodiversity than

[130] Anaya, J. (2004). Indigenous Peoples in International Law (2nd ed.). New York: Oxford University Press.

[131] Truth and Reconciliation Commission of Canada (TRC). (2015). Honouring the Truth, Reconciling for the Future: Summary of the Final Report. Ottawa: Government of Canada.

[132] Borrows, J. (2002). Recovering Canada: The Resurgence of Indigenous Law. Toronto: University of Toronto Press.

[133] Brysk, A. (2013). Speaking Rights to Power: Constructing Political Will. Oxford: Oxford University Press.

[134] Demsetz, H. (1967). Toward a Theory of Property Rights. American Economic Review, 57(2), 347–359.

those under state or private ownership, undermining orthodox assumptions.[135] Communist regimes likewise subordinated Indigenous land systems to state planning. In Latin America during the Cold War, leftist governments in countries such as Peru redistributed land through agrarian reforms but frequently failed to respect Indigenous governance structures, treating communities as peasants rather than sovereign nations.[136] Thus, both capitalist and communist models sidelined Indigenous sovereignty, highlighting why global Indigenous advocacy insists on land rights not only as a matter of justice but also as a foundation for sustainable development. These advocacy movements underscore a broader transformation in the politics of land. Indigenous peoples are reframing land not as a commodity but as a living entity central to cultural survival, ecological stewardship, and political sovereignty. By leveraging international norms, domestic legal systems, and grassroots mobilization, they are reshaping the global discourse on rights, justice, and sustainability.

5.3 *Integrating Indigenous Practices into Modern Conservation Efforts*

In recent decades, global environmental policy has increasingly recognized the value of Indigenous ecological knowledge (IEK) as essential to sustainable resource management. Unlike neoclassical economics, which conceptualises land and resources primarily as commodities subject to market allocation, Indigenous worldviews emphasise stewardship, reciprocity, and interdependence between people and ecosystems. This perspective has begun to reshape conservation models, shifting from exclusionary state-led "fortress conservation" to co-management systems that include Indigenous governance. In northern Canada, the establishment of the Gwaii Haanas National Park Reserve represents a landmark example: jointly managed by the Haida Nation and the Government of Canada, it integrates Haida spiritual principles of respect for land

[135] Ricketts, T., Soares-Filho, B., da Fonseca, G., Nepstad, D., Pfaff, A., Petsonk, A., Kormos, C. (2010). Indigenous Lands, Protected Areas, and Slowing Climate Change. PLoS Biology, 8(3), e1000331.

[136] Kay, C. (1982). Achievements and Contradictions of Agrarian Reform in Latin America. Journal of Development Studies, 18(2), 141–170.

with modern conservation science, resulting in both biodiversity protection and cultural revitalization.[137] Similarly, in Australia, Indigenous Protected Areas (IPAs) now cover more than 40% of the national reserve system, with Aboriginal ranger groups employing traditional fire management (mosaic burning) to reduce wildfire risks and restore ecological balance.[138] These initiatives demonstrate the capacity of Indigenous practices to achieve ecological outcomes often overlooked by state or market logics. Comparisons with communist systems highlight further complexities. Under Soviet collectivization, Indigenous and local land management practices were suppressed in favour of centralized state planning. This approach mirrored the exclusionary nature of early state conservation, where communities were often displaced from parks in the name of ecological protection.[139] Both capitalist and communist models tended to marginalise Indigenous autonomy, albeit through different ideological justifications. In contrast, contemporary co-management frameworks attempt to reconcile ecological conservation with Indigenous sovereignty, offering a pathway beyond these binaries. Despite notable successes, challenges remain in balancing Indigenous autonomy with state-led conservation goals. Co-management often requires Indigenous groups to operate within bureaucratic frameworks that limit their decision-making authority, raising concerns about tokenism rather than genuine power-sharing.[140] Moreover, the expansion of global carbon markets and biodiversity offset schemes risks subsuming Indigenous lands into new forms of commodification, echoing neoclassical assumptions of resource fungibility. Yet empirical evidence indicates that forests under Indigenous stewardship exhibit lower deforestation rates and higher biodiversity than comparable state or private lands.[141] This suggests that full recognition of Indigenous

[137] Jones, R., Rigg, C., & Lee, L. (2010). Haida Marine Planning: First Nations as a Partner in Marine Conservation. Ecology and Society, 15(1), 12.

[138] Altman, J., & Kerins, S. (Eds.). (2012). People on Country: Vital Landscapes, Indigenous Futures. Sydney: Federation Press.

[139] Wegren, S. (1998). Agriculture and the State in Soviet and Post-Soviet Russia. Pittsburgh: University of Pittsburgh Press.

[140] Stevens, S. (Ed.). (2014). Indigenous Peoples, National Parks, and Protected Areas: A New Paradigm Linking Conservation, Culture, and Rights. Tucson: University of Arizona Press.

[141] Ricketts, T., Soares-Filho, B., da Fonseca, G., Nepstad, D., Pfaff, A., Petsonk, A., Kormos, C. (2010). Indigenous Lands, Protected Areas, and Slowing Climate Change. PLoS Biology, 8(3), e1000331.

ecological knowledge and governance is not only a matter of justice but also a pragmatic necessity for achieving global conservation targets in the face of climate change.

6 Conclusion

The analysis in this chapter has demonstrated that Indigenous perspectives on land and resource management fundamentally challenge dominant economic and political frameworks. Across diverse contexts, from the Zuni water systems and Inca terraces to the Plains tribes'bison stewardship and the Sámi's reindeer herding, Indigenous societies have articulated philosophies of land as a sacred, communal, and relational entity. These perspectives are not vestiges of a pre-modern past but sophisticated systems of governance and ecological knowledge that continue to sustain biodiversity and cultural survival. By contrast, both neoclassical economics and communist centralization have consistently commodified land, treating it as either a private asset to be maximized through markets or a productive input to be mobilized for state objectives. In both cases, the result has been ecological degradation, dispossession, and the erosion of cultural autonomy. The historical encounters between Indigenous peoples and European settlers highlighted the depth of these divergences. Colonial doctrines such as terra nullius and the Doctrine of Discovery institutionalized the idea that Indigenous lands were "empty" or "underutilised", legitimizing expropriation in the name of efficiency. Yet the evidence presented undermines these justifications: Indigenous systems of rotational agriculture, fire management, and communal tenure frequently produced more sustainable and resilient outcomes than settler monocultures or industrial extraction. The comparative analysis also revealed the limitations of communist collectivization, which, while rejecting private property, nevertheless subordinated Indigenous governance to state bureaucracy, producing social dislocation and ecological collapse. Thus, Indigenous dispossession was not an unintended by-product of either capitalism or communism, but a structural outcome of their shared instrumentalist view of land. Case studies across North America, Australia, Latin America, Africa, and the Arctic demonstrate both the devastating consequences of dispossession and the resilience of Indigenous resistance. From the Trail of Tears and the Mau Mau uprising to the Mabo case and Sarayaku mobilization in Ecuador, Indigenous peoples have continually adapted strategies of legal challenge, political advocacy, and cultural revival. These struggles highlight that land is not merely a material resource but a foundation of sovereignty, identity, and ecological reciprocity. At the same time, they reveal how the legacies of colonial land policies remain embedded in modern inequalities, where systemic poverty, ecological vulnerability, and political marginalization persist in many Indigenous communities. The broader implications of these findings are profound. First, they challenge the orthodoxy that efficiency or equality can only be achieved through private markets or centralized states, showing instead that Indigenous governance systems offer viable and empirically grounded alternatives. Second, they underscore that reconciliation and reparations must centre on land restitution and recognition of Indigenous sovereignty, not simply symbolic gestures. Without addressing land rights, poverty alleviation and environmental sustainability efforts risk reproducing the very inequalities they claim to overcome. Finally, the growing incorporation of Indigenous ecological knowledge into conservation frameworks points to an emerging paradigm: one in which Indigenous peoples are not passive stakeholders but central actors in global responses to climate change and biodiversity loss. Critically, however, the chapter also cautions against romanticization. Co-management systems, biodiversity offsets, and carbon markets risk appropriating Indigenous knowledge while constraining Indigenous autonomy within state or corporate frameworks. The persistence of these tensions demonstrates that the recognition of Indigenous rights must go beyond instrumental use of ecological practices to affirm self-determination in its fullest sense. This chapter has shown that the political economy of Indigenous land rights is not only a matter of historical redress but a question of humanity's collective ecological future. By learning from Indigenous philosophies of reciprocity, stewardship, and interdependence, societies can envision pathways beyond the binaries of capitalism and communism, towards models of governance that are ecologically sustainable and socially just. The challenge is not whether Indigenous practices can be integrated into modern systems, but whether modern systems can transform themselves to respect and empower Indigenous sovereignty.

The ideology of terra nullius did more than justify territorial acquisition; it redefined the very meaning of land, sovereignty, and law in ways that displaced Indigenous governance systems and reconfigured global political order. As Chapter 6 will demonstrate, these processes of dispossession were not merely legal or economic in nature, but part of a broader conflict between decentralized, consensus-based Indigenous governance models and the hierarchical, centralized state structures that underpinned European imperialism. In confronting the long-term consequences of this clash, Chapter 6 explores how Indigenous peoples resisted, adapted, and continue to assert alternative frameworks of self-determination that challenge dominant conceptions of sovereignty and statehood.

References

Abele, F. (2009). The State and the Northern Social Economy: Research Prospects. The Northern Review, 30, 37–56.

Alfred, T. (2009) Wasáse: Indigenous Pathways of Action and Freedom. Toronto: University of Toronto Press.

Allard, C. (2018). The Nordic Countries' Sami Policy and Law from a Human Rights Perspective. Arctic Review on Law and Politics, 9, 40–62.

Alpers, C. N., Hunerlach, M. P., May, J. T., & Hothem, R. L. (2005). Mercury Contamination from Historic Gold Mining in California. Fact Sheet 2005-3014. U.S. Geological Survey.

Altman, J. (2012). People on Country as Alternative Development. In J. Altman & S. Kerins (Eds.), People on Country: Vital Landscapes, Indigenous Futures (pp. 1–25). Sydney: Federation Press.

Altman, J. & Kerins, S. (2012) People on Country: Vital Landscapes, Indigenous Futures. Sydney: Federation Press.

AMAP (Arctic Monitoring and Assessment Programme). (2021). Arctic Climate Change Update 2021: Key Trends and Impacts. Oslo: AMAP.

Anaya, S.J. (2004) Indigenous Peoples in International Law. Oxford: Oxford University Press.

Anderson, D. (2002). Eroding the Commons: The Politics of Ecology in Baringo, Kenya, 1890s–1963. Oxford: James Currey.

Anderson, D. (2005). Histories of the Hanged: Britain's Dirty War in Kenya and the End of Empire. New York: W. W. Norton.

Anderson, T., & Lee, G. (2010). Land and Livelihoods in Melanesia: Customary Land Tenure and Poverty Reduction. Canberra: Australian National University, Crawford School of Economics and Government, Discussion Paper 2010/6.

Asner, G. P., Llactayo, W., Tupayachi, R., & Luna, E. R. (2013). Elevated Rates of Gold Mining in the Amazon Revealed through High-Resolution Monitoring. Proceedings of the National Academy of Sciences, 110(46), 18454–18459.

Assies, W. (2006). Land Tenure Legislation in a Pluri-cultural and Multi-ethnic Society: The Case of Bolivia. Journal of Peasant Studies, 33(4), 569–611.

Banner, S. (2005) How the Indians Lost Their Land: Law and Power on the Frontier. Cambridge, MA: Harvard University Press.

Benhin, J., & Barbier, E. (2004). Structural Adjustment Programme, Deforestation and Biodiversity Loss in Ghana. Environmental and Resource Economics, 27(3), 337–366.

Berkes, F. (2018) Sacred Ecology. 4th edn. New York: Routledge.

Berry, S. (1993). No Condition is Permanent: The Social Dynamics of Agrarian Change in Sub-Saharan Africa. Madison: University of Wisconsin Press.

Boone, C. (2014). Property and Political Order in Africa: Land Rights and the Structure of Politics. Cambridge: Cambridge University Press.

Borrows, J. (2002). Recovering Canada: The Resurgence of Indigenous Law. Toronto: University of Toronto Press.

Brysk, A. (2013). Speaking Rights to Power: Constructing Political Will. Oxford: Oxford University Press.

Carlson, L. (1981). Indians, Bureaucrats, and Land: The Dawes Act and the Decline of Indian Farming. Westport, CT: Greenwood Press.

Coase, R. (1960). The Problem of Social Cost. Journal of Law and Economics, 3, 1–44.

Conley, R. J. (2005). The Cherokee Nation: A History. Albuquerque: University of New Mexico Press.

Coulthard, G.S. (2014) Red Skin, White Masks: Rejecting the Colonial Politics of Recognition. Minneapolis: University of Minnesota Press.

Davidson-Hunt, I. & Berkes, F. (2003) 'Learning as you journey: Anishinaabe perception of social-ecological environments and adaptive learning', Conservation Ecology, 8(1), p. 5.

Demsetz, H. (1967). Toward a Theory of Property Rights. American Economic Review, 57(2), 347–359.

Durie, M. (1998). Te Mana, Te Kāwanatanga: The Politics of Māori Self-Determination. Auckland: Oxford University Press.

Fondahl, G. (1998) Gaining Ground? Evenkis, Land, and Reform in Southeastern Siberia. Boulder, CO: Westview Press.

Ford, J. D., Clark, D. G., Pearce, T., Berrang-Ford, L., Copland, L., Dawson, J., McDowell, G. (2020). Changing Access to Ice, Land and Water in Arctic Communities. Nature Climate Change, 10(2), 135–142.

Foster, J.B. & Clark, B. (2009) 'The Paradox of Wealth: Capitalism and Ecological Destruction', Monthly Review, 61(6).

Gammage, B. (2011) The Biggest Estate on Earth: How Aborigines Made Australia. Sydney: Allen & Unwin.

Garnett, S.T., Burgess, N.D., Fa, J.E., Fernández-Llamazares, Á., Molnár, Z., Robinson, C.J., Watson, J.E.M., Zander, K.K., Austin, B., Brondizio, E.S., Collier, N.F., Duncan, T., Ellis, E., Geyle, H., Jackson, M.V., Jonas, H.D., Malmer, P., McGowan, B., Sivongxay, A. & Leiper, I. (2018) 'A spatial

overview of the global importance of Indigenous lands for conservation', Nature Sustainability, 1(7), pp. 369–374.
Guillet, D. (1987). Terracing and Irrigation in the Peruvian Highlands. Current Anthropology, 28(4), 409–430.
Hardin, G. (1968). The Tragedy of the Commons. Science, 162(3859), 1243–1248.
Harrell, S. (2001) Perspectives on the Yi of Southwest China. Berkeley: University of California Press.
Homburg, J. A., Sandor, J. A., & Lightfoot, D. R. (2005). Agricultural Sustainability in Zuni Farming Systems. Journal of Ethnobiology, 25(2), 301–321.
Hunn, E. (1990). Nch'i-Wána, "The Big River": Mid-Columbia Indians and Their Land. Seattle: University of Washington Press.
Inuit Circumpolar Council (ICC). (2019). Circumpolar Inuit Protocols for Equitable and Ethical Engagement. Ottawa: ICC.
Isenberg, A. (2000). The Destruction of the Bison: An Environmental History, 1750–1920. Cambridge: Cambridge University Press.
Kanogo, T. (1987). Squatters and the Roots of Mau Mau, 1905–1963. London: James Currey.
Kay, C. (1982). Achievements and Contradictions of Agrarian Reform in Latin America. Journal of Development Studies, 18(2), 141–170.
Kimmerer, R.W. (2013) Braiding Sweetgrass: Indigenous Wisdom, Scientific Knowledge, and the Teachings of Plants. Minneapolis: Milkweed Editions.
McRae, H., Nettheim, G., & Beacroft, L. (2009). Indigenous Legal Issues: Commentary and Materials (4th ed.). Sydney: Thomson Reuters.
Marx, K., & Engels, F. (1998). The Communist Manifesto (original work published 1848). London: Verso.
Micklin, P. (2007). The Aral Sea Disaster. Annual Review of Earth and Planetary Sciences, 35, 47–72.
Miller, R. J. (2006/2010). Native America, Discovered and Conquered: Thomas Jefferson, Lewis & Clark, and Manifest Destiny. Lincoln: University of Nebraska Press.
Miller, R.J., Ruru, J., Behrendt, L. & Lindberg, T. (2010) Discovering Indigenous Lands: The Doctrine of Discovery in the English Colonies. Oxford: Oxford University Press.
Mwangi, E. (2007). Subdividing the Commons: Distributional Conflict in the Transition from Collective to Individual Property Rights in Kenya's Maasailand. World Development, 35(5), 815–834.
Myers, F. (2002). Painting Culture: The Making of an Aboriginal High Art. Durham: Duke University Press.

Natcher, D., & Hickey, C. (2002). Putting the Community Back into Community-Based Resource Management: A Criteria and Indicators Approach to Sustainability. Canadian Journal of Native Studies, 22(1), 1–26.

Nepstad, D., Schwartzman, S., Bamberger, B., Santilli, M., Ray, D., Schlesinger, P., … Rolla, A. (2006). Inhibition of Amazon Deforestation and Fire by Parks and Indigenous Lands. Conservation Biology, 20(1), 65–73.

Niezen, R. (2003) The Origins of Indigenism: Human Rights and the Politics of Identity. Berkeley: University of California Press.

Nuttall, M. (2000). Indigenous Peoples, Self-determination and the Arctic Environment. In M. Nuttall & T. Callaghan (Eds.), The Arctic: Environment, People, Policy (pp. 377–409). Amsterdam: Harwood Academic Publishers.

Perdue, T., & Green, M. D. (2007). The Cherokee Nation and the Trail of Tears. New York: Penguin.

Posey, D. (1985). Indigenous Management of Tropical Forest Ecosystems: The Case of the Kayapó Indians of the Brazilian Amazon. Agroforestry Systems, 3(2), 139–158.

Rahmato, D. (1984). Agrarian Reform in Ethiopia. Uppsala: Scandinavian Institute of African Studies.

Regenvanu, R. (2009). The Traditional Economy as Source of Resilience in Vanuatu. In S. Feeny & S. McDonald (Eds.), Pacific Island Countries: Growth, Welfare and Governance in the Twenty-First Century (pp. 91–106). Cheltenham: Edward Elgar.

Reynolds, H. (1996). Aboriginal Sovereignty: Reflections on Race, State and Nation. St. Leonards: Allen & Unwin.

Ricardo, D. (1951). On the Principles of Political Economy and Taxation. Edited by Piero Sraffa with Maurice Dobb. Cambridge: Cambridge University Press. (Works and Correspondence of David Ricardo, Vol. 1).

Ricardo, D. (1996). Principles of Political Economy and Taxation. Amherst, NY: Prometheus Books. (Original work published 1817).

Ricketts, T., Soares-Filho, B., da Fonseca, G., Nepstad, D., Pfaff, A., Petsonk, A., … Kormos, C. (2010). Indigenous Lands, Protected Areas, and Slowing Climate Change. PLoS Biology, 8(3), e1000331.

Rodríguez-Garavito, C. (2011). Ethnicity.gov: Global Governance, Indigenous Peoples, and the Right to Prior Consultation in Social Minefields. Indiana Journal of Global Legal Studies, 18(1), 263–305.

Rose, D.B. (1996) Nourishing Terrains: Australian Aboriginal Views of Landscape and Wilderness. Canberra: Australian Heritage Commission.

Samuelson, P., & Nordhaus, W. (2009). Economics (19th ed.). New York: McGraw-Hill.

Sandor, J. A., & Homburg, J. A. (2017). Zuni Agricultural History and Ecology: Resilience and Sustainability. Journal of Ethnobiology, 37(2), 195–216.

Sawyer, S. (2004). Crude Chronicles: Indigenous Politics, Multinational Oil, and Neoliberalism in Ecuador. Durham: Duke University Press.
Sheridan, M., & Nyamweru, C. (2008). African Sacred Groves: Ecological Dynamics and Social Change. Oxford: James Currey.
Stammler, F., & Wilson, E. (2006). Dialogue for Development: An Exploration of Relations between Oil and Gas Companies, Communities, and the State. Sibirica, 5(2), 1–42.
Truth and Reconciliation Commission of Canada (TRC). (2015). Honouring the Truth, Reconciling for the Future: Summary of the Final Report. Ottawa: Government of Canada.
Turner, T. (1995) 'An Indigenous People's Struggle for Socially Equitable and Ecologically Sustainable Production: The Kayapo Revolt against Extractivism', Journal of Latin American Anthropology, 1(1), pp. 98–121.
Ubink, J. (2008). In the Land of the Chiefs: Customary Law, Land Conflicts, and the Role of the State in Peri-Urban Ghana. Leiden: Leiden University Press.
United Nations (2007) United Nations Declaration on the Rights of Indigenous Peoples (UNDRIP). New York: United Nations.
Veracini, L. (2010) Settler Colonialism: A Theoretical Overview. Basingstoke: Palgrave Macmillan.
Watson, I. (2014) Aboriginal Peoples, Colonialism and International Law: Raw Law. Abingdon: Routledge.
Wegren, S. (1998). Agriculture and the State in Soviet and Post-Soviet Russia. Pittsburgh: University of Pittsburgh Press.
Whyte, K.P. (2018) 'Indigenous science (fiction) for the Anthropocene: Ancestral dystopias and fantasies of climate change crises', Environment and Planning E: Nature and Space, 1(1–2), pp. 224–242.
Wilkins, D. E., & Lomawaima, K. T. (2001). Uneven Ground: American Indian Sovereignty and Federal Law. Norman: University of Oklahoma Press.
Williams, N. (1986). The Yolngu and Their Land: A System of Land Tenure and the Fight for Its Recognition. Canberra: Australian Institute of Aboriginal Studies.
Wilson, S. (2008) Research is Ceremony: Indigenous Research Methods. Halifax: Fernwood Publishing.
World Bank. (2010). Rising Global Interest in Farmland: Can It Yield Sustainable and Equitable Benefits? Washington, DC: World Bank.
World Bank. (2018). Overcoming Poverty and Inequality in South Africa: An Assessment of Drivers, Constraints and Opportunities. Washington, DC: World Bank.

Yazzie, R. (2010) 'Indigenous Peoples and Sacred Lands: A Navajo Perspective', University of Colorado Law Review, 81(4), pp. 1031–1045.
Zimmerer, K. (1996). Changing Fortunes: Biodiversity and Peasant Livelihood in the Peruvian Andes. Berkeley: University of California Press.

CHAPTER 6

Governance, Self-Determination, and European Imperial Systems

1 Introduction

The encounter between Indigenous governance systems and European imperial state-building represents one of the most transformative and destructive processes in global history. While Indigenous peoples across the world developed governance systems that were deeply embedded in local ecologies, kinship structures, and consensus-based decision-making, European powers exported centralized, hierarchical, and bureaucratic models designed to consolidate authority, mobilize resources, and extend imperial control. These contrasting models of governance were not simply institutional variations: they reflected fundamentally different ontologies of power, sovereignty, and human relationships with land and community.[1] The consequences of these encounters have been enduring, shaping patterns of dispossession, resistance, and the continuing struggle for self-determination. Indigenous governance systems were typically decentralized, flexible, and rooted in collective responsibility. For example, the Iroquois Confederacy in North America operated under the Great Law of Peace, a sophisticated federal system that balanced clan, nation, and

[1] Cornell, S. and Kalt, J. (1998). 'Sovereignty and Nation-Building: The Development Challenge in Indian Country Today', American Indian Culture and Research Journal, 22(3), pp. 187–214.

S. Ramesh, *The Political Economy of the Indigenous Peoples of the World, Volume I*, https://doi.org/10.1007/978-3-032-24041-5_6

confederacy-level decision-making, influencing even Enlightenment political thought, including models later embedded in the U.S. Constitution.[2] In Southern Africa, the San people relied on egalitarian forms of governance through group consensus, with leadership emerging situationally rather than through rigid hierarchy.[3] Similarly, clan-based governance in the Pacific Islands tied authority to stewardship over land and sea, with chiefs serving as custodians rather than owners, embedding political leadership within ecological and spiritual obligations.[4] Such governance frameworks emphasized adaptability, reciprocity, and legitimacy derived from participation and consensus, in stark contrast to European centralization. European governance models, emerging during the consolidation of early modern states, were designed to exert control over expanding populations and economies. The development of professional bureaucracies, standing armies, and taxation systems facilitated the rise of centralized authority.[5] Mercantilist policies and imperial expansion further reinforced these structures, with states like Spain and Portugal building empires through control of trade routes and resource extraction. The Spanish crown's reliance on silver from Potosí, where Indigenous labour was coerced through the mita system, underwrote European state-building and global commerce.[6] Similarly, Britain's parliamentary dominance and administrative capacity allowed it to manage a far-flung empire, embedding legal and bureaucratic institutions that replaced and often undermined Indigenous governance systems.[7] These diverging notions of governance were crystallized in different understandings of sovereignty and territory. Indigenous peoples conceptualized

[2] Lyons, O., Mohawk, J., Deloria, V., Hauptman, L. M., Berman, H., Grinde, D. A., Shaaf, R. and Wilkinson, C. (1992). Exiled in the Land of the Free: Democracy, Indian Nations and the U.S. Constitution. Santa Fe: Clear Light Publishers.

[3] Lee, R. (1979; 2nd ed. 1984). The!Kung San: Men, Women and Work in a Foraging Society. Cambridge: Cambridge University Press.

[4] Hviding, E. (1996). Guardians of Marovo Lagoon: Practice, Place, and Politics in Maritime Melanesia. Honolulu: University of Hawai'i Press.

[5] Tilly, C. (1990). Coercion, Capital, and European States, AD 990–1990. Oxford: Blackwell.

[6] Bakewell, P. (1984). Silver Mining and Society in Colonial Mexico: Zacatecas 1546–1700. Cambridge: Cambridge University Press.

[7] Mamdani, M. (1996). Citizen and Subject: Contemporary Africa and the Legacy of Late Colonialism. Princeton: Princeton University Press.

land as a shared, relational entity, with governance rooted in stewardship and balance. In contrast, European imperial states advanced doctrines of absolute sovereignty and rigid borders, codified in legal instruments such as the Doctrine of Discovery and terra nullius. The result was the widespread denial of Indigenous territorial authority, often justified through treaties that were either coercively imposed or systematically violated. For instance, treaties in North America were routinely reinterpreted by colonial courts in ways that favoured settler expansion, while in Australia the legal fiction of terra nullius erased Indigenous sovereignty altogether until its overturn in the 1992 Mabo v Queensland decision.[8] This chapter situates Indigenous governance and self-determination within this global history of European imperial expansion. It examines the contrasts between Indigenous consensus-based systems and European centralized state-building; explores how European institutions of military, bureaucracy, and religion facilitated colonization; and analyses Indigenous responses ranging from armed resistance to diplomatic alliances. Importantly, it also traces the survival and revitalization of Indigenous governance into the present, including movements for autonomy, international recognition, and the integration of customary law into modern political systems. By juxtaposing Indigenous governance with both capitalist and communist state systems, the chapter demonstrates that Indigenous approaches not only resisted imperial domination but also offer enduring lessons for contemporary debates on sovereignty, sustainability, and global governance.

This chapter builds directly upon the themes explored in Chapters 4 and 5. While Chapter 4 examined the epistemological shifts brought by European Enlightenment thought and Chapter 5 deconstructed the legal and institutional mechanisms of dispossession through colonialism and settler law, Chapter 6 turns to the heart of Indigenous resistance: the struggle for land back and sovereignty. It delves into contemporary movements that reclaim not only territory but also governance, culture, and spiritual ties to place. Through these acts of resurgence, Indigenous peoples contest both the historical erasure and the modern commodification of land, asserting models of custodianship rooted in kinship and law. This chapter thus represents a pivot—from critique to resurgence, from the imposition of colonial rule to the articulation of Indigenous futures.

[8] Nettheim, G., Meyers, G. and Craig, D. (2002). Indigenous Peoples and the Law in Australia. Sydney: Butterworths.

2 Contrasts Between Indigenous Governance Models and European State-Building and Imperial Strategies

2.1 Indigenous Governance: Decentralization and Consensus-Based Systems

Indigenous governance systems across the world were characterized by decentralization, consensus-based decision-making, and an adaptive flexibility that enabled communities to align political authority with ecological and social realities. Unlike European state-building models, which concentrated power in hierarchical institutions, Indigenous governance generally derived legitimacy from kinship ties, reciprocal obligations, and collective participation. Among the Haudenosaunee (Iroquois) Confederacy, the Great Law of Peace established a federal structure where clans, nations, and the confederacy shared responsibilities through a council system that prioritized consensus rather than majority rule. This system not only ensured that minority voices were protected but also offered a degree of political stability that influenced Enlightenment thinkers, including Benjamin Franklin and the framers of the U.S. Constitution.[9] In Southern Africa, the San people exemplify egalitarian governance, where authority is exercised through group deliberation rather than coercion. Leadership among the San is situational and based on skills or knowledge rather than inherited or coercive power. Richard Lee's classic ethnography demonstrates how disputes are resolved through lengthy communal discussions, often taking days, in which consensus is required to prevent divisions that could jeopardise survival in arid environments.[10] Such mechanisms ensured both social cohesion and adaptability, allowing San groups to respond to fluctuating ecological conditions. Pacific Island societies offer further illustrations of decentralized and flexible governance. In the Solomon Islands, clan-based chieftaincy is embedded in custodianship over land and marine resources. Leaders are expected to

[9] Lyons, O., Mohawk, J., Deloria, V., Hauptman, L. M., Berman, H., Grinde, D. A., Shaaf, R. and Wilkinson, C. (1992). Exiled in the Land of the Free: Democracy, Indian Nations and the U.S. Constitution. Santa Fe: Clear Light Publishers.

[10] Lee, R. (1979, 2nd ed. 1984). The!Kung San: Men, Women and Work in a Foraging Society. Cambridge: Cambridge University Press.

mediate disputes, manage resource use, and uphold spiritual responsibilities tied to the environment. Edvard Hviding's research on Marovo Lagoon shows that chiefs' legitimacy derives not from coercive authority but from their ability to maintain harmony within the community and with ecological systems.[11] Such governance was not static: it evolved with ecological pressures such as changing fish stocks and shifting agricultural conditions, highlighting its adaptability. Contrasting these systems with European political economy highlights their distinctiveness. Neoclassical economic theory views collective governance as inefficient, arguing that property rights evolve towards privatization to reduce transaction costs and prevent overuse.[12] Yet the resilience of Indigenous systems challenges this orthodoxy. Empirical studies show that consensus-based governance and communal tenure can sustain resources over centuries, as seen in the Iroquois agricultural system of "Three Sisters" planting, which maintained soil fertility while sustaining dense populations.[13] Similarly, the San's hunting and gathering practices ensured sustainable use of resources without private property regimes. By contrast, communist systems, while rejecting private property, also imposed centralized authority over land and governance. Under the Soviet Union, Indigenous communities in Siberia were collectivized into state farms, with decisions imposed from above rather than reached through consensus, eroding cultural autonomy and damaging local ecologies.[14] The key distinction, therefore, lies in the relational and participatory nature of Indigenous governance. Authority was distributed, adaptive, and accountable to community consensus, enabling societies to thrive in diverse and often fragile ecological contexts. Both capitalist and communist systems subordinated governance to external ideologies of efficiency or equality, disregarding local autonomy. By highlighting Indigenous models, it becomes evident that decentralized, consensus-based governance not only

[11] Hviding, E. (1996). Guardians of Marovo Lagoon: Practice, Place, and Politics in Maritime Melanesia. Honolulu: University of Hawai'i Press.

[12] Demsetz, H. (1967). 'Toward a Theory of Property Rights', American Economic Review, 57(2), pp. 347–359.

[13] Mt. Pleasant, J. (2011). 'The Science Behind the Three Sisters Mound System: An Agronomic Assessment of an Indigenous Agricultural System in the Northeast', Agronomy Journal, 103(4), pp. 1136–1146.

[14] Fondahl, G. (1998). Gaining Ground? Evenkis, Land, and Reform in Southeastern Siberia. Boston: Allyn and Bacon.

sustained social cohesion but also provided a viable alternative to hierarchical state-building, one that continues to inspire contemporary debates about democracy, sustainability, and self-determination.

2.2 European State-Building: Centralization of Power and Bureaucracy

The rise of European nation-states during the early modern period was defined by the centralization of political authority, the development of bureaucratic institutions, and the consolidation of military and fiscal power. Charles Tilly's seminal analysis describes the European state as the product of "war-making and state-making", whereby rulers who could extract resources efficiently through taxation and bureaucracy were better positioned to field standing armies and defend territorial sovereignty.[15] This process stood in stark contrast to Indigenous governance systems, which were more decentralized, consensus-based, and adapted to local ecological conditions. In Spain and Portugal, the centralization of power was closely linked to imperial expansion. The Spanish monarchy established a sophisticated administrative system to manage its vast overseas empire, including the Council of the Indies and the vice royalties, which integrated colonial wealth into the metropolitan economy. Silver from Potosí, extracted through systems of forced Indigenous labour such as the mita, provided up to a third of the Spanish crown's revenues by the late sixteenth century, fuelling both European wars and the consolidation of royal authority.[16] Portugal followed a similar trajectory, with its overseas empire in Brazil and Asia organized through royal charters and monopolies such as the Casa da India, which centralized trade and taxation under state supervision.[17] Britain's path reflected a different but equally centralizing model. Parliamentary supremacy and the rise of a permanent bureaucracy provided the institutional foundation for colonial governance. The establishment of the Colonial Office in 1801

[15] Tilly, C. (1990). Coercion, Capital, and European States, AD 990–1990. Oxford: Blackwell.

[16] Bakewell, P. (1984). Silver Mining and Society in Colonial Mexico: Zacatecas 1546–1700. Cambridge: Cambridge University Press.

[17] Bethencourt, F. (2007). The Portuguese Oceanic Expansion, 1400–1800. Aldershot: Ashgate.

and the development of civil services in India and Africa institutionalized rule through layers of legal and administrative control.[18] British colonial officials implemented uniform systems of taxation, codified law, and census-taking to render populations "legible" to the state, a hallmark of bureaucratic rationalization.[19] From an economic perspective, mercantilism reinforced this centralization. European states regulated trade through monopolies, tariffs, and chartered companies such as the Dutch East India Company (VOC) and the British East India Company. These institutions served as extensions of state power, extracting resources and controlling markets in ways that reinforced the fiscal-military state.[20] Unlike Indigenous governance, which emphasized relational stewardship of resources, mercantilism commodified land and labour for metropolitan accumulation. When compared to neoclassical economics, which valorises market competition and efficiency, European state-building appears as a paradox. Centralized mercantilist policies constrained free markets, yet they were justified as necessary to protect national interests and consolidate state revenues. In contrast, communist systems replicated centralization under a different ideological banner. Soviet collectivization and planned economies similarly subordinated local governance and resource management to state bureaucracies, often producing inefficiency and ecological degradation.[21] Both European mercantilism and communist planning shared a reliance on bureaucratic centralization, distinguishing them from Indigenous governance, which distributed authority and embedded decision-making within ecological and social contexts. The European model of state-building thus exemplifies how bureaucracy, taxation, and military mobilization intertwined to create powerful centralized states. While successful in projecting power globally, these systems also displaced and delegitimized Indigenous governance, replacing consensus and ecological reciprocity with hierarchical control and economic exploitation.

[18] Mamdani, M. (1996). Citizen and Subject: Contemporary Africa and the Legacy of Late Colonialism. Princeton: Princeton University Press.

[19] Scott, J.C. (1998). Seeing Like a State: How Certain Schemes to Improve the Human Condition Have Failed. New Haven: Yale University Press.

[20] Findlay, R. and O'Rourke, K.H. (2007). Power and Plenty: Trade, War, and the World Economy in the Second Millennium. Princeton: Princeton University Press.

[21] Wegren, S. (1998). Agriculture and the State in Soviet and Post-Soviet Russia. Pittsburgh: University of Pittsburgh Press.

2.3 *Diverging Notions of Sovereignty and Territory*

The clash between Indigenous and European notions of sovereignty and territory represents one of the most fundamental disjunctions in world history. Indigenous governance systems generally understood land not as a commodity to be owned but as a relational and fluid entity, embedded in networks of stewardship, kinship, and spiritual responsibility. Sovereignty was collective and distributed, exercised through consensus and anchored in reciprocal obligations to land and community. Among the Canadian and American tribes, Anishinaabe sovereignty was conceived as flowing from the Creator, with leaders holding responsibilities rather than absolute authority, and land use organized through shared stewardship rather than exclusive ownership.[22] Similarly, in Pacific Island societies, territorial claims over sea and land were overlapping and negotiated through kinship ties, creating flexible systems of governance adapted to shifting ecological and social realities.[23] By contrast, European state-building and imperial expansion were predicated on notions of absolute sovereignty, demarcated borders, and territorial control. The "Westphalian order", originating with the Peace of Westphalia in 1648, established a framework of international relations based on state sovereignty, territorial integrity, legal equality, and non-intervention.[24,25] This model defined states as supreme authorities within fixed borders, contrasting sharply with Indigenous governance systems that understood sovereignty as relational, overlapping, and grounded in stewardship rather than rigid territorial demarcation.[26] European colonial expansion drew legitimacy from this order: sovereignty was applied to European states but denied to Indigenous nations, often through doctrines such as terra nullius, which declared Indigenous lands legally "empty" if they did not conform

[22] Simpson, A. (2014). Mohawk Interruptus: Political Life Across the Borders of Settler States. Durham: Duke University Press.

[23] Hviding, E. (1996). Guardians of Marovo Lagoon: Practice, Place, and Politics in Maritime Melanesia. Honolulu: University of Hawai'i Press.

[24] Osiander, A. (2001). 'Sovereignty, International Relations, and the Westphalian Myth', International Organization, 55(2), pp. 251–287.

[25] Philpott, D. (2001). Revolutions in Sovereignty: How Ideas Shaped Modern International Relations. Princeton: Princeton University Press.

[26] Simpson, A. (2014). Mohawk Interruptus: Political Life Across the Borders of Settler States. Durham: Duke University Press.

to European notions of statehood.[27] Thus, the Westphalian model of sovereignty that crystallized in Europe during the seventeenth century defined states as entities with exclusive authority over bounded territories, a concept that was later exported globally through colonization. Land was surveyed, mapped, and divided into property parcels or administrative units, erasing Indigenous fluidity and relationality. Doctrines such as terra nullius in Australia epitomized this imposition by declaring Indigenous lands legally "empty" despite continuous occupation and stewardship. It was only in the landmark Mabo v Queensland (No 2) decision of 1992 that the High Court of Australia overturned terra nullius and recognized native title, acknowledging that Indigenous systems of law and land tenure pre-existed colonial sovereignty. The Westphalian order is increasingly under strain. Globalization has blurred the boundaries of sovereignty as economies, communications, and security threats transcend borders.[28] Transnational challenges such as climate change and pandemics demand cooperative governance that exceeds the capacity of individual states.[29] At the same time, Indigenous rights movements and legal frameworks like the United Nations Declaration on the Rights of Indigenous Peoples (UNDRIP) challenge the universality of Westphalian sovereignty by asserting relational and overlapping claims to land, identity, and governance.[30,31] Together, these developments illustrate that the rigid, state-centric system forged in 1648 is giving way to more plural, networked, and contested forms of global governance. In North America, treaties between European powers and Indigenous nations were frequently misinterpreted or deliberately reinterpreted by colonial courts to erode Indigenous sovereignty. For example, while the Haudenosaunee negotiated treaties as agreements between sovereign entities, colonial authorities increasingly construed them as instruments of land cession.

[27] Banner, S. (2005). How the Indians Lost Their Land: Law and Power on the Frontier. Cambridge, MA: Harvard University Press.

[28] Held, D. and McGrew, A. (2002). Globalization/Anti-Globalization. Cambridge: Polity Press.

[29] Keohane, R.O. (2005). After Hegemony: Cooperation and Discord in the World Political Economy. Princeton: Princeton University Press.

[30] Anaya, J. (2004). Indigenous Peoples in International Law. 2nd ed. New York: Oxford University Press.

[31] Wilkins, D.E. and Lomawaima, K.T. (2001). Uneven Ground: American Indian Sovereignty and Federal Law. Norman: University of Oklahoma Press.

The 1831 U.S. Supreme Court case Cherokee Nation v. Georgia reduced tribes to the status of "domestic dependent nations", undermining their sovereignty and legitimizing federal encroachment.[32] These legal frameworks entrenched European notions of exclusive sovereignty while denying Indigenous systems of shared governance and relational territory. When compared to economic theories, these divergences become sharper. Neoclassical economics assumes clearly defined property rights and demarcated boundaries as prerequisites for efficiency and the prevention of overuse.[33] This logic paralleled European legal doctrines that sought to individualize and commodify land. Yet Indigenous practices, such as rotational agriculture, shared hunting territories, and overlapping clan-based rights, demonstrated that fluid and collective systems could manage resources sustainably over centuries.[34] Communist systems similarly denied Indigenous relational sovereignty, but instead of privatizing land, collectivization in the Soviet Union and China subsumed Indigenous territories into state ownership. This replaced communal autonomy with bureaucratic centralization, often leading to ecological degradation and cultural erasure.[35] Both neoclassical and communist models thus subordinated Indigenous governance to external ideologies of land control, disregarding the relational and fluid understandings at the heart of Indigenous systems. The imposition of European territorial frameworks has had enduring consequences. By redefining sovereignty as absolute and territorial, European empires justified dispossession, transformed landscapes into commodities, and undermined Indigenous governance. Contemporary struggles for recognition, such as native title in Australia, land restitution in Canada, and constitutional reforms in Bolivia, are not simply legal claims but fundamental challenges to the Westphalian order. They represent efforts to reassert relational sovereignty in a global system that remains dominated by rigid territorial logics.

[32] Wilkins, D.E. and Lomawaima, K.T. (2001). Uneven Ground: American Indian Sovereignty and Federal Law. Norman: University of Oklahoma Press.

[33] Demsetz, H. (1967). 'Toward a Theory of Property Rights', American Economic Review, 57(2), pp. 347–359.

[34] Ostrom, E. (1990). Governing the Commons: The Evolution of Institutions for Collective Action. Cambridge: Cambridge University Press.

[35] Wegren, S. (1998). Agriculture and the State in Soviet and Post-Soviet Russia. Pittsburgh: University of Pittsburgh Press.

2.4 *The Role of Alliances and Diplomacy in Indigenous Governance*

Indigenous governance systems were not confined to localized decision-making but extended into sophisticated forms of diplomacy and alliance-building that managed inter-tribal relations and responded to external threats. Unlike European diplomacy, which was codified through treaties between sovereign states under the Westphalian model, Indigenous diplomacy was rooted in reciprocity, gift-giving, and ceremonial practices that emphasized relationship-building over rigid territorial agreements. For example, the Haudenosaunee (Iroquois) Confederacy utilized wampum belts not only as symbolic records of treaties but also as living instruments of accountability, ensuring that agreements were embedded in shared memory and moral obligation rather than static legal documents.[36] Gift-giving and exchange were central to Indigenous diplomatic practices. In the Pacific Northwest, potlatch ceremonies reinforced alliances between communities, redistributing wealth while affirming obligations of mutual support.[37] Similarly, in the Great Plains, peace and war alliances were often negotiated through ceremonial exchanges that recognized the interconnectedness of communities and ecosystems.[38] These systems reflected a relational ontology, where diplomacy was inseparable from social cohesion and ecological stewardship. European colonizers exploited these traditions of alliance-making to expand control. During the French and Indian War (1754–1763), both French and British authorities courted Indigenous coalitions, promising trade goods and military support in exchange for loyalty.[39] While Indigenous nations such as the Huron and Mohawk engaged strategically, switching alliances when advantageous, the imbalance of power and European manipulation ultimately weakened Indigenous sovereignty. The pattern repeated globally: in Africa, European colonial powers deepened divisions by manipulating

[36] Lyons, O., Mohawk, J., Deloria, V., Hauptman, L.M., Berman, H., Grinde, D.A., Shaaf, R. and Wilkinson, C. (1992). Exiled in the Land of the Free: Democracy, Indian Nations and the U.S. Constitution. Santa Fe: Clear Light Publishers.

[37] Codere, H. (1950) Fighting with Property: A Study of Kwakiutl Potlatching and Warfare, 1792–1930. Locust Valley, NY: J. J. Augustin.

[38] Fowler, C.S. (1986) 'Subsistence' (or relevant chapter by Fowler), in d'Azevedo, W.L. (ed.) Handbook of North American Indians, Vol. 11: Great Basin. Washington, DC: Smithsonian Institution.

[39] Dowd, G.E. (2002) War under Heaven: Pontiac, the Indian Nations, and the British Empire. Baltimore: Johns Hopkins University Press.

customary alliances and rivalries to entrench indirect rule.[40] In economic terms, Indigenous diplomacy challenges the assumptions of neoclassical economics. Where economic theory presumes that rational actors engage in exchange to maximize self-interest, Indigenous diplomatic systems emphasized reciprocity, redistribution, and the preservation of long-term relationships over immediate gain.[41] By contrast, communist systems subordinated diplomacy to state-centric internationalism, often forcing Indigenous nations into centrally determined alliances, as seen in the Soviet Union's treatment of Indigenous Siberian groups whose political autonomy was erased under collectivization.[42] In both capitalist and communist systems, Indigenous forms of diplomacy were marginalized, yet their endurance illustrates the resilience of relational governance. Contemporary Indigenous diplomacy continues to draw on these traditions. The Sámi Parliaments of Norway, Sweden, and Finland, for example, serve as institutionalized forms of Indigenous diplomacy, negotiating transboundary rights to reindeer herding, land use, and cultural preservation across nation-state borders.[43] Similarly, Indigenous representatives at the United Nations Permanent Forum on Indigenous Issues have adapted traditional diplomatic principles of consensus and collective advocacy to global institutions, pressing for recognition of Indigenous rights under international law.[44] These modern practices reveal continuity: Indigenous diplomacy remains rooted in relational sovereignty while engaging with new arenas of governance, challenging the dominance of Westphalian frameworks and contributing to the pluralization of global political order.

[40] Mamdani, M. (1996) Citizen and Subject: Contemporary Africa and the Legacy of Late Colonialism. Princeton, NJ: Princeton University Press.

[41] Mauss, M. (1990 [1925]) The Gift: The Form and Reason for Exchange in Archaic Societies. London: Routledge.

[42] Fondahl, G. (1998) Gaining Ground? Evenkis, Land, and Reform in Southeastern Siberia. Boulder, CO: Westview Press.

[43] Josefsen, E. (2010) 'The Saami and the National Parliaments: Channels for Political Influence', Geneva: Inter-Parliamentary Union and UNDP.

[44] Anaya, J. (2004) Indigenous Peoples in International Law. 2nd edn. New York: Oxford University Press.

2.5 Governance in Practice: Indigenous Responses to Imperial Encroachment

Indigenous governance systems demonstrated remarkable adaptability in the face of European imperial expansion. Far from collapsing under colonial pressures, many Indigenous nations reconfigured their political structures to preserve autonomy and cultural continuity. The Lakota Sioux, for example, developed highly mobile governance institutions that enabled them to adapt to the military and economic challenges of European westward expansion in North America. Organized around tiyospaye (extended family groups), leadership was situational and merit-based, allowing for flexibility in decision-making during conflict and migration.[45] This decentralized model stood in stark contrast to the hierarchical structures of the U.S. government, yet it provided the Lakota with resilience in resisting encroachment until the late nineteenth century, most notably during conflicts such as the Battle of the Little Bighorn in 1876. In Aotearoa/New Zealand, the Māori demonstrated similar adaptability by reasserting tribal authority in response to British colonization. The creation of the Kingitanga (Māori King Movement) in 1858 united previously autonomous iwi (tribes) under a single symbolic authority to resist land sales and colonial domination.[46] This adaptation blended traditional chiefly authority with a centralized leadership model designed to negotiate with colonial power on equal terms. Although ultimately undermined by British military campaigns and land confiscations, the Kingitanga survives today as a vital cultural and political institution, exemplifying the endurance of Indigenous governance under settler colonialism. These adaptations can be contrasted with the logics of neoclassical economics, which assumes that efficient governance arises through centralized authority and clearly defined property rights.[47] The Lakota and Māori examples illustrate instead that decentralization and fluid alliances could provide resilience and efficiency under conditions of external pressure. Similarly, communist governance models

[45] Ostler, J. (2004). The Plains Sioux and U.S. Colonialism from Lewis and Clark to Wounded Knee. Cambridge: Cambridge University Press.

[46] Belich, J. (1996). Making Peoples: A History of the New Zealanders from Polynesian Settlement to the End of the Nineteenth Century. Auckland: Penguin.

[47] Demsetz, H. (1967). 'Toward a Theory of Property Rights', American Economic Review, 57(2), pp. 347–359.

imposed centralized, state-led authority in Indigenous regions, such as the Soviet collectivization of Siberian reindeer herders, which dismantled clan-based governance and eroded cultural autonomy.[48] In both capitalist and communist contexts, Indigenous governance principles, such as collective stewardship, distributed authority, and consensus-building, were dismissed as "inefficient", yet historical evidence shows they enabled survival, adaptation, and even resistance. The survival of Indigenous governance principles despite displacement and coercion underscores their resilience. Institutions such as the Lakota tiyospaye and the Māori Kingitanga reveal that Indigenous nations did not passively succumb to imperial authority but strategically reconfigured their governance to preserve autonomy. These practices highlight a vital comparative insight: while European models sought to impose sovereignty through rigid centralization, Indigenous governance thrived through flexibility, adaptability, and relational forms of authority that remain influential in contemporary struggles for self-determination.

3 How Centralized Political Systems Enabled European Colonial Efforts

3.1 Military Power and Resource Mobilization

The emergence of centralized political systems in early modern Europe provided the institutional framework for large-scale colonial expansion. Strong states were able to mobilize both human and financial resources in ways that smaller polities could not. As noted, "war made the state, and the state made war".[49] The development of professional standing armies and naval fleets depended on the extraction of regular taxation and the centralization of fiscal capacity. Unlike Indigenous governance systems, which typically organized defence through kinship networks and seasonal alliances, European states institutionalized permanent military structures supported by bureaucratic administrations. The Spanish empire illustrates the fiscal-military state at its height. Silver from Potosí (modern Bolivia) and Zacatecas (Mexico) underpinned Spain's imperial finances. Between

[48] Fondahl, G. (1998). Gaining Ground? Evenkis, Land, and Reform in Southeastern Siberia. Boulder, CO: Westview Press.

[49] Tilly, C. (1990). Coercion, Capital, and European States, AD 990–1990. Oxford: Blackwell.

Table 1 Estimated silver production from the Americas, 1500–1650

Region	*Approx. Output (tons of silver)*	*% to royal treasury*
Potosí (Bolivia)	60,000	~33
Zacatecas (Mexico)	40,000	~33
Other mines	50,000	~33
Total	150,000	~33 (~50,000 tons)

Source Bakewell (1984), Hamilton (1934)

1500 and 1650, an estimated 150,000 tons of silver were extracted from the Americas, with approximately one-third flowing directly into the royal treasury, Table 1.[50,51] These revenues financed Habsburg wars in Europe and sustained Spain's vast standing army. Portugal similarly depended on wealth from Brazil's sugar plantations and later gold mines to underwrite its naval expansion into Asia and Africa.[52]

Britain and France followed similar trajectories. Britain's introduction of excise taxes, customs duties, and the creation of public credit markets allowed it to sustain wars against France while financing colonial ventures. By the mid-eighteenth century, Britain's Royal Navy had become the largest in the world, with naval expenditures accounting for more than half of state spending during wartime.[53] A dominance rooted in its unique fiscal, institutional, and geopolitical advantages. The development of the "fiscal-military state" enabled Britain to outspend rivals through a combination of excise taxes, customs duties, and an innovative system of public credit, which allowed long-term borrowing to sustain naval expansion.[54] The "innovative system of public credit" refers to the financial revolution of late seventeenth- and eighteenth-century Britain, which fundamentally

[50] Bakewell, P. (1984). Silver Mining and Society in Colonial Mexico: Zacatecas 1546–1700. Cambridge: Cambridge University Press.

[51] Hamilton, E.J. (1934). American Treasure and the Price Revolution in Spain, 1501–1650. Cambridge, MA: Harvard University Press.

[52] Bethencourt, F. (2007). The Portuguese Oceanic Expansion, 1400–1800. Aldershot: Ashgate.

[53] Brewer, J. (1989). The Sinews of Power: War, Money and the English State, 1688–1783. London: Unwin Hyman.

[54] Brewer, J. (1989). The Sinews of Power: War, Money and the English State, 1688–1783. London: Unwin Hyman.

transformed how the state financed war and naval expansion. Prior to this shift, monarchs relied on short-term loans from wealthy individuals or coercive exactions, which were often unreliable and prone to default. After the Glorious Revolution of 1688, however, Britain developed a durable framework of institutions that secured creditor confidence. Central to this system was the creation of the Bank of England in 1694, which provided substantial loans to the Crown in exchange for the right to issue banknotes, creating a stable mechanism for long-term borrowing. The introduction of consols (consolidated annuities), a form of permanent government bond paying fixed interest but never requiring repayment of principal, allowed the state to borrow indefinitely. Crucially, the establishment of a funded national debt, supported by predictable streams of excise and customs taxation, ensured that interest payments were guaranteed, reassuring investors of repayment. Finally, parliamentary oversight of fiscal policy enhanced creditor trust by preventing arbitrary repudiation of debts, in contrast to absolutist monarchies. These innovations enabled Britain to borrow at relatively low interest rates and on an unprecedented scale. By the mid-eighteenth century, Britain's national debt exceeded 150 percent of GDP, yet confidence remained strong, allowing the state to maintain and expand the Royal Navy far more effectively than its rivals.[55,56] In contrast, France, despite its larger population and greater tax potential, failed to construct an equally credible system of public credit. The French monarchy continued to rely heavily on tax farming and short-term loans from financiers, with weak institutional guarantees and frequent defaults, which undermined investor confidence.[57,58] Unlike Britain's parliamentary system, the absence of credible checks on royal authority meant creditors feared arbitrary confiscation or repudiation. As a result, France faced higher borrowing costs and was unable to sustain prolonged naval investment at the same scale as Britain. During the

[55] Brewer, J. (1989). The Sinews of Power: War, Money and the English State, 1688–1783. London: Unwin Hyman.

[56] Neal, L. (1990). The Rise of Financial Capitalism: International Capital Markets in the Age of Reason. Cambridge: Cambridge University Press.

[57] Bonney, R. (1995). The King's Debts: Finance and Politics in France 1589–1661. Oxford: Oxford University Press.

[58] White, E.N. (2010). 'Was There a Solution to the Ancien Régime's Financial Dilemma?', Journal of Economic History, 50(3), pp. 545–568.

Seven Years' War, for instance, France struggled to finance fleet construction, contributing directly to British naval dominance and the erosion of French imperial power.[59] The failure to replicate Britain's financial revolution thus crippled France's ability to project maritime power, despite its demographic and economic advantages. British naval supremacy was further reinforced by the integration of commerce and strategy: the Royal Navy protected lucrative Atlantic trade routes and colonial markets, which in turn financed further naval investment.[60] Geopolitical insularity gave Britain a structural incentive to invest more in sea power than in continental armies, unlike France or Spain, whose resources were tied down by large standing armies.[61] Institutional reforms, such as the professionalization of the officer corps and improved naval administration, also provided Britain with organizational advantages that outstripped rivals hampered by corruption and inefficiency.[62] By sustaining naval expenditures that often exceeded half of total wartime budgets, Britain forged a system where financial capacity, trade protection, and naval power formed a mutually reinforcing cycle, securing its global maritime dominance.[63,64] (Table 2).

Table 2 British government expenditure by function, c. 1756–1783

Category	*% of Total Expenditure*
Navy	55
Army	25
Debt service	15
Civil government	5

Source Brewer (1989)

[59] Baugh, D.A. (2011). The Global Seven Years War, 1754–1763: Britain and France in a Great Power Contest. Harlow: Pearson.

[60] Rodger, N.A.M. (2004). The Command of the Ocean: A Naval History of Britain, 1649–1815. London: Allen Lane.

[61] Kennedy, P. (1987). The Rise and Fall of the Great Powers: Economic Change and Military Conflict from 1500 to 2000. New York: Random House.

[62] Baugh, D.A. (2011). The Global Seven Years War, 1754–1763: Britain and France in a Great Power Contest. Harlow: Pearson.

[63] Brewer, J. (1989). The Sinews of Power: War, Money and the English State, 1688–1783. London: Unwin Hyman.

[64] Rodger, N.A.M. (2004). The Command of the Ocean: A Naval History of Britain, 1649–1815. London: Allen Lane.

Comparatively, this pattern of resource mobilization diverges from neoclassical economics, which assumes that efficient markets and voluntary exchange allocate resources optimally. The fiscal-military state reveals instead how coercive taxation and imperial extraction funded militaries that did not conform to "market efficiency" but ensured strategic dominance. Similarly, communist states in the twentieth century mobilized resources for military purposes through centralized planning. The Soviet Union devoted an estimated 15–17% of GDP to defence spending in the 1980s, compared to about 5% in the U.S.[65] This mirrors early modern Europe in subordinating domestic welfare to military capacity. Indigenous governance, by contrast, mobilized resources for collective defence only as needed, often relying on kinship-based militias, seasonal alliances, and mobility rather than permanent militarization.[66] Thus, the centralization of fiscal and military power was decisive in enabling European colonial expansion. By institutionalizing taxation, public debt, and standing armies, European states projected power across oceans and continents, reshaping global political economies. Unlike neoclassical or Indigenous systems, this was a model built on coercion and extraction, a logic later replicated in communist regimes, which privileged expansion and military dominance over sustainability.

3.2 Bureaucracy and Administration as Tools of Control

The expansion of European colonial empires relied not only on military force but also on the construction of bureaucratic institutions that enabled the governance of vast and diverse territories. The rise of the modern "fiscal-military" state in Europe was accompanied by an equally important administrative revolution, in which colonial offices, hierarchies, and legal frameworks were created to translate imperial authority into

[65] Wegren, S. (1998). Agriculture and the State in Soviet and Post-Soviet Russia. Pittsburgh: University of Pittsburgh Press.

[66] Simpson, A. (2014). Mohawk Interruptus: Political Life Across the Borders of Settler States. Durham: Duke University Press.

everyday control.[67,68] In British India, the centralized civil service established first by the East India Company and later expanded under the Crown systematically subordinated Indigenous institutions of governance, law, and education. The Mughal system of revenue collection, based on zamindars (inherited) and jagirdars (appointed) who were key landholding and revenue-collecting elites under the Mughal Empire in India, was transformed by the Permanent Settlement of 1793 in Bengal, which recast zamindars as tax collectors for the Company and eroded reciprocal obligations between the Mughal rulers and cultivators.[69] Village-level panchayats, which had traditionally mediated disputes, allocated land, and organized irrigation on the basis of consensus and community norms, were displaced by colonial courts and revenue officers that imposed hierarchical authority.[70] Similarly, Indigenous legal traditions, plural and flexible in their application, were codified into rigid "Anglo-Hindu" and "Anglo-Muhammadan" law filtered through English categories, while the Indian Penal Code of 1860 imposed a uniform criminal code that curtailed the authority of qazis (Muslim judges trained in Islamic law (sharia)) and pandits (Hindu legal scholars and interpreters of dharmaśāstra (Hindu religious law)).[71] Caste councils (jati panchayats), once central to regulating kinship, trade, and local order, lost legitimacy as colonial courts monopolized dispute resolution and delegitimized customary sanctions.[72] Indigenous educational systems, pathshalas, madrasas, and gurukuls, which transmitted not only literacy but also cultural and spiritual worldviews, were subordinated to colonial curricula privileging English and Western science, particularly after Macaulay's 1835 "Minute on Indian

[67] Brewer, J. (1989). The Sinews of Power: War, Money and the English State, 1688–1783. London: Unwin Hyman.

[68] Tilly, C. (1990). Coercion, Capital, and European States, AD 990–1990. Oxford: Blackwell.

[69] Washbrook, D.A. (1981). 'Law, State and Agrarian Society in Colonial India'. Modern Asian Studies, 15(3), pp. 649–721.

[70] Cohn, B.S. (1996). Colonialism and Its Forms of Knowledge: The British in India. Princeton, NJ: Princeton University Press.

[71] Derrett, J.D.M. (1968). Religion, Law and the State in India. London: Faber & Faber.

[72] Dirks, N.B. (2001). Castes of Mind: Colonialism and the Making of Modern India. Princeton, NJ: Princeton University Press.

Education".[73] In contrast to these plural, decentralized, and consensus-based systems, colonial bureaucracy sought uniformity and centralization, embedding a legal and administrative order that prioritized extractive efficiency and state authority over social cohesion and cultural continuity. The introduction of the Indian Penal Code (1860) and the replacement of customary practices with English-style jurisprudence illustrate how colonial bureaucracies sought to standardize and universalize governance in the service of imperial power.[74] Similarly, in Africa, the British relied on the Indian Civil Service model to build administrative cadres that both extracted resources and mediated relations with Indigenous populations, often using "indirect rule" under colonial officials' supervision.[75] The French adopted a different but equally intrusive system in West Africa, emphasizing "direct rule" that imposed metropolitan laws and dismantled customary legal orders. The establishment of cercles (administrative districts) and the authority of colonial governors subordinated local chiefs, integrating them into a centralized system that denied Indigenous autonomy.[76] These administrative hierarchies enabled the French to enforce taxation, mobilize labour, and regulate trade, consolidating the extraction of wealth to the metropole. Such systems replaced the plural and adaptive nature of Indigenous governance, which relied on negotiation, kinship ties, and flexible customary norms.

From the perspective of neoclassical economics, colonial bureaucracies appear as rational instruments for reducing "transaction costs" by imposing uniform rules and predictable enforcement mechanisms.[77] Yet in practice, they often generated inefficiencies, corruption, and resistance, as Indigenous societies resisted the destruction of customary norms that had sustained social cohesion. In British India, the introduction

[73] Bayly, C.A. (1996). Empire and Information: Intelligence Gathering and Social Communication in India, 1780–1870. Cambridge: Cambridge University Press.

[74] Cohn, B.S. (1996). Colonialism and Its Forms of Knowledge: The British in India. Princeton, NJ: Princeton University Press.

[75] Mamdani, M. (1996). Citizen and Subject: Contemporary Africa and the Legacy of Late Colonialism. Princeton, NJ: Princeton University Press.

[76] Crowder, M. (1964). 'Indirect Rule: French and British Style'. Africa: Journal of the International African Institute, 34(3), pp. 197–205.

[77] North, D.C. (1990). Institutions, Institutional Change and Economic Performance. Cambridge: Cambridge University Press.

of the Permanent Settlement of Bengal (1793) created new opportunities for exploitation. Zamindars, tasked with remitting fixed revenues to the colonial state, frequently overtaxed peasants, using the threat of eviction to extract surplus. Colonial officials turned a blind eye so long as revenue quotas were met, while court clerks (munshis) often accepted bribes to delay hearings or falsify documents, undermining trust in the new judicial system.[78,79] Similarly, in French West Africa, the system of direct rule imposed rigid tax obligations without reference to customary norms. Chiefs appointed under colonial authority often inflated head tax demands, keeping the surplus for themselves, while French administrators tolerated graft in exchange for compliance and labour recruitment.[80,81] In both contexts, corruption thrived because colonial bureaucracies dismantled local institutions of accountability, replacing consensus-based mechanisms with hierarchical systems that prioritized extraction and obedience. Under communist regimes, a similar drive towards centralization and administrative uniformity emerged. In the Soviet Union, for instance, Indigenous peoples of Siberia were integrated into centrally planned bureaucratic structures, with collectivization and state law displacing clan-based governance.[82] In both colonial and communist contexts, bureaucratic centralization subordinated Indigenous governance to overarching systems that prioritized extraction, uniformity, and state authority over local autonomy and sustainability. Thus, colonial bureaucracies served as the everyday machinery of empire. By embedding European legal and administrative practices in colonized territories, they extended imperial sovereignty into the most local domains of life, undermining Indigenous governance while normalizing state dominance as the only legitimate form of political authority.

[78] Sarkar, S. (1983). Modern India: 1885–1947. Delhi: Macmillan.

[79] Cohn, B.S. (1996). Colonialism and Its Forms of Knowledge: The British in India. Princeton, NJ: Princeton University Press.

[80] Crowder, M. (1964). 'Indirect Rule: French and British Style'. Africa: Journal of the International African Institute, 34(3), pp. 197–205.

[81] Mamdani, M. (1996). Citizen and Subject: Contemporary Africa and the Legacy of Late Colonialism. Princeton, NJ: Princeton University Press.

[82] Fondahl, G. (1998). Gaining Ground? Evenkis, Land, and Reform in Southeastern Siberia. Boulder, CO: Westview Press.

3.3 Economic Centralization and the Rise of Mercantilism

Economic centralization was a defining feature of European imperial expansion in the early modern period, with mercantilism providing the ideological and practical framework through which states mobilized resources for colonial conquest. Mercantilist policy viewed global trade as a zero-sum competition in which state power depended on accumulating bullion and controlling markets. Centralized monarchies such as Spain, Portugal, and the Dutch Republic used monopolies, tariffs, and regulated trading companies to extract wealth from overseas colonies and funnel it into national treasuries.[83] Spain's control of silver mines in Potosí (in present-day Bolivia) exemplifies this system: vast quantities of bullion, estimated at over 150,000 tons between the 16th and 18th centuries, were shipped to Europe and used to finance Habsburg imperial ambitions. However, the influx of silver also produced inflationary pressures, the so-called "Price Revolution", revealing both the power and the limits of resource extraction as a basis for state power.[84] The "Price Revolution" refers to the sustained period of inflation that swept across Europe between the late 15th and early 17th centuries, most dramatically between 1500 and 1650. Its most significant driver was the massive influx of precious metals, especially silver, from Spain's American colonies, notably the mines at Potosí (modern Bolivia) and Zacatecas (Mexico). Estimates suggest that by 1600 Spain had imported more than 150,000 tons of silver, much of which entered European markets through Seville.[85] As bullion flooded Europe, the supply of money vastly expanded while the supply of goods and agricultural production remained relatively fixed. This imbalance created sustained upward pressure on prices.

The implications were profound. On the one hand, the Price Revolution enhanced state revenues in the short term. Because monarchs like the Spanish Habsburgs collected taxes in nominal terms, they initially benefited from increased cash flows tied to bullion imports. This allowed Spain to fund its imperial ambitions, including wars in the Netherlands,

[83] Findlay, R. and O'Rourke, K.H. (2007). Power and Plenty: Trade, War, and the World Economy in the Second Millennium. Princeton, NJ: Princeton University Press.

[84] Hamilton, E.J. (1934). American Treasure and the Price Revolution in Spain, 1501–1650. Cambridge, MA: Harvard University Press.

[85] Hamilton, E.J. (1934). American Treasure and the Price Revolution in Spain, 1501–1650. Cambridge, MA: Harvard University Press.

Italy, and against the Ottoman Empire. On the other hand, the inflation eroded the real value of fixed incomes, disproportionately harming peasants, wage labourers, and small landholders while benefiting landowners and merchants who could pass higher prices onto consumers. The erosion of purchasing power generated social unrest and widened inequality.[86] Crucially, the inflationary impact exposed the limits of resource extraction as a sustainable foundation for imperial power. Spain became heavily reliant on silver imports to finance military expenditures, but much of the bullion quickly flowed out to northern Europe, especially to Dutch and English merchants and financiers, who controlled trade networks and provided credit to the Spanish crown. By the early seventeenth century, Spain's dependence on silver revenues had created deep structural vulnerabilities in its economy. Between 1503 and 1660, Spain imported an estimated 16,000 tons of silver and 181 tons of gold from the Americas, with silver from Potosí (Bolivia) and Zacatecas (Mexico) forming the backbone of royal finance.[87] This bullion was crucial in funding Spain's imperial military commitments, from the Eighty Years' War with the Dutch (1568–1648) to its campaigns in Italy and against the Ottoman Empire. However, the very scale of reliance led to fragility. The Spanish Crown declared bankruptcies in 1557, 1575, 1596, and again in 1607, each time suspending payments on its debts to Genoese and other European bankers.[88] At the same time, the flood of silver drove the Price Revolution, where prices across Europe rose approximately sixfold between 1500 and 1650.[89] While Spanish landowners initially benefited from higher rents, the inflation eroded the real wages of urban workers and destabilized peasant subsistence. Worse, Spain's own manufacturing base declined: the easy flow of bullion allowed the

[86] Munro, J. (2003). 'The Monetary Origins of the "Price Revolution": South German Silver Mining, Merchant-Banking, and Venetian Commerce, 1470–1540'. In: J. Munro, Textiles, Merchants and Money in Late Medieval and Early Modern Europe. Aldershot: Ashgate.

[87] Barrett, W. (1983). World Bullion Flows, 1450–1800. In: J.F. Richards (ed.), Precious Metals in the Later Medieval and Early Modern Worlds. Durham, NC: Carolina Academic Press, pp. 224–254.

[88] Drelichman, M. and Voth, H-J. (2014). Lending to the Borrower from Hell: Debt, Taxes, and Default in the Age of Philip II. Princeton, NJ: Princeton University Press.

[89] Hamilton, E.J. (1934). American Treasure and the Price Revolution in Spain, 1501–1650. Cambridge, MA: Harvard University Press.

monarchy and nobility to import luxury goods, woollens, and armaments from northern Europe rather than fostering domestic industry. By the seventeenth century, regions such as Castile faced economic stagnation and depopulation, while cities in the Low Countries and England expanded their manufacturing sectors, financed in part by silver that had passed through Spain.[90] Thus, bullion extraction sustained Spanish imperial grandeur in the short term but undermined its long-term fiscal stability and industrial competitiveness, leaving the empire increasingly dependent on foreign creditors and suppliers. Thus, while silver fuelled Spain's rise as the first global empire, the Price Revolution revealed the structural weaknesses of an economy overly dependent on bullion rather than productive development. However, the Dutch East India Company (VOC) represented a different model of economic centralization. Granted monopoly rights by the Dutch state, the VOC combined public and private capital to dominate spice trade networks in Southeast Asia. Its ability to raise funds through the Amsterdam stock exchange enabled sustained military and naval investment, illustrating how financial innovation could underpin mercantilist strategies.[91] In both Spain and the Dutch Republic, economic centralization rested on the state's ability to regulate trade, impose tariffs, and direct colonial extraction, ensuring that imperial centres captured the benefits of overseas expansion. From the perspective of neoclassical economics, mercantilist monopolies appear inefficient, generating deadweight losses by restricting competition and distorting prices.[92] Yet within their historical context, these policies reduced uncertainty, secured revenue streams, and ensured the predictable flow of resources necessary to sustain fiscal-military states. By contrast, communist economic centralization in the twentieth century shared with mercantilism the reliance on state monopolies and the suppression of market mechanisms, but its goals differed. In the Soviet Union, central planning subordinated resource allocation to ideological aims of industrialization and class transformation, often at the expense of efficiency

[90] Flynn, D.O. and Giráldez, A. (1995). 'Born with a "Silver Spoon": The Origin of World Trade in 1571'. Journal of World History, 6(2), pp. 201–221.

[91] Israel, J.I. (1989). Dutch Primacy in World Trade, 1585–1740. Oxford: Clarendon Press.

[92] North, D.C. (1990). Institutions, Institutional Change and Economic Performance. Cambridge: Cambridge University Press.

and local autonomy.[93] The comparison highlights how both mercantilist and communist systems used economic centralization to project power, though with divergent rationales and outcomes. For Indigenous peoples, however, both systems meant dispossession: mercantilism commodified land and resources for extraction, while communist collectivization eroded traditional forms of stewardship and subsistence.

3.4 *Religious and Ideological Centralization*

Religious and ideological centralization was a core dimension of European imperial expansion, functioning not only as a moral justification for conquest but also as a practical mechanism of political control. Christianity was presented as a "civilizing" force, yet in practice missionary activities frequently served to undermine Indigenous governance structures and social cohesion. The Spanish missions in Latin America, most notably the Franciscan and Jesuit reductions in Paraguay and Mexico, aimed to convert Indigenous populations while simultaneously restructuring their communities into grid-like towns (reducciones) designed for surveillance and taxation.[94,95] Conversion was often accompanied by the suppression of Indigenous spiritual practices, festivals, and land-based rituals, which weakened the cultural legitimacy of local leadership. Similarly, in Portuguese territories such as Goa and Brazil, the Inquisition and Jesuit missions sought to eradicate "pagan" practices, imposing European legal and moral norms through schools, churches, and courts.[96] The institutionalization of Christianity thus reinforced colonial bureaucracies, embedding religious conformity into governance. From the perspective of neoclassical economics, these missionary interventions appear as a form of social engineering designed to reduce "transaction costs" for empire. By homogenizing belief systems and enforcing obedience to Christian institutions, colonial powers sought to minimize resistance and facilitate

[93] Wegren, S.K. (1998). Agriculture and the State in Soviet and Post-Soviet Russia. Pittsburgh, PA: University of Pittsburgh Press.

[94] Pagden, A. (1995). Lords of All the World: Ideologies of Empire in Spain, Britain and France c.1500–c.1800. New Haven, CT: Yale University Press.

[95] Wilde, G. (2009). Religious Power and Everyday Life in Jesuit Missions: The Guaraní and the Making of Colonial South America. Durham, NC: Duke University Press.

[96] Boxer, C.R. (1969). The Portuguese Seaborne Empire, 1415–1825. London: Hutchinson.

resource extraction.[97] Yet this suppression of plural Indigenous practices also destroyed informal institutions of cooperation and reciprocity that had governed resource management and social life. In this sense, religious centralization imposed hidden efficiency losses, as communities were destabilized and alienated from their own cultural frameworks. Comparisons with communist regimes highlight similar dynamics of ideological centralization: in the Soviet Union, for instance, the suppression of religious institutions and local identities under state atheism mirrored the missionary destruction of Indigenous governance, as both subordinated cultural diversity to a centralizing political project.[98] Empirically, the costs and consequences of this religious centralization were stark. In colonial Mexico, by 1650 more than 90% of the Indigenous population had been baptized, but this did not reflect voluntary acceptance of Christianity so much as the coercive integration of Indigenous people into parish systems that doubled as taxation and labour registers.[99] In Brazil, Jesuit missions became major landholders, exploiting Indigenous labour under the guise of religious education.[100] Religious and ideological centralization thus served imperial expansion not only by disciplining subject populations but also by providing empires with an enduring justification for dispossession, which continues to reverberate in debates over cultural erasure and Indigenous rights today.

3.5 Technological Coordination and Expansion

The expansion of European empires from the fifteenth century onwards was underpinned by the capacity of centralized states to coordinate technological innovation and exploration. Maritime powers such as Portugal and Spain invested heavily in navigation, shipbuilding, and cartography, providing the infrastructure for long-distance oceanic voyages. Centralized European states were able to channel resources into technological

[97] North, D.C. (1990). Institutions, Institutional Change and Economic Performance. Cambridge: Cambridge University Press.

[98] Wegren, S.K. (1998). Agriculture and the State in Soviet and Post-Soviet Russia. Pittsburgh, PA: University of Pittsburgh Press.

[99] Taylor, W.B. (1991996). Magistrates of the Sacred: Priests and Parishioners in Eighteenth-Century Mexico. Stanford, CA: Stanford University Press.

[100] Alden, D. (1996). The Making of an Enterprise: The Society of Jesus in Portugal, Its Empire, and Beyond, 1540–1750. Stanford, CA: Stanford University Press.

innovations that transformed global navigation, warfare, and imperial administration. Maritime advances such as the caravel and later the galleon gave Portugal and Spain the ability to sustain transoceanic voyages and protect bullion fleets, while instruments like the astrolabe and magnetic compass enabled open-ocean navigation with greater precision. Cartographic breakthroughs, most notably the Mercator projection (1569) and the establishment of centralized map-making institutions such as Spain's Casa de la Contratación (1503), provided empires with a systematic way to claim and administer overseas territories. In naval warfare, the mounting of heavy cannon on ships and the standardization of muskets revolutionized European military dominance, while in Britain, innovations such as Harrison's marine chronometer (mid-eighteenth century) solved the "longitude problem", reducing maritime risk and enhancing the efficiency of global trade. These developments were not isolated scientific achievements but products of state coordination and long-term investment, which allowed imperial powers to outcompete rivals and subordinate Indigenous knowledge systems such as Polynesian navigation or Inca resource coordination (Table 3).

Similarly, the Spanish monarchy financed expeditions like that of Columbus in 1492 and Magellan's circumnavigation in 1519–1522, projects that required coordination between royal treasuries, naval engineers, and international financiers.[101] By the eighteenth century, technological coordination had expanded beyond maritime exploration to include scientific mapping and surveying. The British Admiralty sponsored expeditions such as Captain James Cook's voyages (1768–1779), which not only claimed territories but also generated vast amounts of cartographic and ethnographic knowledge. Such expeditions linked the state to emerging scientific institutions like the Royal Society, reflecting how imperial expansion and the Enlightenment were mutually reinforcing.[102] This centralization of knowledge production gave imperial powers a strategic advantage: Indigenous cartographies and navigational systems were often relational and ecological, prioritizing landmarks,

[101] Pagden, A. (1995). Lords of All the World: Ideologies of Empire in Spain, Britain and France c.1500–c.1800. New Haven, CT: Yale University Press.

[102] Gascoigne, J. (2007). Encountering the Pacific in the Age of the Enlightenment. Cambridge: Cambridge University Press.

Table 3 Comparative table: Centralized technological advances in imperial expansion

Empire	*Key maritime innovations*	*Cartography & scientific coordination*	*Military/ weaponry advances*	*Strategic outcomes*
Portugal	Caravel design; adoption of lateen sails; early use of astrolabe	Navigation school at Sagres; early Atlantic charts	Fortified outposts (Ceuta, Goa) with artillery	Opened Sea routes around Africa; established early global trading empire
Spain	Galleon fleets for bullion transport; standardized oceanic routes	Casa de la Contratación (1503); Mercator projection (adopted)	Heavy cannon on ships; bastion fortifications in Havana, Manila	Dominated transatlantic trade; secured silver flows from Americas
Britain	Advanced shipbuilding; integration of cargo and warship design	Admiralty charts; Royal Society support; Harrison's chronometer	Standardized musket and cannon production	Long-term naval supremacy; global commercial dominance by eighteenth century

Source Author

kinship, and seasonal use of space.[103] By contrast, European mapping practices imposed fixed territorial grids and borders, legitimizing imperial claims in accordance with the emerging Westphalian system of sovereignty. From a neoclassical economic perspective, this coordination of technological innovation reduced transaction costs by improving navigation reliability, lowering the risks of long-distance trade, and standardizing information flows.[104] State patronage effectively subsidized exploration and military dominance, making imperial expansion more predictable and profitable. In comparison, under communist regimes,

[103] Harley, J.B. (2001). The New Nature of Maps: Essays in the History of Cartography. Baltimore, MD: Johns Hopkins University Press.

[104] North, D.C. (1990). Institutions, Institutional Change and Economic Performance. Cambridge: Cambridge University Press.

technological coordination was also centralized but often subordinated to ideological and industrial priorities rather than commercial expansion. The Soviet Union's rapid development of aerospace and military technology in the twentieth century exemplifies how centralized states could mobilize resources to achieve global projection of power, albeit without the commercial integration characteristic of mercantilist empires.[105] In both systems, centralization allowed states to marshal technological innovation towards political and strategic goals, though at the expense of suppressing local and Indigenous knowledge systems. The consequences of this dynamic were profound. Indigenous knowledge of navigation, such as the Polynesian stick charts used to cross the Pacific, or the Inca's quipu-based record-keeping for coordinating resources, was systematically marginalized or appropriated without recognition. For example, Captain James Cook's Pacific voyages relied heavily on the expertise of the Tahitian navigator Tupaia, whose detailed mental maps of hundreds of islands were central to the success of British exploration, yet European accounts framed these as scientific achievements of the Royal Navy.[106] Similarly, in the Andes, the Spanish initially exploited the quipu system (knotted cords for record-keeping) to manage tribute and resources, but gradually erased Indigenous record-keepers (quipucamayocs) from official governance, even as quipu logic influenced colonial administration.[107] In North America, Indigenous cartographic traditions such as the Chitimacha and Catawba deerskin maps informed treaty-making and territorial demarcations, but were later recast in European cartography without acknowledging their sources.[108] Even in the Arctic, British explorers depended on Inuit ecological knowledge of sea-ice and migration routes for survival, yet expedition reports attributed success to European bravery and technology.[109] These examples illustrate how

[105] Josephson, P.R. (1996). Red Atom: Russia's Nuclear Power Program from Stalin to Today. New York: W.H. Freeman.

[106] Finney, B. (1994). Voyage of Rediscovery: A Cultural Odyssey through Polynesia. Berkeley: University of California Press.

[107] Salomon, F. (2004). The Cord Keepers: Khipus and Cultural Life in a Peruvian Village. Durham, NC: Duke University Press.

[108] Harley, J.B. (2001). The New Nature of Maps: Essays in the History of Cartography. Baltimore, MD: Johns Hopkins University Press.

[109] Bravo, M. (1996). 'Ethnographic Navigation and the Geographies of Knowledge in the Arctic'. Arctic, 49(4), pp. 397–412.

Indigenous epistemologies were not only sidelined but also appropriated into imperial systems that claimed authority while erasing their original creators. European technological expansion thus illustrates how centralization not only advanced state power but also erased or subordinated alternative epistemologies of space and resource management.

4 Indigenous Movements for Self-Determination and Political Autonomy

4.1 Early Forms of Resistance to European Imperial Systems

Indigenous peoples across the globe mounted sustained resistance to European imperial systems from the very outset of colonial encroachment, drawing on both warfare and diplomacy to defend their autonomy. In North America, the Pueblo Revolt of 1680 stands as one of the most successful uprisings against Spanish domination. Pueblo communities coordinated a multi-village alliance under the leadership of Popé, driving Spanish settlers out of New Mexico for over a decade and reasserting traditional religious and political practices.[110] Similarly, King Philip's War (1675–1676), led by the Wampanoag sachem Metacom (known to the English as King Philip), united several Native American nations in New England against English settlers. Although brutally suppressed, the conflict inflicted proportionally higher casualties on colonists than any later American war, revealing the costs of dispossession and the intensity of Indigenous resistance.[111] In Africa, the Zulu kingdom under leaders such as Cetshwayo kaMpande resisted British imperial expansion during the Anglo-Zulu War of 1879. Despite eventual defeat, the Zulu demonstrated the capacity of Indigenous polities to mobilize disciplined armies and exploit terrain knowledge against technologically superior European forces.[112] In South America, Tupac Amaru II's rebellion (1780–1783) in the Andes mobilized tens of thousands of Indigenous and mestizo peasants against Spanish colonial rule, combining demands for lower tribute

[110] Knaut, A.L. (1995). The Pueblo Revolt of 1680: Conquest and Resistance in Seventeenth-Century New Mexico. Norman: University of Oklahoma Press.

[111] Lepore, J. (1998). The Name of War: King Philip's War and the Origins of American Identity. New York: Knopf.

[112] Laband, J. (1997). The Rise and Fall of the Zulu Nation. London: Arms and Armour Press.

burdens with appeals to Inca sovereignty.[113] In Africa's Portuguese and Dutch-controlled territories, Queen Nzinga of Ndongo and Matamba (seventeenth century) employed both guerrilla warfare and shrewd diplomacy, including alliances with the Dutch, to resist Portuguese enslavement and territorial encroachment.[114] Finally, in North America's Great Lakes region, Tecumseh, leader of the Shawnee, envisioned a pan-Indigenous confederacy to counter U.S. expansion in the early nineteenth century, rejecting the commodification of land in favour of collective sovereignty.[115] From the perspective of neoclassical economics, these resistance movements can be seen as rational responses to the economic displacement wrought by colonialism, particularly the erosion of access to land and resources that underpinned Indigenous livelihoods. The loss of property rights, as framed by colonial legal regimes, represented a catastrophic reduction in Indigenous welfare and spurred collective action to defend customary systems of ownership and reciprocity. By contrast, communist analyses have emphasized how Indigenous revolts reflected class struggles within colonial contexts, with leaders such as Tupac Amaru II articulating demands that fused anti-colonial nationalism with proto-socialist calls for redistribution.[116] Empirical evidence underscores the scale of resistance: in the Andes alone, Tupac Amaru's rebellion mobilized over 100,000 insurgents, and the Anglo-Zulu War at Isandlwana (1879) remains one of the rare Indigenous victories against a modern European army.[117] These cases reveal not only the resilience of Indigenous governance systems but also the global interconnectedness of resistance as a political economy of survival and defiance.

[113] Walker, C. (2014). The Tupac Amaru Rebellion. Cambridge, MA: Harvard University Press.

[114] Heywood, L.M. (2017). Njinga of Angola: Africa's Warrior Queen. Cambridge, MA: Harvard University Press.

[115] Edmunds, R.D. (2007). Tecumseh and the Quest for Indian Leadership. New York: Pearson Longman.

[116] Kay, C. (1982). 'Achievements and Contradictions of Agrarian Reform in Latin America'. Journal of Development Studies, 18(2), pp. 141–170.

[117] Laband, J. (1997). The Rise and Fall of the Zulu Nation. London: Arms and Armour Press.

4.2 *Twentieth-Century Movements for Political Autonomy*

The twentieth century marked a decisive transformation in Indigenous struggles for sovereignty, as grassroots uprisings gave way to organized political movements demanding recognition, autonomy, and self-determination. In North America, the Pan-Indian movement emerged in the early twentieth century as Indigenous leaders sought to transcend tribal divisions and unify their demands in response to U.S. and Canadian assimilationist policies. The founding of the National Congress of American Indians (1944) and later the American Indian Movement (AIM, 1968) reflected this shift towards mass mobilization, blending legal challenges with direct action protests, such as the occupation of Alcatraz (1969–1971) and the standoff at Wounded Knee (1973).[118] These movements reframed Indigenous issues not as isolated grievances but as structural questions of sovereignty and treaty rights, echoing broader struggles for racial justice during the Civil Rights era. In New Zealand, Maori land-rights campaigns intensified during the mid-twentieth century, culminating in the Waitangi Tribunal (established 1975), which provided a legal framework to address breaches of the Treaty of Waitangi. Movements such as the 1975 Maori Land March, led by Whina Cooper, spotlighted the ongoing alienation of Maori land and catalysed reforms that returned certain lands and financial compensation to iwi (tribes).[119] Meanwhile, in Africa, decolonization after World War II saw Indigenous and colonized peoples mobilize for independence through nationalist movements. Leaders such as Kwame Nkrumah in Ghana and Julius Nyerere in Tanzania fused anti-colonial nationalism with ideologies of social justice and collective development. These struggles highlighted the convergence between Indigenous sovereignty movements and broader global anti-imperial campaigns.[120] Institutional recognition of Indigenous political autonomy also advanced through the establishment of representative bodies. In Canada, the Assembly

[118] Smith, P.C. and Warrior, R. (1996). Like a Hurricane: The Indian Movement from Alcatraz to Wounded Knee. New York: New Press.

[119] Hill, R.S. (2009). Maori and the State: Crown–Maori Relations in New Zealand/Aotearoa, 1950–2000. Wellington: Victoria University Press.

[120] Cooper, F. (2002). Africa Since 1940: The Past of the Present. Cambridge: Cambridge University Press.

of First Nations (AFN), formed in 1982, provided a national platform for Indigenous leaders to negotiate land claims, resource rights, and constitutional recognition.[121] In Europe, the creation of the Sami Parliament in Norway (1989) institutionalized Indigenous political voice in northern governance, granting the Sami authority over language, culture, and land-use policies in ways that signalled a rebalancing of power within the state.[122] From the lens of neoclassical economics, these movements can be interpreted as rational attempts to restore lost property rights and to secure more efficient allocation of resources through self-governance, as colonial and state-led management often generated inefficiencies and rent-seeking. Conversely, in a communist framework, Indigenous mobilizations have been framed as struggles against capitalist dispossession, aligning them with broader movements for redistribution and collective ownership, particularly visible in African socialism during the independence period.[123] Empirical data underscores the impact of these movements: the Waitangi Tribunal has led to settlements worth over NZ$2 billion by the early twenty-first century, while the AFN represents over 600 First Nations across Canada, influencing constitutional debates and federal policy. These examples demonstrate how twentieth-century Indigenous political autonomy movements not only reshaped national politics but also advanced new models of sovereignty that challenged the Westphalian framework of the nation-state.

4.3 International Recognition of Indigenous Self-Determination

The late twentieth century marked a turning point in the recognition of Indigenous self-determination, as global frameworks and landmark legal cases challenged centuries of colonial dispossession. A key milestone was the adoption of the United Nations Declaration on the Rights of Indigenous Peoples (UNDRIP) in 2007, the result of decades of

[121] Cornell, S. and Kalt, J.P. (1998). 'Sovereignty and Nation-Building: The Development Challenge in Indian Country Today'. American Indian Culture and Research Journal, 22(3), pp. 187–214.

[122] Josefsen, E. (2010). 'The Saami and the National Parliaments: Channels for Political Influence'. Inter-Parliamentary Union and UNDP Reports on Indigenous Peoples and Parliament. Geneva: IPU/UNDP.

[123] Mamdani, M. (1996). Citizen and Subject: Contemporary Africa and the Legacy of Late Colonialism. Princeton, NJ: Princeton University Press.

Indigenous advocacy at the UN Working Group on Indigenous Populations. UNDRIP articulated the principle that Indigenous peoples possess inherent rights to land, culture, and governance, explicitly affirming their entitlement to "self-determination" and "free, prior, and informed consent" in matters affecting their territories.[124] While initially opposed by settler colonial states such as Australia, Canada, New Zealand, and the United States, all eventually endorsed the declaration, reflecting the growing moral and legal authority of Indigenous movements on the international stage.[125] Concrete legal victories reinforced these international norms. In Australia, the landmark Mabo v Queensland (No. 2) case of 1992 overturned the doctrine of terra nullius and recognized the concept of native title, acknowledging that Aboriginal and Torres Strait Islander peoples held pre-existing land rights under customary law. This decision restructured Australian property law and led to the Native Title Act of 1993, enabling Indigenous communities to make claims to traditional lands.[126] In Latin America, Bolivia's 2009 Constitution, spearheaded under the presidency of Evo Morales, the country's first Indigenous leader, declared the nation a "plurinational state" and enshrined Indigenous autonomy, customary justice systems, and territorial rights.[127] Similar developments occurred across Latin America, with Ecuador's 2008 Constitution also embedding Indigenous rights and environmental protections inspired by the Andean concept of sumak kawsay ("good living").[128] From the perspective of neoclassical economics, these developments can be seen as attempts to correct the inefficiencies caused by insecure property rights and legal exclusion. By recognizing Indigenous land tenure, systems such as Australia's native title aimed to provide clearer incentives for sustainable investment and resource management, albeit within a capitalist framework. In contrast,

[124] Anaya, S.J. (2004). Indigenous Peoples in International Law. 2nd ed. New York: Oxford University Press.

[125] Lightfoot, S. (2016). Global Indigenous Politics: A Subtle Revolution. Abingdon: Routledge.

[126] Nettheim, G., Meyers, G. and Craig, D. (2015). Indigenous Peoples and the Law in Australia. Sydney: LexisNexis Butterworths.

[127] Postero, N. (2017). The Indigenous State: Race, Politics, and Performance in Plurinational Bolivia. Berkeley: University of California Press.

[128] Van Cott, D.L. (2005). From Movements to Parties in Latin America: The Evolution of Ethnic Politics. Cambridge: Cambridge University Press.

communist and post-colonial approaches emphasize the redistributive and anti-capitalist dimensions of Indigenous victories: Bolivia's plurinational constitution sought not only to formalize land rights but also to redistribute political power away from an elite-dominated state towards historically marginalized communities. Empirical data show that recognition is uneven; by 2020, Indigenous peoples had achieved legal ownership or tenure rights over only 10% of global land, despite their stewardship of territories containing 80% of the world's biodiversity.[129] Nevertheless, these legal and institutional reforms highlight the increasing convergence of Indigenous struggles with global debates over sovereignty, equity, and environmental sustainability.

4.4 *The Role of Customary Governance in Modern Political Autonomy*

The revitalization of customary governance has become a cornerstone of Indigenous self-determination in the modern era, reflecting both a rejection of colonial structures and a creative adaptation to contemporary political realities. Across the globe, Indigenous peoples have sought to reassert traditional governance institutions alongside or within state frameworks, challenging the monopoly of Western legal and administrative models. In Canada, co-management arrangements between Indigenous communities and the state illustrate this dynamic. For example, the Nunavut Land Claims Agreement (1993) established the Nunavut Wildlife Management Board, granting Inuit communities authority to regulate hunting and resource use in collaboration with federal authorities. This model has not only strengthened Inuit cultural practices around subsistence but has also been recognized internationally as a successful example of integrating Indigenous ecological knowledge into modern environmental policy.[130] In New Zealand, the revitalization of Māori fisheries governance has been central to contemporary autonomy. Following the 1992 Fisheries Settlement, Māori iwi (tribes) were allocated a substantial share of commercial fisheries quota, enabling them to establish tribally owned corporations while retaining customary fishing rights.

[129] Rights and Resources Initiative (2020). Who Owns the World's Land? A Global Baseline of Indigenous and Community Land Rights. Washington, DC: RRI.

[130] Berkes, F. (2018). Sacred Ecology. 4th ed. New York: Routledge.

This arrangement blends modern economic enterprises with traditional governance principles rooted in kaitiakitanga (guardianship), balancing commercial profitability with stewardship responsibilities towards marine ecosystems.[131] Similarly, in Norway and Sweden, the establishment of Sami parliaments has been complemented by the recognition of traditional reindeer herding rights, embedding customary governance within national resource-management systems.[132] From a neoclassical economics perspective, these arrangements can be seen as mechanisms for reducing transaction costs and aligning incentives by leveraging local knowledge for efficient resource allocation.[133] Indigenous governance ensures that decision-making is informed by those with the greatest stake in sustainable resource use, thereby overcoming the inefficiencies of centralized state control. By contrast, communist and post-colonial interpretations emphasize these cases as forms of collective ownership and resistance to capitalist dispossession, where customary governance challenges the primacy of private property and market logics. For instance, Māori fisheries governance represents not only economic empowerment but also a critique of the commodification of natural resources, positioning collective stewardship as an alternative to neoliberal resource exploitation. Empirical data underscores the importance of customary governance. Indigenous-managed lands comprise approximately 25% of the world's surface area, overlapping with regions of highest biodiversity.[134] In Canada, Indigenous co-management regimes have been shown to improve conservation outcomes while enhancing community livelihoods. These examples demonstrate that customary governance is not a relic of the past but a living institution that provides innovative models for sustainable development and political autonomy in the twenty-first century.

[131] Kawharu, M. (ed.) (2010). Tāhuhu Kōrero: The Sayings of Taitokerau. Auckland: Auckland University Press.

[132] Josefsen, E. (2010). 'The Saami and the National Parliaments: Channels for Political Influence'. Inter-Parliamentary Union and UNDP Reports on Indigenous Peoples and Parliament. Geneva: IPU/UNDP.

[133] Ostrom, E. (1990). Governing the Commons: The Evolution of Institutions for Collective Action. Cambridge: Cambridge University Press.

[134] Garnett, S.T., Burgess, N.D., Fa, J.E., Fernández-Llamazares, Á., Molnár, Z., Robinson, C.J., Watson, J.E.M., Zander, K.K., Austin, B., Brondizio, E.S., Collier, N.F., Duncan, T., Ellis, E., Geyle, H., Jackson, M.V., Jonas, H., Malmer, P., McGowan, B., Sivongxay, A. and Leiper, I. (2018). 'A spatial overview of the global importance of Indigenous lands for conservation'. Nature Sustainability, 1(7), pp. 369–374.

4.5 Contemporary Challenges to Self-Determination

Despite notable advances in recognition and institutional reforms since the late twentieth century, Indigenous peoples continue to face profound structural barriers to genuine self-determination. In many settler states, sovereignty is only partially recognized, with governance powers ultimately subordinated to national legal frameworks. For instance, in Canada, modern treaties and comprehensive land claims have granted partial recognition, but often at the cost of ceding significant territorial or resource rights in exchange for financial compensation, thereby constraining political autonomy.[135] Similarly, in Australia, the landmark recognition of native title in the Mabo v Queensland (No 2) case (1992) was subsequently undermined by Wik Peoples v Queensland (1996), which subordinated native title to pastoral leases, entrenching limitations on Indigenous sovereignty despite rhetorical advances.[136] These examples illustrate how state recognition frequently consolidates state authority rather than redistributing genuine decision-making power. Economic exploitation compounds these structural barriers. Extractive industries such as mining, oil, and large-scale logging remain persistent threats to Indigenous territories, frequently sanctioned by governments eager for investment or export revenues. In Latin America, for example, Indigenous communities in Bolivia and Ecuador, despite constitutional guarantees of autonomy, face continual encroachment from oil and mining projects, revealing the contradictions of plurinational frameworks under conditions of resource dependency.[137] Similar dynamics are evident in North America, where Indigenous-led mobilizations such as the Standing Rock protests of 2016 against the Dakota Access Pipeline highlighted the deep entanglement of corporate energy projects, state security apparatuses, and the erosion of Indigenous land rights. Standing Rock was not an isolated event but part of a long tradition of Indigenous resistance to extractive

[135] Papillon, M. (2012). 'Adapting Federalism: Indigenous Multilevel Governance in Canada and the United States'. Publius: The Journal of Federalism, 42(2), pp. 289–312.

[136] Nettheim, G., Meyers, G. and Craig, D. (2015). Indigenous Peoples and the Law in Australia. Sydney: LexisNexis Butterworths.

[137] Postero, N. (2017). The Indigenous State: Race, Politics, and Performance in Plurinational Bolivia. Berkeley: University of California Press.

colonial capitalism.[138] Climate change has exacerbated these pressures, eroding both the ecological bases of Indigenous sovereignty and the cultural practices linked to them. In the Arctic, Inuit communities face shrinking hunting grounds and unsafe travel routes as melting sea ice undermines subsistence economies central to cultural identity. Research demonstrates how Inuit hunters are responding by combining Indigenous ecological knowledge (IEK) with satellite mapping and scientific data to create adaptive, hybrid governance systems, ensuring continuity of subsistence practices in radically altered conditions.[139] These adaptations underscore the resilience of Indigenous governance but also highlight structural vulnerabilities to global climate disruption. The Intergovernmental Panel on Climate Change[140] has recognized that Indigenous peoples are disproportionately exposed to climate impacts, while simultaneously being critical actors in adaptation strategies. Beyond adaptation, Indigenous land stewardship is increasingly recognized as crucial to planetary sustainability. A major study estimates that Indigenous territories overlap with approximately 80% of the world's remaining biodiversity hotspots, underscoring the global importance of Indigenous ecological governance.[141] From the perspective of neoclassical economics, however, such lands are often mischaracterized as "underutilised resources" in need of "productive investment". This framing legitimizes dispossession under the guise of efficiency. By contrast, scholars[142] have demonstrated that communal institutions are often more efficient than markets or states

[138] Estes, N. (2019). Our History is the Future: Standing Rock versus the Dakota Access Pipeline, and the Long Tradition of Indigenous Resistance. London: Verso.

[139] Ford, J.D., Clark, D.G., Pearce, T., Berrang-Ford, L., Copland, L., Dawson, J. and McDowell, G. (2020). 'Changing Access to Ice, Land and Water in Arctic Communities'. Nature Climate Change, 10(2), pp. 135–142.

[140] IPCC (2022). Climate Change 2022: Impacts, Adaptation and Vulnerability. Contribution of Working Group II to the Sixth Assessment Report of the Intergovernmental Panel on Climate Change. Cambridge: Cambridge University Press.

[141] Garnett, S.T., Burgess, N.D., Fa, J.E., Fernández-Llamazares, Á., Molnár, Z., Robinson, C.J., Watson, J.E.M., Zander, K.K., Austin, B., Brondizio, E.S., Collier, N.F., Duncan, T., Ellis, E., Geyle, H., Jackson, M.V., Jonas, H., Malmer, P.,

McGowan, B., Sivongxay, A. and Leiper, I. (2018). 'A spatial overview of the global importance of Indigenous lands for conservation'. Nature Sustainability, 1(7), pp. 369–374.

[142] Ostrom, E. (1990). Governing the Commons: The Evolution of Institutions for Collective Action. Cambridge: Cambridge University Press.

in governing common-pool resources, while others[143] argue that true self-determination must be rooted in sustainable practices of land-based governance rather than narrowly defined political recognition. This means that Indigenous sovereignty depends not only on legal or constitutional acknowledgment by states but also on the ability of communities to exercise authority over their lands, waters, and resources in ways consistent with their cultural values and ecological knowledge. For example, the recognition of the Whanganui River in New Zealand as a legal person in 2017 illustrates this principle: Māori iwi did not simply seek symbolic recognition, but the embedding of their cosmology of river guardianship into state law, ensuring that governance is tied to ecological stewardship as well as political rights. The implication is that legal innovation has also become a key avenue for advancing Indigenous autonomy within state systems. The case of the Whanganui River in New Zealand is illustrative: after decades of Māori activism, the river was recognized as a legal person in 2017, with guardianship jointly held by the Crown and iwi representatives. This legal pluralism reflects Indigenous cosmologies of rivers as living ancestors, embedding them within state law.[144] Such cases point to the possibility of transforming governance through recognition of Indigenous epistemologies, though they remain rare and contested.

At the international level, Indigenous peoples are increasingly mobilizing under the banner of climate justice and human rights. Scholars argue that Indigenous sovereignty cannot be separated from environmental sovereignty, since land, law, and ecological knowledge are indivisible.[145] Activists have linked their struggles to transnational networks, reframing climate politics as a struggle against what has been referred to as the "structural violence of colonial capitalism".[146] In this sense, Indigenous movements resonate with critiques familiar from communist

[143] Corntassel, J. (2008). 'Toward Sustainable Self-Determination: Rethinking the Contemporary Indigenous-Rights Discourse'. Alternatives: Global, Local, Political, 33(1), pp. 105–132.

[144] Charpleix, L. (2018). 'The Whanganui River as Te Awa Tupua: Place-based law in a legally pluralistic society'. The Geographical Journal, 184(1), pp. 19–30.

[145] Whyte, K.P. (2017). 'Indigenous Climate Change Studies: Indigenizing Futures, Decolonizing the Anthropocene'. English Language Notes, 55(1–2), pp. 153–162.

[146] Whyte, K.P. (2018). 'Indigenous Science (Fiction) for the Anthropocene: Ancestral Dystopias and Fantasies of Climate Change Crises'. Environment and Planning E: Nature and Space, 1(1–2), pp. 224–242.

and dependency theory traditions, which highlight resource dispossession as a necessary condition for capital accumulation. Contemporary challenges therefore highlight a paradox: Indigenous peoples represent less than 5% of the world's population yet steward over 80% of its biodiversity, making their marginalization not only a matter of justice but of planetary survival.[147] The persistence of state-centric legal constraints, extractive economies, and climate disruptions reveals the limits of formal recognition when broader political-economic structures remain unchanged. The implication is that even when Indigenous rights are acknowledged in law, they continue to be undermined by the dominance of capitalist market logics, resource-driven development models, and centralized state authority that prioritize profit and control over Indigenous governance and ecological sustainability. However, Indigenous-led governance innovations, from hybrid IEK-scientific adaptation systems in the Arctic, to personhood recognition for rivers in New Zealand, to mass grassroots resistance at Standing Rock, demonstrate that Indigenous nations are not passive victims but active shapers of alternative futures. These movements expose the inadequacies of neoclassical frameworks, align with post-colonial critiques of resource exploitation, and offer vital models for rethinking sovereignty, sustainability, and global political economy in the twenty-first century.

5 Broader Themes and Implications

5.1 Comparative Governance: Lessons from Indigenous Systems

Indigenous governance systems offer valuable insights for addressing the governance crises of the twenty-first century, particularly in relation to climate change and ecological sustainability. Many Indigenous societies developed consensus-based decision-making structures that emphasized dialogue, reciprocity, and accountability to both human and non-human communities. For instance, the Haudenosaunee Confederacy's Great Law of Peace institutionalized deliberation among clan representatives

[147] Garnett, S.T., Burgess, N.D., Fa, J.E., Fernández-Llamazares, Á., Molnár, Z., Robinson, C.J., Watson, J.E.M., Zander, K.K., Austin, B., Brondizio, E.S., Collier, N.F., Duncan, T., Ellis, E., Geyle, H., Jackson, M.V., Jonas, H., Malmer, P.,

McGowan, B., Sivongxay, A. and Leiper, I. (2018). 'A spatial overview of the global importance of Indigenous lands for conservation'. Nature Sustainability, 1(7), pp. 369–374.

to achieve consensus rather than majority rule, demonstrating an early form of democratic practice centred on collective responsibility.[148] Similarly, among the San of Southern Africa, decision-making often emerged from prolonged discussion and consultation, with leadership dependent on persuasion and respect rather than coercion.[149] These models stand in stark contrast to the hierarchical and centralized bureaucracies that developed in Europe, where sovereignty and decision-making authority became concentrated in states and ruling elites.[150] Indigenous ecological governance also presents a critical alternative to dominant economic paradigms. Systems of land stewardship, such as Māori kaitiakitanga in Aotearoa/New Zealand or the co-management of fisheries by Pacific Northwest tribes in North America, demonstrate that resource management can be embedded in cultural values of care, intergenerational responsibility, and sustainability.[151] Empirical evidence underscores their effectiveness: Indigenous-managed lands, though only covering around 25% of the global terrestrial surface, coincide with over 80% of remaining biodiversity hotspots.[152] Such outcomes challenge neoclassical economics, which tends to treat land and resources as factors of production optimized through individual property rights and market exchange.[153] By contrast, Indigenous systems highlight that collective governance and long-term ecological planning can outperform market-driven models in terms of sustainability and resilience. From the perspective of communist and post-capitalist thought, Indigenous governance has often been interpreted as embodying forms of "primitive communism",

[148] Lyons, O., Mohawk, J., Deloria, V., Hauptman, L.M., Berman, H., Grinde, D.A., Shaaf, R. and Wilkinson, C. (1992). Exiled in the Land of the Free: Democracy, Indian Nations and the U.S. Constitution. Santa Fe: Clear Light Publishers.

[149] Lee, R. (2017). The!Kung San: Men, Women and Work in a Foraging Society. 3rd ed. Cambridge: Cambridge University Press.

[150] Tilly, C. (1990). Coercion, Capital, and European States, AD 990–1990. Oxford: Blackwell.

[151] Berkes, F. (2018). Sacred Ecology. 4th ed. New York: Routledge.

[152] Garnett, S.T., Burgess, N.D., Fa, J.E., Fernández-Llamazares, Á., Molnár, Z., Robinson, C.J., Watson, J.E.M., Zander, K.K., Austin, B., Brondizio, E.S., Collier, N.F., Duncan, T., Ellis, E., Geyle, H., Jackson, M.V., Jonas, H., Malmer, P., McGowan, B., Sivongxay, A. and Leiper, I. (2018). 'A spatial overview of the global importance of Indigenous lands for conservation'. Nature Sustainability, 1(7), pp. 369–374.

[153] Demsetz, H. (1967). 'Toward a Theory of Property Rights'. American Economic Review, 57(2), pp. 347–359.

in which property is held collectively, and production is organized around shared survival rather than private accumulation.[154] While such framings risk oversimplification, they nevertheless highlight how Indigenous systems challenge the assumption that private property and competitive markets are the natural foundations of political economy. Instead, Indigenous governance offers an alternative paradigm where social cohesion, ecological sustainability, and cultural continuity are prioritized over profit maximization.

The lessons from Indigenous governance are particularly relevant in the era of climate crisis. International frameworks, such as the Intergovernmental Panel on Climate Change,[155] increasingly acknowledge Indigenous ecological knowledge as essential for adaptation strategies. Hybrid models, such as co-management regimes in Canada's Arctic or the recognition of the Whanganui River as a legal person in New Zealand, suggest pathways towards integrating Indigenous governance with state systems to create more pluralistic and sustainable frameworks.[156,157] These examples demonstrate that consensus-based and ecological governance are not simply relics of the past but provide viable models for rethinking global governance in the Anthropocene.

5.2 *Reclaiming Sovereignty in a Globalized World*

In the twenty-first century, Indigenous sovereignty is increasingly being redefined beyond the boundaries of nation-states, as Indigenous peoples mobilize across borders to confront shared challenges such as environmental degradation, human rights violations, and the ongoing legacies of colonialism. Globalization has intensified pressures on Indigenous lands and cultures through extractive industries, trade liberalization, and climate

[154] Marx, K. and Engels, F. (1848 [1998]). The Communist Manifesto. London: Verso.

[155] IPCC (2022). Climate Change 2022: Impacts, Adaptation and Vulnerability. Contribution of Working Group II to the Sixth Assessment Report of the Intergovernmental Panel on Climate Change. Cambridge: Cambridge University Press.

[156] Charpleix, L. (2018). 'The Whanganui River as Te Awa Tupua: Place-based law in a legally pluralistic society'. The Geographical Journal, 184(1), pp. 19–30.

[157] Ford, J.D., Clark, D.G., Pearce, T., Berrang-Ford, L., Copland, L., Dawson, J. and McDowell, G. (2020). 'Changing Access to Ice, Land and Water in Arctic Communities'. Nature Climate Change, 10(2), pp. 135–142.

change, but it has also opened opportunities for new forms of transnational advocacy and cooperation. Indigenous leaders have emerged at the forefront of global environmental and human rights movements, articulating critiques of neoliberal globalization while advancing alternative governance models rooted in ecological stewardship and collective rights. The 2007 adoption of the United Nations Declaration on the Rights of Indigenous Peoples (UNDRIP) represented a landmark victory for Indigenous diplomacy, achieved through decades of coalition-building among Indigenous nations worldwide.[158] This achievement demonstrated the capacity of Indigenous networks to influence international law despite resistance from powerful states. Concrete examples illustrate the expanding role of Indigenous leadership in transnational governance. The participation of Sámi leaders in the Arctic Council has institutionalized Indigenous voices in regional policymaking, shaping debates on climate adaptation and sustainable development in the circumpolar North.[159] Similarly, the international visibility of the Standing Rock protests (2016) against the Dakota Access Pipeline positioned Indigenous sovereignty at the heart of global climate justice debates, drawing solidarity from human rights organizations, environmental NGOs, and other Indigenous nations.[160] In Latin America, the plurinational constitutions of Bolivia and Ecuador, influenced by Indigenous mobilization, have integrated Indigenous concepts such as buen vivir into state frameworks, challenging the neoliberal model of development.[161] These examples underscore how Indigenous sovereignty is being reframed not only as a domestic political issue but as a global concern linked to sustainability and justice. Furthermore, theoretical comparisons illuminate the broader significance of these struggles. From the perspective of neoclassical economics, sovereignty conflicts are often framed in terms of property rights and efficient

[158] Anaya, S.J. (2009). International Human Rights and Indigenous Peoples. New York: Aspen Publishers.

[159] Josefsen, E. (2015). "Political Systems and the Sami." In C. Keskitalo (ed.), The Sami People: Traditions in Transition. Fairbanks: University of Alaska Press, pp. 123–140.

[160] Estes, N. (2019). Our History is the Future: Standing Rock versus the Dakota Access Pipeline, and the Long Tradition of Indigenous Resistance. London: Verso.

[161] Postero, N. (2017). The Indigenous State: Race, Politics, and Performance in Plurinational Bolivia. Berkeley: University of California Press.

resource allocation, treating Indigenous lands as inputs to be optimized for productivity.[162] By contrast, Marxist and dependency-theory traditions interpret Indigenous sovereignty movements as challenges to capitalist accumulation and imperial domination, highlighting the structural exploitation of Indigenous lands and labour within global economic systems.[163,164] These critiques align with Indigenous intellectual traditions that stress the indivisibility of land, governance, and culture, rejecting the commodification of sovereignty into narrowly defined political rights,[165] The persistence of Indigenous-led transnational activism demonstrates that sovereignty in a globalized world is not simply about recognition within state structures but about reshaping the global political economy to value sustainability, reciprocity, and justice. Empirical data underscores the urgency of these efforts. Indigenous peoples make up less than 5% of the world's population but manage more than 25% of global land area, including territories that overlap with 80% of the planet's biodiversity.[166] This reality positions Indigenous nations as indispensable actors in confronting the ecological crises of globalization. Reclaiming sovereignty in this context means asserting the legitimacy of Indigenous governance not only as a matter of rights but as a critical foundation for planetary survival. Indigenous movements for transnational solidarity therefore represent both a resistance to the destructive logics of global capitalism and an articulation of alternative pathways for human societies in the Anthropocene epoch.

[162] Demsetz, H. (1967). 'Toward a Theory of Property Rights'. American Economic Review, 57(2), pp. 347–359.

[163] Mamdani, M. (1996). Citizen and Subject: Contemporary Africa and the Legacy of Late Colonialism. Princeton, NJ: Princeton University Press.

[164] Kay, C. (1982). 'Achievements and Contradictions of Agrarian Reform in Latin America'. Journal of Development Studies, 18(2), pp. 141–170.

[165] Corntassel, J. (2008). 'Toward Sustainable Self-Determination: Rethinking the Contemporary Indigenous-Rights Discourse'. Alternatives: Global, Local, Political, 33(1), pp. 105–132.

[166] Garnett, S.T., Burgess, N.D., Fa, J.E., Fernández-Llamazares, Á., Molnár, Z., Robinson, C.J., Watson, J.E.M., Zander, K.K., Austin, B., Brondizio, E.S., Collier, N.F., Duncan, T., Ellis, E., Geyle, H., Jackson, M.V., Jonas, H., Malmer, P., McGowan, B., Sivongxay, A. and Leiper, I. (2018). 'A spatial overview of the global importance of Indigenous lands for conservation'. Nature Sustainability, 1(7), pp. 369–374.

5.3 *The Future of Indigenous Self-Determination*

The future of Indigenous self-determination is increasingly shaped by the intersection of technology, education, and activism, which together provide new avenues for advancing governance and cultural preservation. Digital platforms, for instance, allow Indigenous nations to amplify their voices in global debates, from climate justice to human rights, while also strengthening internal governance through the use of mapping technologies and digital archives that document land claims and cultural heritage.[167,168] Renewable energy initiatives have become particularly significant, demonstrating how Indigenous communities can simultaneously achieve economic autonomy and ecological sustainability. The O'Chiese First Nation in Alberta, for example, has invested in solar energy projects that reduce dependence on external power sources, while in New Zealand, Māori iwi have pioneered geothermal energy ventures that combine cultural values with long-term economic independence.[169] Such projects challenge the neoclassical economic framing of Indigenous lands as "underutilized resources" by illustrating how collective, community-driven management can yield both efficiency and sustainability. Education and language revitalization programs represent another critical pathway. Efforts such as the Hawaiian Pūnana Leo immersion schools and Sámi language revitalization initiatives in Norway show how Indigenous peoples use education to reinforce cultural sovereignty, ensuring intergenerational continuity of governance systems.[170] These projects contrast sharply with the homogenizing tendencies of communist regimes, which often sought to subsume Indigenous governance under centralized state authority, as seen in the Soviet Union's repression of

[167] Corntassel, J. (2008). 'Toward Sustainable Self-Determination: Rethinking the Contemporary Indigenous-Rights Discourse'. Alternatives: Global, Local, Political, 33(1), pp. 105–132.

[168] Kukutai, T. and Taylor, J. (eds.) (2016). Indigenous Data Sovereignty: Toward an Agenda. Canberra: ANU Press.

[169] Krupa, J. (2012). Identifying barriers to aboriginal renewable energy deployment in Canada. Energy Policy, 42, pp. 710–714.

[170] May, S. (2012). Language and Minority Rights: Ethnicity, Nationalism and the Politics of Language. 2nd ed. New York: Routledge.

Evenki and Nenets institutions.[171] Instead, contemporary Indigenous-led educational efforts embody a pluralist model of governance that reaffirms distinct identities while engaging modern pedagogical tools. Activism further strengthens these pathways. Movements such as Idle No More in Canada and the global Indigenous climate justice network illustrate how grassroots mobilization links local struggles with transnational advocacy, positioning Indigenous self-determination as integral to global debates on sustainability and equity.[172] These movements also highlight the contradictions of capitalist globalization: while Indigenous communities are disproportionately affected by extractive industries and climate change, they are also among the most effective stewards of biodiversity, safeguarding over 80% of the world's biodiversity hotspots despite constituting less than 5% of the global population.[173] Taken together, these initiatives suggest that the future of Indigenous self-determination lies not simply in achieving formal political recognition but in embedding sovereignty within sustainable economic practices, cultural renewal, and transnational advocacy. By drawing on both traditional governance and modern tools, Indigenous nations are reframing sovereignty as a living practice that challenges the logics of both neoliberal capitalism and centralized communist models, offering alternative pathways for equitable governance in an increasingly globalized world.

6 Conclusion

The analysis in this chapter has demonstrated that the encounter between Indigenous governance systems and European imperial state-building was not simply a clash of political institutions but a profound confrontation between different ontologies of sovereignty, land, and community. Indigenous governance, rooted in decentralization, consensus, and

[171] Fondahl, G. (1998). Gaining Ground? Evenkis, Land, and Reform in Southeastern Siberia. Boulder, CO: Westview Press.

[172] Estes, N. (2019). Our History is the Future: Standing Rock versus the Dakota Access Pipeline, and the Long Tradition of Indigenous Resistance. London: Verso.

[173] Garnett, S.T., Burgess, N.D., Fa, J.E., Fernández-Llamazares, Á., Molnár, Z., Robinson, C.J., Watson, J.E.M., Zander, K.K., Austin, B., Brondizio, E.S., Collier, N.F., Duncan, T., Ellis, E., Geyle, H., Jackson, M.V., Jonas, H., Malmer, P., McGowan, B., Sivongxay, A. and Leiper, I. (2018). 'A spatial overview of the global importance of Indigenous lands for conservation'. Nature Sustainability, 1(7), pp. 369–374.

ecological stewardship, provided sustainable frameworks for managing resources and maintaining social cohesion across diverse environments.[174,175] By contrast, European imperial powers developed highly centralized, bureaucratic, and militarized systems designed to maximize extraction and control, underpinned by mercantilist logics, religious justifications, and technological coordination.[176,177,178] The asymmetry of power allowed European models to displace and subordinate Indigenous systems, but this process was never uncontested. Indigenous peoples resisted through warfare, diplomacy, and adaptation, and, crucially, many of their governance principles have endured into the present.[179,180,181] The chapter has also shown how fiscal-military states in Europe, such as Britain, leveraged financial innovations and bureaucratic capacity to sustain imperial expansion.[182,183] However, Indigenous nations mobilized flexible and relational forms of governance to defend their autonomy.[184,185] These divergences illustrate the limits of both capitalist and communist frameworks, which, despite their ideological

174 Berkes, F. (2018). Sacred Ecology. 4th ed. New York: Routledge.

175 Ostrom, E. (1990). Governing the Commons: The Evolution of Institutions for Collective Action. Cambridge: Cambridge University Press.

176 Brewer, J. (1989). The Sinews of Power: War, Money and the English State, 1688–1783. London: Unwin Hyman.

177 Tilly, C. (1990). Coercion, Capital, and European States, AD 990–1990. Oxford: Blackwell.

178 Pagden, A. (1995). Lords of All the World: Ideologies of Empire in Spain, Britain and France c.1500–c.1800. New Haven, CT: Yale University Press.

179 Lepore, J. (1998). The Name of War: King Philip's War and the Origins of American Identity. New York: Knopf.

180 Knaut, A.L. (1995). The Pueblo Revolt of 1680: Conquest and Resistance in Seventeenth-Century New Mexico. Norman: University of Oklahoma Press.

181 Laband, J. (2009). The Rise and Fall of the Zulu Nation. Johannesburg: Jonathan Ball.

182 Brewer, J. (1989). The Sinews of Power: War, Money and the English State, 1688–1783. London: Unwin Hyman.

183 Neal, L. (1990). The Rise of Financial Capitalism: International Capital Markets in the Age of Reason. Cambridge: Cambridge University Press.

184 Lyons, O. et al. (1992). Exiled in the Land of the Free: Democracy, Indian Nations and the U.S. Constitution. Santa Fe: Clear Light Publishers.

185 Belich, J. (1996). Making Peoples: A History of the New Zealanders from Polynesian Settlement to the End of the Nineteenth Century. Auckland: Penguin.

differences, share a reliance on centralization and disregard for local autonomy.[186,187] Indigenous governance exposes alternative logics, based on reciprocity, collective responsibility, and ecological embeddedness, that challenge dominant paradigms of political economy.[188,189] Contemporary Indigenous struggles for self-determination, from legal victories such as Mabo v Queensland to transnational activism at Standing Rock, underscore that Indigenous governance is not a relic of the past but a living system actively shaping political futures.[190,191] These movements highlight the contradictions of state recognition, which often reproduces state authority rather than redistributing power[192,193]; and expose the ongoing violence of extractive economies and climate disruption.[194,195] At the same time, Indigenous-led innovations, such as legal personhood for rivers, co-management of resources, and renewable energy initiatives, demonstrate how traditional knowledge can be revitalized and integrated

[186] Demsetz, H. (1967). 'Toward a Theory of Property Rights'. American Economic Review, 57(2), pp. 347–359

[187] Marx, K. and Engels, F. (1998). The Communist Manifesto. London: Verso.

[188] Corntassel, J. (2008). 'Toward Sustainable Self-Determination: Rethinking the Contemporary Indigenous-Rights Discourse'. Alternatives: Global, Local, Political, 33(1), pp. 105–132.

[189] Simpson, A. (2014). Mohawk Interruptus: Political Life Across the Borders of Settler States. Durham, NC: Duke University Press.

[190] Nettheim, G., Meyers, G. and Craig, D. (2002). Indigenous Peoples and the Law in Australia. Sydney: LexisNexis Butterworths.

[191] Estes, N. (2019). Our History is the Future: Standing Rock versus the Dakota Access Pipeline, and the Long Tradition of Indigenous Resistance. London: Verso.

[192] Papillon, M. (2012). 'Adapting Federalism: Indigenous Multilevel Governance in Canada and the United States'. Publius: The Journal of Federalism, 42(2), pp. 289–312.

[193] Wilkins, D.E. and Lomawaima, K.T. (2001). Uneven Ground: American Indian Sovereignty and Federal Law. Norman: University of Oklahoma Press.

[194] Postero, N. (2017). The Indigenous State: Race, Politics, and Performance in Plurinational Bolivia. Berkeley: University of California Press.

[195] Ford, J.D. et al. (2020). 'Changing Access to Ice, Land and Water in Arctic Communities'. Nature Climate Change, 10(2), pp. 135–142.

into global governance debates.[196,197,198] The broader implication is that the resilience of Indigenous governance offers not only a counter-narrative to colonial domination but also vital lessons for the twenty-first century. In an era defined by ecological crisis, widening inequality, and contested sovereignty, Indigenous systems provide models of governance that are adaptive, sustainable, and relational. They challenge the state-centric assumptions of both neoclassical and Marxist frameworks and reveal pathways towards a more plural and just political economy. Far from being peripheral, Indigenous governance and self-determination stand at the centre of reimagining sovereignty, sustainability, and global cooperation in the Anthropocene epoch.[199,200,201]

The reclamation of land and the reassertion of Indigenous governance discussed in this chapter underscore the foundational role that territory plays in sustaining Indigenous economies and worldviews. These acts of resurgence are not merely reactive but generative; they reveal new/old economic paradigms rooted in spiritual responsibility, ecological stewardship, and collective governance. As we turn to the final chapter, the narrative broadens to synthesize these practices across diverse Indigenous and ancient traditions. Chapter 7critically interrogates neoclassical and Marxist economic models, introducing Symbiotic Gaian Economics as a pluralistic and ecological alternative grounded in Indigenous thought. It proposes a paradigm shift—one where Indigenous frameworks do not supplement existing economic theory but redefine its very foundations.

[196] Charpleix, L. (2018). 'The Whanganui River as Te Awa Tupua: Place-based law in a legally pluralistic society'. The Geographical Journal, 184(1), pp. 19–30.

[197] Kukutai, T. and Taylor, J. (eds.) (2016). Indigenous Data Sovereignty: Toward an Agenda. Canberra: ANU Press.

[198] Garnett, S.T. et al. (2018). 'A spatial overview of the global importance of Indigenous lands for conservation'. Nature Sustainability, 1(7), pp. 369–374.

[199] Whyte, K.P. (2017). 'Indigenous Climate Change Studies: Indigenizing Futures, Decolonizing the Anthropocene'. English Language Notes, 55(1–2), pp. 153–162.

[200] Anaya, S.J. (2004). Indigenous Peoples in International Law. 2nd ed. Oxford: Oxford University Press.

[201] Lightfoot, S. (2016). Global Indigenous Politics: A Subtle Revolution. Abingdon: Routledge.

References

Alden, D. (1996). The Making of an Enterprise: The Society of Jesus in Portugal, Its Empire, and Beyond, 1540–1750. Stanford, CA: Stanford University Press.

Anaya, J. (2004). Indigenous Peoples in International Law. 2nd ed. New York: Oxford University Press.

Anaya, S.J. (2009). International Human Rights and Indigenous Peoples. New York: Aspen Publishers.

Bakewell, P. (1984). Silver Mining and Society in Colonial Mexico: Zacatecas 1546–1700. Cambridge: Cambridge University Press.

Banner, S. (2005). How the Indians Lost Their Land: Law and Power on the Frontier. Cambridge, MA: Harvard University Press.

Barrett, W. (1983). 'World Bullion Flows, 1450–1800'. In: J.F. Richards (ed.), Precious Metals in the Later Medieval and Early Modern Worlds. Durham, NC: Carolina Academic Press, pp. 224–254.

Baugh, D.A. (2011). The Global Seven Years War, 1754–1763: Britain and France in a Great Power Contest. Harlow: Pearson.

Bayly, C.A. (1996). Empire and Information: Intelligence Gathering and Social Communication in India, 1780–1870. Cambridge: Cambridge University Press.

Belich, J. (1996). Making Peoples: A History of the New Zealanders from Polynesian Settlement to the End of the Nineteenth Century. Auckland: Penguin.

Berkes, F. (2018). Sacred Ecology. 4th ed. New York: Routledge.

Bethencourt, F. (2007). The Portuguese Oceanic Expansion, 1400–1800. Aldershot: Ashgate.

Bethencourt, F. (2009). The Portuguese Empire, 1415–1808. Cambridge: Cambridge University Press.

Bonney, R. (1981). The King's Debts: Finance and Politics in France, 1589–1661. Oxford: Clarendon Press.

Boxer, C.R. (1969). The Portuguese Seaborne Empire, 1415–1825. London: Hutchinson.

Bravo, M. (1996). 'Ethnographic Navigation and the Geographies of Knowledge in the Arctic'. Arctic, 49(4), pp. 397–412.

Brewer, J. (1989). The Sinews of Power: War, Money and the English State, 1688–1783. London: Unwin Hyman.

Charpleix, L. (2018). 'The Whanganui River as Te Awa Tupua: Place-based law in a legally pluralistic society'. The Geographical Journal, 184(1), pp. 19–30.

Codere, H. (1950) Fighting with Property: A Study of Kwakiutl Potlatching and Warfare, 1792–1930. Locust Valley, NY: J. J. Augustin.

Cohn, B.S. (1996). Colonialism and Its Forms of Knowledge: The British in India. Princeton, NJ: Princeton University Press.

Cooper, F. (2002). Africa Since 1940: The Past of the Present. Cambridge: Cambridge University Press.
Cornell, S. and Kalt, J. (1998). 'Sovereignty and Nation-Building: The Development Challenge in Indian Country Today', American Indian Culture and Research Journal, 22(3), pp. 187–214.
Corntassel, J. (2008). 'Toward Sustainable Self-Determination: Rethinking the Contemporary Indigenous-Rights Discourse'. Alternatives: Global, Local, Political, 33(1), pp. 105–132.
Crowder, M. (1964). 'Indirect Rule: French and British Style'. Africa: Journal of the International African Institute, 34(3), pp. 197–205.
Demsetz, H. (1967). 'Toward a Theory of Property Rights', American Economic Review, 57(2), pp. 347–359.
Derrett, J.D.M. (1968). Religion, Law and the State in India. London: Faber & Faber.
Diffie, B.W. and Winius, G.D. (1977). Foundations of the Portuguese Empire, 1415–1580. Minneapolis: University of Minnesota Press.
Dirks, N.B. (2001). Castes of Mind: Colonialism and the Making of Modern India. Princeton, NJ: Princeton University Press.
Dowd, G.E. (2002) War under Heaven: Pontiac, the Indian Nations, and the British Empire. Baltimore: Johns Hopkins University Press.
Drelichman, M. and Voth, H-J. (2014). Lending to the Borrower from Hell: Debt, Taxes, and Default in the Age of Philip II. Princeton, NJ: Princeton University Press.
Edmunds, R.D. (2007). Tecumseh and the Quest for Indian Leadership. New York: Pearson Longman.
Estes, N. (2019). Our History is the Future: Standing Rock versus the Dakota Access Pipeline, and the Long Tradition of Indigenous Resistance. London: Verso.
Findlay, R. and O'Rourke, K.H. (2007). Power and Plenty: Trade, War, and the World Economy in the Second Millennium. Princeton: Princeton University Press.
Finney, B. (1994). Voyage of Rediscovery: A Cultural Odyssey through Polynesia. Berkeley: University of California Press.
Flynn, D.O. and Giráldez, A. (1995). 'Born with a "Silver Spoon": The Origin of World Trade in 1571'. Journal of World History, 6(2), pp. 201–221.
Fondahl, G. (1998). Gaining Ground? Evenkis, Land, and Reform in Southeastern Siberia. Boston: Allyn and Bacon.
Ford, J.D., Clark, D.G., Pearce, T., Berrang-Ford, L., Copland, L., Dawson, J. and McDowell, G. (2020). 'Changing Access to Ice, Land and Water in Arctic Communities'. Nature Climate Change, 10(2), pp. 135–142.

Fowler, C.S. (1986) 'Subsistence' (or relevant chapter by Fowler), in d'Azevedo, W.L. (ed.) Handbook of North American Indians, Vol. 11: Great Basin. Washington, DC: Smithsonian Institution.

Garnett, S.T., Burgess, N.D., Fa, J.E., Fernández-Llamazares, Á., Molnár, Z., Robinson, C.J., Watson, J.E.M., Zander, K.K., Austin, B., Brondizio, E.S., Collier, N.F., Duncan, T., Ellis, E., Geyle, H., Jackson, M.V., Jonas, H., Malmer, P., McGowan, B., Sivongxay, A. and Leiper, I. (2018). 'A spatial overview of the global importance of Indigenous lands for conservation'. Nature Sustainability, 1(7), pp. 369–374.

Gascoigne, J. (2007). Encountering the Pacific in the Age of the Enlightenment. Cambridge: Cambridge University Press.

Hamilton, E.J. (1934). American Treasure and the Price Revolution in Spain, 1501–1650. Cambridge, MA: Harvard University Press.

Harley, J.B. (2001). The New Nature of Maps: Essays in the History of Cartography. Baltimore, MD: Johns Hopkins University Press.

Held, D. and McGrew, A. (2002). Globalization/Anti-Globalization. Cambridge: Polity Press.

Heywood, L.M. (2017). Njinga of Angola: Africa's Warrior Queen. Cambridge, MA: Harvard University Press.

Hill, R.S. (2009). Maori and the State: Crown–Maori Relations in New Zealand/ Aotearoa, 1950–2000. Wellington: Victoria University Press.

Hviding, E. (1996). Guardians of Marovo Lagoon: Practice, Place, and Politics in Maritime Melanesia. Honolulu: University of Hawai'i Press.

IPCC (2022). Climate Change 2022: Impacts, Adaptation and Vulnerability. Contribution of Working Group II to the Sixth Assessment Report of the Intergovernmental Panel on Climate Change. Cambridge: Cambridge University Press.

Israel, J.I. (1989). Dutch Primacy in World Trade, 1585–1740. Oxford: Clarendon Press.

Josefsen, E. (2010a) 'The Saami and the National Parliaments: Channels for Political Influence'. Geneva: Inter-Parliamentary Union and UNDP.

Josefsen, E. (2010b). 'The Saami and the National Parliaments: Channels for Political Influence'. Inter-Parliamentary Union and UNDP Reports on Indigenous Peoples and Parliament. Geneva: IPU/UNDP.

Josefsen, E. (2015). "Political Systems and the Sami." In C. Keskitalo (ed.), The Sami People: Traditions in Transition. Fairbanks: University of Alaska Press, pp. 123–140.

Josephson, P.R. (1996). Red Atom: Russia's Nuclear Power Program from Stalin to Today. New York: W.H. Freeman.

Kawharu, M. (ed.) (2010). Tāhuhu Kōrero: The Sayings of Taitokerau. Auckland: Auckland University Press.

Kay, C. (1982). 'Achievements and Contradictions of Agrarian Reform in Latin America'. Journal of Development Studies, 18(2), pp. 141–170.
Kennedy, P. (1987). The Rise and Fall of the Great Powers: Economic Change and Military Conflict from 1500 to 2000. New York: Random House.
Keohane, R.O. (1984). After Hegemony: Cooperation and Discord in the World Political Economy. Princeton: Princeton University Press.
Knaut, A.L. (1995). The Pueblo Revolt of 1680: Conquest and Resistance in Seventeenth-Century New Mexico. Norman: University of Oklahoma Press.
Krupa, J. (2012). Identifying barriers to aboriginal renewable energy deployment in Canada. Energy Policy, 42, pp. 710–714.
Kukutai, T. and Taylor, J. (eds.) (2016). Indigenous Data Sovereignty: Toward an Agenda. Canberra: ANU Press.
Laband, J. (1997). The Rise and Fall of the Zulu Nation. London: Arms and Armour Press.
Lee, R. (1979; 2nd ed. 1984). The !Kung San: Men, Women and Work in a Foraging Society. Cambridge: Cambridge University Press.
Lee, R. (2017). The !Kung San: Men, Women and Work in a Foraging Society. 3rd ed. Cambridge: Cambridge University Press.
Lepore, J. (1998). The Name of War: King Philip's War and the Origins of American Identity. New York: Knopf.
Lightfoot, S. (2016). Global Indigenous Politics: A Subtle Revolution. Abingdon: Routledge.
Lyons, O., Mohawk, J., Deloria, V., Hauptman, L. M., Berman, H., Grinde, D. A., Shaaf, R. and Wilkinson, C. (1992). Exiled in the Land of the Free: Democracy, Indian Nations and the U.S. Constitution. Santa Fe: Clear Light Publishers.
Mamdani, M. (1996). Citizen and Subject: Contemporary Africa and the Legacy of Late Colonialism. Princeton: Princeton University Press.
Marx, K. and Engels, F. (1848 [1998]). The Communist Manifesto. London: Verso
Mauss, M. (1990 [1925]) The Gift: The Form and Reason for Exchange in Archaic Societies. London: Routledge.
May, S. (2012). Language and Minority Rights: Ethnicity, Nationalism and the Politics of Language. 2nd ed. New York: Routledge.
Mt. Pleasant, J. (2011). 'The Science Behind the Three Sisters Mound System: An Agronomic Assessment of an Indigenous Agricultural System in the Northeast', Agronomy Journal, 103(4), pp. 1136–1146.
Munro, J. (2003). 'The Monetary Origins of the "Price Revolution": South German Silver Mining, Merchant-Banking, and Venetian Commerce, 1470–1540'. In: J. Munro, Textiles, Merchants and Money in Late Medieval and Early Modern Europe. Aldershot: Ashgate.

Neal, L. (1990). The Rise of Financial Capitalism: International Capital Markets in the Age of Reason. Cambridge: Cambridge University Press.
Nettheim, G., Meyers, G. and Craig, D. (2002). Indigenous Peoples and the Law in Australia. Sydney: Butterworths.
Nettheim, G., Meyers, G. and Craig, D. (2014). Indigenous Peoples and the Law in Australia (2nd ed.). Sydney: LexisNexis Butterworths.
North, D.C. (1990). Institutions, Institutional Change and Economic Performance. Cambridge: Cambridge University Press.
Osiander, A. (2001). 'Sovereignty, International Relations, and the Westphalian Myth', International Organization, 55(2), pp. 251–287.
Ostler, J. (2004). The Plains Sioux and U.S. Colonialism from Lewis and Clark to Wounded Knee. Cambridge: Cambridge University Press.
Ostrom, E. (1990). Governing the Commons: The Evolution of Institutions for Collective Action. Cambridge: Cambridge University Press.
Pagden, A. (1995). Lords of All the World: Ideologies of Empire in Spain, Britain and France c.1500–c.1800. New Haven, CT: Yale University Press.
Papillon, M. (2012). 'Adapting Federalism: Indigenous Multilevel Governance in Canada and the United States'. Publius: The Journal of Federalism, 42(2), pp. 289–312.
Philpott, D. (2001). Revolutions in Sovereignty: How Ideas Shaped Modern International Relations. Princeton: Princeton University Press.
Postero, N. (2017). The Indigenous State: Race, Politics, and Performance in Plurinational Bolivia. Berkeley: University of California Press.
Rights and Resources Initiative (2020). Who Owns the World's Land? A Global Baseline of Indigenous and Community Land Rights. Washington, DC: RRI.
Rodger, N.A.M. (2004). The Command of the Ocean: A Naval History of Britain, 1649–1815. London: Allen Lane.
Salomon, F. (2004). The Cord Keepers: Khipus and Cultural Life in a Peruvian Village. Durham, NC: Duke University Press.
Sarkar, S. (1983). Modern India: 1885–1947. Delhi: Macmillan.
Scott, J.C. (1998). Seeing Like a State: How Certain Schemes to Improve the Human Condition Have Failed. New Haven: Yale University Press.
Simpson, A. (2014). Mohawk Interruptus: Political Life Across the Borders of Settler States. Durham: Duke University Press.
Smith, P.C. and Warrior, R. (1996). Like a Hurricane: The Indian Movement from Alcatraz to Wounded Knee. New York: New Press.
Taylor, W.B. (1996). Magistrates of the Sacred: Priests and Parishioners in Eighteenth-Century Mexico. Stanford, CA: Stanford University Press.
Tilly, C. (1990). Coercion, Capital, and European States, AD 990–1990. Oxford: Blackwell.
Van Cott, D.L. (2005). From Movements to Parties in Latin America: The Evolution of Ethnic Politics. Cambridge: Cambridge University Press.

Walker, C. (2014). The Tupac Amaru Rebellion. Cambridge, MA: Harvard University Press.
Washbrook, D.A. (1981). 'Law, State and Agrarian Society in Colonial India'. Modern Asian Studies, 15(3), pp. 649–721.
Wegren, S. (1998). Agriculture and the State in Soviet and Post-Soviet Russia. Pittsburgh: University of Pittsburgh Press.
White, E.N. (1995). 'Was There a Solution to the Ancien Régime's Financial Dilemma?' Journal of Economic History, 49(3), pp. 545–568.
Whyte, K.P. (2017). 'Indigenous Climate Change Studies: Indigenizing Futures, Decolonizing the Anthropocene'. English Language Notes, 55(1–2), pp. 153–162.
Whyte, K.P. (2018). 'Indigenous Science (Fiction) for the Anthropocene: Ancestral Dystopias and Fantasies of Climate Change Crises'. Environment and Planning E: Nature and Space, 1(1–2), pp. 224–242.
Wilde, G. (2009). Religious Power and Everyday Life in Jesuit Missions: The Guaraní and the Making of Colonial South America. Durham, NC: Duke University Press.
Wilkins, D.E. and Lomawaima, K.T. (2001). Uneven Ground: American Indian Sovereignty and Federal Law. Norman: University of Oklahoma Press.

CHAPTER 7

Conclusion—Reclaiming the Past, Reimagining the Future

1 Introduction

The final chapter of this volume brings into focus the core insights gathered across Indigenous economic systems and ancient economic traditions, offering a reframing of what political economy can mean in a pluriversal world. It synthesizes the material covered in earlier chapters by revisiting the historical and ontological ruptures caused by colonialism, interrogating the assumptions of Western economic theory, and exploring how Indigenous frameworks offer alternative pathways grounded in ecological care, collective responsibility, and spiritual sovereignty. Land, in Indigenous thought, is not an input to be priced but a living entity with which relationships are maintained through reciprocity and law.[1,2] This relational ontology challenges dominant paradigms where utility maximization and commodification underpin modern economic models.[3,4] Instead, Indigenous economies are embedded in kinship systems, spiritual

[1] Berkes, F. (2012) Sacred Ecology: Traditional Ecological Knowledge and Resource Management. 3rd edn. London: Routledge.

[2] Kimmerer, R.W. (2013) Braiding Sweetgrass: Indigenous Wisdom, Scientific Knowledge and the Teachings of Plants. Minneapolis: Milkweed Editions.

[3] Sen, A. (1999) Development as Freedom. Oxford: Oxford University Press.

[4] Polanyi, K. (1944) The Great Transformation: The Political and Economic Origins of Our Time. Boston: Beacon Press.

S. Ramesh, *The Political Economy of the Indigenous Peoples of the World, Volume I*, https://doi.org/10.1007/978-3-032-24041-5_7

practice, and multigenerational stewardship, a pattern that resonates with other ancient systems, such as Confucian agrarianism, Kautilyan public investment strategies, and Aristotelian critiques of chrematistics.[5,6,7] This chapter also confronts the enduring legacy of colonialism, not simply as a historical phenomenon, but as an ongoing structural force that continues to marginalize Indigenous sovereignty and economic autonomy.[8,9] In doing so, it recognizes the significance of revitalization movements, from food sovereignty to Indigenous data governance, as acts of epistemic resistance and economic innovation.[10,11] In response to the ecological and political limits of both capitalism and communism, this concluding chapter introduces Symbiotic Gaian Economics (SGE) as a future-facing framework. SGE draws from Earth-system science,[12] Indigenous relationality, and capabilities-based approaches to propose an economy based on consent, regeneration, and embedded pluralism.[13,14] It is not a utopian blueprint, but a design philosophy for living economies that prioritize resilience, equity, and ontological dignity. Ultimately, this chapter invites a reorientation of economic thought—from abstract universalism to situated, plural, and relational models. It positions Indigenous economies

[5] Elman, B.A. (2000) A Cultural History of Civil Examinations in Late Imperial China. Berkeley: University of California Press.

[6] Rangarajan, L.N. (trans.) (1992) Kautilya: The Arthashastra. New Delhi: Penguin Books.

[7] Finley, M.I. (1973) The Ancient Economy. Berkeley: University of California Press.

[8] Federici, S. (2004) Caliban and the Witch: Women, the Body and Primitive Accumulation. New York: Autonomedia.

[9] Nadasdy, P. (2003) Hunters and Bureaucrats: Power, Knowledge, and Aboriginal-State Relations in the Southwest Yukon. Vancouver: UBC Press.

[10] Corntassel, J. (2008) 'Toward Sustainable Self-Determination: Rethinking the Contemporary Indigenous-Rights Discourse', Alternatives: Global, Local, Political, 33(1), pp. 105–132.

[11] Kukutai, T. and Taylor, J. (eds.) (2016) Indigenous Data Sovereignty: Toward an Agenda. Canberra: ANU Press.

[12] Rockström, J. et al. (2009) 'A Safe Operating Space for Humanity', Nature, 461(7263), pp. 472–475.

[13] Raworth, K. (2017) Doughnut Economics: Seven Ways to Think Like a 21st-Century Economist. White River Junction: Chelsea Green Publishing.

[14] Ostrom, E. (2010) 'Beyond Markets and States: Polycentric Governance of Complex Economic Systems', American Economic Review, 100(3), pp. 641–672.

not at the margins but at the centre of planetary survival and collective flourishing.

This final chapter of Volume 1 draws together the conceptual, historical, and comparative insights developed throughout the preceding chapters to synthesize an understanding of the foundational structures of Indigenous political economies. Chapters 1–6 have explored the spiritual, philosophical, economic, and legal dimensions of Indigenous relationships to land, sovereignty, and communal systems of value, consistently contrasting them with the individualistic and extractive logics of neoclassical and Marxist economic paradigms. From the embeddedness of Indigenous economies in kinship and ecology (Chapters 1–3) to the impacts of colonial epistemologies and institutional displacement (Chapters 4–6), this volume has sought to challenge the idea that Indigenous economic systems are marginal or pre-modern. This chapter thus brings these threads together by exploring how a holistic Indigenous worldview can form the basis for a radically different economic paradigm—Symbiotic Gaian Economics—rooted in reciprocity, ecological sustainability, and sovereignty. This chapter serves as both culmination and bridge, linking foundational understandings of Indigenous economies to a transformative vision of economic theory that will be further explored in Volume 2 through the lenses of resistance, resurgence, and justice in contemporary global contexts.

1.1 Revisiting the Foundations

This volume has traced the roots, frameworks, and implications of Indigenous political economy across a broad spectrum of societies, from the Andean ayllu and the Māori hapū to the Cree traplines and Yolŋu governance systems. A foundational insight unifies these diverse traditions: land is not merely a factor of production, nor a tradable asset, but a living entity, a source of law, responsibility, and existence itself.[15,16] Among the Navajo (Diné), for example, the land is considered sacred and endowed with moral agency. Economies are structured around hózhó, harmony, balance, and beauty, not around profit maximization or material surplus.

[15] Berkes, F. (2012). Sacred Ecology: Traditional Ecological Knowledge and Resource Management. 3rd edn. London: Routledge.

[16] Kimmerer, R. W. (2013). Braiding Sweetgrass: Indigenous Wisdom, Scientific Knowledge and the Teachings of Plants. Minneapolis: Milkweed Editions.

Contrary to the marginalization of Indigenous systems in mainstream economic theory, these are not underdeveloped or alternative versions of capitalism. Rather, they represent ontologically distinct models of economic life rooted in interdependence, reciprocity, and ecological stewardship.[17,18] In the Sámi reindeer economies of Fennoscandia, economic decisions are made based on migratory cycles, herd well-being, and intergenerational obligations, not according to supply and demand or state quotas.[19] Similarly, the Zapatista communities in Chiapas operate under the principle of "mandar obedeciendo" (lead by obeying), rejecting both capitalist accumulation and statist centralization in favour of bottom-up, deliberative economic governance. Neoclassical economics, by contrast, is founded on assumptions of individual rationality, utility maximization, and market equilibrium, where land is an input and value is determined by marginal productivity. Efficiency is defined as Pareto optimality, which presumes scarcity, competitive markets, and no externalities, an abstraction that obscures real-world inequities and ecological degradation.[20] In contrast, Indigenous economies often prioritize sufficiency, regeneration, and social harmony. For instance, the rotational farming systems of the Karen people in Northern Thailand preserve biodiversity and maintain soil fertility, defying the neoclassical logic that sees such practices as "inefficient" due to low yield per acre.[21] Marxist political economy, while critiquing capitalism's exploitative nature, still centres production, labour, and material surplus as the driving forces of history. Its emphasis on class struggle and industrial ownership largely overlooks the spiritual and ecological dimensions of Indigenous economies. Marx's notion of "primitive accumulation"[22] rightly critiques the expropriation of communal

[17] Escobar, A. (2018). Designs for the Pluriverse: Radical Interdependence, Autonomy, and the Making of Worlds. Durham: Duke University Press.

[18] De la Cadena, M. and Blaser, M. (eds.) (2018). A World of Many Worlds. Durham: Duke University Press.

[19] Mustonen, T. et al. (2022). "Co-management of Reindeer Herding and Climate Adaptation among Sámi Peoples", Sustainability Science, 17(3), pp. 765–778.

[20] Sen, A. (1999). Development as Freedom. Oxford: Oxford University Press.

[21] FAO (2015). Indigenous Peoples' Food Systems and Agriculture. Rome: Food and Agriculture Organization of the United Nations Nations.

[22] Marx, K. (1867). Capital: A Critique of Political Economy. Volume I. London: Penguin Classics (1990 edition).

lands, but offers no viable framework for valuing the kin-centric ontologies of Indigenous peoples. In contrast, many Indigenous economic systems embed surplus within protocols of redistribution and ceremonial exchange. The potlatch of the Pacific Northwest, for example, was outlawed by colonial authorities because it challenged capitalist logics of hoarding and accumulation through its ritualized giving and social cohesion functions.[23] Terms like "efficiency", "rationality", and "growth" are exposed as culturally contingent rather than universal. The Māori concept of kaitiakitanga, guardianship, frames wealth as the ability to uphold one's responsibilities to land and kin, not the amassing of capital. Similarly, the Haida Nation's land-use plans incorporate species protection thresholds and spiritual considerations into forestry decisions, challenging cost–benefit analysis as the primary tool of policy evaluation.[24] These examples reveal that Indigenous economies are not static relics of a pre-modern past. They offer contemporary, scalable alternatives to the ecological and social crises of global capitalism. What emerges, then, is not nostalgia but a philosophical and political rupture with the epistemic foundations of modern economics. The challenge is not only to recognize these systems, but to reconfigure development, policy, and governance in ways that honour plural ontologies of economy.

1.2 The Enduring Legacy of Colonialism

Colonialism was not merely a geopolitical event or territorial conquest; it was a foundational rupture that restructured Indigenous political economies and erased ontological systems. Through land alienation, forced labour regimes, and extractive infrastructure, colonial powers forcibly integrated Indigenous territories into the global capitalist economy as peripheral resource frontiers. In Africa, colonial land ordinances, such as the 1913 Natives Land Act in South Africa, formally dispossessed Black communities of over 80% of arable land, confining

[23] Cole, D., and Chaikin, I. (1990). An Iron Hand Upon the People: The Law Against the Potlatch on the Northwest Coast. Vancouver: Douglas & McIntyre.

[24] Mason, R., Borrows, J. and Napoleon, V. (2021). "Indigenous Legal Orders and Forest Stewardship", in Curran, D. (ed.) Living within Limits: Regenerating Canada's Forests. Vancouver: UBC Press.

them to reserves and enforcing dependency on wage labour in settler-owned mines and farms.[25] In North America, the enclosure of communal territories through the Dawes Act (1887) resulted in a loss of over 90 million acres of Native American land by 1934.[26]

The economic logic underpinning colonialism often reflected elements of both neoclassical and state-socialist doctrines, albeit filtered through imperial control. Like neoclassical economics, colonial regimes sought to commodify land and labour to generate maximum resource extraction, prioritizing efficiency and market integration. Simultaneously, the command-and-control features of colonial governance, monopolized trade, fixed labour obligations, and centralized planning, resembled certain aspects of planned economies under communism. However, unlike either system in theory, colonialism lacked any genuine concern for the welfare or consent of the subject populations; both economic output and political power were extracted, not negotiated. Colonial economic systems were enforced through an architecture of legal erasure and ontological imposition. Indigenous governance structures, such as the Gadaa system of the Oromo in Ethiopia, the ayllu networks of the Andes, or the potlatch economies of the Northwest Coast, were either criminalized, dismantled, or rendered invisible under foreign property law and bureaucratic administration.[27,28] The Potlatch economies of the Northwest Coast refer to traditional Indigenous systems of wealth distribution and governance practiced by First Nations such as the Haida, Tlingit, Kwakwaka'wakw, and Tsimshian peoples in what is now British Columbia and Alaska. Potlatch economies of the Northwest Coast invert conventional capitalist logic by redistributing wealth through ceremonial gift-giving, reinforcing social status not through accumulation but through generosity, reciprocity, and community obligation. Taxation systems and administrative hierarchies imposed hierarchical categories that ignored Indigenous relationality and reciprocity, reducing

[25] Bundy, C. (1988) The Rise and Fall of the South African Peasantry. London: James Currey.

[26] Wilkins, D. E. and Lomawaima, K. T. (2001) Uneven Ground: American Indian Sovereignty and Federal Law. Norman: University of Oklahoma Press.

[27] Cole, D. and Chaikin, I. (1990) An Iron Hand Upon the People: The Law Against the Potlatch on the Northwest Coast. Vancouver: Douglas & McIntyre.

[28] Mamdani, M. (1996) Citizen and Subject: Contemporary Africa and the Legacy of Late Colonialism. Princeton: Princeton University Press.

complex systems of stewardship to exploitable 'vacant' land or labour pools. Education systems further advanced this ontological colonization. Schools became mechanisms for assimilation, embedding Western epistemologies while delegitimizing Indigenous knowledge, languages, and cosmologies.[29] The legacies of these disruptions remain present. Across continents, Indigenous peoples face disproportionately high rates of poverty, ecological degradation, and marginalization from economic decision-making. Extractive industries continue to operate on territories without Free, Prior and Informed Consent (FPIC), often under the banner of national development. In the Amazon, for example, Indigenous resistance to illegal mining and logging reflects a deeper struggle for jurisdictional and epistemic recognition, not merely environmental protection.[30] These are not just economic injustices but manifestations of epistemic violence. Structural underdevelopment, criminalization, and social exclusion are the result of ongoing efforts to deny the legitimacy of Indigenous governance, law, and cosmology. What is at stake is not just land or livelihood, but the right to define what constitutes economy, value, and life itself. Against this backdrop, Indigenous resurgence does not seek inclusion into existing systems, but the recovery and articulation of political economies grounded in consent, custodianship, and cosmological continuity.

1.3 Indigenous Resilience and Revitalization

Despite centuries of dispossession, Indigenous economies have not disappeared; they have persisted, evolved, and are now undergoing significant revitalization. This endurance is not simply a matter of survival but reflects a profound capacity for adaptation and transformation. In many regions, Indigenous communities have advanced food sovereignty movements that challenge the global agri-food system's commodification of land and life. For example, the White Earth Land Recovery Project in Minnesota, founded by Winona LaDuke, exemplifies how Anishinaabe people are reclaiming land and reviving traditional wild rice harvesting

[29] Smith, L. T. (2012) Decolonizing Methodologies: Research and Indigenous Peoples. 2nd edn. London: Zed Books.

[30] De la Cadena, M. and Blaser, M. (eds.) (2018) A World of Many Worlds. Durham: Duke University Press.

methods in defiance of genetically modified alternatives and environmentally harmful practices.[31] Land-back campaigns across North America, Australia, and Latin America demonstrate the political dimensions of economic restoration. In Canada, the Haida Nation's co-management agreement over Gwaii Haanas National Park Reserve represents a reclamation not only of land but of governance, stewardship, and economic autonomy rooted in ancestral responsibilities.[32] These movements starkly contrast with neoclassical economic models that prioritize efficiency and individual ownership. Where neoclassical frameworks reduce land to an input or asset, Indigenous economies treat it as a living relation, one that entails reciprocal obligations rather than extractive rights.

Adaptive subsistence practices, such as rotational hunting in the Arctic, transhumant pastoralism among the Sámi, or shifting cultivation by the Karen in Southeast Asia, are not vestiges of the past. Rather, they reflect dynamic, experimental systems of resilience and ecological intelligence. A study on Sámi reindeer herding under climate change shows how Indigenous governance structures integrate observation, cosmology, and adaptation strategies in ways that elude conventional state-centric environmental planning.[33] This stands in contrast to both neoclassical and communist models. While the former promotes market-based solutions, and the latter often imposed industrial agricultural schemes, both tended to undermine the social and ecological embeddedness of local practices. Unlike the technocratic approach often seen in state socialism, where planning was centralized and rural collectives (e.g. China's People's Communes or Soviet kolkhozy) aimed at maximizing output, Indigenous economic strategies remain plural, decentralized, and attuned to local ecologies. Whereas centralized planning often ignored local variability, leading, for example, to ecological crises like the Aral Sea disaster, Indigenous land use systems, such as Andean ayllu structures or Zapatista agroecological farming in Chiapas, embed social and environmental

[31] LaDuke, W. (2005). Recovering the Sacred: The Power of Naming and Claiming. Cambridge, MA: South End Press.

[32] Borrows, J. (2010). Canada's Indigenous Constitution. Toronto: University of Toronto Press.

[33] Mustonen, T., Feodoroff, P., Gaup, E., Lempinen, H., Morimoto, J., Mustonen, K., and Nieminen, S. (2022). 'Co-management of Reindeer Herding and Climate Adaptation among Sámi Peoples', Sustainability Science, 17(3), pp. 765–778.

knowledge into every stage of decision-making.[34,35] Importantly, Indigenous knowledge is not only ecological but deeply political. It constitutes a resistance through cosmology, a refusal to sever economy from culture, law, or spirit. The rise of Indigenous data sovereignty initiatives, such as those led by the Aotearoa-based Te Mana Raraunga collective, reflects this holistic perspective. By reclaiming the right to define, collect, and use data in ways that reflect Indigenous values and priorities, these movements challenge both capitalist metrics of productivity and statist instruments of surveillance.[36] Revitalization extends to law, language, and learning. Indigenous legal orders, like the Cree concept of Wahkohtowin or the Navajo principle of Hózhó, articulate economic relationships as fundamentally moral and relational, structured around duties of care rather than commodified exchange.[37] In this way, education itself becomes a site of decolonial economic transformation. Initiatives such as Canada's First Nations University or the Māori immersion kura kaupapa schools work to reconstruct economic literacy not in abstraction from land and people, but in deep alignment with them.

Ultimately, these examples point towards a reassertion of Indigenous sovereignty not just over territory, but over thought, governance, and futurity. The goal is not a return to the past but a forward-looking reconstitution of economic life on terms that reflect ancestral wisdom and present-day realities. Indigenous political economies present a compelling alternative to both market fundamentalism and state socialism, a pluriversal vision grounded in respect, responsibility, and regeneration.

1.4 Interrogating Western Economic Thought

This volume has paired Indigenous philosophies with a critical re-evaluation of economic traditions from ancient India, China, and Greece,

[34] Escobar, A. (2018). Designs for the Pluriverse: Radical Interdependence, Autonomy, and the Making of Worlds. Durham: Duke University Press.

[35] De la Cadena, M. and Blaser, M. (eds.) (2018). A World of Many Worlds. Durham: Duke University Press.

[36] Kukutai, T. and Taylor, J. (eds.) (2016). Indigenous Data Sovereignty: Towards an Agenda. Canberra: ANU Press.

[37] Napoleon, V. and Friedland, H. (2016). 'An Inside Job: Engaging with Indigenous Legal Traditions through Stories', McGill Law Journal, 61(4), pp. 725–754.

demonstrating that the moral and ecological foundations of economic life were historically central across cultures. In ancient Indian Arthashastra, for example, Kautilya's prescriptions on statecraft, taxation, and land management were deeply tied to dharma, or moral duty, with the king bearing responsibility for the welfare of all beings, not merely subjects but also forests, animals, and rivers.[38] Similarly, in Confucian China, the ideal of harmonious governance embedded the economy within a framework of filial piety and ritual propriety, placing ethical constraints on accumulation and advocating redistribution in times of scarcity.[39] Ancient Greek oikonomia, the root of our term "economy", referred not to market efficiency but to household management and civic virtue, where wealth was not to be pursued limitlessly, but with moderation, as Aristotle warned against chrematistics, the art of wealth acquisition for its own sake.[40] These traditions contrast sharply with the dominant assumptions of neoclassical economics, which models society as an aggregate of self-interested individuals optimizing utility within markets that are assumed to function best when left unregulated. Land, labour, and capital are abstracted from historical, ecological, and cultural context. Economic "rationality" becomes defined by individual maximization, while collective responsibilities, sacred landscapes, and intergenerational obligations are rendered invisible. Indigenous economies challenge this by rooting value in relationality rather than scarcity or price. For instance, in the Andean ayllu system, land is not a commodity but a living relative, and agricultural labour is embedded in reciprocal obligations (ayni) among kin and non-human entities.[41] Communist economic models, while rejecting capitalist private property, often reproduce universalizing assumptions. Classical Marxism reduces social life to class relations and material production, underestimating the role of cosmology, language, and place in structuring Indigenous economies.[42] For example, Soviet collectivization policies

[38] Rangarajan, L.N. (trans.) (1992). Kautilya: The Arthashastra. New Delhi: Penguin Books.

[39] Elman, B.A. (2005). Classicism, Politics, and Kinship: The Ch'ing Imperial Examinations. Cambridge: Cambridge University Press.

[40] Finley, M.I. (1973). The Ancient Economy. Berkeley: University of California Press.

[41] De la Cadena, M. and Blaser, M. (eds.) (2018). A World of Many Worlds. Durham: Duke University Press.

[42] Marx, K. (1867). Capital: A Critique of Political Economy. Volume I. London: Penguin Classics (1990 edition).

in Central Asia ignored nomadic patterns of pastoralism and sacred geographies, leading to widespread ecological disruption and cultural dislocation.[43] Similarly, in China, the imposition of commune systems during the Great Leap Forward displaced intricate village economies attuned to seasonal cycles and ancestral rites.[44] Both neoclassical and Marxist traditions, despite their differences, carry a universalist epistemology that presumes a single model of rationality, value, and progress. By contrast, Indigenous economic thought centres ontological plurality, the recognition that there is not one world, but many. Legal orders, moral economies, and land relations are diverse and place-specific. This is evident in the governance systems of the Yolŋu people in northern Australia, where land tenure is expressed through songlines and ancestral narratives rather than title deeds or state registries.[45,46] In North America, Potlatch economies among the Haida and Kwakwaka'wakw nations regulated surplus distribution through ceremonial exchange and social status, not accumulation or price mechanisms.[47] Contemporary Indigenous movements are not merely resistance projects, they are epistemic innovations. The Sámi Council's co-management of reindeer herding in Arctic Finland integrates satellite data and climate modelling with oral traditions and seasonal calendars, demonstrating how Indigenous data sovereignty can guide adaptive governance.[48,49] Such examples call for a profound reconstruction of economic theory, not simply to include Indigenous voices, but to shift its foundations, from extraction

[43] Mamdani, M. (1996). Citizen and Subject: Contemporary Africa and the Legacy of Late Colonialism. Princeton: Princeton University Press.

[44] Escobar, A. (2018). Designs for the Pluriverse: Radical Interdependence, Autonomy, and the Making of Worlds. Durham: Duke University Press.

[45] Kimmerer, R.W. (2013). Braiding Sweetgrass: Indigenous Wisdom, Scientific Knowledge and the Teachings of Plants. Minneapolis: Milkweed Editions.

[46] Smith, L.T. (2012). Decolonizing Methodologies: Research and Indigenous Peoples. 2nd edn. London: Zed Books.

[47] Cole, D., and Chaikin, I. (1990). An Iron Hand Upon the People: The Law Against the Potlatch on the Northwest Coast. Vancouver: Douglas & McIntyre.

[48] Mustonen, T. et al. (2022). 'Co-management of Reindeer Herding and Climate Adaptation among Sámi Peoples', *Sustainability Science*, 17(3), pp. 765–778.

[49] Kukutai, T. and Taylor, J. (eds.) (2016). *Indigenous Data Sovereignty: Toward an Agenda*. Canberra: ANU Press.

to relation, from abstraction to emplacement, and from universality to plurality.

1.5 Looking Ahead: Towards Symbiotic Gaian Economics

As humanity confronts intersecting crises, climate change, biodiversity collapse, and widening social inequality, the limitations of prevailing economic systems have become increasingly clear. Neoclassical economics, with its emphasis on individual utility maximization, competitive equilibrium, and infinite growth, has proven ill-equipped to account for ecological thresholds or the social cost of environmental degradation.[50,51] Meanwhile, the centrally planned economies of communist regimes, although more egalitarian in ambition, often fell into extractive industrial models that sidelined both environmental sustainability and local agency.[52] In this context, Symbiotic Gaian Economics (SGE) emerges as a pluralistic and ecologically grounded alternative. SGE challenges the growth imperatives of conventional models by foregrounding ecological carrying capacity and interdependence, principles long central to Indigenous economies and cosmologies.[53,54] Ecological carrying capacity refers to the maximum level of resource use and waste generation that an ecosystem can sustain without degrading its ability to support life over time. Rather than viewing the Earth as a passive backdrop for production, SGE sees the biosphere as an active participant in economic life, a living system with which humans must enter respectful and regenerative relationships.[55] One key distinction between SGE and traditional economic frameworks lies in its valuation metrics. Instead of GDP or

[50] Raworth, K. (2017) Doughnut Economics: Seven Ways to Think Like a 21st-Century Economist. White River Junction: Chelsea Green Publishing.

[51] Rockström, J. et al. (2009) 'A Safe Operating Space for Humanity', Nature, 461(7263), pp. 472–475.

[52] Malm, A. (2016) Fossil Capital: The Rise of Steam Power and the Roots of Global Warming. London: Verso.

[53] Kimmerer, R.W. (2013) Braiding Sweetgrass: Indigenous Wisdom, Scientific Knowledge and the Teachings of Plants. Minneapolis: Milkweed Editions.

[54] Berkes, F. (2012) Sacred Ecology: Traditional Ecological Knowledge and Resource Management, 3rd edn. London: Routledge.

[55] Latour, B. (2017) Facing Gaia: Eight Lectures on the New Climatic Regime. Cambridge: Polity Press.

output maximization, SGE turns to multidimensional indicators such as Amartya Sen's capabilities approach,[56] biodiversity integrity indices, and measures of intergenerational well-being.[57] For example, Bhutan's Gross National Happiness index operationalizes well-being not as consumption, but as holistic life satisfaction, spiritual fulfilment, and environmental health. To construct a robust multidimensional index aligned with the theoretical commitments of Sustainable Green Economics (SGE), the included variables must span social, ecological, and temporal or intergenerational dimensions. From a social perspective, Amartya Sen's capabilities approach offers a foundational framework. This focuses on what people can and do, the "functionings" they value. Core variables in this domain include indicators of health (such as life expectancy, access to healthcare, and nutrition), education (encompassing literacy rates and access to all levels of schooling), political agency and freedom (including civic participation and legal rights), income security (focusing not just on absolute income levels but on the security and equity of access to income), and general living conditions (housing quality, access to utilities, and safety). While some of these are captured in Human Development Index-style measures, SGE requires greater disaggregation and context sensitivity, for example, by gender or region. On the ecological side, the index should reflect planetary boundaries and ecological carrying capacity, capturing the health of natural systems and biodiversity. Relevant indicators include species richness and abundance, habitat integrity (e.g. deforestation rates and protected area coverage), carbon emissions per capita, and water and air quality indices. A combined measure such as the ecological footprint compared against national biocapacity is also valuable. National biocapacity can be quantified by estimating the biological productivity of a country's ecosystems, such as cropland, forests, and fisheries, based on their ability to regenerate renewable resources and absorb waste, especially carbon emissions, using standardized land productivity factors. These components may be drawn from established sources such as the Living Planet Index, the Environmental Performance Index, or the Planetary Boundaries framework. The third core domain is intergenerational well-being, which addresses the sustainability and fairness of economic

[56] Sen, A. (1999) Development as Freedom. Oxford: Oxford University Press.

[57] O'Neill, D.W., Fanning, A.L., Lamb, W.F. and Steinberger, J.K. (2018) 'A Good Life for All within Planetary Boundaries', Nature Sustainability, 1, pp. 88–95.

and ecological systems over time. Variables here include the net stock of natural capital (e.g. forests, minerals, freshwater), public investment in education (as a proxy for future capabilities), the debt-to-GDP ratio (to assess fiscal sustainability), youth employment trends, and measures of climate resilience and infrastructure durability. The Genuine Progress Indicator (GPI) and the Inclusive Wealth Index (IWI) are two tools that already incorporate elements of these concerns. To construct such an index robustly from a theoretical standpoint, several criteria must be met. First, normative justification is crucial: each selected dimension must reflect the central values of SGE, namely equity, sustainability, human capability, and ecological integrity. The framework should be pluralistic, moving beyond income to reflect multiple axes of well-being, in line with thinkers like Sen and Nussbaum. Indicator selection should prioritize policy-relevance, measurability, and reliability, while ensuring representativeness across the three key domains. In terms of aggregation, indicators must first be normalized, using methods such as min–max scaling or z-scores, and then weighted. These weights can be determined through participatory processes or empirical techniques such as principal component analysis, but they must also reflect ethical constraints: for instance, recognizing that some dimensions (such as biodiversity loss) may not be substitutable by gains in others (like income). Additive or geometric means may be used for index construction, with careful attention paid to the implications of each method. Further, sensitivity analysis should be employed to test the robustness of the index against changes in weights or variable inclusion. Disaggregation by region, gender, or class should be built into the index architecture, reflecting Sen's emphasis on distributional outcomes and social justice. Thus, replacing GDP with a multidimensional index marks a paradigmatic shift from output maximization towards a broader notion of flourishing, one that captures human capabilities, respects ecological limits, and safeguards intergenerational well-being. However, constructing such an index demands both theoretical coherence and methodological rigour to avoid the pitfalls of over-aggregation and to ensure the framework remains responsive to real-world complexity.

SGE also draws upon Earthsystem science, especially the concept of planetary boundaries[58] to embed biophysical limits within economic

[58] Rockström, J. et al. (2009) 'A Safe Operating Space for Humanity', Nature, 461(7263), pp. 472–475.

design. Circular and regenerative models inspired by Indigenous systems, such as Andean ayllu-based agriculture or First Nations forestry co-management, provide tangible pathways for aligning economic life with long-term ecological balance.[59,60] Governance under SGE is polycentric and consent-based, rejecting both top-down state control and unregulated market forces. It favours overlapping institutions, from clan councils and watershed assemblies to intergovernmental climate panels, that coordinate across scales while remaining grounded in place-specific knowledge.[61] Coordinating across scales means aligning decision-making and action from the local to the global level, ensuring that policies are coherent, mutually reinforcing, and responsive to both grassroots realities and broader systemic challenges. For example, the Sámi Parliament's participation in reindeer herding regulation represents a form of Indigenous sovereignty operating within national and transnational policy spheres.[62] Unlike Marxist approaches that emphasize historical materialism and class struggle, SGE is deeply ontological. It recognizes that economic relationships are not merely distributive, but constitutive of worldviews, identities, and responsibilities. Wealth is measured not by surplus accumulation, but by the health of relationships, human and non-human, intergenerational and interspecies.[63,64] Rather than prescribing a universal solution, SGE advocates for situated economic design. This means that economic institutions and practices must be developed in alignment with local cosmologies, land relations, and ecological rhythms. In the Māori concept of kaitiakitanga (guardianship), for instance, stewardship is not a policy choice, but a sacred duty rooted in genealogy

[59] Mustonen, T. et al. (2022) 'Co-management of Reindeer Herding and Climate Adaptation among Sámi Peoples', Sustainability Science, 17(3), pp. 765–778.

[60] Mason, L., Shearer, C., Baldwin, E., Tovar, A., & Buzzard, V. (2021) Co-stewardship as a pathway to strengthen Indigenous land rights and improve environmental outcomes, Ecological Applications, 31(2), e02259.

[61] Ostrom, E. (2010) 'Beyond Markets and States: Polycentric Governance of Complex Economic Systems', American Economic Review, 100(3), pp. 641–672.

[62] Mustonen, T. et al. (2022) 'Co-management of Reindeer Herding and Climate Adaptation among Sámi Peoples', Sustainability Science, 17(3), pp. 765–778.

[63] Escobar, A. (2018) Designs for the Pluriverse: Radical Interdependence, Autonomy, and the Making of Worlds. Durham: Duke University Press.

[64] LaDuke, W. (2005) Recovering the Sacred: The Power of Naming and Claiming. Cambridge, MA: South End Press.

and place.[65] In the Zapatista territories of Chiapas, autonomous municipalities organize production through cooperatives and assemblies that blend Indigenous traditions with contemporary resistance to neoliberal globalization.[66]

Symbiotic Gaian Economics is not a utopian escape from reality but a rigorous and pragmatic framework for transition. It opens the possibility of economic sovereignty that is both planetary and plural, capable of sustaining diverse lifeways while responding to the planetary emergency. It builds towards Volume 2, which will explore the institutional architectures, legal frameworks, and pedagogical tools necessary to enact such a transition.

1.6 *Final Reflections*

This volume has traced the historical ruptures and the resilient continuities of Indigenous economic systems, positioning them not as marginal or obsolete, but as viable foundations for rethinking political economy in the twenty-first century. Far from being passive victims of modernity, Indigenous peoples are active agents in crafting alternative modernities, rooted in values of relationality, reciprocity, and ecological embeddedness. These are not abstract ideals, but grounded practices that guide production, distribution, and stewardship across diverse geographies. For example, the Tŝilhqot'in Nation in British Columbia governs its forests through Indigenous legal orders that prioritize biodiversity and intergenerational accountability, operating alongside provincial regulatory systems through negotiated consent-based co-management.[67] Similarly, Sámi herders in the Nordic countries adapt transhumant practices in response to climate change through flexible governance structures that blend traditional ecological knowledge and modern scientific monitoring.[68] By contrast, neoclassical economics frames the economy as a

[65] Smith, L.T. (2012) Decolonizing Methodologies: Research and Indigenous Peoples, 2nd edn. London: Zed Books.

[66] EZLN (2001) Our Word is Our Weapon: Selected Writings. Edited by J.P. Ponce de León. New York: Seven Stories Press.

[67] Napoleon, V. (2013). Thinking About Indigenous Legal Orders. In: M. Asch, ed. Aboriginal Rights and Canada's Constitution. Vancouver: UBC Press, pp. 229–245.

[68] Mustonen, T. et al. (2022). 'Co-management of Reindeer Herding and Climate Adaptation among Sámi Peoples', Sustainability Science, 17(3), pp. 765–778.

closed system of rational, self-interested agents maximizing utility through market exchange. It abstracts individuals from communities, and land from its ecological and spiritual meanings. This worldview has justified extractive development models that devastate Indigenous territories, from Amazonian oil extraction to Canadian tar sands.[69,70] Even when framed as growth or development, the underlying logic privileges accumulation over care, efficiency over equity, and control over consent. Communism, while critiquing capitalist exploitation, often replicated its universalizing tendencies. State socialism in the Soviet Union, for example, suppressed Indigenous economies like the Evenki reindeer herders, enforcing collectivization schemes that disrupted kin-based land stewardship and spiritual cosmologies.[71] In China, ethnic minority regions have frequently been targeted for state-led development that marginalizes Indigenous governance, replacing plural economic forms with homogenized production quotas and infrastructure megaprojects.[72] Indigenous resurgence challenges both paradigms by insisting that economy is not separate from society or ecology, it is embedded in place-based law, kinship, and moral responsibility. The Zapatista communities in Chiapas, Mexico, exemplify this refusal. Since their 1994 uprising, they have sustained autonomous governance and economic self-determination through cooperatives, communal land ownership, and participatory democracy.[73] Their model is not anti-modern, but counter-modern, proposing a pluriversal future where many worlds fit. Such examples demonstrate that the struggle for epistemic justice is not merely theoretical or symbolic, it is material, legal, and infrastructural. It requires the recognition of Indigenous metrics, data governance, planning logics, and legal systems as

[69] LaDuke, W. (2005). Recovering the Sacred: The Power of Naming and Claiming. Cambridge, MA: South End Press.

[70] Escobar, A. (2018). Designs for the Pluriverse: Radical Interdependence, Autonomy, and the Making of Worlds. Durham: Duke University Press.

[71] Mamdani, M. (1996). Citizen and Subject: Contemporary Africa and the Legacy of Late Colonialism. Princeton: Princeton University Press.

[72] Smith, L.T. (2012). Decolonizing Methodologies: Research and Indigenous Peoples. 2nd edn. London: Zed Books.

[73] EZLN (2001). Our Word is Our Weapon: Selected Writings. Edited by Juana Ponce de León. New York: Seven Stories Press.

legitimate forms of world-making.[74,75] Initiatives such as Indigenous data sovereignty, land-back movements, and language revitalization campaigns are vital strategies for reclaiming authority over knowledge, territory, and time. Looking ahead, global challenges such as climate breakdown, ecological overshoot, and social inequality demand paradigms that can hold complexity and interdependence. Symbiotic Gaian Economics (SGE), introduced in this volume, begins to sketch such a framework, drawing from Indigenous philosophies, Earth-system science, and ethical economic traditions beyond the West.[76,77] It reframes prosperity through capabilities, care, and regeneration, rather than GDP or surplus value. Volume 2 will deepen this analysis, examining how neoliberal globalization, financialization and planetary governance structures intersect with Indigenous sovereignty. But the foundation is already clear: there is no sustainable or just future without Indigenous economic resurgence. This is not an inclusion into dominant systems, it is a re-worlding from below, through the plural rationalities and ecological intelligence of Indigenous nations.

2 Conclusion

This chapter has reaffirmed a critical proposition running throughout this volume: Indigenous political economies are not remnants of a bygone era, nor are they romanticized alternatives to capitalism; they are dynamic, living systems with contemporary relevance and future-facing potential. As global societies confront escalating crises of ecological degradation, inequality, and cultural dislocation, the insights of Indigenous economies offer not only critique but concrete pathways to reimagined futures. Indigenous communities across continents, from the Sámi in northern Europe to the Zapatistas in Chiapas, have demonstrated remarkable adaptability through legal pluralism, decentralized governance, and

[74] Kukutai, T. and Taylor, J. (eds.) (2016). Indigenous Data Sovereignty: Toward an Agenda. Canberra: ANU Press.

[75] Borrows, J. (2010). Canada's Indigenous Constitution. Toronto: University of Toronto Press.

[76] Latour, B. (2017). Facing Gaia: Eight Lectures on the New Climatic Regime. Cambridge: Polity Press.

[77] Raworth, K. (2017). Doughnut Economics: Seven Ways to Think Like a 21st-Century Economist. White River Junction: Chelsea Green Publishing.

ecological stewardship. These are not merely survival strategies; they are sophisticated responses to colonial disruption and neoliberal extraction.[78,79] The continued vitality of Indigenous economies, seen in food sovereignty movements, water protectors' actions, and language revitalization campaigns, constitutes a form of resurgence, not reactionary, but generative and visionary.[80] Where dominant economic theories such as neoclassical economics privilege scarcity, competition, and rational individualism, Indigenous frameworks embed economy within kinship, territory, and cosmology.[81] Unlike communism, which often replaces markets with state control but retains extractivist logics, Indigenous models decentralize power and emphasize relational accountability. For example, the Yolŋu people of Arnhem Land manage marine zones through a system of ancestral law that recognizes interspecies responsibilities.[82] Similarly, Sámi reindeer herding communities use polycentric governance to respond to climate disruption in ways that national governments struggle to emulate.[83] The call for epistemic justice is not symbolic. Indigenous legal orders, such as those articulated in Cree, Māori, or Anishinaabe traditions, hold authority over environmental and economic governance and challenge Eurocentric models of property, development, and time.[84,85] They do so by embedding law in relationships with land, kinship, and seasonal cycles, offering frameworks that prioritize reciprocity, restoration, and long-term ecological balance. Reclaiming narrative sovereignty, through

[78] Mason, R., Borrows, J. and Napoleon, V. (2021). 'Indigenous Legal Orders and Forest Stewardship', in Curran, D. (ed.) Living within Limits: Regenerating Canada's Forests. Vancouver: UBC Press.

[79] EZLN (2001) Our Word is Our Weapon: Selected Writings. Edited by J.P. Ponce de León. New York: Seven Stories Press.

[80] Tuck, E. and Yang, K.W. (2012). 'Decolonization is not a metaphor', Decolonization: Indigeneity, Education & Society, 1(1), pp. 1–40.

[81] Escobar, A. (2018). Designs for the Pluriverse: Radical Interdependence, Autonomy, and the Making of Worlds. Durham: Duke University Press.

[82] Berkes, F. (2012). Sacred Ecology: Traditional Ecological Knowledge and Resource Management. 3rd edn. London: Routledge.

[83] Mustonen, T. et al. (2022). 'Co-management of Reindeer Herding and Climate Adaptation among Sámi Peoples', Sustainability Science, 17(3), pp. 765–778.

[84] Borrows, J. (2010). Canada's Indigenous Constitution. Toronto: University of Toronto Press.

[85] Smith, L.T. (2012). Decolonizing Methodologies: Research and Indigenous Peoples. 2nd edn. London: Zed Books.

Indigenous media, scholarship, and pedagogy, is foundational to decolonizing the institutions that shape knowledge and policy. Looking ahead, the urgency of planetary instability demands a rethinking of economics itself. Symbiotic Gaian Economics (SGE), introduced here as a conceptual bridge to Volume 2, draws from these insights. By reconfiguring value around care, consent, ecological thresholds, and plural worldviews, SGE challenges the linear temporality and universalizing logics of both capitalist and socialist paradigms. It offers a model for economies that are not only sustainable but just, responsive, and culturally rooted.[86,87] Thus, this volume concludes not with finality, but with a proposition: that Indigenous political economies are indispensable to our collective future. They ask us to reframe prosperity, to reorder power, and to reclaim the ethical foundations of economic life. Volume 2 will extend this analysis into the contested terrain of global development and planetary governance. But the compass remains the same; economic thought must turn towards resurgence, relationality, and a pluriverse of futures.

As we conclude this volume, it becomes clear that Indigenous economic systems are not only resilient legacies of the past but are also powerful frameworks for shaping sustainable and just futures. The development of Symbiotic Gaian Economics as an alternative to neoclassical and Marxist thought marks a conceptual shift towards a model of the economy that foregrounds interdependence, ecological stewardship, and communal flourishing. However, the challenges Indigenous peoples face today—structural marginalization, climate threats, legal dispossession, and globalization—require not only theoretical alternatives but practical resistance and strategic resurgence. These contemporary dynamics are the focus of Volume 2, which moves from foundational analysis to the active struggles of Indigenous communities around the world. It interrogates how Indigenous peoples are reclaiming autonomy through political mobilization, legal reform, cultural revitalization, and the creation of alternative institutions. In doing so, Volume 2 deepens the analytical framework established here and provides a global account of Indigenous economic justice in action.

[86] Raworth, K. (2017). Doughnut Economics: Seven Ways to Think Like a 21st-Century Economist. White River Junction: Chelsea Green Publishing.

[87] Rockström, J. et al. (2009). 'A Safe Operating Space for Humanity', Nature, 461(7263), pp. 472–475.

References

Berkes, F. (2012) *Sacred Ecology: Traditional Ecological Knowledge and Resource Management*. 3rd edn. London: Routledge.

Borrows, J. (2010). Canada's Indigenous Constitution. Toronto: University of Toronto Press.

Borrows, J. (2016). Freedom and Indigenous Constitutionalism. Toronto: University of Toronto Press.

Bundy, C. (1988) The Rise and Fall of the South African Peasantry. London: James Currey.

Cole, D. and Chaikin, I. (1990). An Iron Hand Upon the People: The Law Against the Potlatch on the Northwest Coast. Vancouver: Douglas & McIntyre.

Corntassel, J. (2008) 'Toward Sustainable Self-Determination: Rethinking the Contemporary Indigenous-Rights Discourse', *Alternatives: Global, Local, Political*, 33(1), pp. 105–132.

De la Cadena, M. and Blaser, M. (eds.) (2018). A World of Many Worlds. Durham: Duke University Press.

Elman, B.A. (2000) *A Cultural History of Civil Examinations in Late Imperial China*. Berkeley: University of California Press.

Elman, B.A. (2005). Classicism, Politics, and Kinship: The Ch'ing Imperial Examinations. Cambridge: Cambridge University Press.

Escobar, A. (2018). Designs for the Pluriverse: Radical Interdependence, Autonomy, and the Making of Worlds. Durham: Duke University Press.

EZLN (2001) Our Word is Our Weapon: Selected Writings. Edited by J.P. Ponce de León. New York: Seven Stories Press.

FAO (2015). Indigenous Peoples' Food Systems and Agriculture. Rome: Food and Agriculture Organization of the United Nations.

Federici, S. (2004) *Caliban and the Witch: Women, the Body and Primitive Accumulation*. New York: Autonomedia.

Finley, M.I. (1973) *The Ancient Economy*. Berkeley: University of California Press.

Kimmerer, R.W. (2013) *Braiding Sweetgrass: Indigenous Wisdom, Scientific Knowledge and the Teachings of Plants*. Minneapolis: Milkweed Editions.

Kukutai, T. and Taylor, J. (eds.) (2016) *Indigenous Data Sovereignty: Toward an Agenda*. Canberra: ANU Press.

LaDuke, W. (2005). Recovering the Sacred: The Power of Naming and Claiming. Cambridge, MA: South End Press.

Latour, B. (2017) Facing Gaia: Eight Lectures on the New Climatic Regime. Cambridge: Polity Press.

Malm, A. (2016) Fossil Capital: The Rise of Steam Power and the Roots of Global Warming. London: Verso.

Mamdani, M. (1996) Citizen and Subject: Contemporary Africa and the Legacy of Late Colonialism. Princeton: Princeton University Press.

Marx, K. (1867). Capital: A Critique of Political Economy. Volume I. London: Penguin Classics (1990 edition).

Mason, R., Borrows, J. and Napoleon, V. (2021). "Indigenous Legal Orders and Forest Stewardship", in Curran, D. (ed.) Living within Limits: Regenerating Canada's Forests. Vancouver: UBC Press.

Mason, L., Shearer, C., Baldwin, E., Tovar, A., & Buzzard, V. (2021) Co-stewardship as a pathway to strengthen Indigenous land rights and improve environmental outcomes, Ecological Applications, 31(2), e02259.

Mustonen, T., Feodoroff, P., Gaup, E., Lempinen, H., Morimoto, J., Mustonen, K., and Nieminen, S. (2022). 'Co-management of Reindeer Herding and Climate Adaptation among Sámi Peoples', Sustainability Science, 17(3), pp. 765–778.

Nadasdy, P. (2003) *Hunters and Bureaucrats: Power, Knowledge, and Aboriginal-State Relations in the Southwest Yukon*. Vancouver: UBC Press.

Napoleon, V. (2013). Thinking About Indigenous Legal Orders. In: M. Asch, ed. Aboriginal Rights and Canada's Constitution. Vancouver: UBC Press, pp. 229–245.

Napoleon, V. and Friedland, H. (2016). 'An Inside Job: Engaging with Indigenous Legal Traditions through Stories', McGill Law Journal, 61(4), pp. 725–754.

O'Neill, D.W., Fanning, A.L., Lamb, W.F. and Steinberger, J.K. (2018) 'A Good Life for All within Planetary Boundaries', Nature Sustainability, 1, pp. 88–95.

Ostrom, E. (1990) *Governing the Commons: The Evolution of Institutions for Collective Action*. Cambridge: Cambridge University Press.

Ostrom, E. (2010) 'Beyond Markets and States: Polycentric Governance of Complex Economic Systems', *American Economic Review*, 100(3), pp. 641–672.

Polanyi, K. (1944) *The Great Transformation: The Political and Economic Origins of Our Time*. Boston: Beacon Press.

Rangarajan, L.N. (trans.) (1992) *Kautilya: The Arthashastra*. New Delhi: Penguin Books.

Raworth, K. (2017) *Doughnut Economics: Seven Ways to Think Like a 21st-Century Economist*. White River Junction: Chelsea Green Publishing.

Reyna, J.D. (ed.) (2014). Words of the Zapatistas: Communiqués and Interviews, 2001–2013. Oakland, CA: PM Press.

Rockström, J. et al. (2009) 'A Safe Operating Space for Humanity', *Nature*, 461(7263), pp. 472–475.

Sen, A. (1999) *Development as Freedom*. Oxford: Oxford University Press.

Smith, L. T. (2012) Decolonizing Methodologies: Research and Indigenous Peoples. 2nd edn. London: Zed Books.
Tuck, E. and Yang, K.W. (2012). 'Decolonization is not a metaphor', Decolonization: Indigeneity, Education & Society, 1(1), pp. 1–40.

Index

S. Ramesh, *The Political Economy of the Indigenous Peoples of the World, Volume I*, https://doi.org/10.1007/978-3-032-24041-5

FSC
www.fsc.org
MIX
Papier | Fördert
gute Waldnutzung
FSC® C083411

Kolibri 360 GmbH
Ferdinand-Jühlke-Straße 7
99095 Erfurt, Deutschland
produktsicherheit@kolibri360.de